Lichter aus Papier in Origami Technik

Vorwort

Lieben Sie auch die tolle Ausstrahlung von Papierlichtern?

Dann ist dieses Buch genau das richtige für Sie. Insgesamt 55 Modelle werden Sie begeistern. Bringen Sie einfach eine neue Stimmung mit nach Hause, oder genießen Sie ein Abendessen im Schein eines exklusiven Lichtmodells. Für Partys und Feste gibt es tolle Leuchten und Lichterketten. Besonderst zur Weihnachtszeit ist das „Deko-Licht“ von der Firma nice papers schon ein Klassiker, siehe Seite 52 bis 57. Ihre Familie und Freunde werden begeistert sein, so dass ein solches Lichtobjekt auch ein schönes Geschenk ist.
Durch die ausführlichen Schritt-für-Schritt Anleitungen mit farbigen Diagrammen und dazugehörigen Texten kommen Sie sicher zum Erfolg. Welch eine Freude entbrennt, sobald Ihr selbstgemachtes Licht erstrahlt!
Auch für Kenner von Papierlichtern ist dieses Buch interessant, denn für dieses Werk wurden exklusiv 34 neue Modelle entwickelt. Für die Lichter, welche mit Teelichtern leuchten, wurden die Lampenpapiere von nice papers verwendet. Diese sind flammsicher, haben hervorragende Falteigenschaften und eine Superleuchtkraft. Im Handel sind sie unter der Marke „Paper Frog“ erhältlich.

Viele schöne Stunden mit den neuen Lichtobjekten wünscht Ihnen

Alexandra Dirk

Do you love the great charisma of paper lights?

Then this book is ideal for you. Altogether 55 light objects will fill you with enthusiasm. Bring a new atmosphere at your home, or enjoy dinner in the shine of an exclusive light model. Also there are lamps and light chains for parties and celebrations. Especially for the Christmas season, the party light from the company nice papers is very popular, see from page 52 to 57. Your family and friends will be enthusiastic, so that such a light object is a beautiful gift, as well.
Because of the detailed step-by-step instructions with coloured charts and text, you will come safely to success. There will be great joy, when your first homemade light shines!
This book is also interesting for people, who already know paper lights, because it includes 34 novelties, developed for this book only. For lights, which shine with tea lights, we did use lamp paper from nice papers. This lamp paper is fire proof, has outstanding folding qualities and super luminous power. The retail offers it under the brand „Paper Frog“.

I wish you lots of great hours with the new paper objects

Alexandra Dirk

Inhaltsverzeichnis

Schwierigkeitsgrad
Level of difficulty

einfach
very easy

mittel
easy

intensiv
intermediate

Modellübersicht

Frühjahr

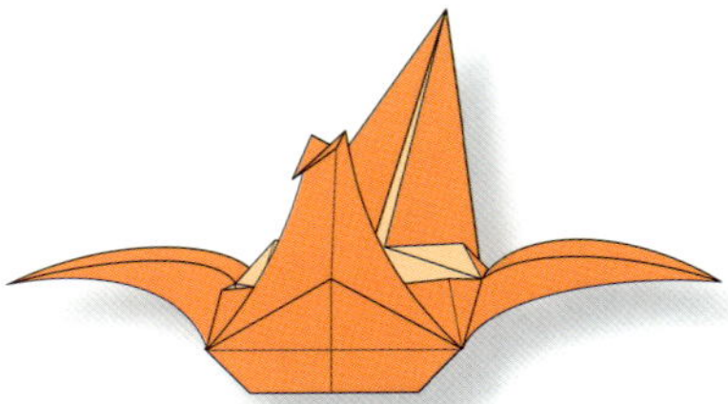

Seite 8

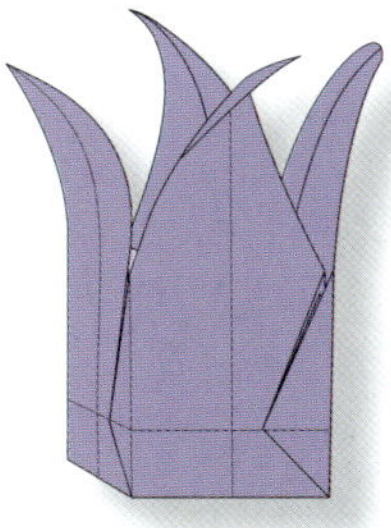

Seite 9

Seite 10

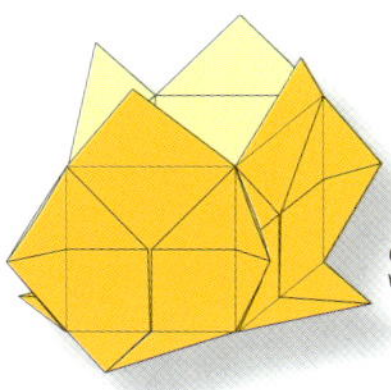

Seite 12

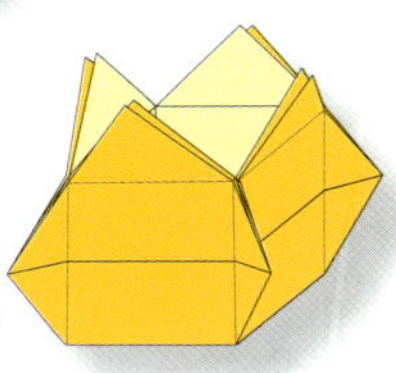

Seite 13

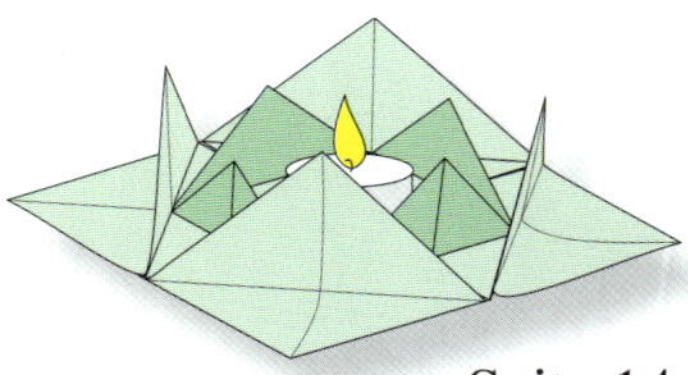

Seite 14

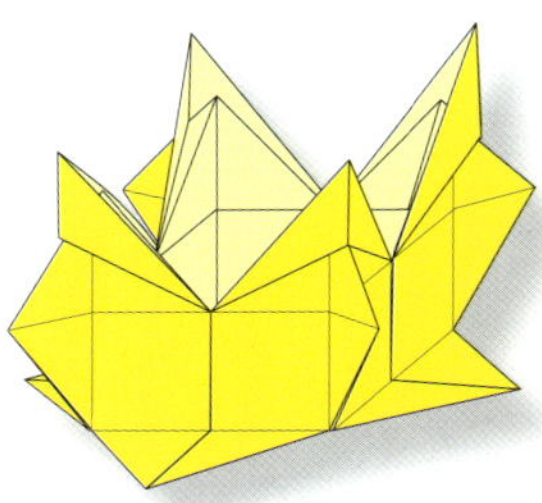

Seite 15

Seite 16

Sommer

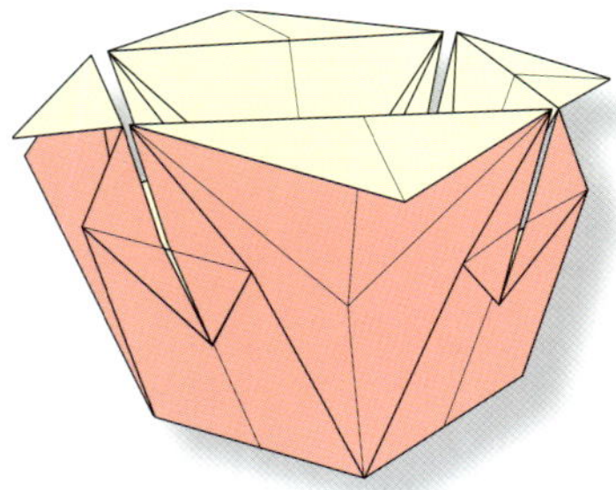

Seite 18

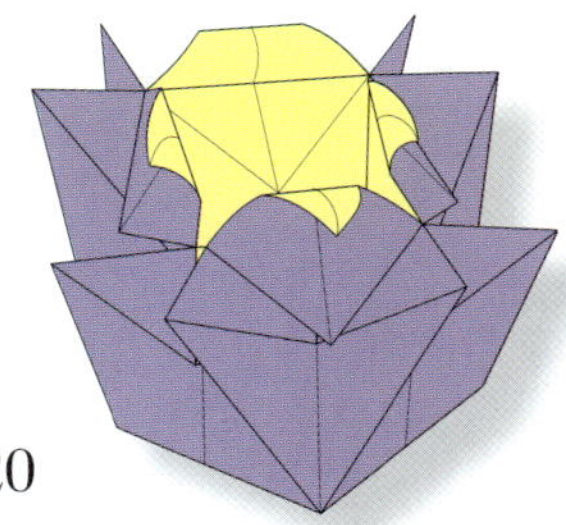

Seite 20

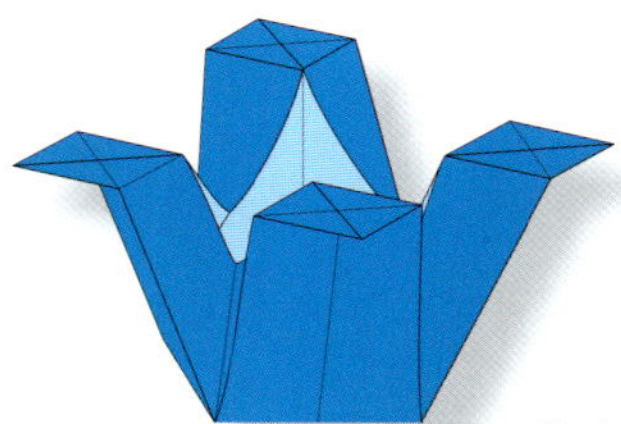

Seite 21

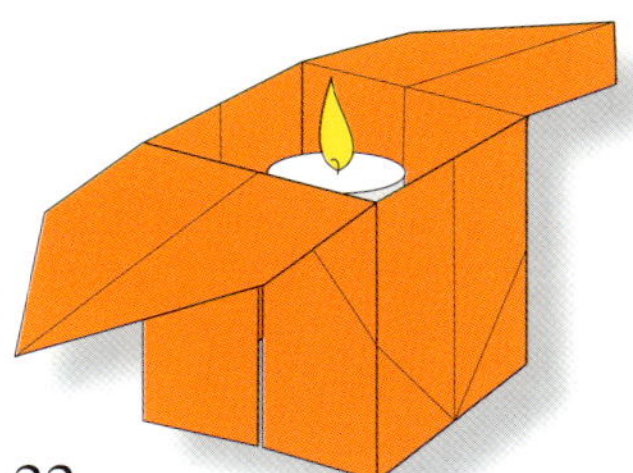

Seite 22

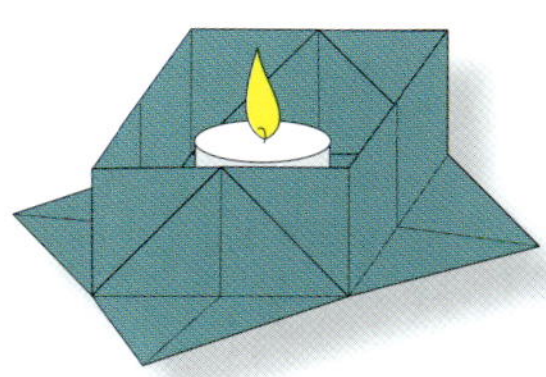

Seite 23

Seite 24

Herbst

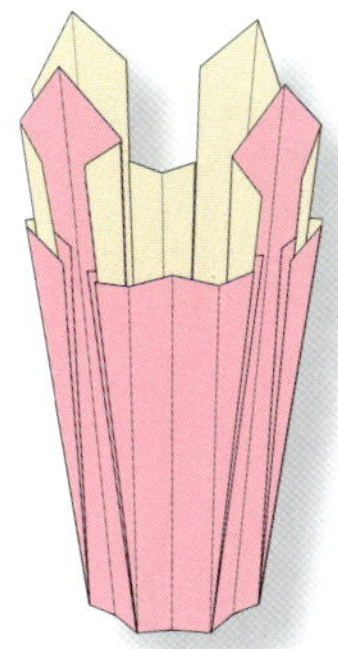

Seite 26

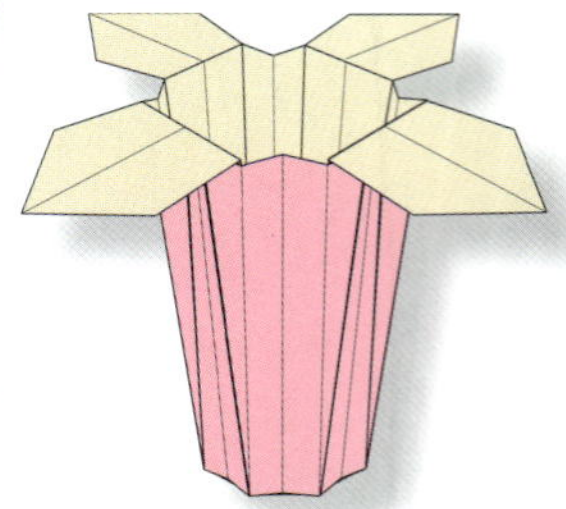

Seite 27

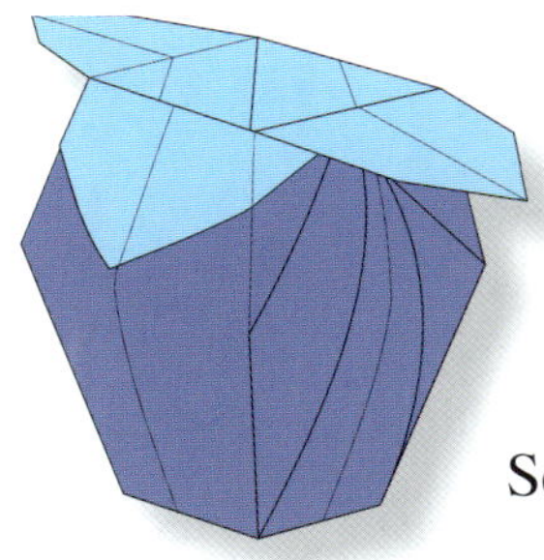

Seite 28

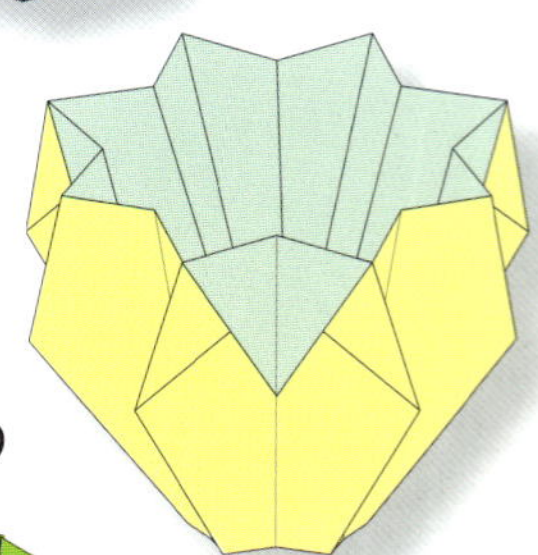

Seite 29

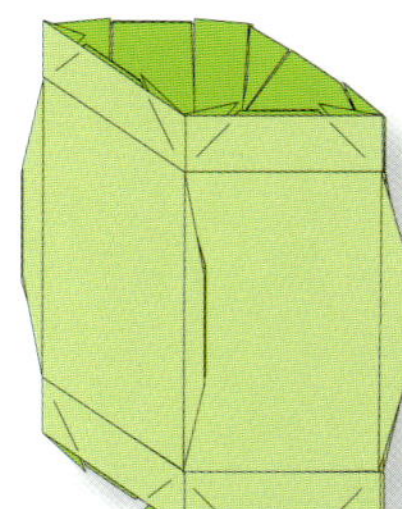

Seite 30

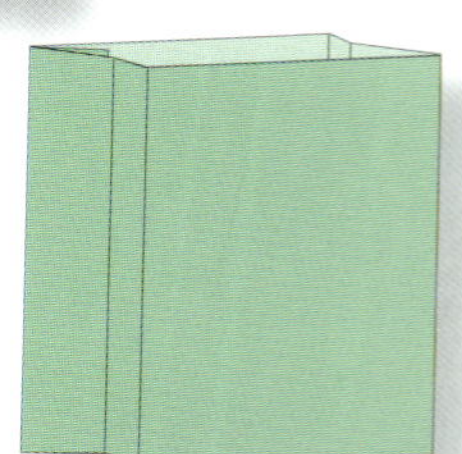

Seite 31

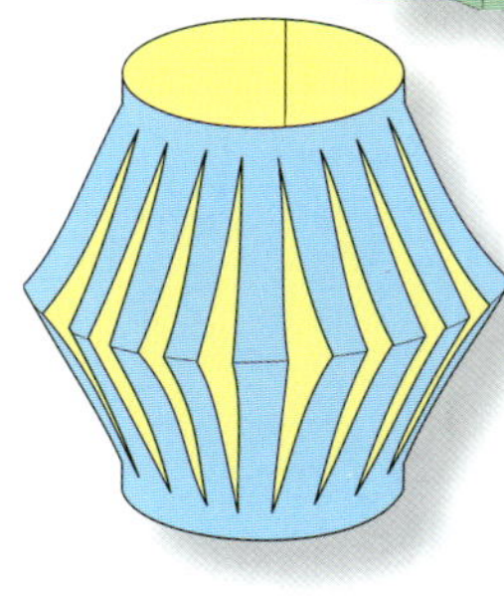

Seite 32

Rauten

Seite 34

Seite 35

Seite 36

Seite 37

Seite 38

Seite 38

Seite 39

Seite 39

Winter

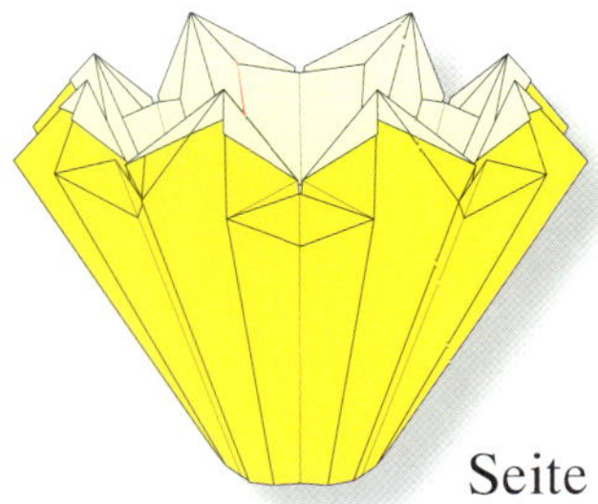
Seite 40

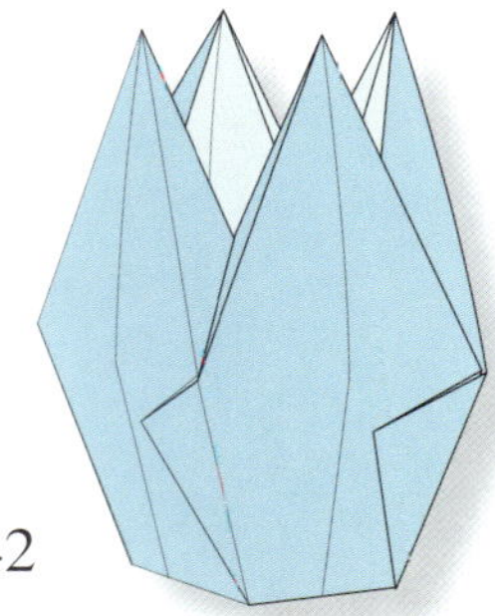
Seite 42

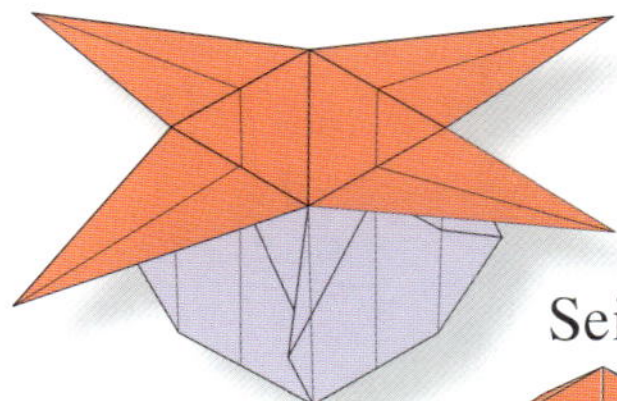
Seite 44

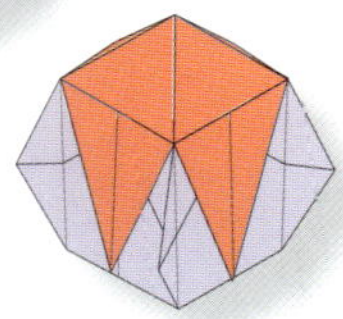
Seite 44

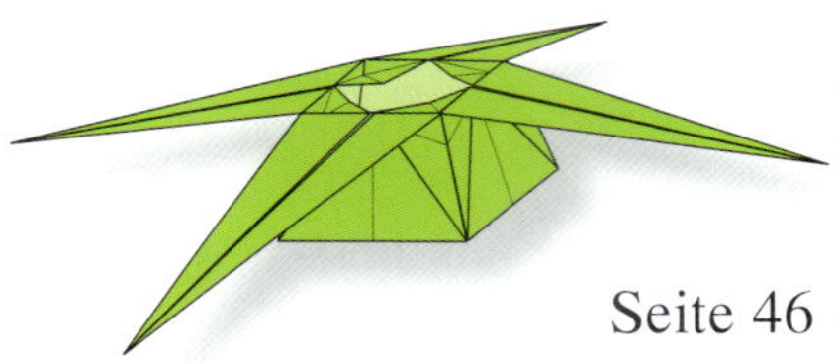
Seite 46

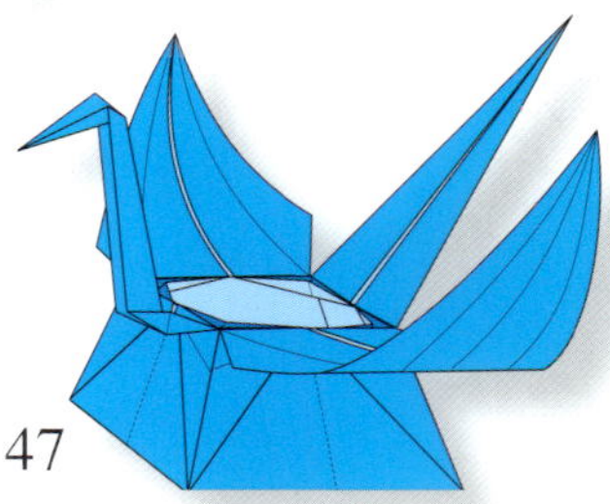
Seite 47

Seite 48

Seite 49

Weihnachten

Seite 52

Seite 53

Seite 54

Seite 55

Seite 55

Seite 56

Seite 57

Seite 60

Lampenpapier MIX
lamp paper mix

Lampenpapiere
lamp paper

Papiere für Lichterketten
paper for light-chains

ORIGAMI Zeichen + Werkzeuge

Origami Zeichnungen

Alle Zeichnungen sind mit Symbolen versehen. Gleichzeitig ist immer noch ausreichend Text angegeben worden, so dass das Gelingen der Arbeit auch gewährleistet ist.
Auf dieser Seite sind die internationalen Origami Zeichen abgebildet.
Zur besseren Darstellung von Vorder- und Rückseite wurden bei allen Zeichnungen verschiedene Farben verwendet, wie auch bei dieser Symbolerklärung.

Origami charts

All charts have symbols and enough text, so that you will come safely to success.
The international Origami symbols are shown on this page.
For a better representation of front and back side of the paper, we did use different colours for all charts, as you can see on this explanation of symbols.

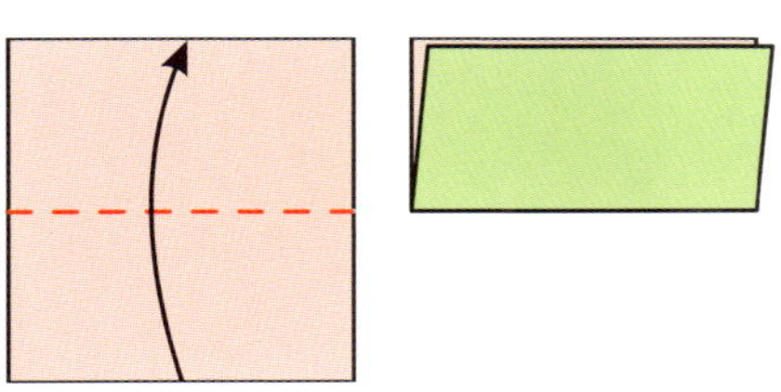

Talfalte
valley-fold

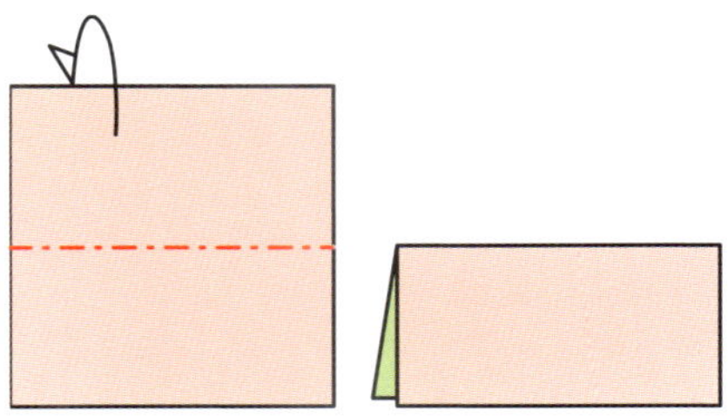

Bergfalte
mountain-fold

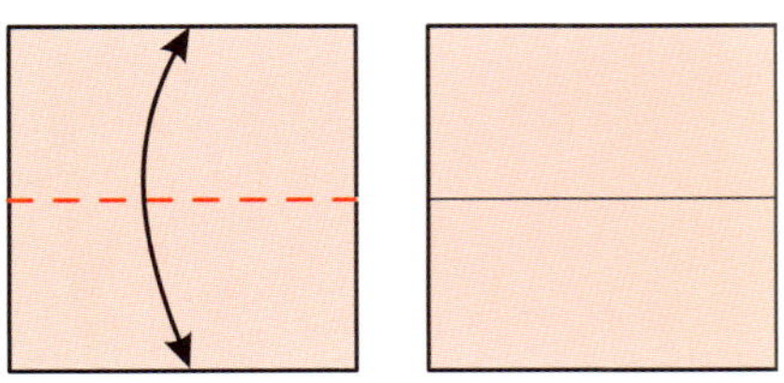

Falten, wieder öffnen.
Fold and open up again.

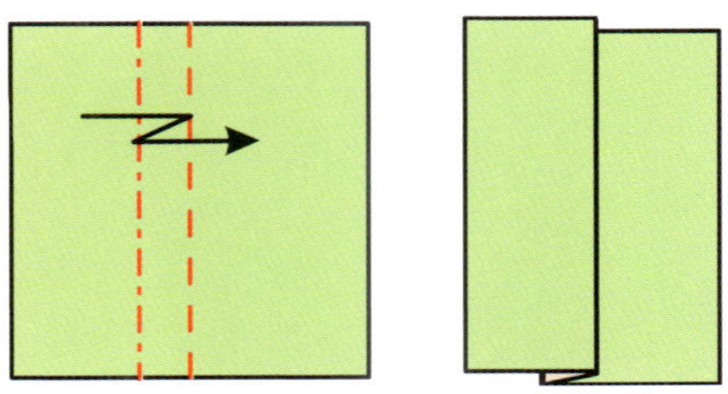

Zickzackfaltung
zigzag fold

Origamiarbeiten benötigen grundsätzlich kein Werkzeug. Bei Faltungen, wo das Papier in mehreren Lagen liegt, ist es sehr angenehm mit einem Falzbein zu arbeiten. Zusätzlich wird bei einigen Modellen auch eine Schere benötigt. Zur Beleuchtung können Sie Teelichter verwenden. Diese sollten Sie zuerst mit einem Glaseinsatz in das fertige Modell stellen. Dann erst das Teelicht anzünden. Wenn das Modell sehr hoch ist, verwenden Sie einen Gasanzünder, damit Sie das Teelicht am Boden des Modells erreichen und sicher anzünden können.

For Origami you fundamentally don't need any tools. If the paper lies in several layers, it is pleasant to work with a bonefolder. In addition you need a scissor for some models. You can use tea lights for the lighting. First of all you should put the tea light in a small glass and then place it at the bottom of the model. Then you can light the tea light. If the model is very high, use a gas lighter, so that you can reach the tea light on the bottom of the model and light it safely.

Symbole

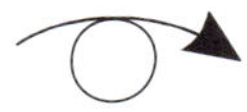

Rückseite nach oben legen.
Turn over to the back.

Gefaltetes Teil nach außen ziehen, siehe nächste Zeichnung.
Pull the folded part outwards, see next chart.

Drehen.
Turn around.

Arbeitsschritte auf der anderen Seite wiederholen.
Repeat working steps on the other side.

Ansicht der Zeichnung wurde vergrößert.
The sight of the chart has been enlarged.

Eindrücken und glatt falten.
Push in and fold flatly.

Papier in gleiche Teile einteilen.
Divide paper into equal parts.

Papier nach innen falten.
Fold paper inwards.

Einschneiden oder abschneiden.
Cut in or cut off.

Aufblasen.
Inflate.

Falzbein
bonefolder

Teelicht+Glas
tea light+glass

Gasanzünder
gas lighter

Licht in Kranichform

Modell von Janina Weinand

MATERIAL

1 Blatt 15x15 cm (kleines Modell), oder 30x30 cm (großes Modell) flammsicheres Lampenpapier. Da bei dem fertigen Modell viel von der Papierrückseite zu sehen ist, sollte durchgefärbtes Papier gewählt werden.

One sheet 15x15 cm (small model), or 30x30 cm (big model) of not inflammable lamp paper. From the finished model, you will see much of the back side of the paper. So you should use paper with a coloured back side.

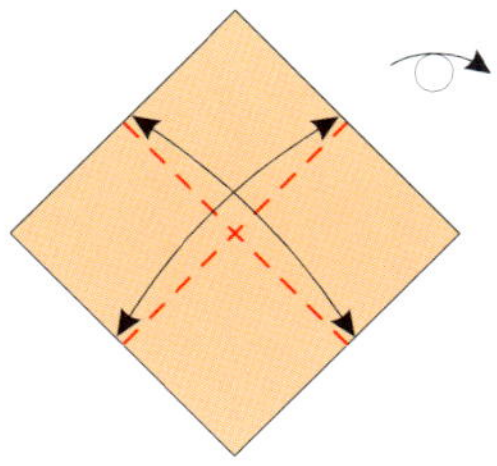

1. Zweimal waagerecht die Mitte falten, wieder öffnen. Rückseite nach oben legen.
Fold twice the horizontal middle and open up again. Turn over to the back.

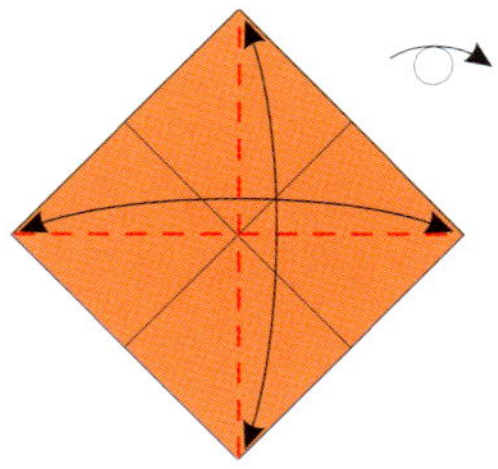

2. Zweimal diagonal die Mitte falten, wieder öffnen. Rückseite nach oben legen.
Fold twice the middle diagonally and open up again. Turn over to the back.

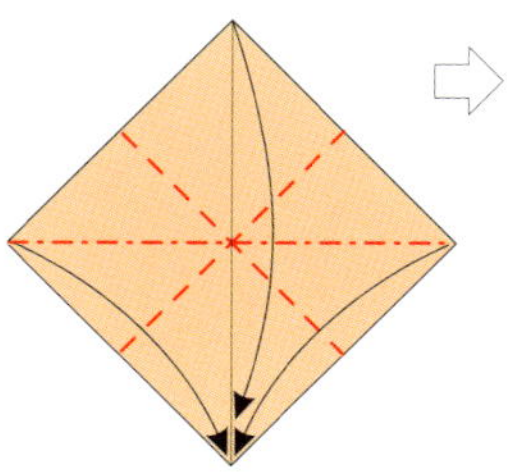

3. Von der waagerechten Mitte (Bergfalte), die seitlichen Ecken zur unteren Ecke legen. Die obere Ecke dann ebenfalls nach unten legen, siehe Pfeile.
From the horizontal middle (mountain-fold), lay the corners from the side to the lower corner. Also lay the upper corner to the lower corner, see arrows.

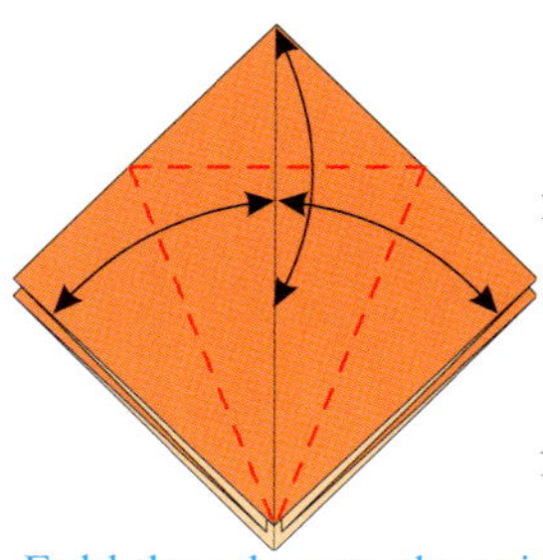

4. Kanten zur Mitte falten, wieder öffnen. Obere Spitze nach unten falten, wieder öffnen.
Fold the edges to the middle and open up again. Fold upper point downwards and open up again.

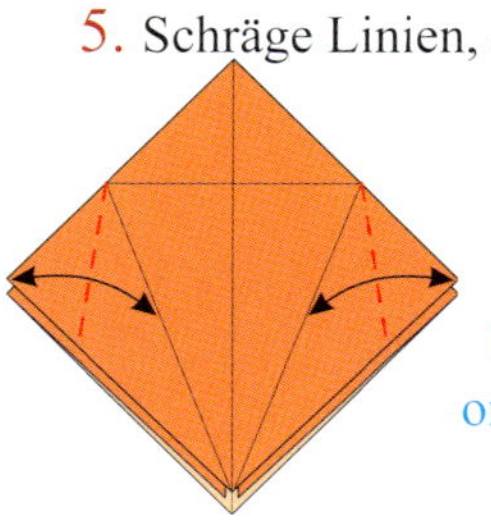

5. Schräge Linien, siehe Pfeile, auf beiden Seiten falten, wieder öffnen.
Fold oblique lines, see arrow, on both sides and open up again.

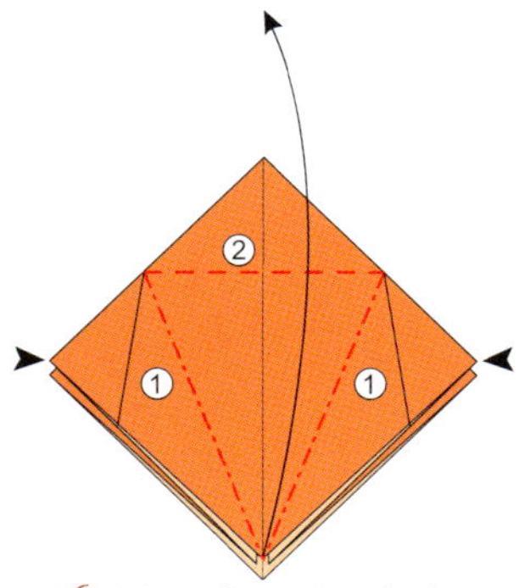

6. Nur obere Papierlage, siehe Pfeil, von unten nach oben an die Linie Nr.2 legen. Dabei werden die seitlichen Linien Nr.1 zur Bergfalte gefaltet. Seitliche Ecken dabei eindrücken.
Using only the top layer of paper, see arrow, lay paper from bottom to top along line No.2. At the same time fold lines No.1 on the sides as a mountain-fold and push in the corners from the side.

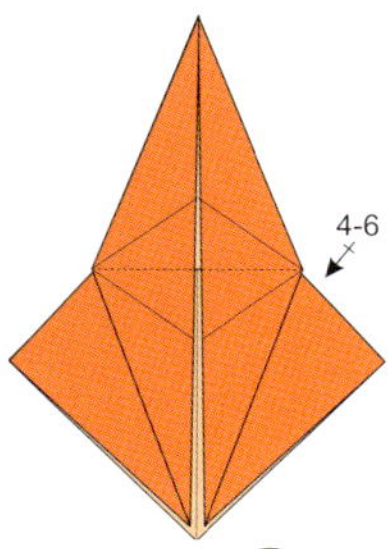

7. Die Arbeitsschritte von Nr.4 bis Nr.6 auf der Rückseite wiederholen.
Repeat working steps from No.4 to No.6 on the back.

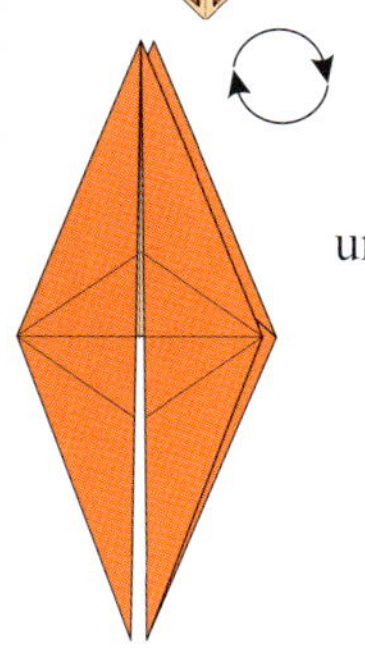

8. Modell um 180 Grad drehen, die unteren offenen Spitzen liegen dann oben.
Turn the model 180 degrees around. Now the lower open points lie on the top.

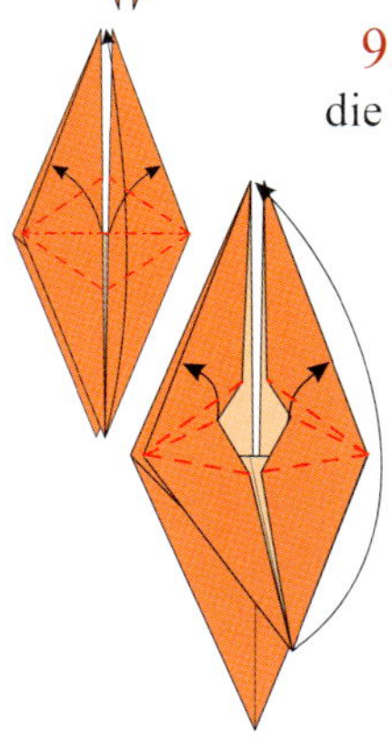

9. Von der Mitte aus die bereits vorhandene waagerechte Linie an die äußeren Kanten legen, liegen lassen.
Starting from the middle, lay the existing horizontal line towards the outer edges and leave.

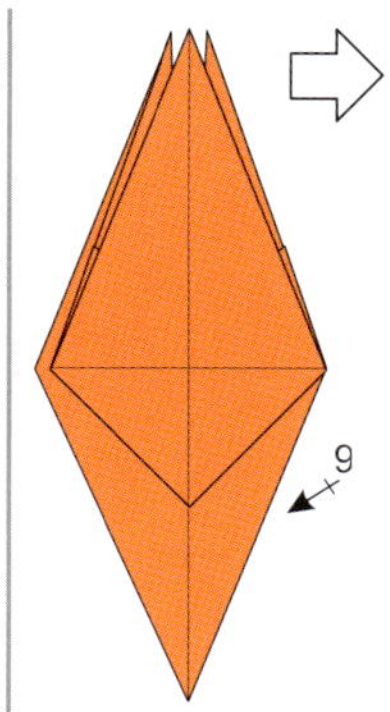

10. Die Arbeitsschritte von Nr.9 auf der Rückseite wiederholen.
Repeat working step No.9 on the back.

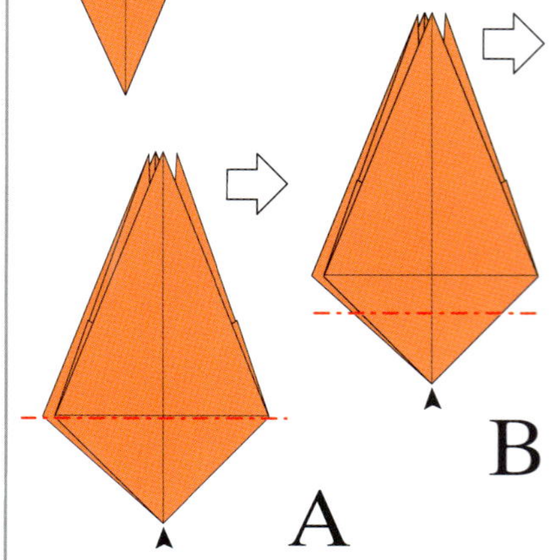

11. Diagramm A nur bei 15x15 cm Papier.
An allen vier Seiten eine Bergfalte formen und dabei die untere Spitze eindrücken.
Diagramm B nur bei 30x30 cm Papier.
In der Mitte der unteren Spitze eine waagerechte Linie falten, wieder öffnen.
Dann auf allen Seiten eine Bergfalte formen und dabei die untere Spitze eindrücken.
Chart A only for 15x15 cm paper.
Form a mountain-fold on all four edges, at the same time push in the lower point.
Chart B only for 30x30 cm paper.
Fold a horizontal line on the middle of the lower point and open up again.
Then form a mountain-fold on all edges, at the same time push in the lower point.

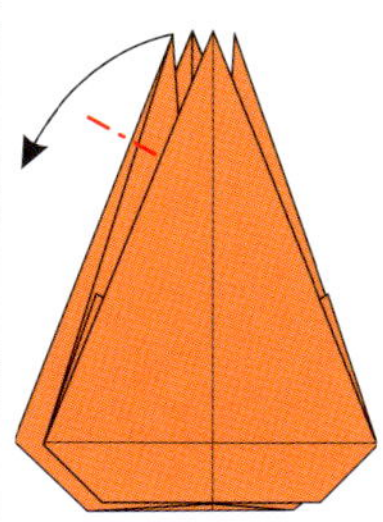

12. Für den Schnabel, siehe Pfeil eine schräge Linie falten und dann die Spitze nach innen versenken.
For the beak, see arrow, fold a oblique line and push the point inwards.

13. Die seitlichen Spitzen über ein Falzbein rollen, dadurch wird das Papier rund und die Flügelform entsteht.
Roll the points on both sides over a bonefolder, so the paper becomes round and the form of a wing arises.

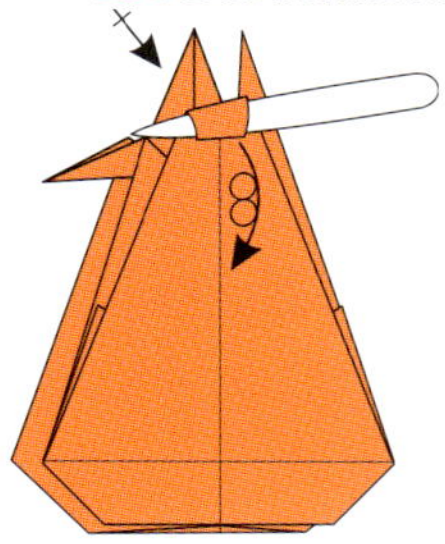

14. Modell von innen auseinanderdrücken, das Modell steht dann flach auf dem Tisch.
Push the model from the inside outwards. Now the model stands flatly on the table.

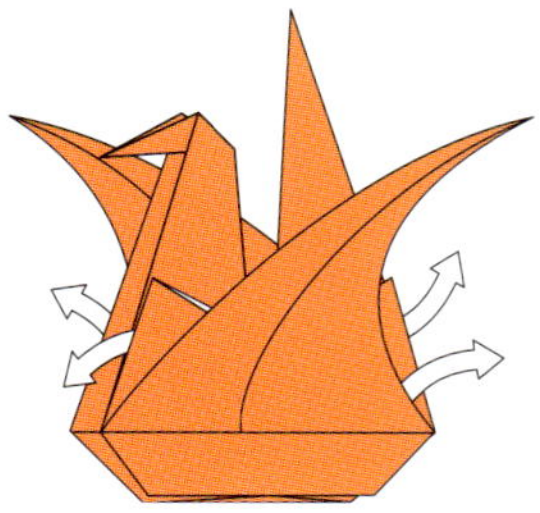

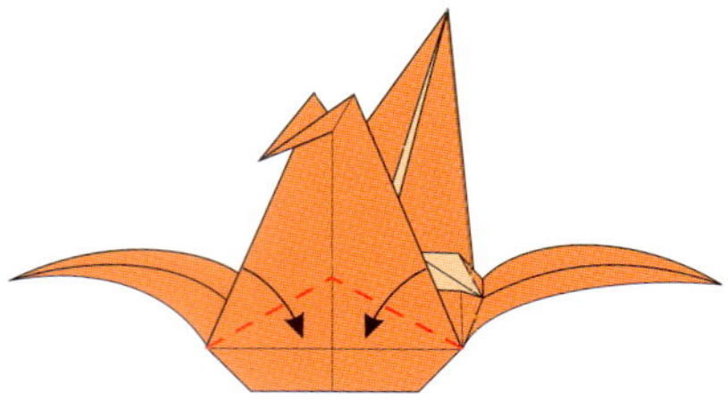

15. Linien nach vorne falten, siehe Pfeile, damit der Kopf seine endgültige Form bekommt.
Fold lines to the front, see arrows, so that the head gets his final shape.

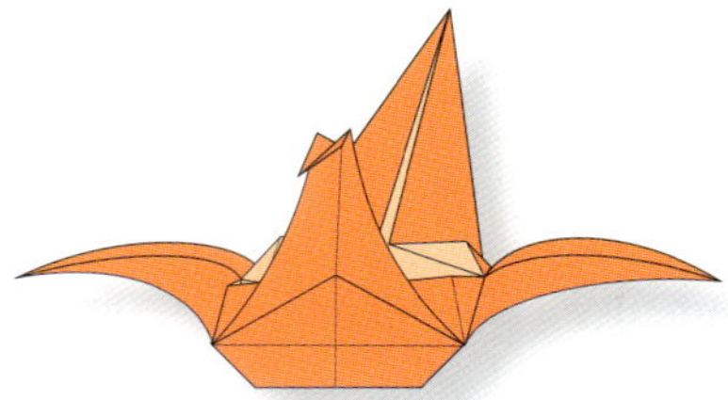

16. Fertiges Modell seitlich gesehen.
Finished model seen from the side.

17. Fertiges Modell von oben gesehen.
Finished model seen from above.

Tulpen-Licht

MATERIAL

1 Blatt 30x30 cm flammsicheres Lampenpapier. Bei dem fertigen Modell ist von der Papierrückseite wenig zu sehen. Es kann also durchgefärbtes Papier oder Papier mit einer weißen Rückseite gewählt werden.
One sheet 30x30 cm of not inflammable lamp paper. From the finished model, you won't see much of the back side of the paper. So you can use paper with a coloured or white back side.

Start. Diagramme von Seite 8 bis Nr.11 falten.
Fold charts of page 8 until step No.11.

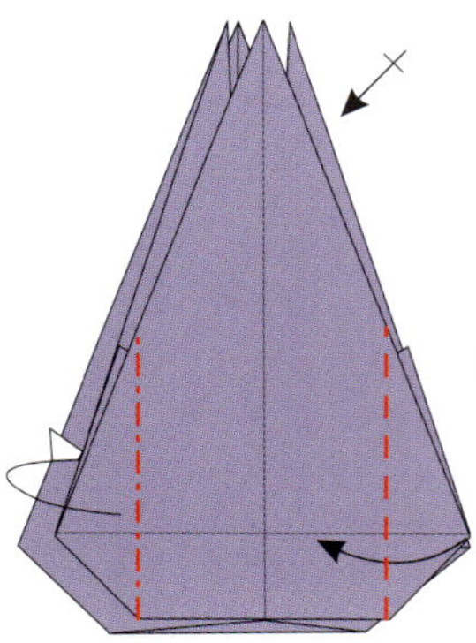

1. Alle vier Ecken zur Mitte falten, liegen lassen.
Fold all four corners to the middle and leave.

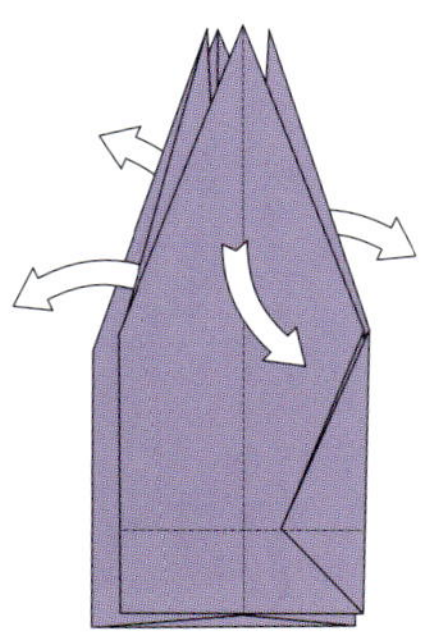

2. Modell von innen auseinanderdrücken, das Modell steht dann flach auf dem Tisch.
Push the model from the inside outwards. Now the model stands flatly on the table.

3. Alle vier Spitzen über ein Falzbein rollen, dadurch wird das Papier rund und die Blütenform entsteht.
Roll all four points over a bonefolder, so that the paper becomes round and the flourish form arises.

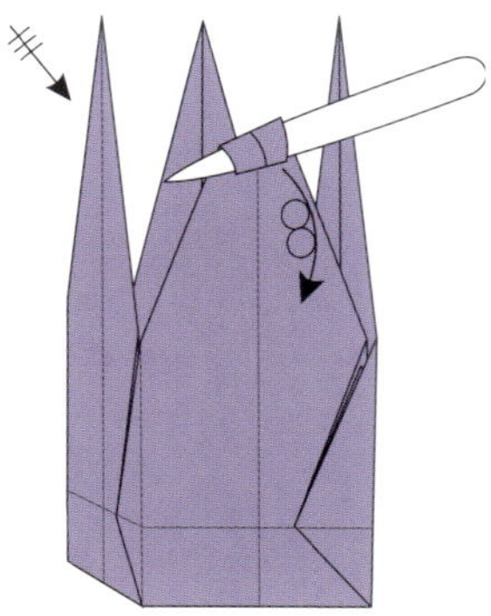

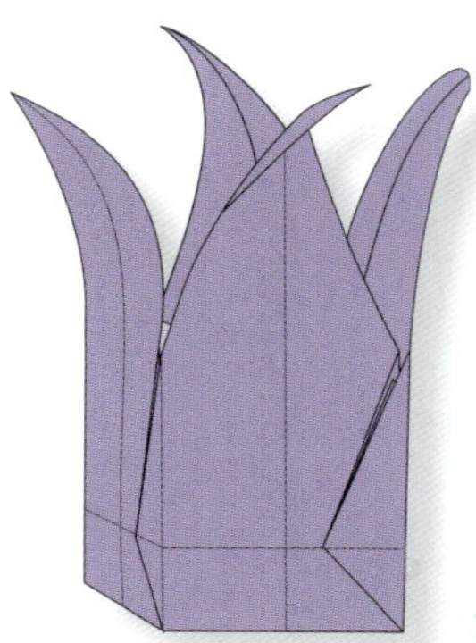

4. Fertiges Modell seitlich gesehen.
Finished model seen from the side.

5. Fertiges Modell von oben gesehen.
Finished model seen from above.

Paradiesvogelblüten-Licht

MATERIAL

1 Blatt 30x30 cm flammsicheres Lampenpapier. Bei dem fertigen Modell ist die Papierrückseite etwas zu sehen. Es kann durchgefärbtes Papier, aber auch Papier mit einer weißen Rückseite gewählt werden.

One sheet 30x30 cm of not inflammable lamp paper. From the finished model, you will see a little bit of the back side of the paper. So you can use paper with a coloured or white back side.

Start. Diagramme von Seite 8 bis Nr.4 falten.

Fold charts of page 8 until step No.4.

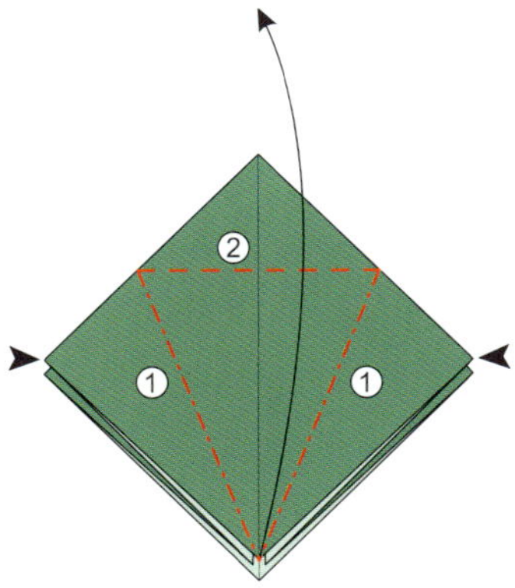

1. Nur obere Papierlage, siehe Pfeil, von unten nach oben an die Linie Nr.2 legen. Dabei werden die seitlichen Linien Nr.1 zur Bergfalte gefaltet. Seitliche Ecken dabei eindrücken.

Using only the top layer of paper, see arrow, lay paper from bottom to top along line No.2. At the same time fold lines No.1 on the sides as a mountain-fold and push in the corners from the side.

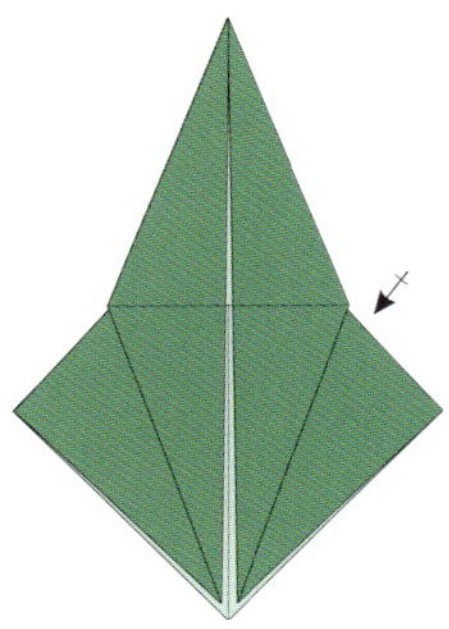

2. Die Arbeitsschritte von Nr.1 auf der Rückseite wiederholen.

Repeat the working steps from No.1 at the back.

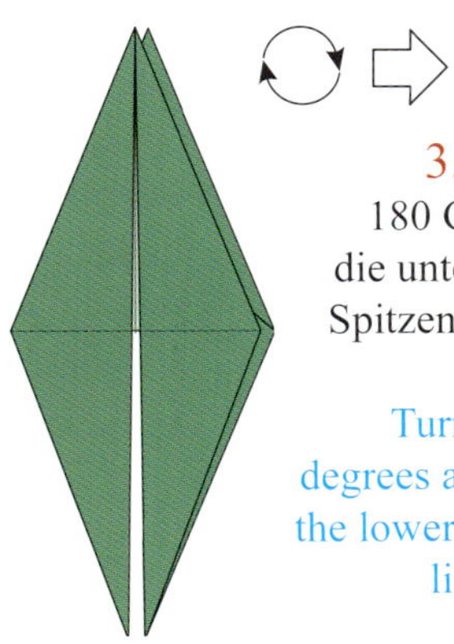

3. Modell um 180 Grad drehen, die unteren offenen Spitzen liegen dann oben.

Turn model 180 degrees around. Now the lower open points lie on the top.

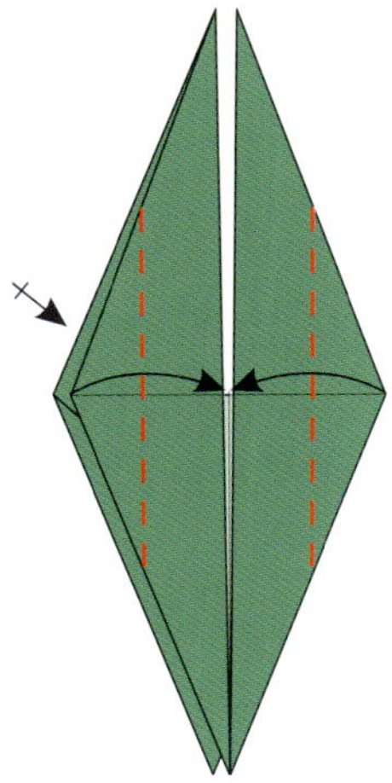

4. Die seitlichen Ecken zur Mitte falten, liegen lassen. Auf der Rückseite wiederholen.

Fold the corners from the side to the middle and leave. Repeat on the back.

5. Spitze nach oben falten, siehe Pfeil, liegen lassen. Auf der Rückseite wiederholen.

Fold point upwards, see arrow, and leave. Repeat on the back.

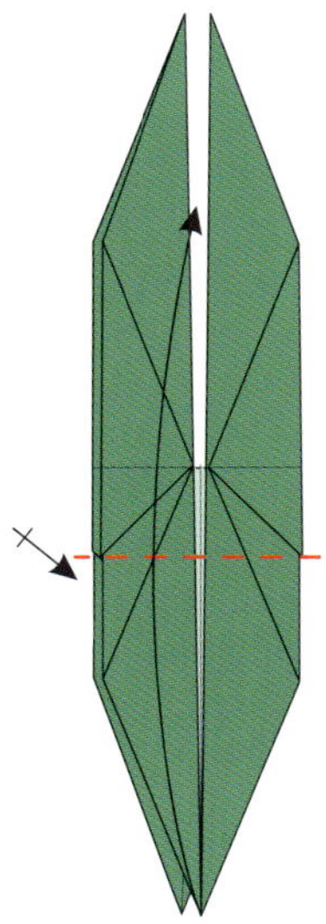

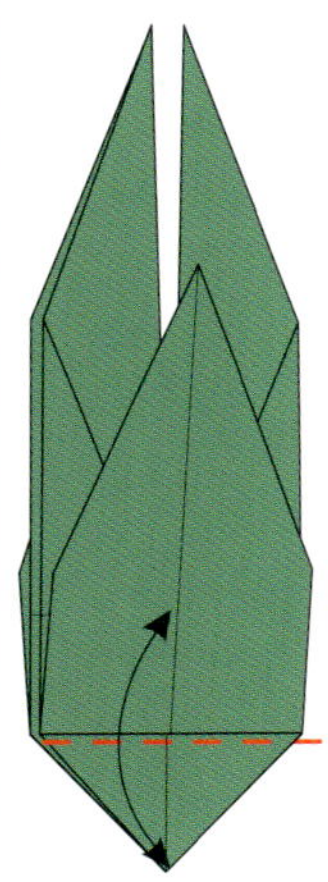

6. Unteres Dreieck nach oben falten, wieder öffnen.

Fold lower triangle upwards and open up again.

7. Spitzen, siehe Pfeile, wieder nach unten legen.

Lay points, see arrow, downwards again.

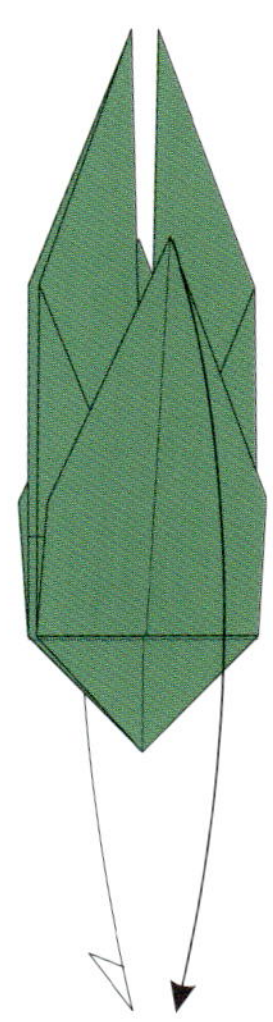

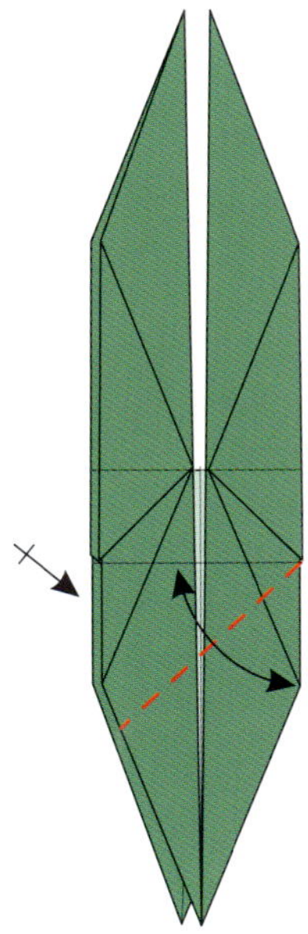

8. Schräge Linie an die waagerechte Linie falten, wieder öffnen. Auf der Rückseite wiederholen.

Fold the oblique line to the horizontal line and open up again. Repeat on the back.

9. Schräge Linie an die waagerechte Linie falten, wieder öffnen. Auf der Rückseite wiederholen.

Fold the oblique line to the horizontal line and open up again. Repeat on the back.

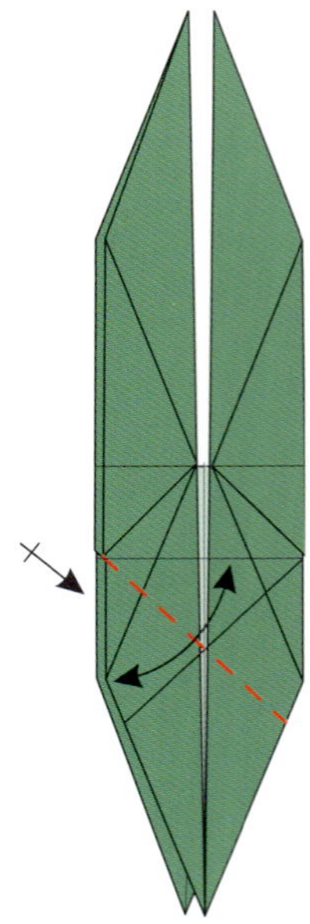

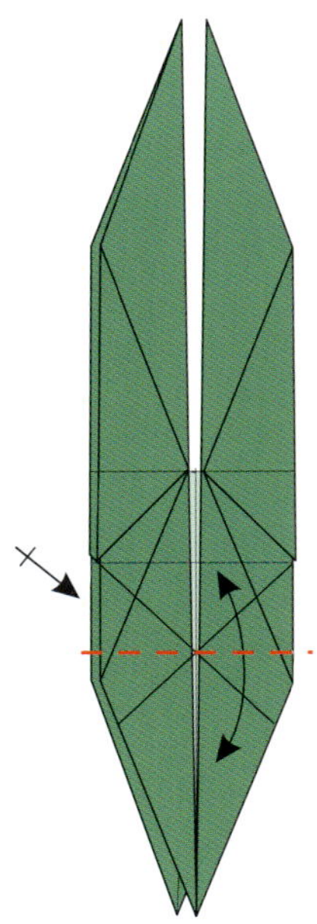

10. Waagerechte Linie nach oben falten, wieder öffnen. Auf der Rückseite wiederholen.

Fold horizontal line upwards and open up again. Repeat on the back.

11. Waagerechte Linie zur Bergfalte formen und von den Seiten zur Mitte legen, siehe Pfeile. Auf der Rückseite wiederholen.
Form horizontal line as a mountain-fold and lay from the side to the middle, see arrows. Repeat on the back.

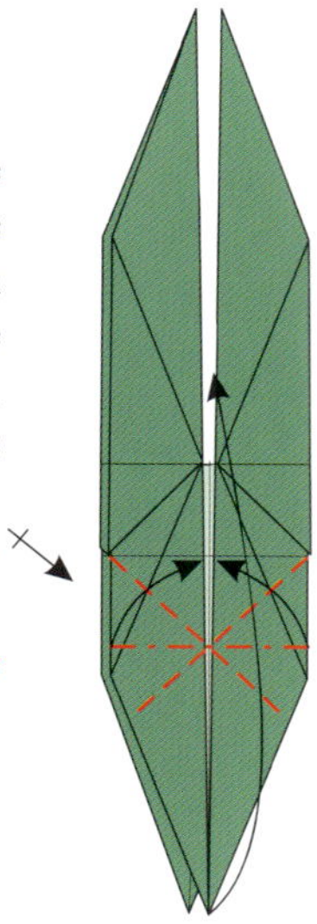

12. Die nun nach oben stehende Spitze über ein Falzbein rollen, dadurch wird das Papier rund und die Blattform entsteht. Auf der Rückseite wiederholen.
Roll the point over a bonefolder, so the paper becomes round and the form of a leaf arises. Repeat on the back.

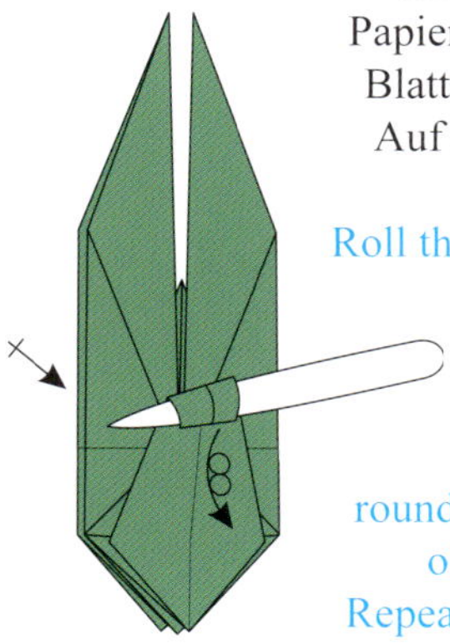

13. Beide Dreiecke seitlich hoch biegen, siehe Pfeile.
Bend both triangles upwards, see arrows.

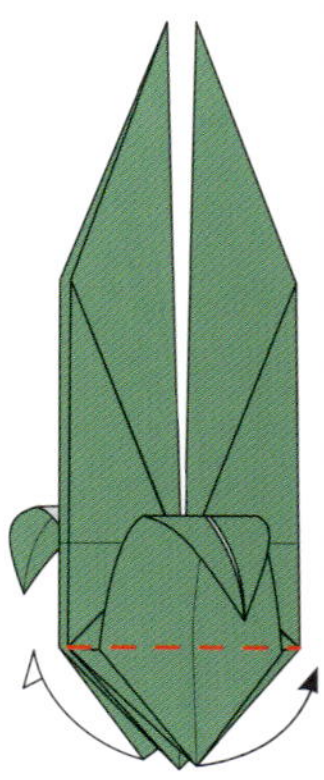

14. Modell von innen mit einem Falzbein auseinanderdrücken, sowie die untere Spitze nach oben eindrücken, so dass es dann flach auf dem Tisch steht.
Push the model with a bonefolder from the inside outwards and push in the lower point upwards. Now the model stands flatly on the table.

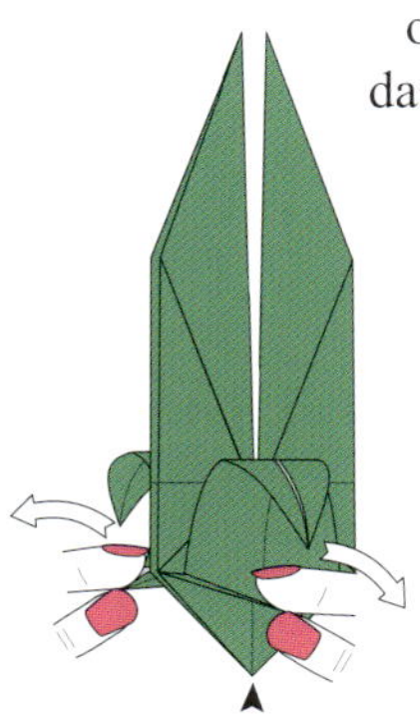

15. Fertiges Modell seitlich gesehen.
Finished model seen from the side.

Modell von Seite 47

Kleine Blüte-Lichteffekte

Modell von Janina Weinand

MATERIAL

1 Blatt 30x30 cm flammsicheres Lampenpapier. Bei dem fertigen Modell ist von der Papierrückseite etwas zu sehen. Es kann also durchgefärbtes Papier oder Papier mit einer weißen Rückseite gewählt werden.

One sheet 30x30 cm of not inflammable lamp paper. From the finished model, you will see a little bit of the back side of the paper. So you can use paper with a coloured or white back side.

1. Zweimal waagerecht die Mitte falten, wieder öffnen.
Fold twice the horizontal middle and open up again.

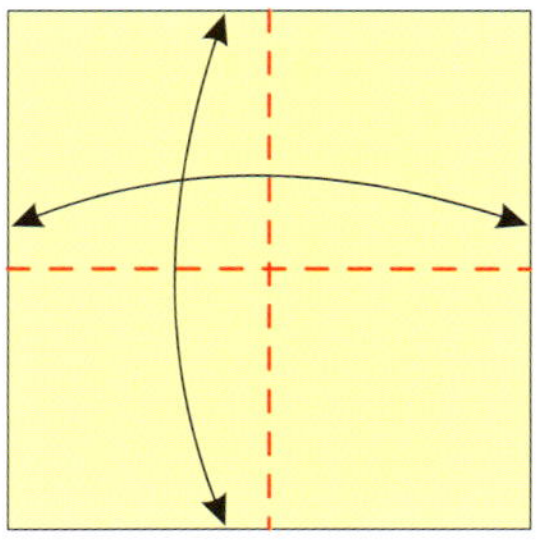

2. Zweimal diagonal die Mitte falten, wieder öffnen.
Fold twice the middle diagonally and open up again.

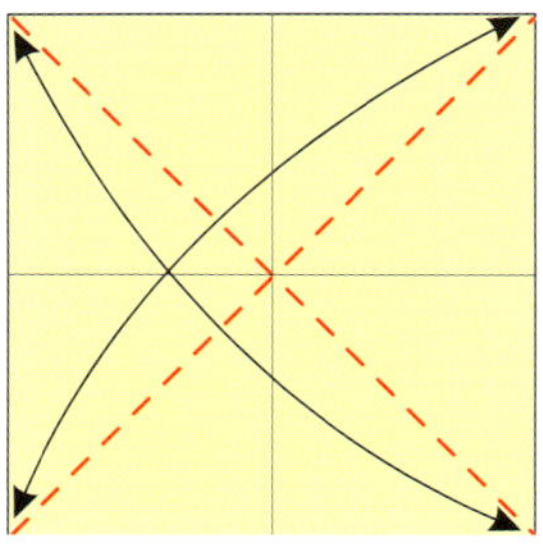

3. Alle vier Ecken zur Mitte falten, liegen lassen.
Fold all four corners to the middle and leave.

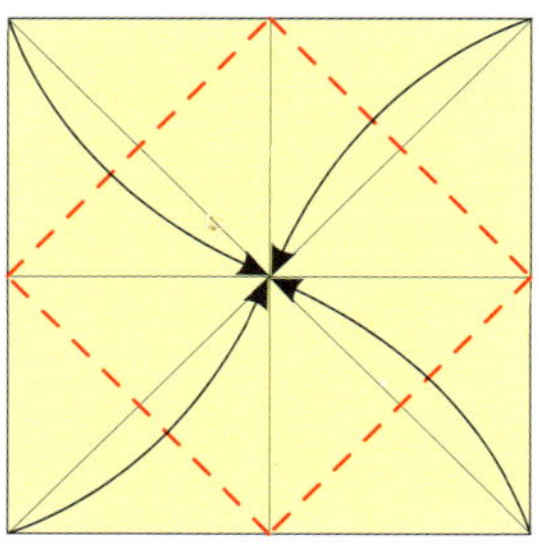

4. Wieder alle vier Ecken zur Mitte falten, liegen lassen.
Again fold all four corners to the middle and leave.

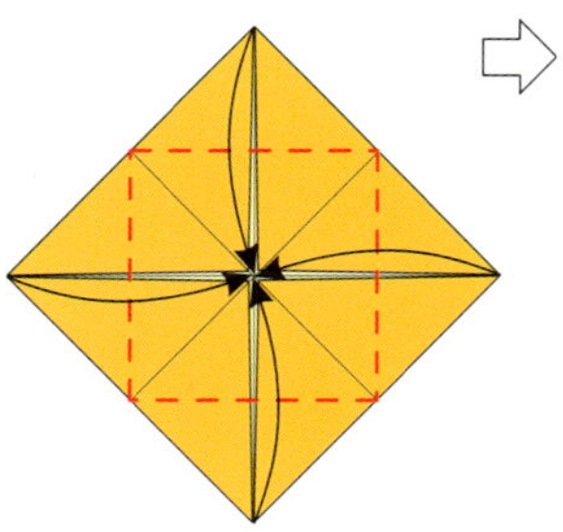

5. Spitzen von der Mitte an die Papierkante falten, liegen lassen.
Fold points from the middle to the edge and leave.

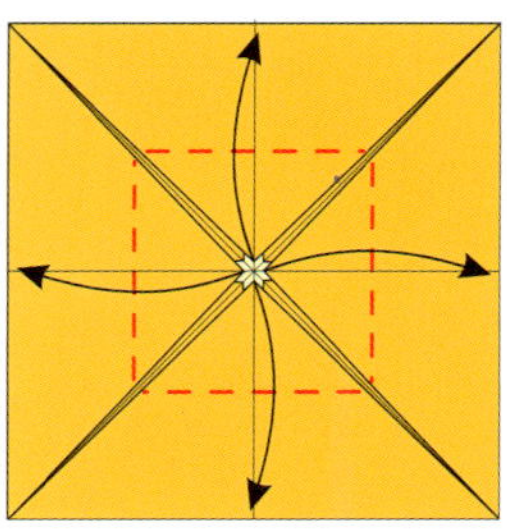

6. Rückseite nach oben legen.
Turn over to the back.

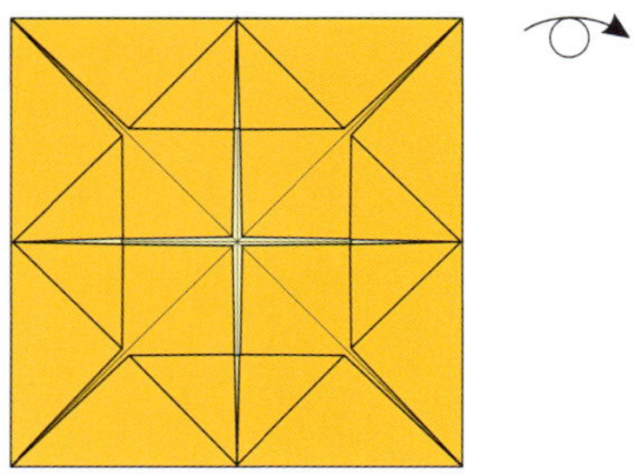

7. Alle vier Ecken zur Mitte falten, liegen lassen.
Fold all four corners to the middle and leave.

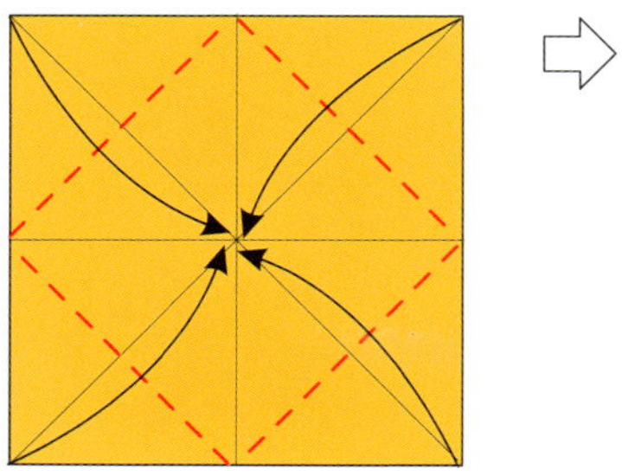

8. Spitzen von der Mitte an die Papierkante falten, liegen lassen.
Fold points from the middle to the edge and leave.

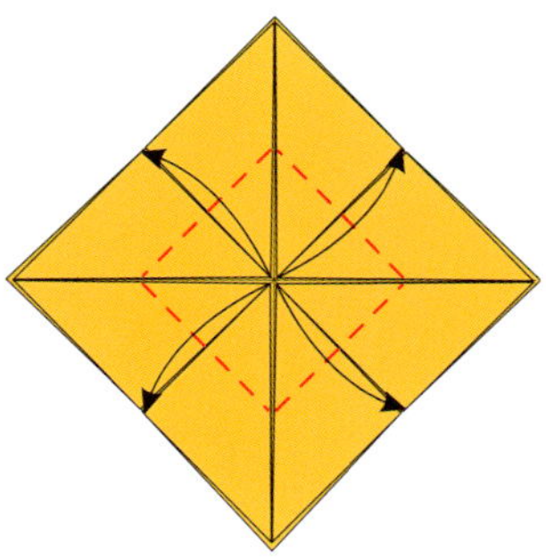

9. Rückseite nach oben legen.
Turn over to the back.

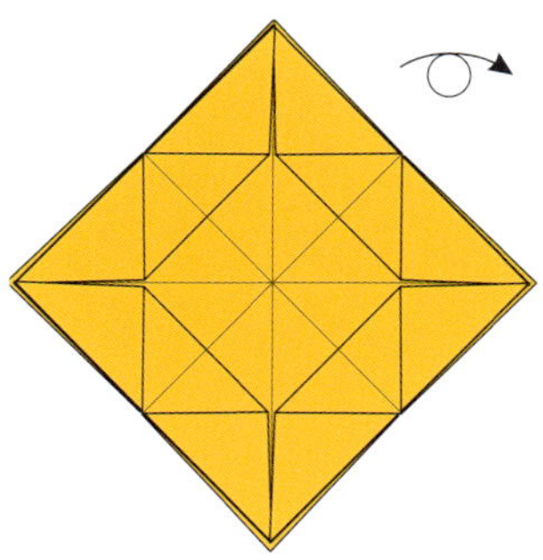

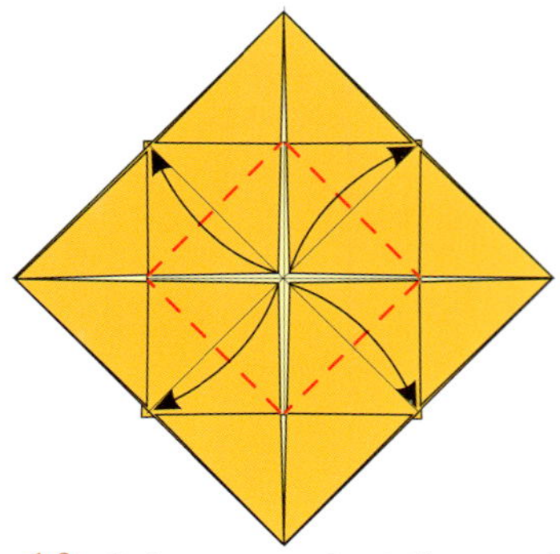

10. Spitzen von der Mitte an die Papierkante falten, liegen lassen.
Fold points from the middle to the edge and leave.

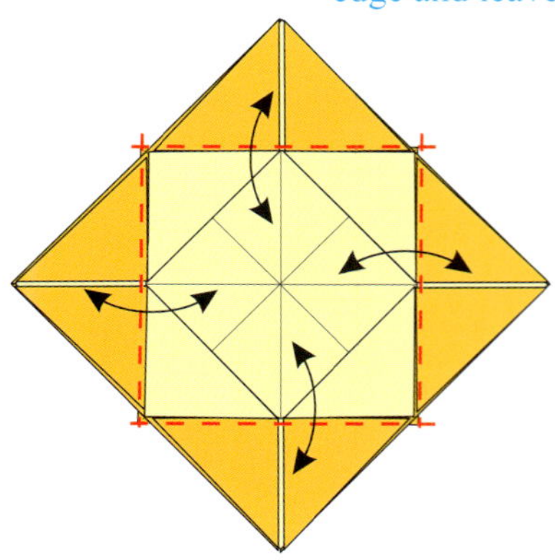

11. Alle vier waagerechten Linien falten, wieder öffnen.
Fold all horizontal lines and open up again.

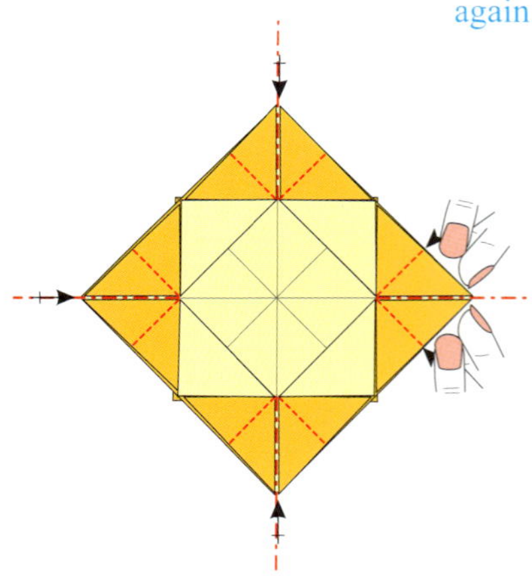

12. An der Ecke Bergfalte formen, dabei seitlich mit den Händen eindrücken. An den anderen drei Ecken wiederholen. Dadurch wird aus dem flachen Papier die aufgestellte Form.
Form a mountain-fold on the corner, at the same time push in from the side. Repeat on the other three corners, so that a erected form arises.

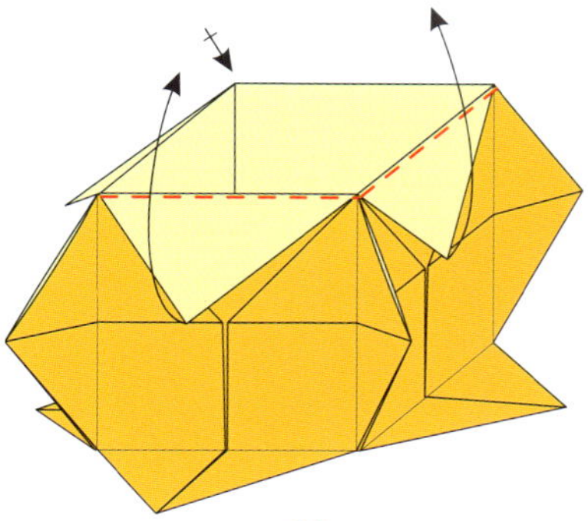

13. Alle vier Ecken nach oben stellen.
Put all four corners upwards.

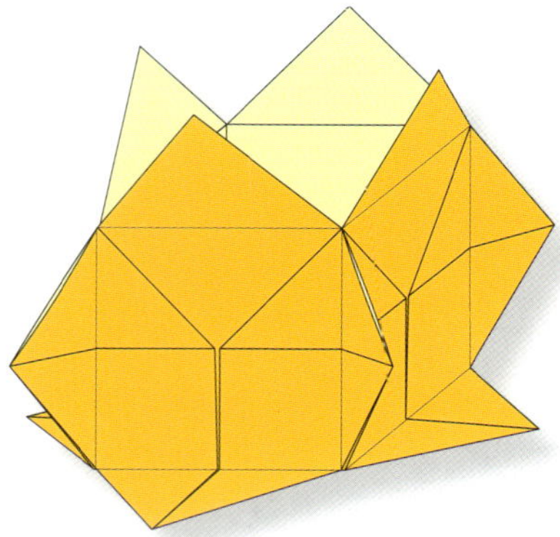

14. Fertiges Modell seitlich gesehen.
Finished model seen from the side.

15. Fertiges Modell von oben gesehen.
Finished model seen from above.

Kleine Blüte-Lichteffekte Variation

Start. Diagramme von Seite 12 bis Nr.13 falten.
Fold charts of page 12 until No.13.

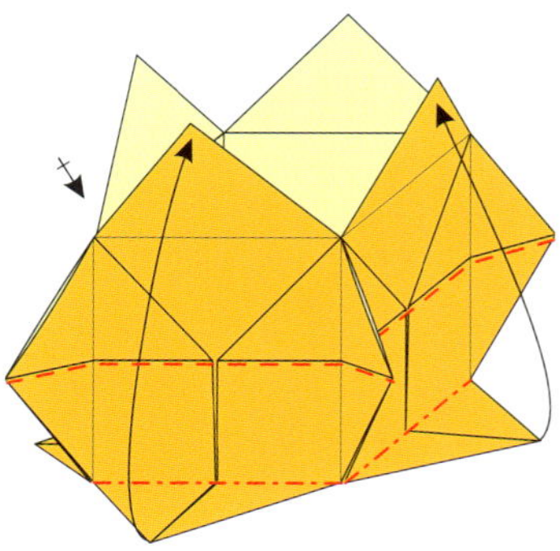

1. Untere Spitze nach oben falten, liegen lassen.
Fold lower point upwards and leave.

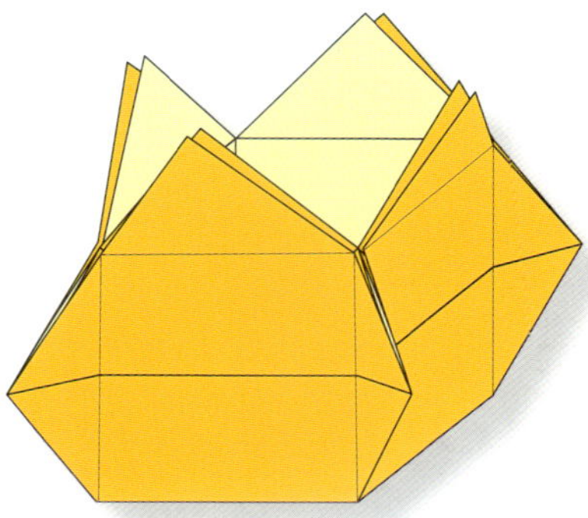

2. Fertiges Modell seitlich gesehen.
Finished model seen from the side.

3. Fertiges Modell von oben gesehen.
Finished model seen from above.

Flache Blüten Lichter

MATERIAL

1 Blatt 30x30 cm flammsicheres Lampenpapier. Bei dem fertigen Modell ist von der Papierrückseite nichts zu sehen. Es kann also jedes Papier gewählt werden.

One sheet 30x30 cm of not inflammable lamp paper. From the finished model, you won't see much of the back side of the paper. So you can choose any design.

1. Zweimal diagonal die Mitte falten, wieder öffnen. Fold twice the middle diagonally and open up again.

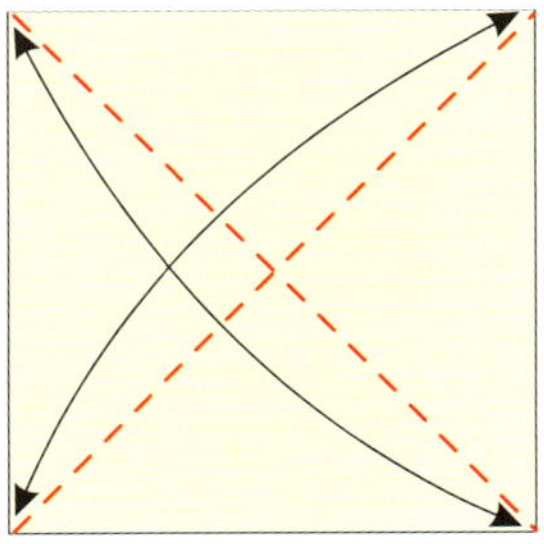

2. Alle vier Ecken zur Mitte falten, liegen lassen. Fold all four corners towards the middle and leave.

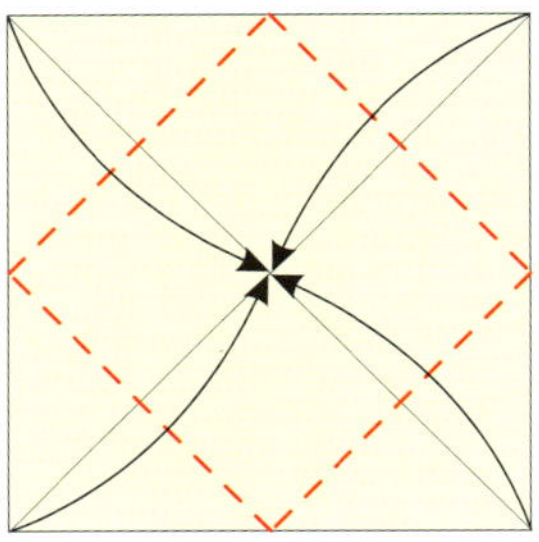

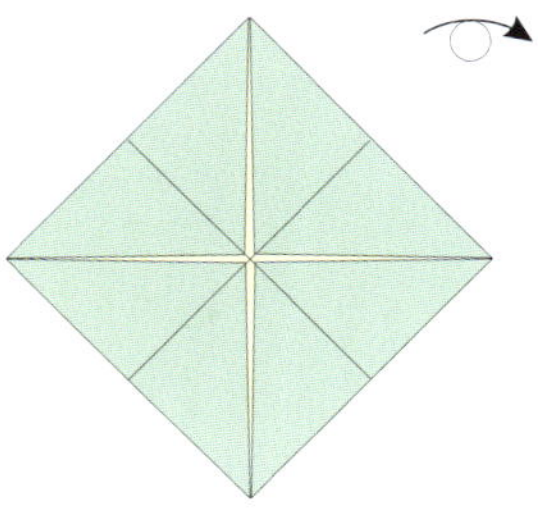

3. Rückseite nach oben legen. Turn over to the back.

4. Wieder alle vier Ecken zur Mitte falten, liegen lassen. Again, fold all four corners towards the middle and leave.

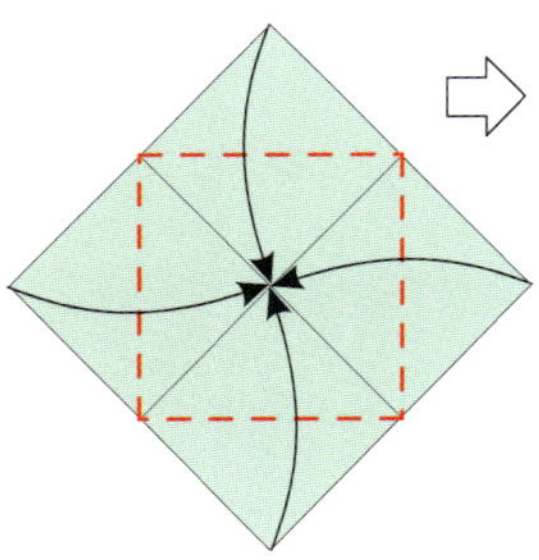

5. Spitzen von der Mitte an die Papierkante falten, wieder öffnen. Fold the points from the middle to the paper edge and open up again.

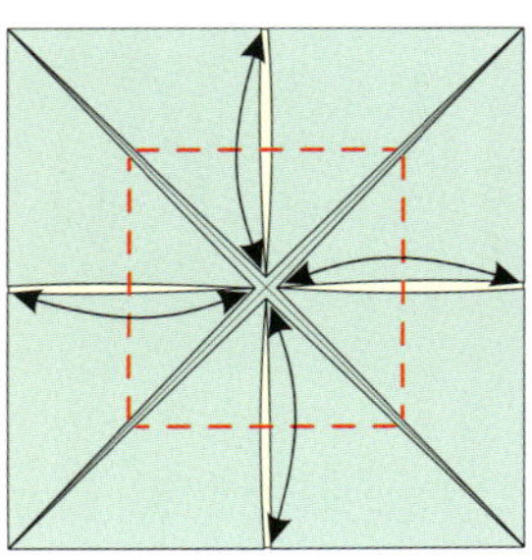

6. Alle vier Ecken zur Mitte falten, liegen lassen. Fold all four corners towards the middle and leave.

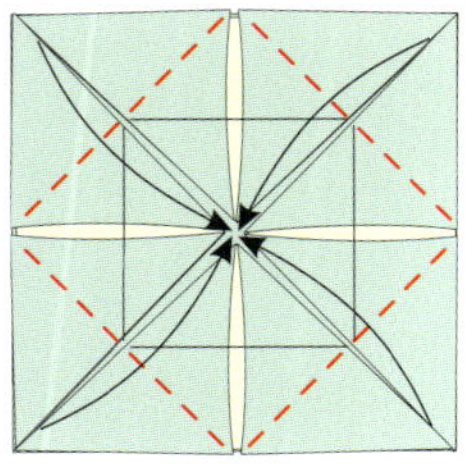

7. Alle vier Papierspitzen von der Rückseite nach oben legen. Put all four points from the back towards the top.

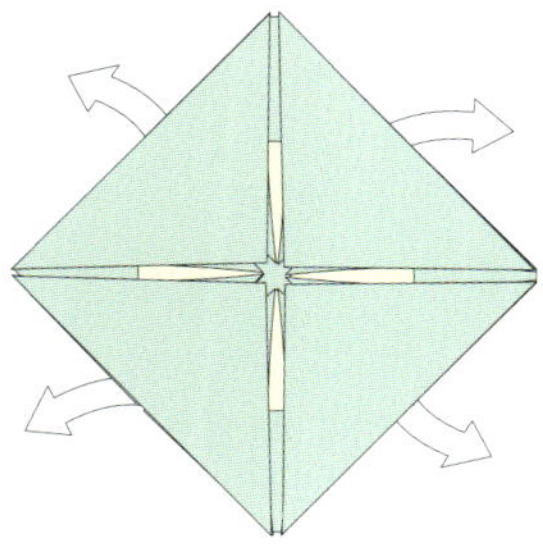

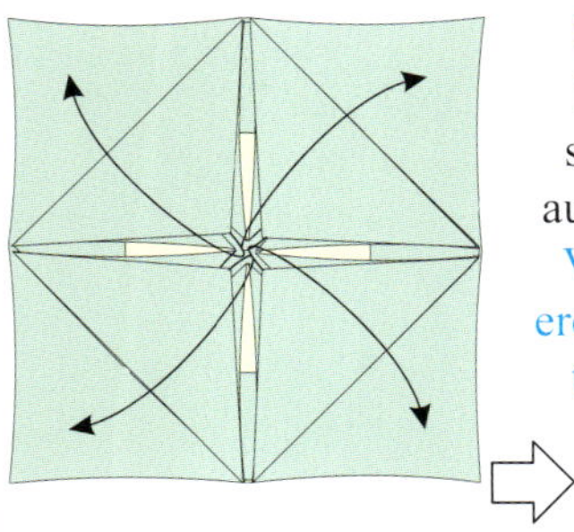

8. Obere Dreiecke senkrecht aufrichten. Vertically erect upper triangles.

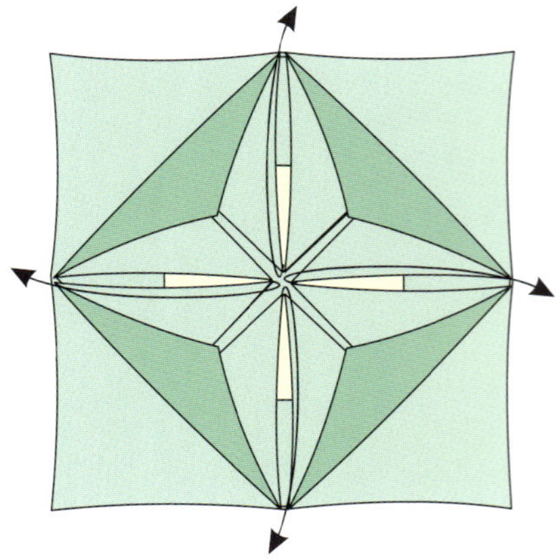

9. Nun die inneren Dreiecke auch senkrecht aufrichten. Also vertically erect the internal triangles.

10. Fertiges Modell von oben gesehen. Finished model seen from above.

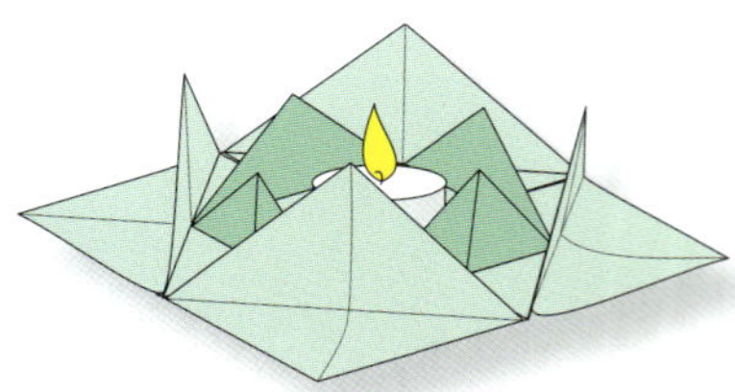

11. Fertiges Modell seitlich gesehen. Finished model seen from the side.

Seerosen-Lichtblätter

Modell von Jannie van Schuylenburg

MATERIAL

1 Blatt 30x30 cm flammsicheres Lampenpapier. Bei dem fertigen Modell ist von der Papierrückseite etwas zu sehen. Es kann durchgefärbtes Papier oder Papier mit weißer Rückseite gewählt werden. Schön ist es auch mit nur weißem Papier.
One sheet 30x30 cm of not inflammable lamp paper. From the finished model, you will see a little bit of the back side of the paper. So you can use paper with a coloured or white back side. It will also look very lovely using white paper only.

Start. Diagramme von Seite 14 bis Nr.2 falten.
Fold charts of page 14 until No.2.

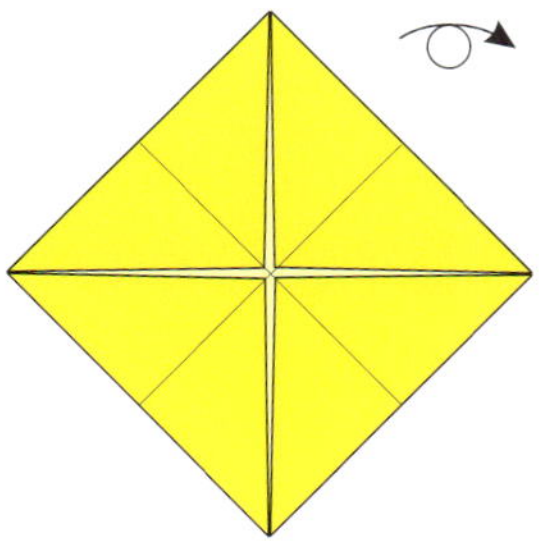

1. Rückseite nach oben legen.
Turn over to the back.

2. Alle vier Ecken zur Mitte falten, liegen lassen.
Fold all four corners to the middle and leave.

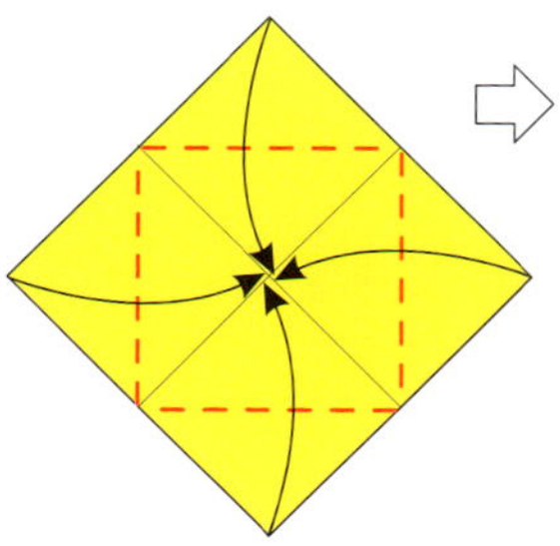

3. Spitzen von der Mitte an die Papierkante falten, liegen lassen.
Fold points from the middle to the edge and leave.

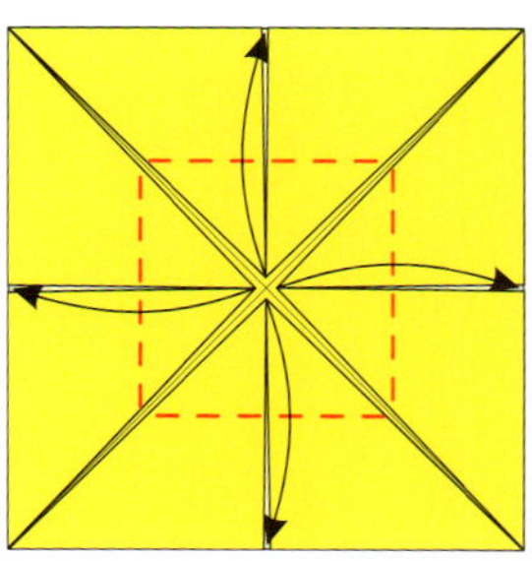

4. Rückseite nach oben legen.
Turn over to the back.

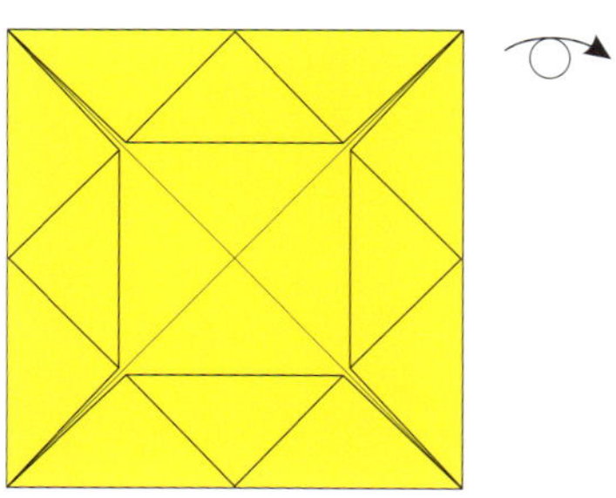

5. Alle vier Spitzen an die Ecken falten, liegen lassen.
Fold all four points to the corners and leave.

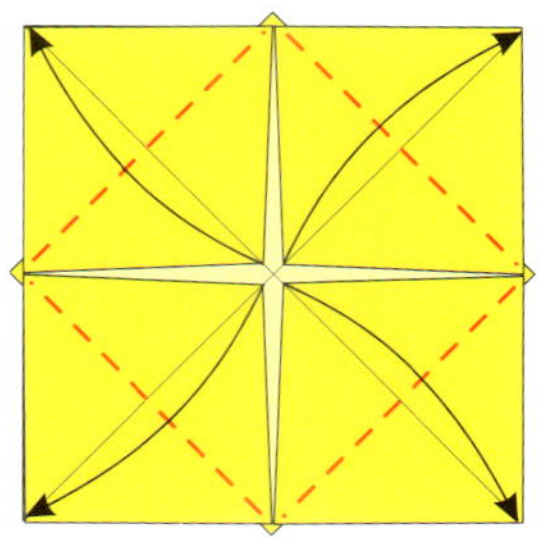

6. Waagerechte Linien, nur im inneren Teil falten, wieder öffnen.
Fold horizontal lines on the inner part only and open up again.

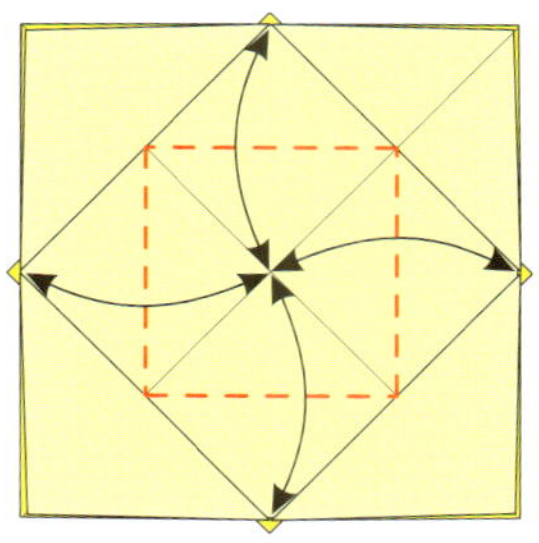

7. Nur mit der oberen Papierlage, schräge Linie falten, wieder öffnen. An den drei anderen Ecken wiederholen.
Using only the top layer of paper, fold oblique lines and open up again. Repeat on the other three corners.

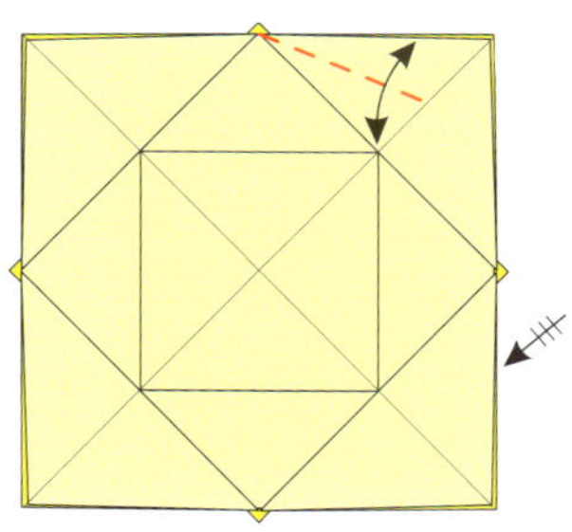

8. Nur mit der oberen Papierlage, schräge Linie falten, wieder öffnen. An den drei anderen Ecken wiederholen.
Using only the top layer of paper, fold oblique lines and open up again. Repeat on the other three corners.

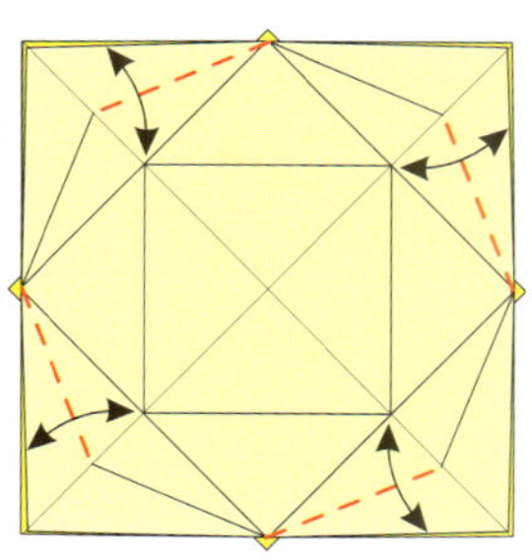

9. An allen vier Ecken die obere Papierlage, siehe Pfeile, senkrecht aufstellen.
Erect the top layer of paper vertically on all four corners.

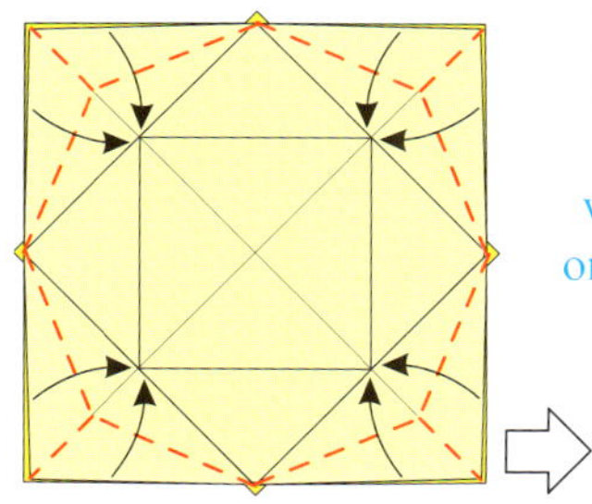

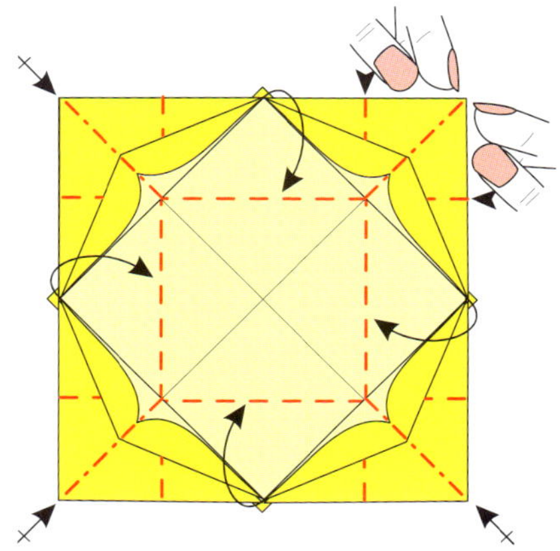

10. Linien an der Ecke zur Bergfalte formen, dabei seitlich mit den Händen eindrücken. An den anderen drei Ecken wiederholen. Dadurch wird aus dem flachen Papier die aufgestellte Form.
Form lines from the corner as a mountain-fold and push in from the side. Repeat on the three other corners, so that the erected form arises.

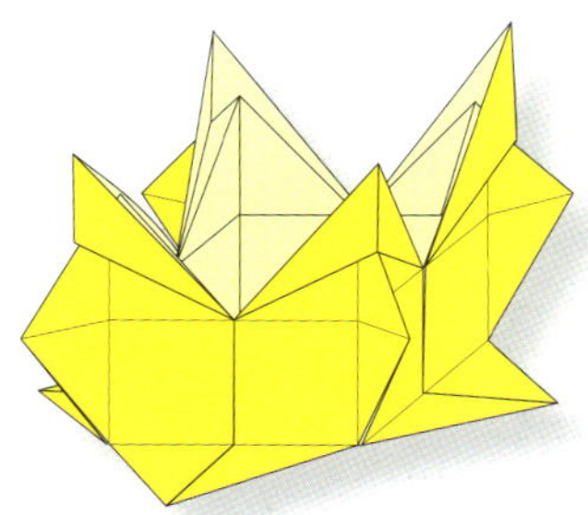

11. Fertiges Modell seitlich gesehen.
Finished model seen from the side.

12. Fertiges Modell von oben gesehen.
Finished model seen from above.

Seerosen-Lichtblätter Variation

Modell von Jannie van Schuylenburg

Start. Diagramme von Seite 15 bis Nr.11 falten.
Fold charts of page 15 until No.11.

1. Untere Spitze an der waagerechten Linie nach oben falten, liegen lassen.
Fold lower point along the horizontal line upwards and leave.

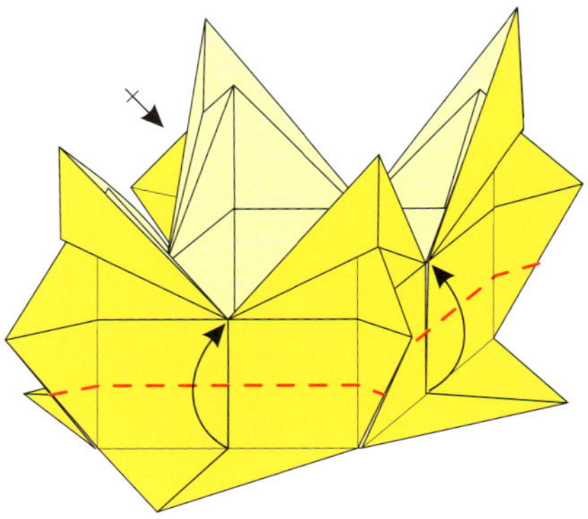

2. Fertiges Modell seitlich gesehen.
Finished model seen from the side.

3. Fertiges Modell von oben gesehen.
Finished model seen from above.

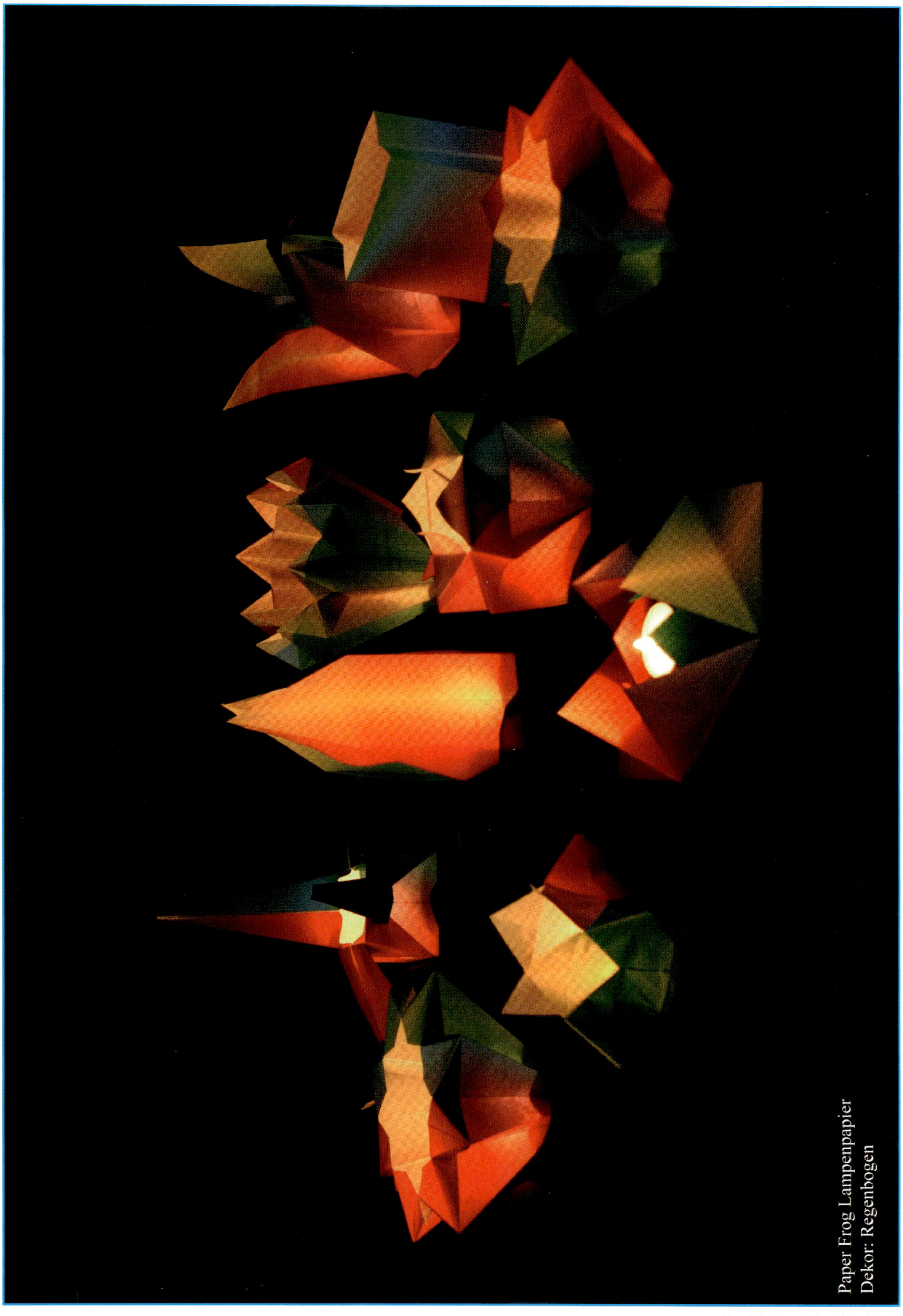
Paper Frog Lampenpapier
Dekor: Regenbogen

Lichtschüssel-standard

Modell von Janina Weinand

MATERIAL

1 Blatt 30x30 cm flammsicheres Lampenpapier. Bei dem fertigen Modell ist von der Papierrückseite sehr viel zu sehen. Es sollte also nur durchgefärbtes Papier gewählt werden. Allerdings sieht das weiße Papier auch sehr schön aus.

One sheet 30x30 cm of not inflammable lamp paper. From the finished model, you will see a lot of the back side of the paper. So you should use paper with a coloured back side. It will also look very lovely using white paper.

1. Zweimal diagonal die Mitte falten, wieder öffnen. Rückseite nach oben legen.

Fold twice the middle diagonally and open up again. Turn over to the back.

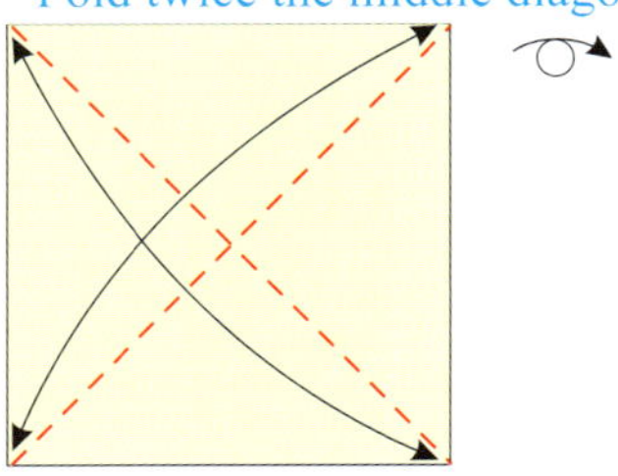

2. Zweimal waagerecht die Mitte falten, wieder öffnen.

Fold twice the middle horizontally and open up again.

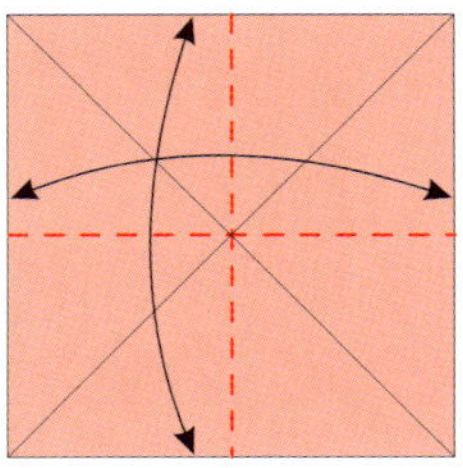

3. Senkrechte Linien falten, aber nur bis zu den schrägen diagonalen Linien, wieder öffnen.

Fold vertical lines, but only until the oblique diagonal lines and open up again.

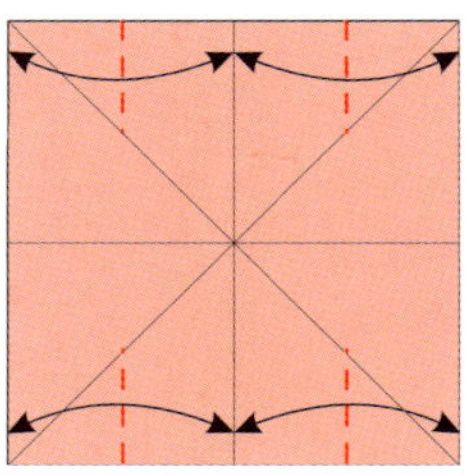

4. Waagerechte Linien falten, aber nur bis zu den schrägen diagonalen Linien, wieder öffnen.

Fold horizontal lines, but only until the oblique diagonal lines and open up again.

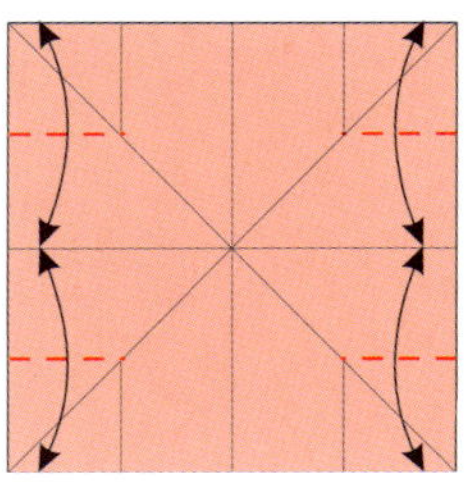

5. Schräge Linien falten, wieder öffnen. Rückseite nach oben legen.

Fold oblique lines and open up again. Turn over to the back.

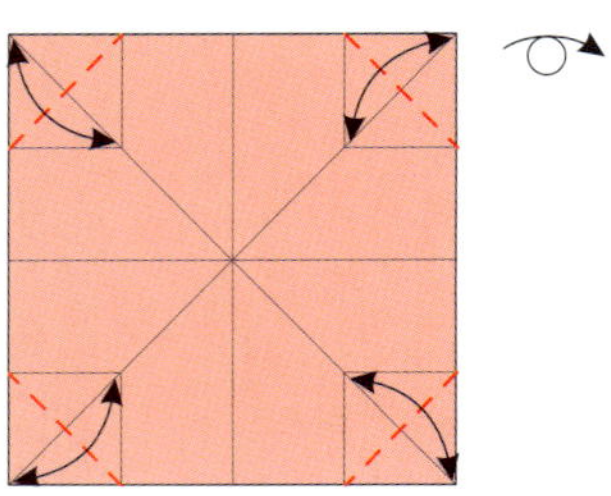

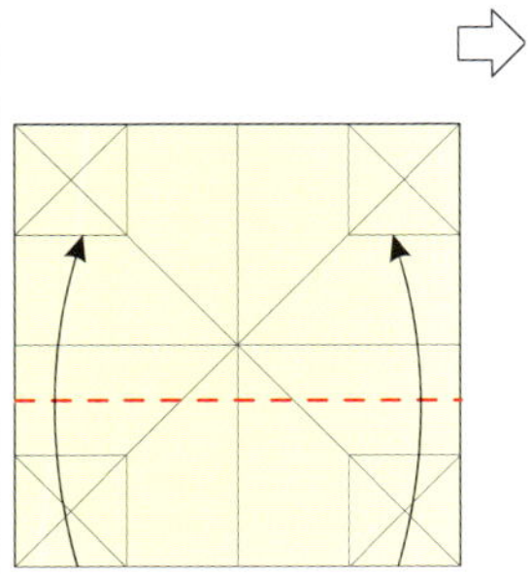

6. Waagerechte Linie falten, liegen lassen.

Fold horizontal line and leave.

7. Schräge Linien falten, wieder öffnen.

Fold oblique lines and open up again.

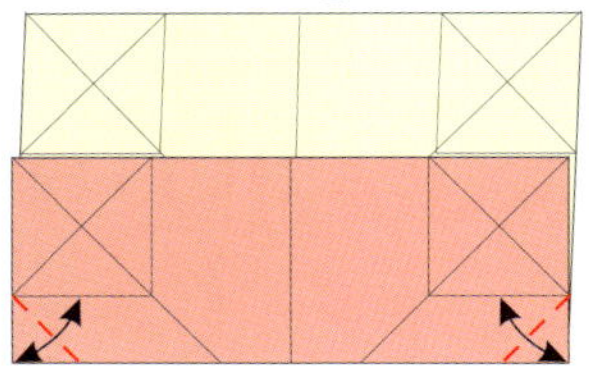

8. Obere Papierlage, siehe Pfeil, wieder öffnen.

Open up the top layer of paper, see arrow.

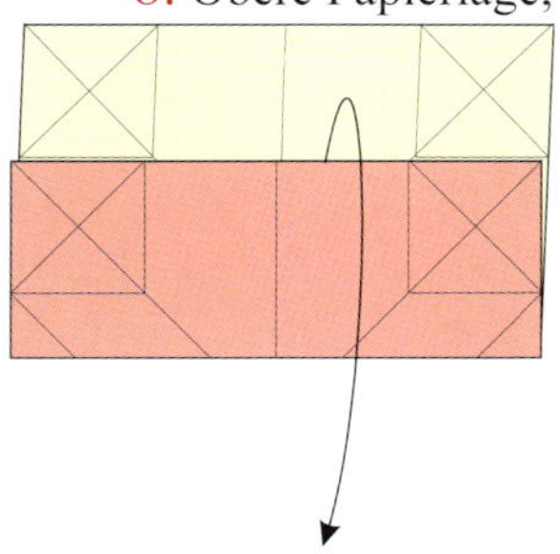

9. Die Arbeitsschritte von Nr.6 bis Nr.8 im oberen Teil, siehe Pfeil, wiederholen. Papier um 90 Grad drehen.

Repeat working steps from No.6 to No.8 in the upper part, see arrow. Turn the model 90 degrees around.

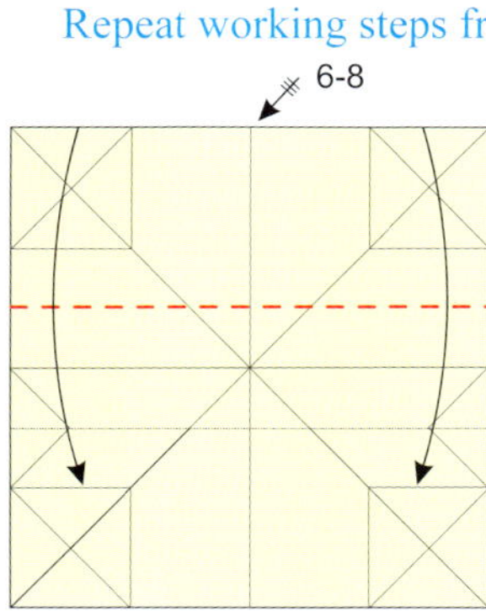

10. Die Arbeitsschritte von Nr.6 bis Nr.9 wiederholen.

Repeat working steps from No.6 to No.9.

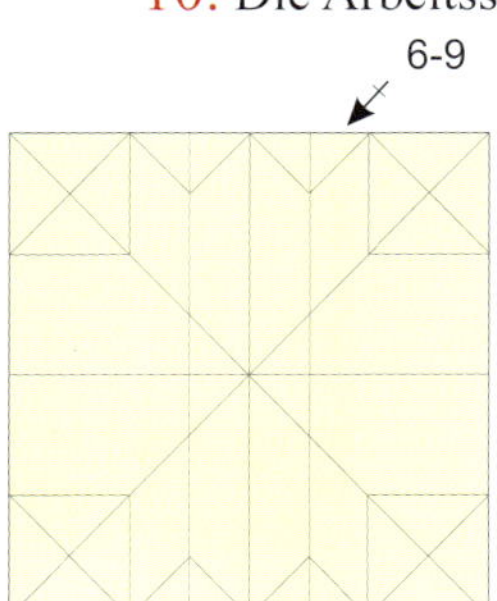

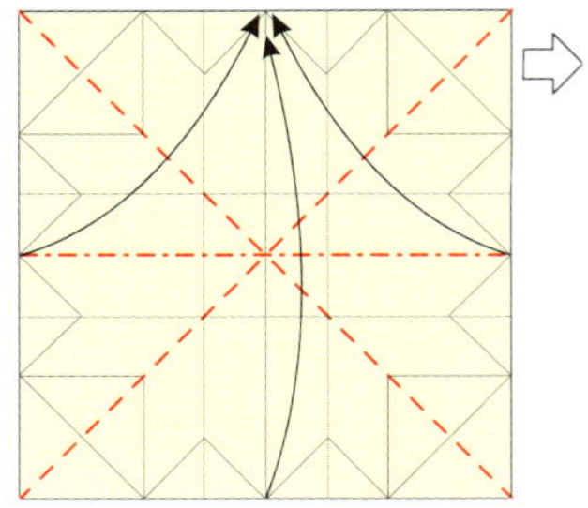

11. Von der waagerechten Mitte (Bergfalte), Papier seitlich zum oberen Mittelpunkt legen, siehe Pfeile. Es entsteht ein Dreieck.

From the horizontal middle (mountain-fold), lay paper from the side to the upper centre, see arrows. A triangle arises.

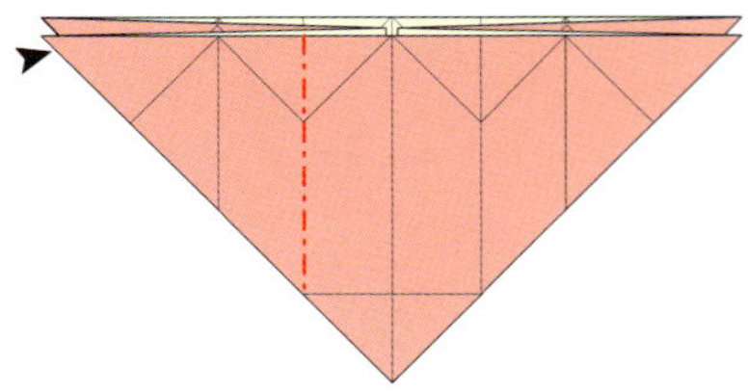

12. Spitze an der roten Linie (bereits gefaltet), nach innen legen.

Lay point along the red line (already folded) inwards.

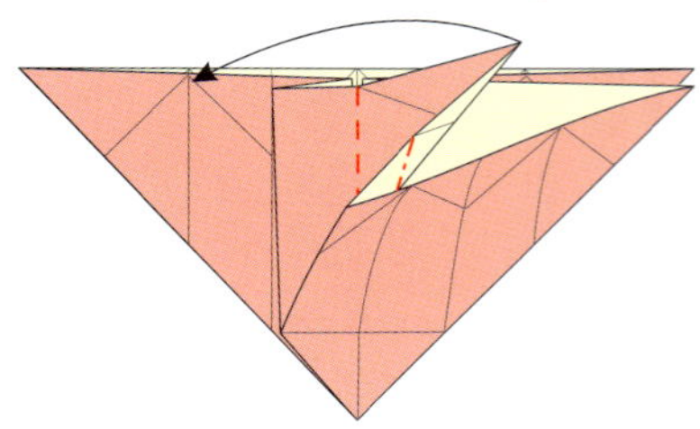

13. Spitze an der roten Linie (bereits gefaltet), wieder nach außen legen, siehe Pfeil.

Lay point along the red line (already folded) back outwards, see arrow.

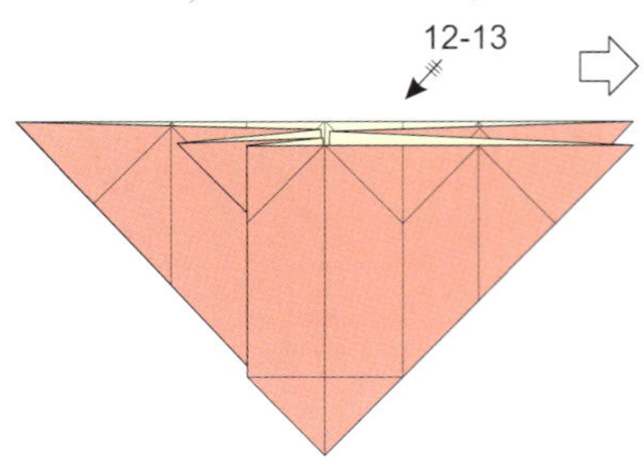

14. Die Arbeitsschritte von Nr.12 bis Nr.13 mit den anderen drei Spitzen wiederholen.

Repeat working steps from No.12 to No.13 with the other three points.

15. Schräge Linien (bereits vorhanden) zur Bergfalte formen, dabei die Ecken nach innen legen. Auf der Rückseite wiederholen.
Form oblique lines (already folded) as a mountain-fold, at the same time lay corners inwards. Turn over to the back.

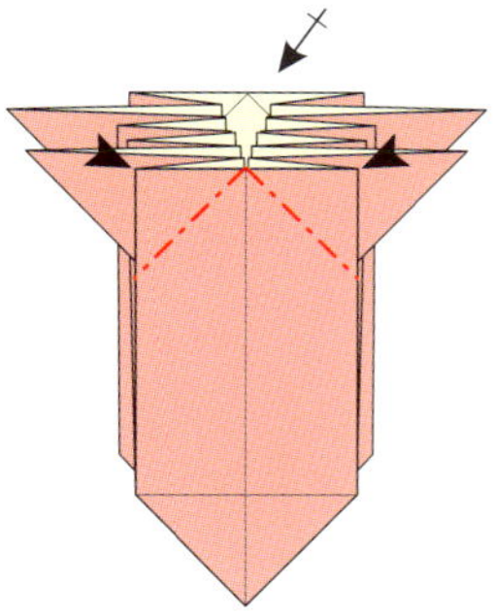

16. Spitze nach unten falten, liegen lassen. Auf der Rückseite wiederholen.
Fold point downwards and leave. Repeat on the back.

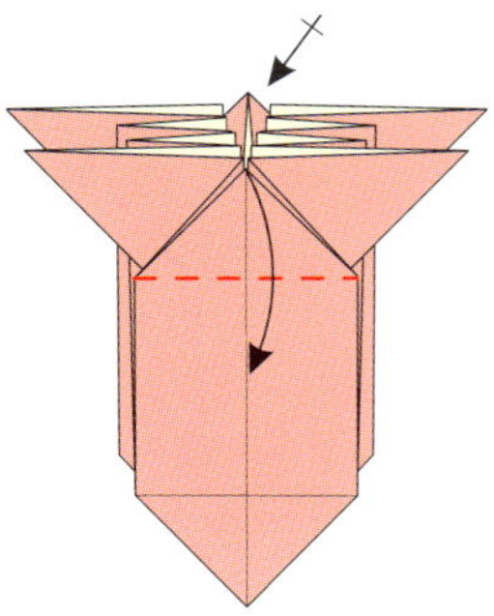

17. Nur mit der oberen Papierlage senkrechte Mitte falten, siehe Pfeil, liegen lassen. Auf der Rückseite wiederholen.
Using only the top layer of paper, fold the vertical middle, see arrow and leave. Repeat on the back.

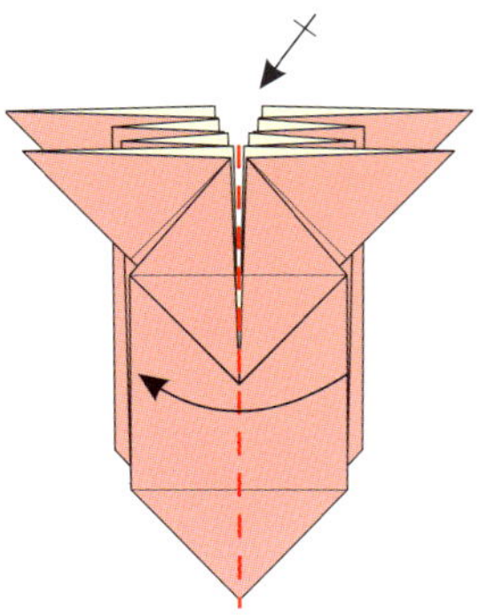

18. Schräge Linien (bereits vorhanden) zur Bergfalte formen, dabei die Ecken nach innen legen. Auf der Rückseite wiederholen.
Form oblique lines (already folded) as a mountain-fold, at the same time lay corners inwards. Turn over to the back.

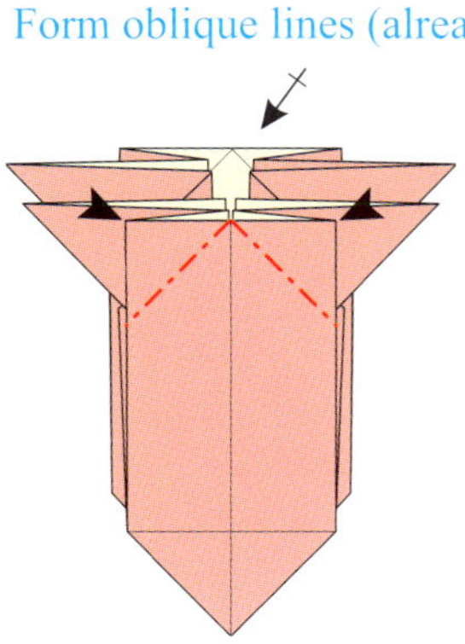

19. Spitze nach unten falten, liegen lassen. Auf der Rückseite wiederholen.
Fold point downwards and leave. Repeat on the back.

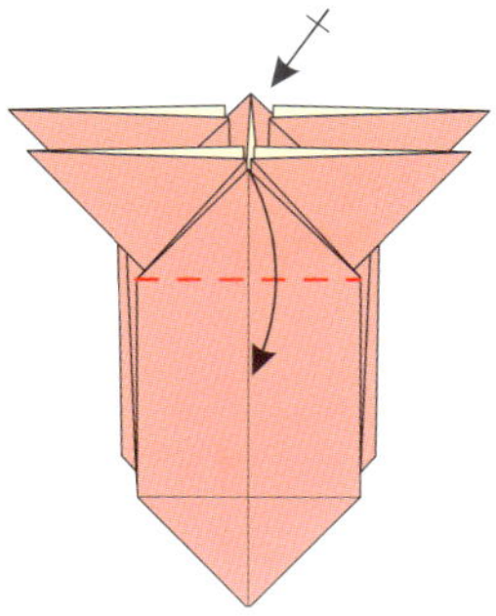

20. Bergfalte an der unteren Spitze arbeiten. Modell von innen auseinanderdrücken, das Modell steht dann flach auf dem Tisch.
Form a mountain-fold on the lower point. Push the model from the inside outwards. Now the model stands flatly on the table.

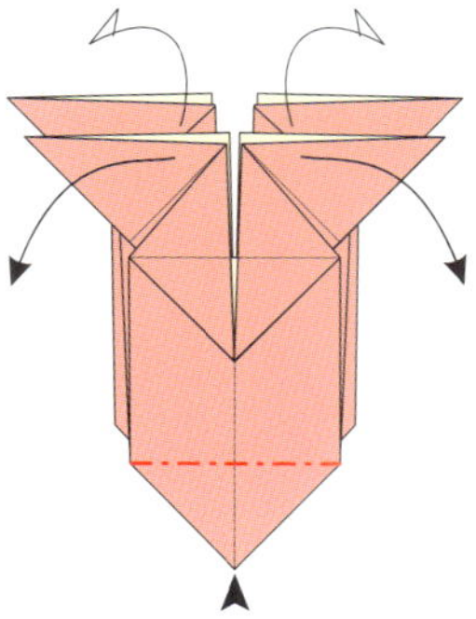

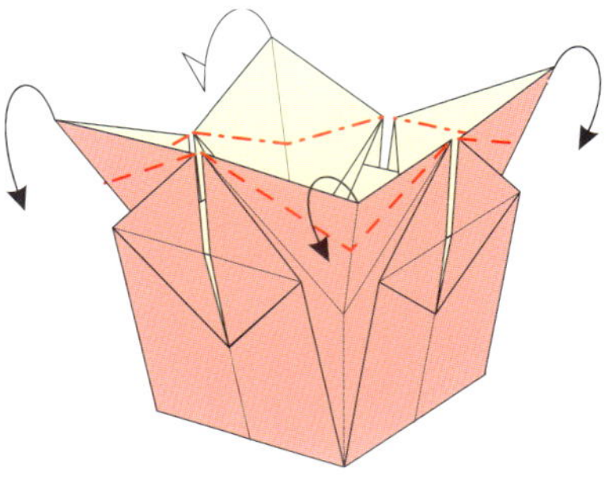

21. Linien nach vorne falten, siehe Pfeile, damit das Modell seine endgültige Form bekommt.
Fold lines to the front, see arrow, so that the model gets his final shape.

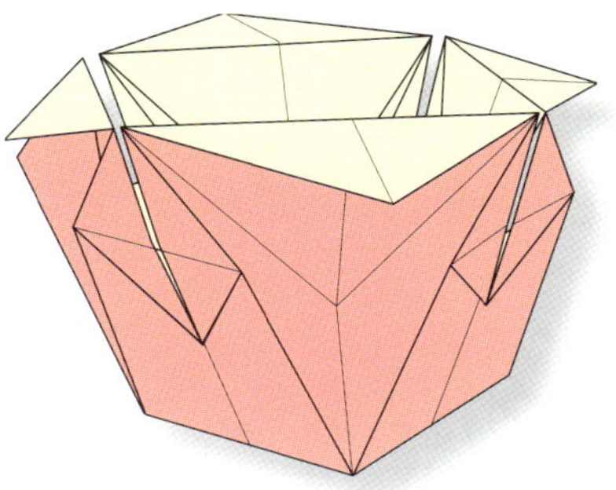

22. Fertiges Modell seitlich gesehen.
Finished model seen from the side.

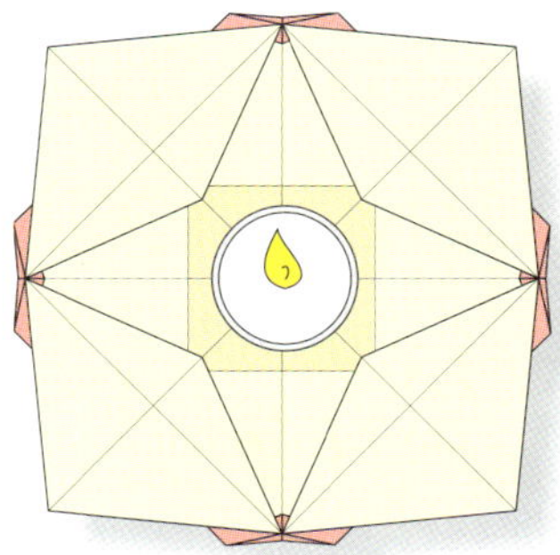

23. Fertiges Modell von oben gesehen.
Finished model seen from above.

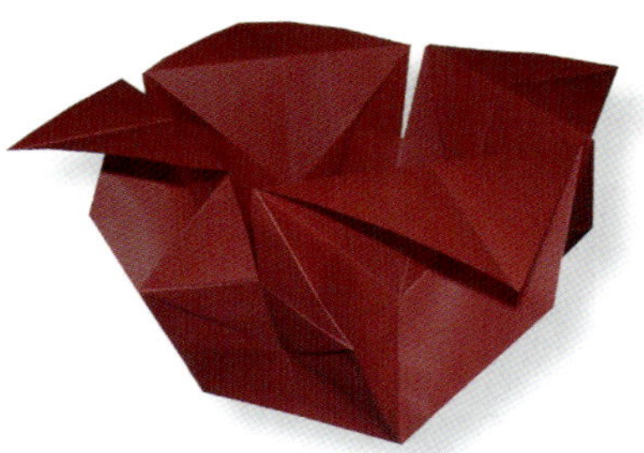

Lichtschüssel-blumig

MATERIAL

1 Blatt 30x30 cm flammsicheres Lampenpapier. Bei dem fertigen Modell ist von der Papierrückseite nur wenig zu sehen. Es kann also durchgefärbtes Papier oder Papier mit einer weißen Rückseite gewählt werden.

One sheet 30x30 cm of not inflammable lamp paper. From the finished model, you won't see much of the back side of the paper. So you can choose any design.

Start. Diagramme von Seite 18 bis Nr.10 falten.

Fold charts of page 18 until step No.10.

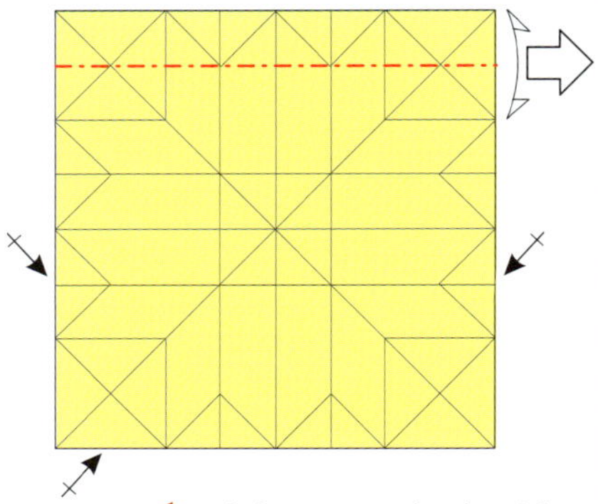

1. Linie zur Rückseite falten (Bergfalte), wieder öffnen. An den anderen drei Seiten wiederholen.

Fold line to the back (mountain-fold) and open up again. Repeat on the other three edges.

2. Nun die Diagramme von Seite 18 Nr. 11 bis Nr.19 falten.

Fold charts of page 18 from step No.11 to step No.19.

3. Schräge Linien falten, wieder öffnen. Auf der Rückseite wiederholen.

Fold oblique lines and open up again. Repeat on the back.

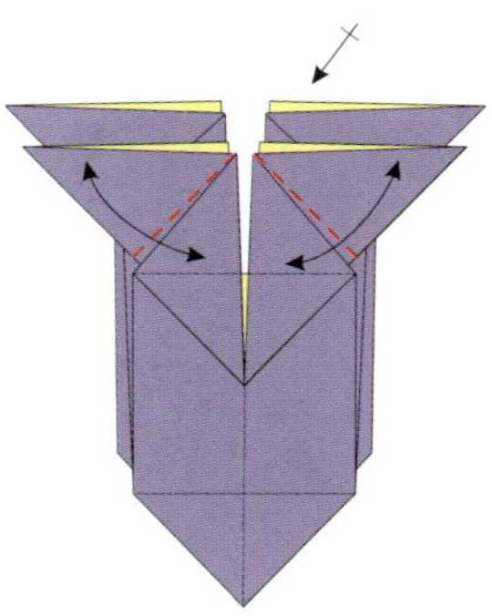

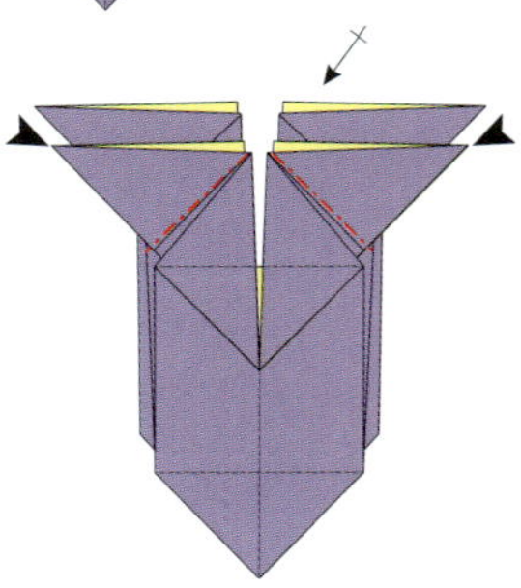

4. Spitzen nach innen legen, dabei die schrägen Linien zur Bergfalte formen. Auf der Rückseite wiederholen.

Lay points inwards, at the same time form oblique lines as a mountain-fold. Repeat on the back.

5. Spitzen, siehe Pfeile, zwischen die einzelnen Papierlagen nach unten falten. Achtung: Vorsichtig arbeiten, damit das Papier nicht einreißen kann. Mit allen oberen Spitzen wiederholen.

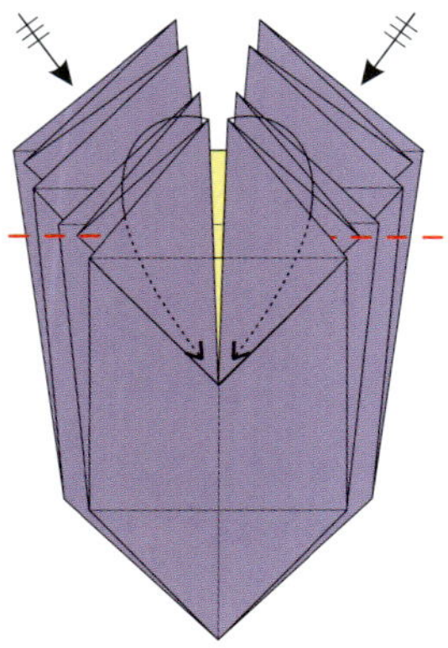

Fold points downwards, see arrow, between the layers of paper. Attention: Work carefully, so that the paper doesn't rip. Repeat with all upper points.

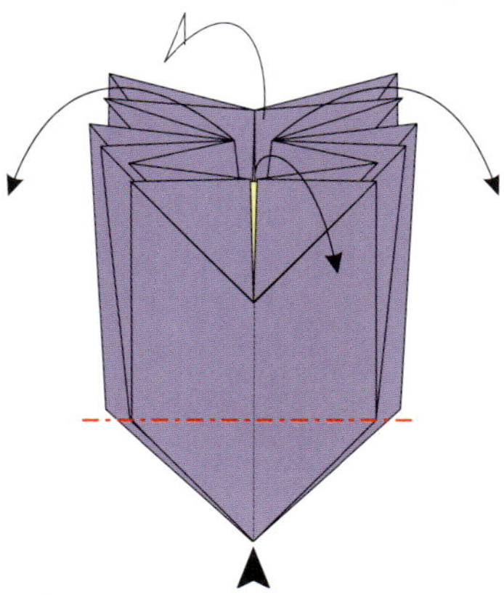

6. Bergfalte an der unteren Spitze arbeiten. Modell von innen auseinanderdrücken, das Modell steht dann flach auf dem Tisch.

Form a mountain-fold on the lower point. Push the model from the inside outwards. Now the model stands flatly on the table.

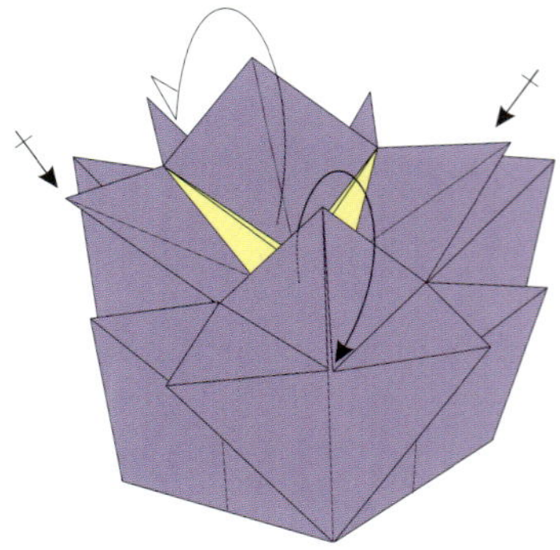

7. Am oberen Rand haben sich vier Spitzen gebildet, die nun nach außen gebogen werden. Dadurch bildet sich ein kleines waagerechtes Quadrat. Achtung: Vorsichtig arbeiten, damit das Papier nicht einreißen kann.

There are four points now on the upper edge, which will be bend now to the outside. Then a little horizontal square arises. Attention: Work carefully, so that the paper doesn't rip.

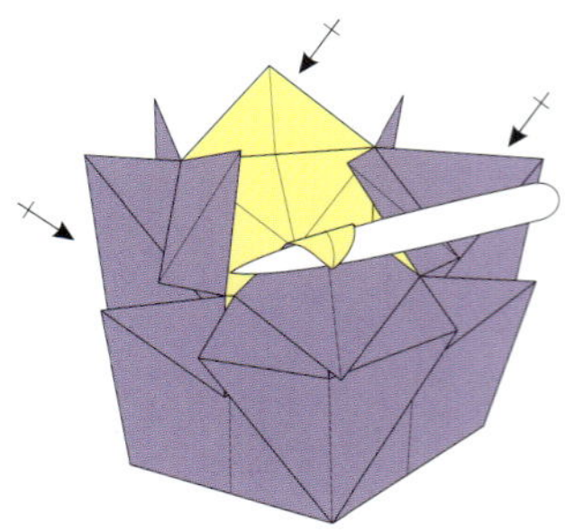

8. Alle vier Spitzen dieser kleinen Quadrate werden jetzt über ein Falzbein gerollt, dadurch wird das Papier rund und die Blütenform entsteht.

Roll all four points of the small squares over a bonefolder, so that the paper becomes round and the flourish form arises.

9. Fertiges Modell seitlich gesehen.

Finished model seen from the side.

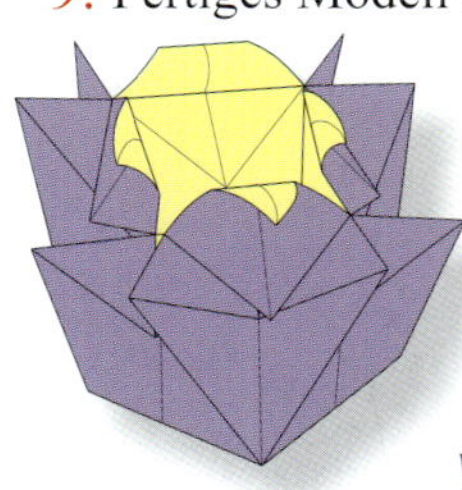

10. Fertiges Modell von oben gesehen.

Finished model seen from above.

Lichtschüssel-futuristisch

Modell von Janina Weinand

MATERIAL

1 Blatt 30x30 cm flammsicheres Lampenpapier. Bei dem fertigen Modell ist von der Papierrückseite nur wenig zu sehen. Es kann also durchgefärbtes Papier oder Papier mit einer weißen Rückseite gewählt werden.

One sheet 30x30 cm of not inflammable lamp paper. From the finished model, you won't see much of the back side of the paper. So you can choose any design.

Start. Diagramme von Seite 18 bis Nr.10 falten.

Fold charts of page 18 until step No.10.

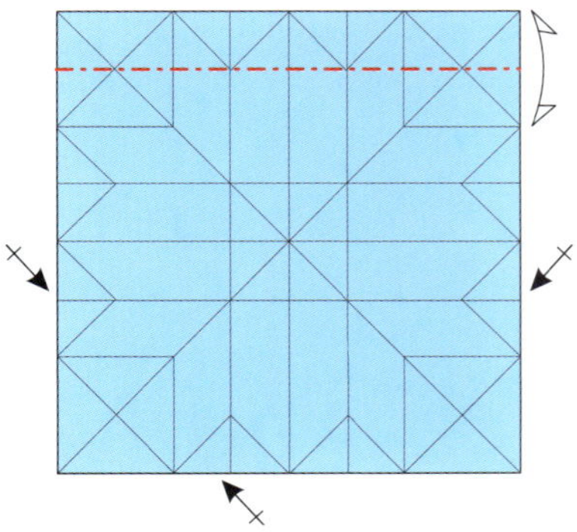

1. Linie zur Rückseite falten (Bergfalte), wieder öffnen. An den anderen drei Seiten wiederholen.

Fold line to the back (mountain-fold) and open up again. Repeat on the other three edges.

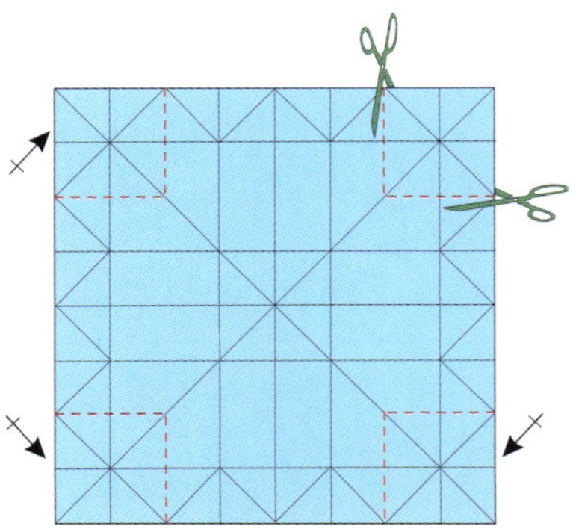

2. An der roten Linie wird jetzt an allen vier Ecken das Papier abgeschnitten.

Cut off the paper along the red line on all four corners.

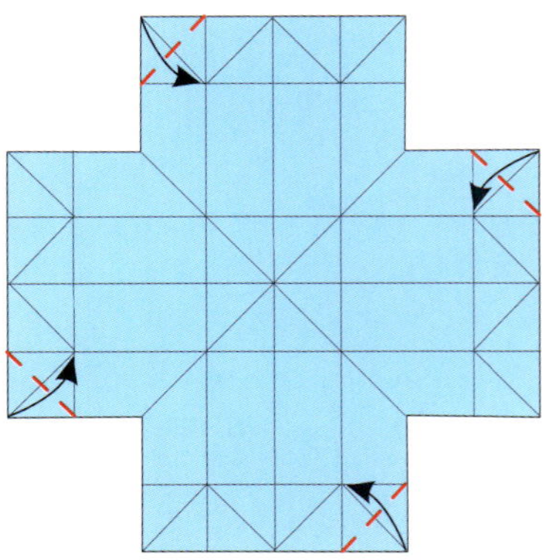

3. Schräge Linien an allen vier Seiten falten, liegen lassen.

Fold oblique lines on all four edges and leave.

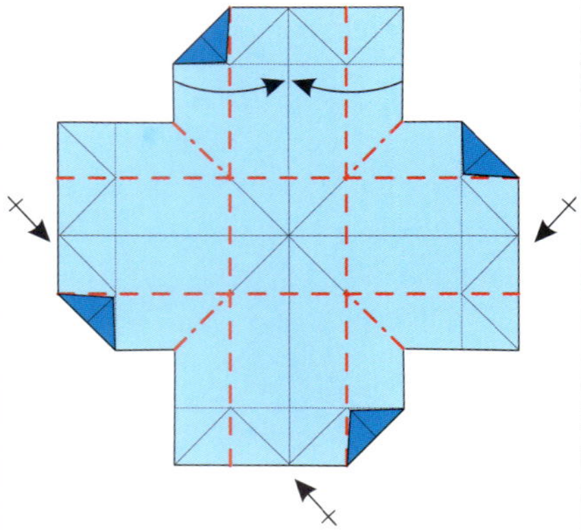

4. Im kleinen waagerechten Papierteil schräge Linie falten, dabei die senkrechte Bergfalte unter das kleine gefaltete Dreieck von Nr.3 schieben. Mit beiden Händen arbeiten, dann ist es einfacher.

Fold oblique line on the small horizontal paper part, at the same time push the vertical mountain-fold under the small folded triangle from No.3. Work with both hands at ease.

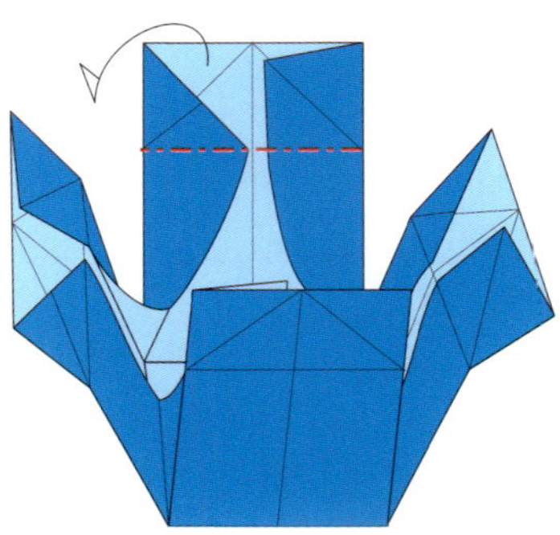

5. Linie als Bergfalte arbeiten, das obere Papierteil muss jetzt waagerecht sein.

Form line as a mountain-fold, so that the upper paper part is horizontally.

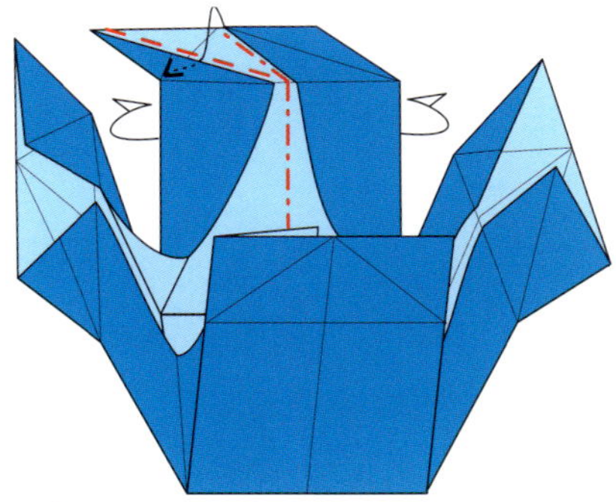

6. Das Papier wird nun an den roten Linien in die gewünschte Form gebracht, dabei die kleinen schrägen Linien zur Bergfalte formen. Siehe auch Diagramm Nr.7.

Get the paper now into shape along the red lines, at the same time form the little oblique lines as a mountain-fold. See also chart No.7.

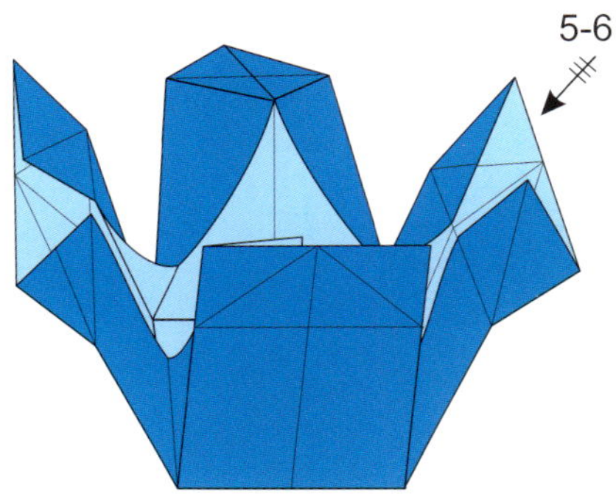

7. Die Arbeitsschritte von Nr.5 und Nr.6 mit den drei anderen Seiten wiederholen.

Repeat working steps No.5 and No.6 with the three other edges.

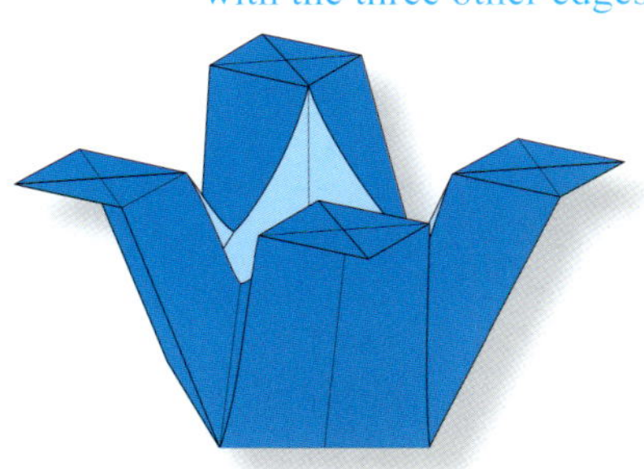

8. Fertiges Modell seitlich gesehen.

Finished model seen from the side.

9. Fertiges Modell von oben gesehen.

Finished model seen from above.

Partyschale hoch

MATERIAL

1 Bogen 30x30 cm flammsicheres Lampenpapier. Bei dem fertigen Modell ist von der Papierrückseite nichts zu sehen. Es kann also jedes Papier gewählt werden.

One sheet 30x30 cm of not inflammable lamp paper. From the finished model, you won't see much of the back side of the paper. So you can choose any design.

1. Zweimal waagerecht die Mitte falten, wieder öffnen.
Fold twice the middle horizontally and open up again.

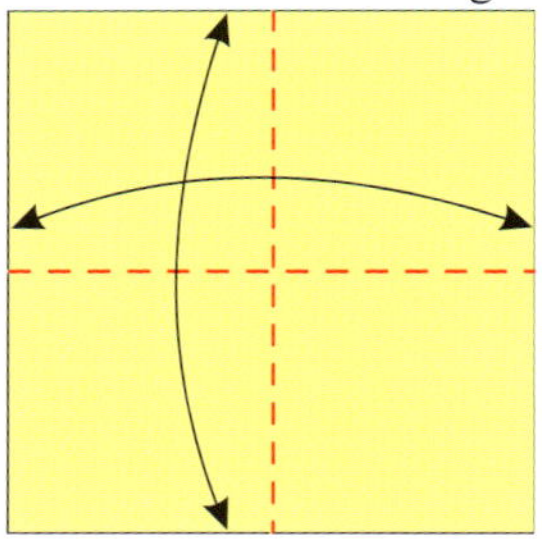

2. Zweimal diagonal die Mitte falten, wieder öffnen.
Fold twice the middle diagonally and open up again.

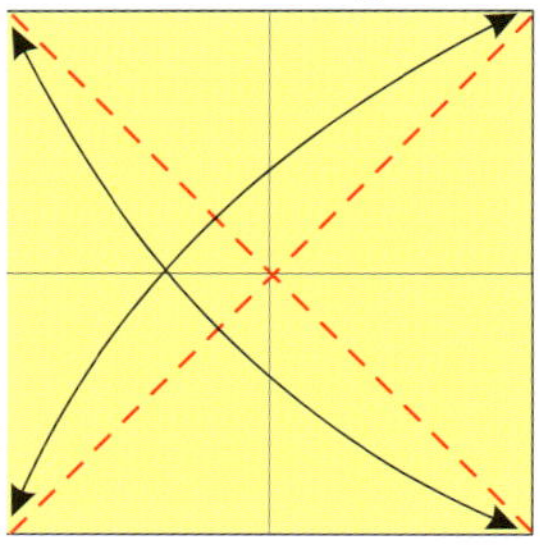

3. Alle vier Ecken zur Mitte falten, liegen lassen.
Fold all four corners to the middle and leave.

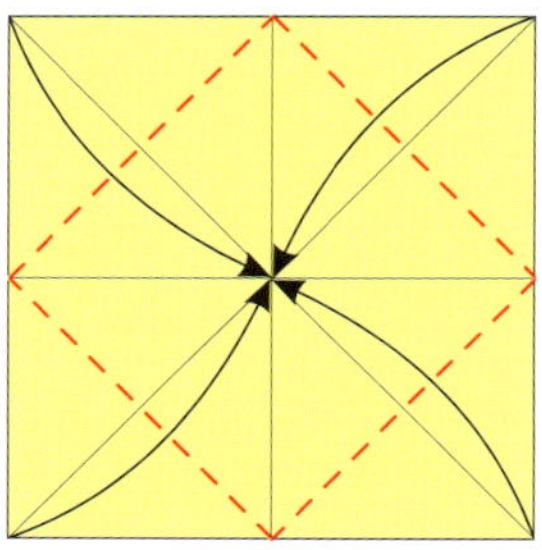

4. Rückseite nach oben legen.
Turn over to the back.

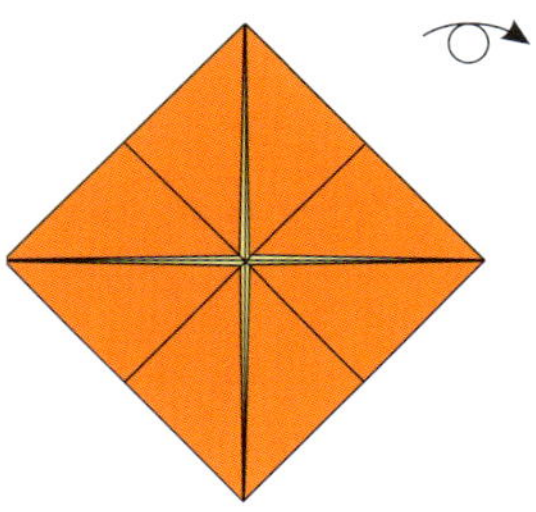

5. Von der waagerechten Mitte (Bergfalte), die seitlichen Ecken zur oberen Mitte legen. Die untere Ecke dann ebenfalls nach oben legen, siehe Pfeile.
From the horizontal middle (mountain-fold), lay the corners from the side to the upper middle. Then lay the lower corner upwards, as well, see arrows.

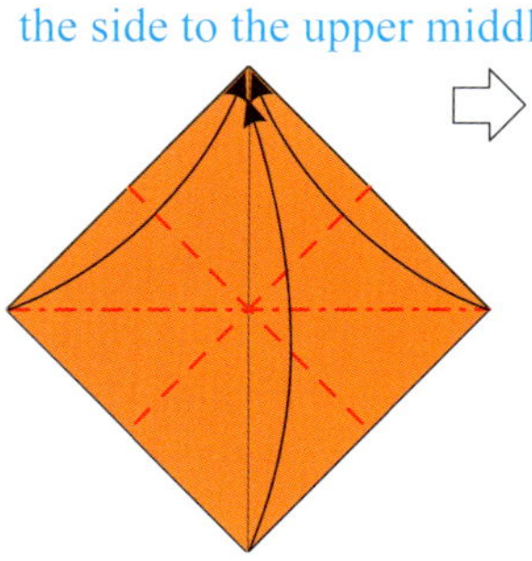

6. Die oberen Papierlagen öffnen (siehe Pfeile), um dann die senkrechte Bergfalte zu arbeiten. Siehe auch Diagramm Nr.7.
Open the upper layers of paper (see arrow) and form the vertical mountain-fold. See also chart No.7.

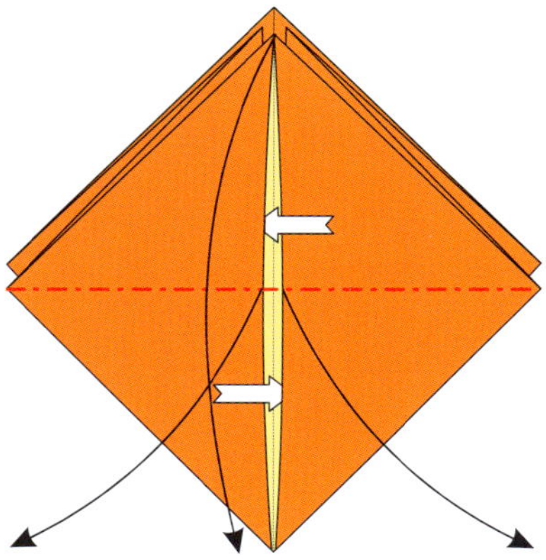

7. Arbeitsschritt von Nr.6 auf der Rückseite wiederholen.
Repeat working step No.6 on the back.

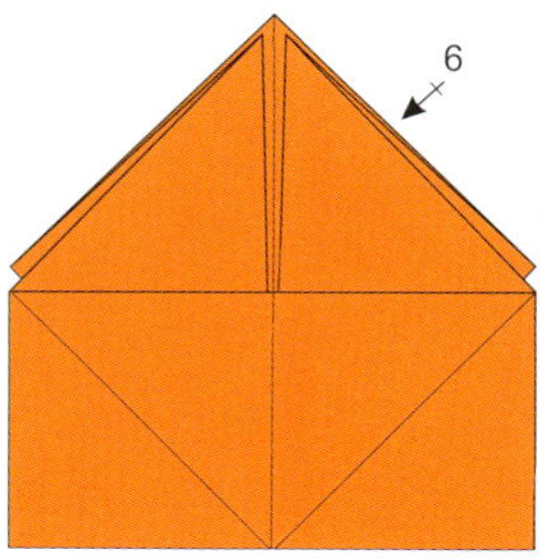

8. Mit der oberen Papierlage senkrechte Mitte falten, siehe Pfeil, liegen lassen. Auf der Rückseite wiederholen.
Using only the top layer of paper, fold the vertical middle, see arrow, and leave. Repeat on the back.

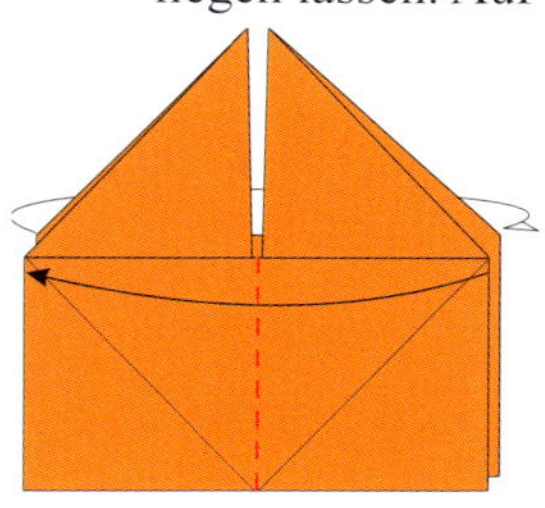

9. Senkrechte Linien falten, liegen lassen. Auf der Rückseite wiederholen.
Fold the vertical lines and leave. Repeat on the back.

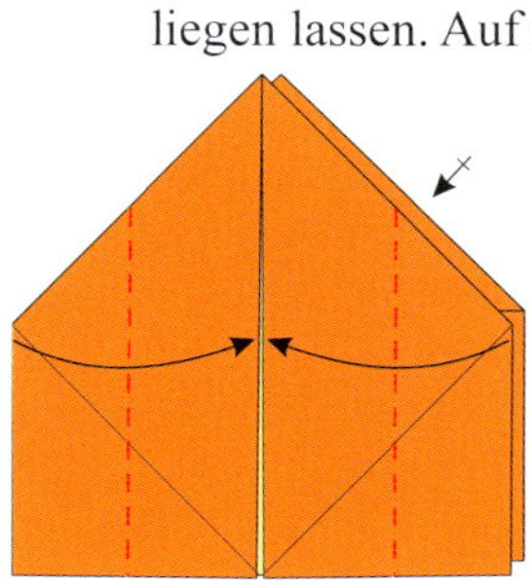

10. Spitzen nach unten falten, liegen lassen. Auf der Rückseite wiederholen.
Fold the point downwards and leave. Repeat on the back.

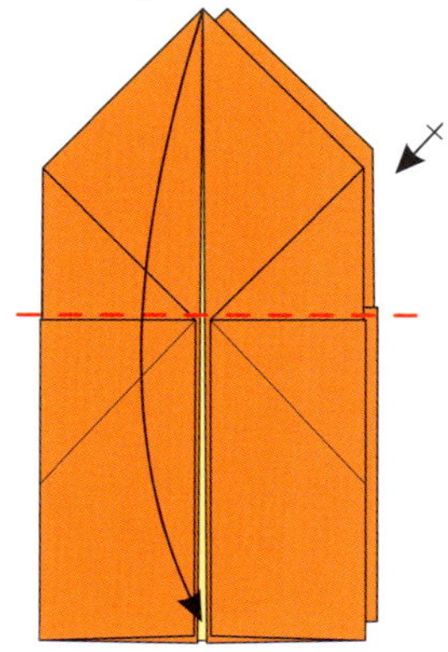

11. Modell von innen auseinanderdrücken, das Papier liegt jetzt nicht unten flach auf dem Tisch. Die Besonderheit dieses Modells ist, das der Boden auf der halben Höhe ist. Dadurch entsteht ein besonderer Leuchteffekt.
Push the model from the inside outwards. Now the paper doesn't lie flatly on the table. The bottom is now on half of the model's height. Now you have a special light effect.

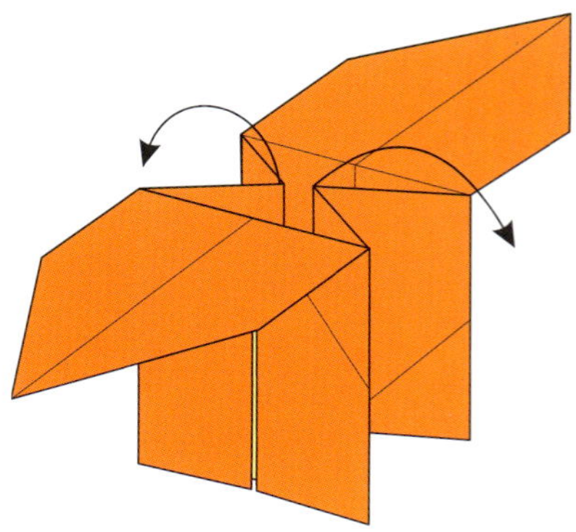

12. Fertiges Modell seitlich gesehen.
Finished model seen from the side.

Partyschale flach

MATERIAL

1 Bogen 15x15 cm flammsicheres Lampenpapier. Bei dem fertigen Modell ist von der Papierrückseite nichts zu sehen. Es kann also jedes Papier gewählt werden.

One sheet 15x15 cm of not inflammable lamp paper. From the finished model, you won't see anything of the back side of the paper. So you can choose any design.

1. Zweimal diagonal die Mitte falten, wieder öffnen.
Fold twice the middle diagonally and open up again.

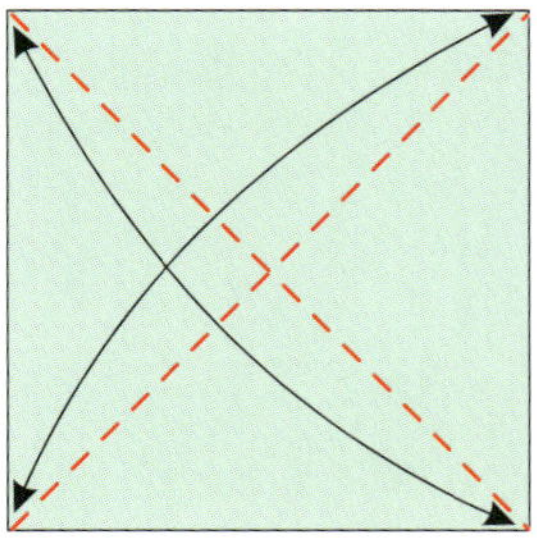

2. Alle vier Ecken zur Mitte falten, liegen lassen.
Fold all four corners to the middle and leave.

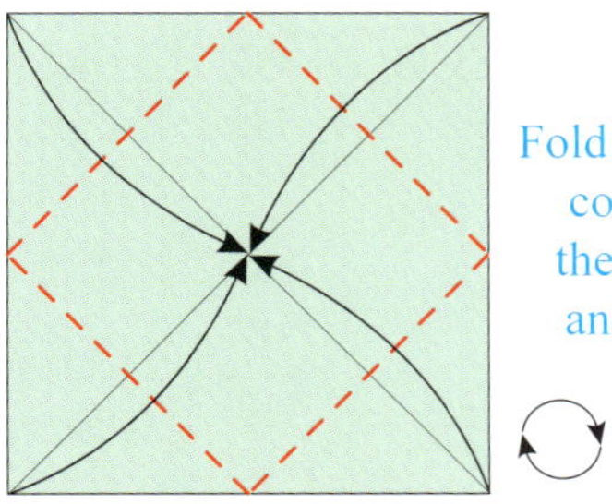

3. Rückseite nach oben legen.
Turn over to the back.

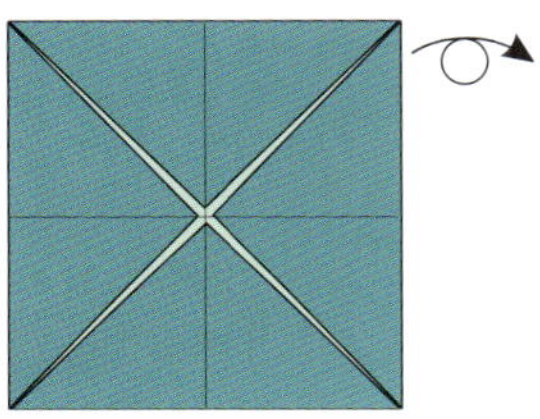

4. Senkrechte Linien falten, aber die Dreiecke von der Rückseite nicht mitfalten, sondern nur flach legen. Siehe auch Diagramm Nr.5.
Fold the vertical lines, but don't fold the triangles of the back, instead lay them flat. See also chart No.5.

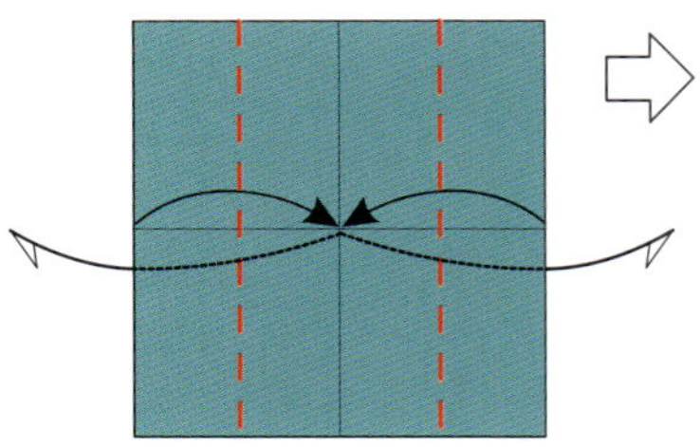

5. Alle vier schrägen Linien falten und dann unter das Dreieck legen.
Fold all four oblique lines and lay them under the triangle.

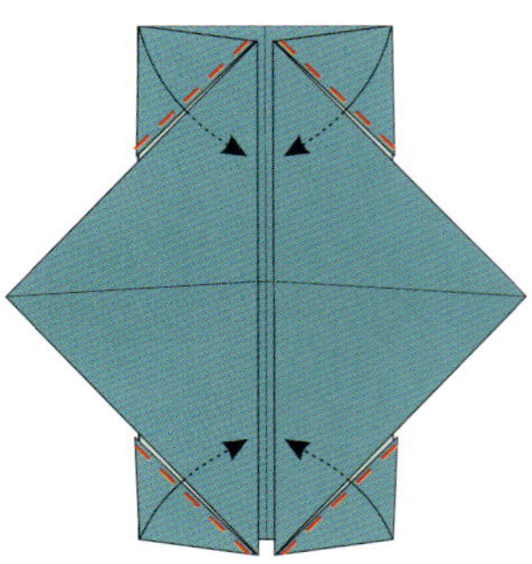

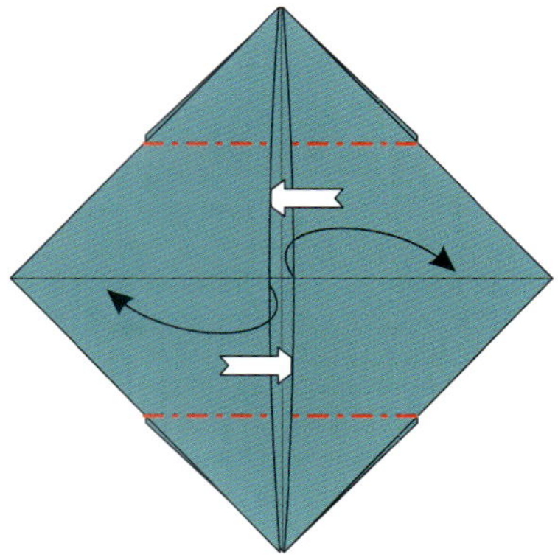

6. Die oberen Papierlagen öffnen (siehe Pfeile), um dann die waagerechten Bergfalten zu arbeiten. Siehe auch Diagramm Nr.7.
Open the upper layers of paper (see arrows) and form the horizontal mountain-folds. See also chart No.7.

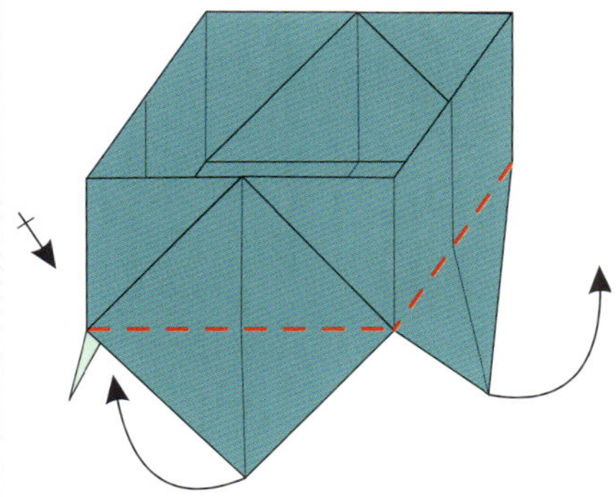

7. An den vier unteren Spitzen waagerechte Linie falten, liegen lassen. Es ist nun ein versetztes Quadrat auf einem Quadrat entstanden.
Fold the horizontal line on the four lower points and leave. Now a square arises on a turned square.

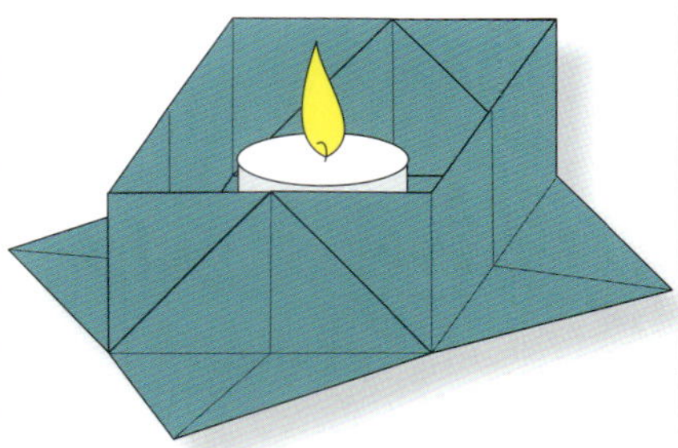

8. Fertiges Modell seitlich gesehen.
Finished model seen from the side.

Lichtfächer

MATERIAL

3 Bogen 30x30 cm flammsicheres Lampenpapier. Bei dem fertigen Modell ist von der Papierrückseite sehr viel zu sehen. Es sollte also nur durchgefärbtes Papier gewählt werden. Allerdings sieht das weiße Papier auch sehr schön aus.
Three sheets 30x30 cm of not inflammable lamp paper. From the finished model, you will see much of the back side of the paper. So you should choose paper with a coloured back. It also will look very lovely, using white paper only.

1. Zweimal waagerecht die Mitte falten, wieder öffnen.
Fold twice the middle horizontally and open up again.

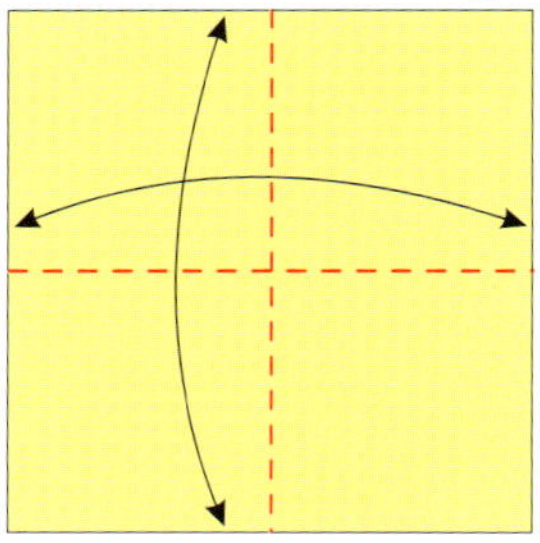

2. Senkrechte Linien zur Mitte falten, wieder öffnen.
Fold the vertical lines to the middle and open up again.

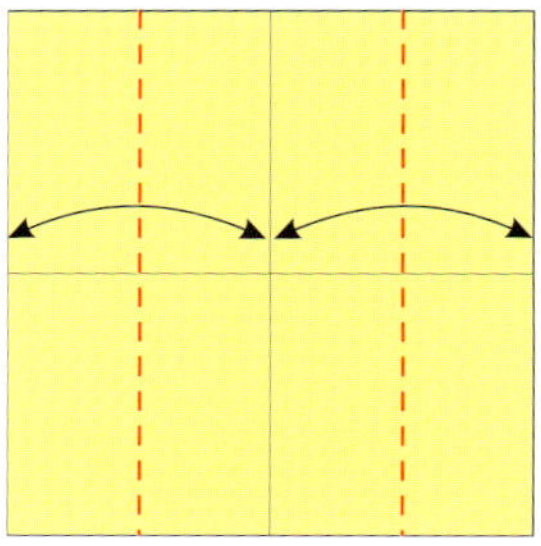

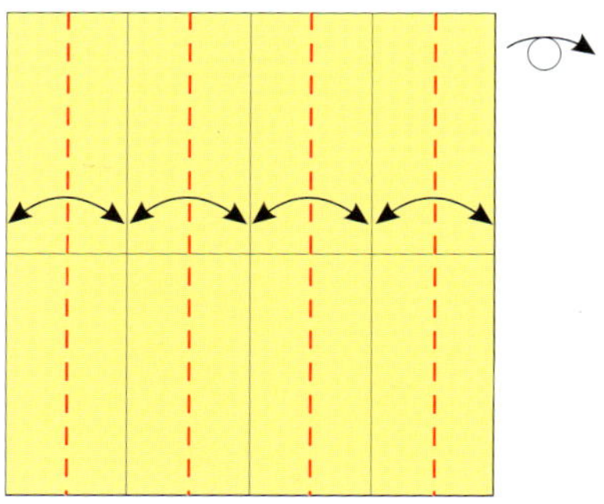

3. In allen vier Teilen jeweils die Mitte falten, wieder öffnen. Rückseite nach oben legen.
Fold on all four parts the middle and open up again. Turn over to the back.

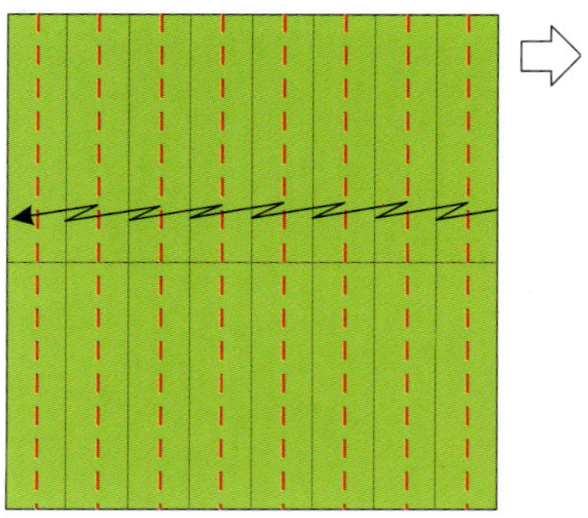

4. In allen acht Teilen wieder jeweils die Mitte falten, liegen lassen. Dadurch ist jetzt die Zickzackfaltung entstanden.
Fold on all eight parts the middle and leave. Now you got the zigzag fold.

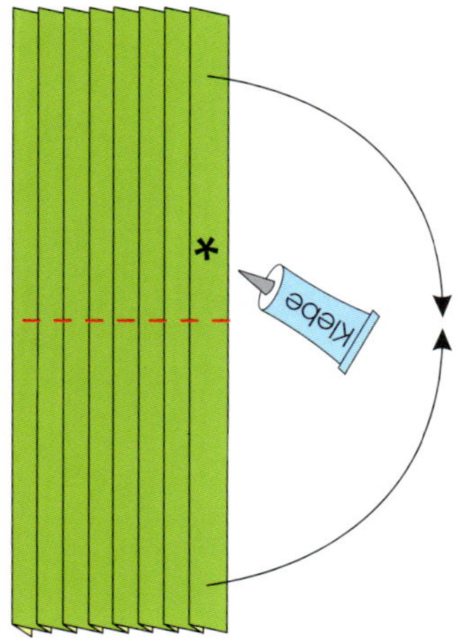

5. Waagerechte Mitte falten, wieder öffnen. Obere Hälfte an die untere Hälfte kleben, siehe Pfeile, damit ein Rundbogen entsteht. Keinen wasserhaltigen Kleber benutzen.
Fold the horizontal middle and open up again. Glue the upper on the lower part, see arrow, so that an arch arises. Do not use water based glue.

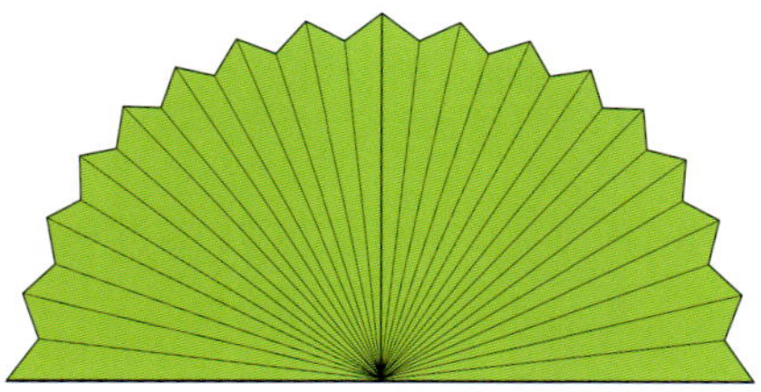

6. So muss das Modell jetzt aussehen. Es werden zwei gleiche Teile benötigt.
Now the model has to look like this. A second equal model is needed.

8. Dicht am Modell nun das überstehende Papier abschneiden. Achtung: Dabei bitte nicht in das Modell schneiden.
Cut off the paper close to the model. Attention: Don't cut the model.

9. Fertiges Modell seitlich gesehen.
Finished model seen from the side.

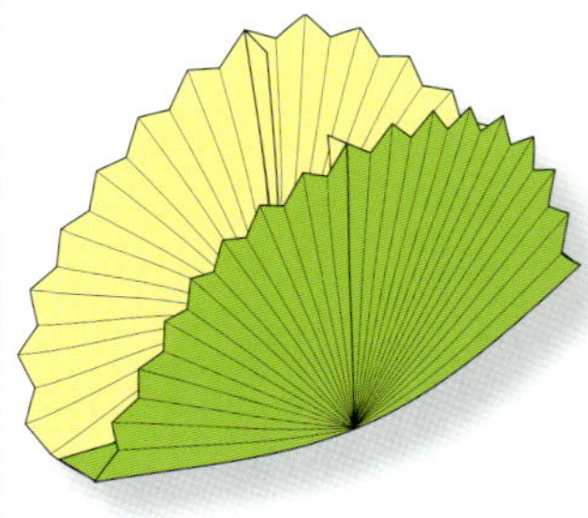

10. Fertiges Modell von oben gesehen.
Finished model seen from above.

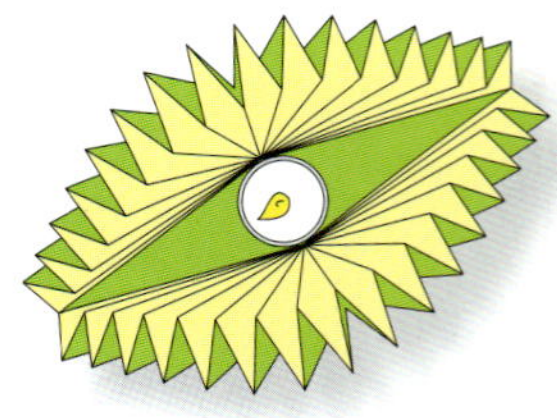

7. Auf einem weiteren Papier werden jetzt diese beiden Rundbogen so aufgeklebt, wie im Diagramm zu sehen.
Glue both arches on a paper, like shown on the chart.

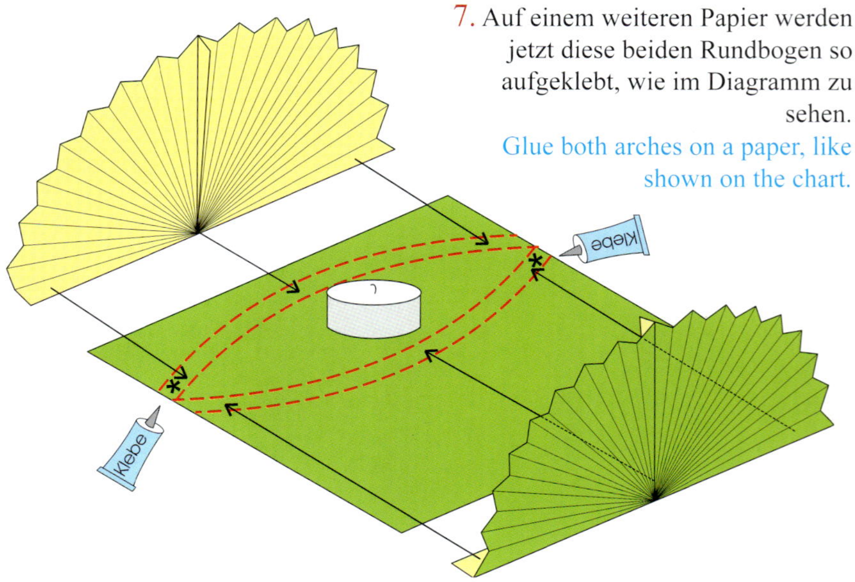

Vasenlicht hoch

MATERIAL

1 Bogen 30x30 cm flammsicheres Lampenpapier. Bei dem fertigen Modell ist von der Papierrückseite sehr viel zu sehen. Es sollte also nur durchgefärbtes Papier gewählt werden. Allerdings sieht das weiße Papier auch sehr schön aus.

One sheet 30x30 cm of not inflammable lamp paper. From the finished model, you will see much of the back side of the paper. So you should choose paper with a coloured back. It also will look very lovely, using white paper only.

1. Zweimal waagerecht die Mitte falten, wieder öffnen. Rückseite nach oben legen.
Fold twice the horizontal middle and open up again. Turn over to the back.

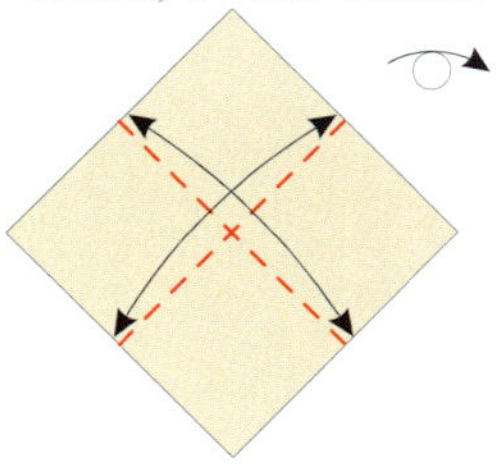

2. Zweimal diagonal die Mitte falten, wieder öffnen. Rückseite nach oben legen.
Fold twice the middle diagonally and open up again. Turn over to the back.

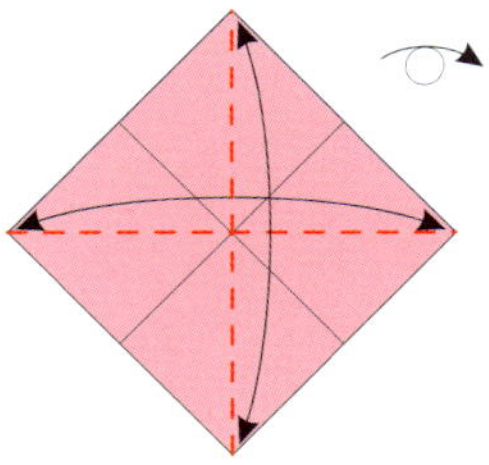

3. Von der waagerechten Mitte (Bergfalte), die seitlichen Ecken zur oberen Ecke legen. Die untere Ecke dann ebenfalls nach oben legen, siehe Pfeile.
From the horizontal middle (mountain-fold), lay the corners from the side to the upper corner. Also lay the lower corner upwards, see arrows.

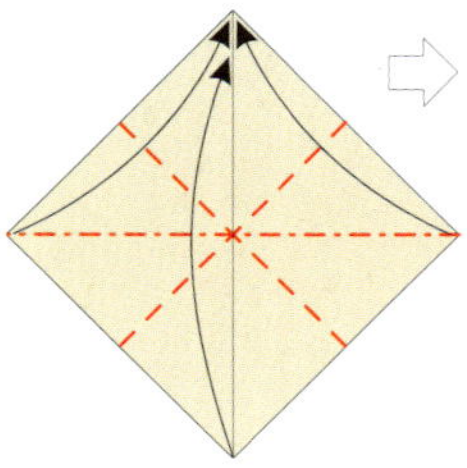

4. Bergfalte nach rechts falten, dabei die Ecke flach drücken.
Fold mountain-fold to the right, at the same time push corner flat.

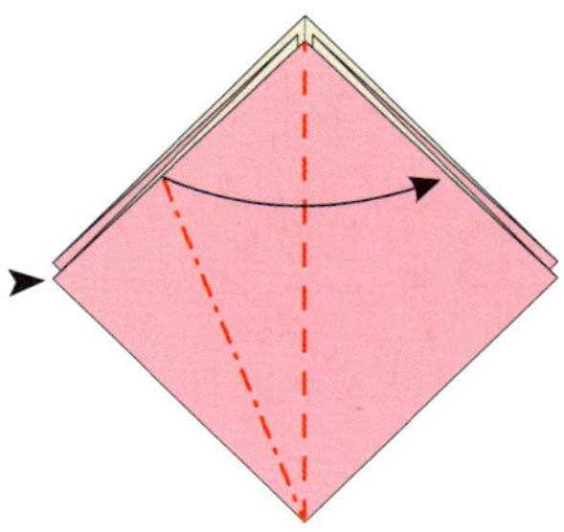

5. Mit den anderen drei Ecken den Arbeitsschritt Nr.4 wiederholen.
Repeat working step No.4 with the other three corners.

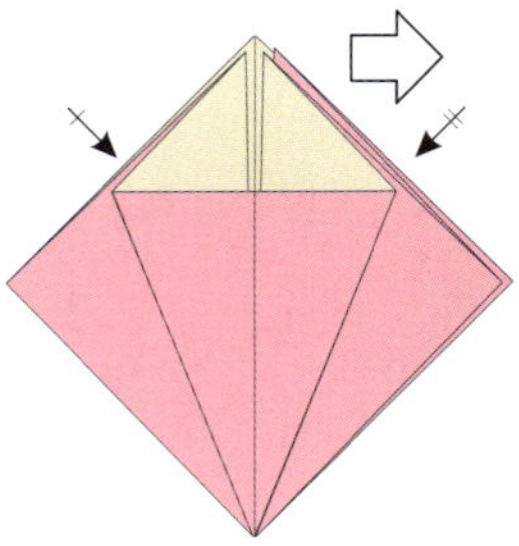

6. Nur mit der oberen Papierlage, siehe Pfeil, von rechts nach links falten. Auf der Rückseite wiederholen.
Using only the top layer of paper, see arrow, fold from right to the left. Repeat on the back.

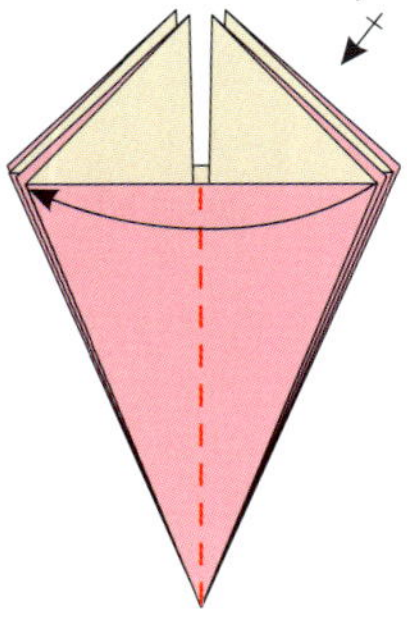

7. An der unteren Spitze die waagerechte Linie falten, wieder öffnen.
On the lower point fold the horizontal line and open up again.

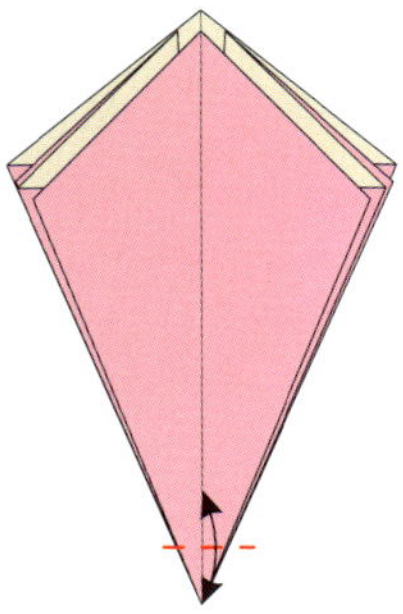

8. Schräge Linien falten, liegen lassen. Auf der Rückseite wiederholen.
Fold the oblique lines and leave. Repeat on the back.

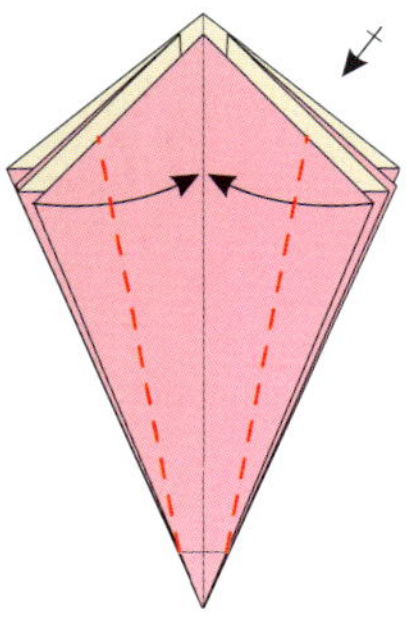

9. Nur mit der oberen Papierlage, siehe Pfeil, von rechts nach links falten. Auf der Rückseite wiederholen.
Using only the top layer of paper, see arrow, fold from right to the left. Repeat on the back.

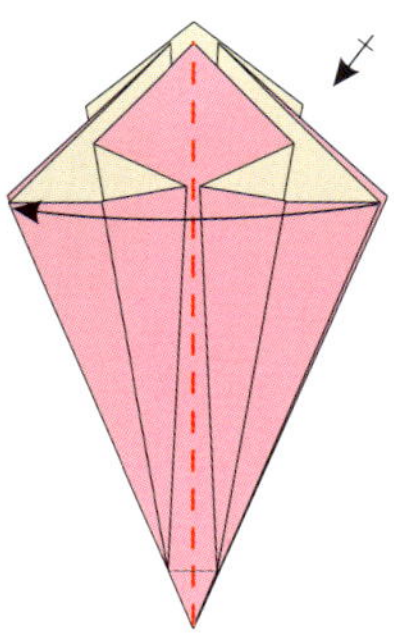

10. Schräge Linien falten, liegen lassen. Auf der Rückseite wiederholen.
Fold oblique lines and leave. Repeat on the back.

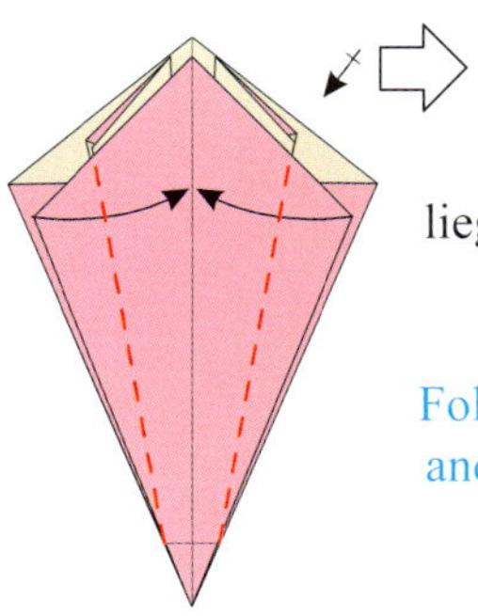

11. Schräge Linien falten, liegen lassen. Auf der Rückseite wiederholen.
Fold oblique lines and leave. Repeat on the back.

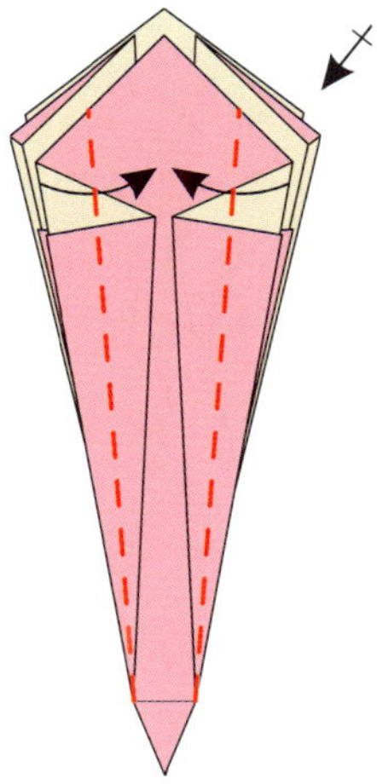

12. Nur mit der oberen Papierlage, siehe Pfeil, von rechts nach links falten. Auf der Rückseite wiederholen.
Using only the top layer of paper, see arrow, fold from right to the left. Repeat on the back.

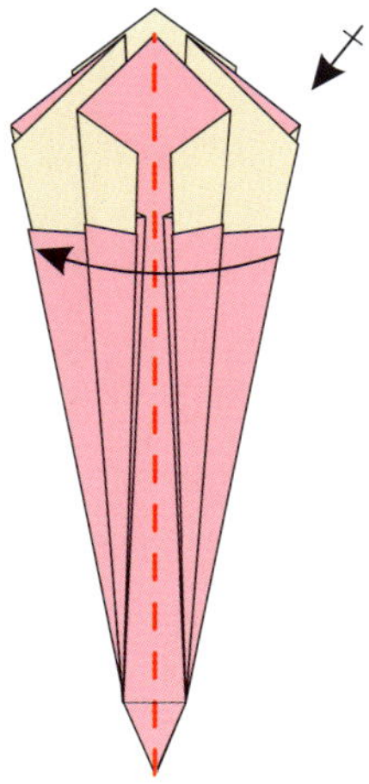

13. Schräge Linien falten, liegen lassen. Auf der Rückseite wiederholen.
Fold oblique lines and leave. Repeat on the back.

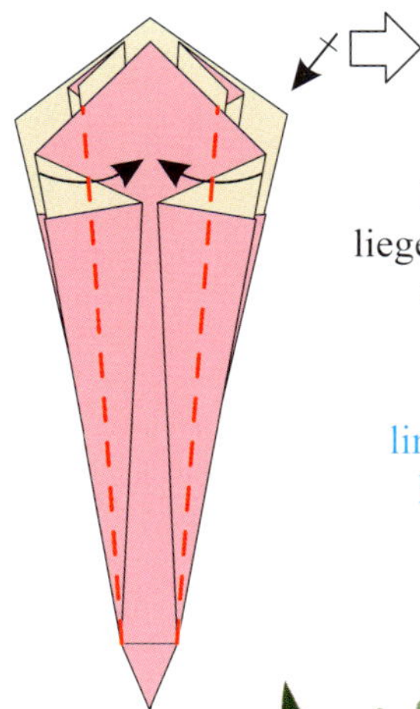

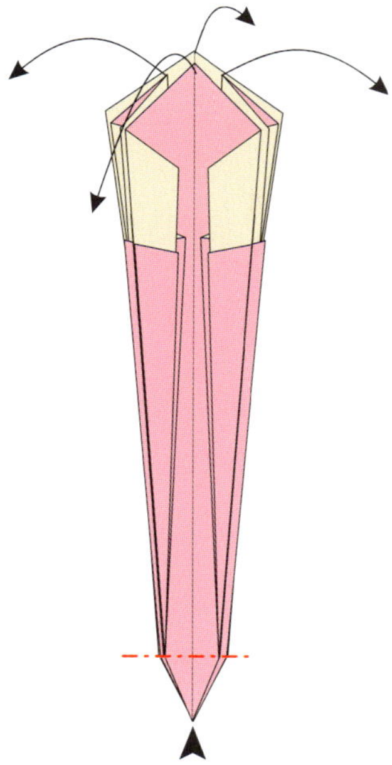

14. An der unteren Spitze eine Bergfalte formen, dabei die Spitze eindrücken. Modell von innen auseinanderdrücken, das Modell steht dann flach auf dem Tisch.
Form a mountain-fold on the lower point, at the same time push in the point. Push the model from the inside outwards. Now the model stands flatly on the table.

15. Fertiges Modell von oben gesehen.
Finished model seen from above.

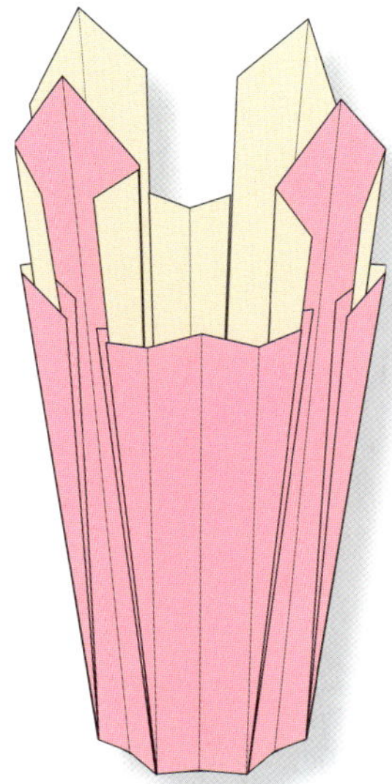

16. Fertiges Modell seitlich gesehen.
Finished model seen from the side.

Vasenlicht hoch Variation

Start. Diagramme von Seite 26 bis Nr.13 falten.
Fold charts of page 26 until No.13.

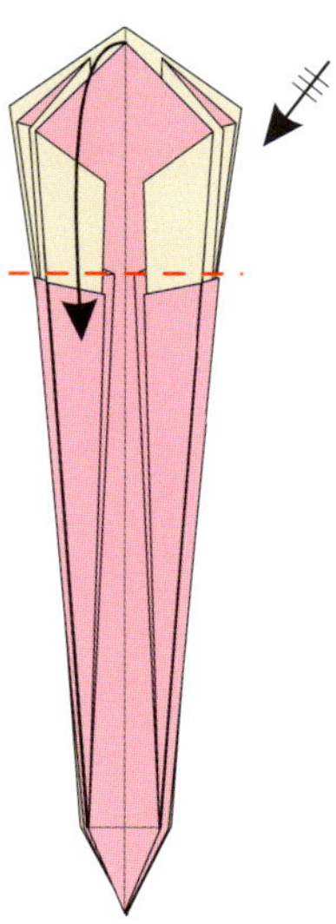

1. Waagerechte Linie falten, liegen lassen. An den anderen drei Spitzen wiederholen.
Fold horizontal line and leave. Repeat on the other three points.

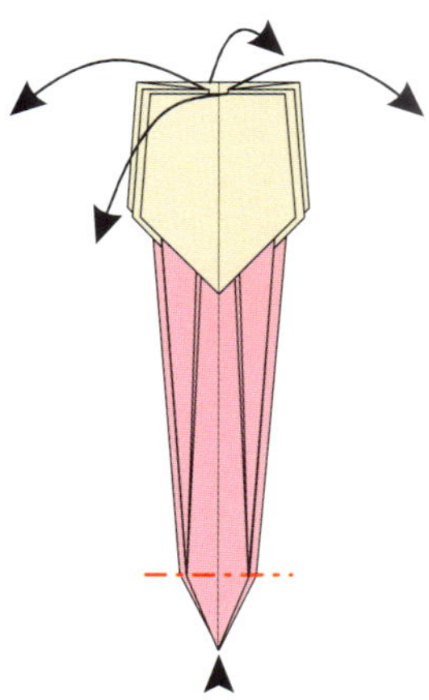

2. An der unteren Spitze eine Bergfalte formen, dabei die Spitze eindrücken. Modell von innen auseinanderdrücken, das Modell steht dann flach auf dem Tisch. Die vier Spitzen waagerecht formen.
Form a mountain-fold on the lower point, at the same time push in the point. Push the model from the inside outwards. Now the model stands flatly on the table. Form the four points horizontally.

3. Fertiges Modell seitlich gesehen.
Finished model seen from the side.

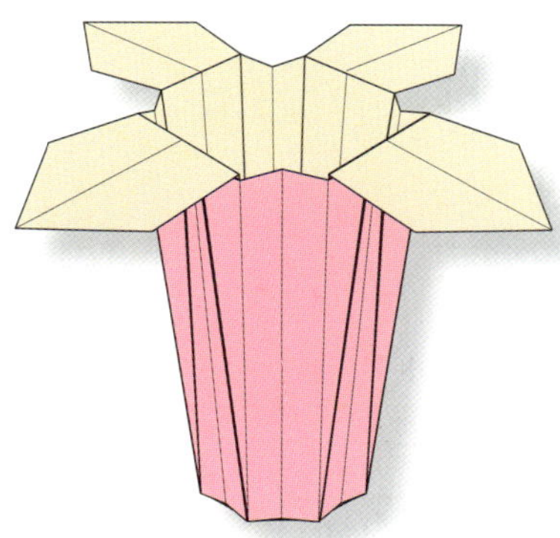

4. Fertiges Modell von oben gesehen.
Finished model seen from above.

Vase bauchig

MATERIAL

1 Bogen 30x30 cm flammsicheres Lampenpapier. Bei dem fertigen Modell ist von der Papierrückseite sehr viel zu sehen. Es sollte also nur durchgefärbtes Papier gewählt werden. Allerdings sieht das weiße Papier auch sehr schön aus.
One sheet 30x30 cm of not inflammable lamp paper. From the finished model, you will see much of the back side of the paper. So you should choose paper with a coloured back. It also will look very lovely, using white paper only.

Start. Diagramme von Seite 26 bis Nr.3 falten.
Fold charts of page 26 until step No.3.

1. Bei der Blattgröße von 30x30 cm, Linie an der unteren Spitze auf 2,5 cm falten, wieder öffnen. Diese Linie ist sehr wichtig, denn damit wird die Form bestimmt. Je höher die Linie gefaltet wird um so bauchiger ist das Vasen-Licht.
If you use a sheet of 30x30 cm, fold on the lower point a line by the height of 2,5 cm and open up again. This line is very important, because it determines the shape. The higher you fold the line, the model becomes more bulbous.

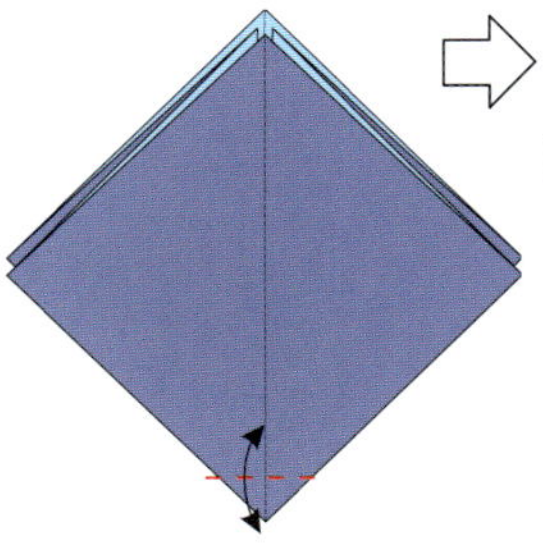

2. Nur mit der oberen Papierlage, siehe Pfeile, Ecken an die Mittellinie falten. Auf der Rückseite wiederholen.
Using only the top layer of paper, see arrows, fold corners to the line in the middle. Repeat on the back.

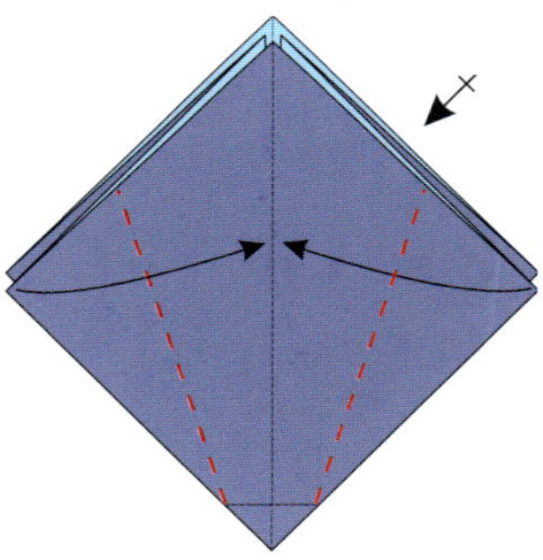

3. Nur mit der oberen Papierlage, siehe Pfeil, von rechts nach links falten. Auf der Rückseite wiederholen.
Using only the top layer of paper, see arrow, fold from right to the left. Repeat on the back.

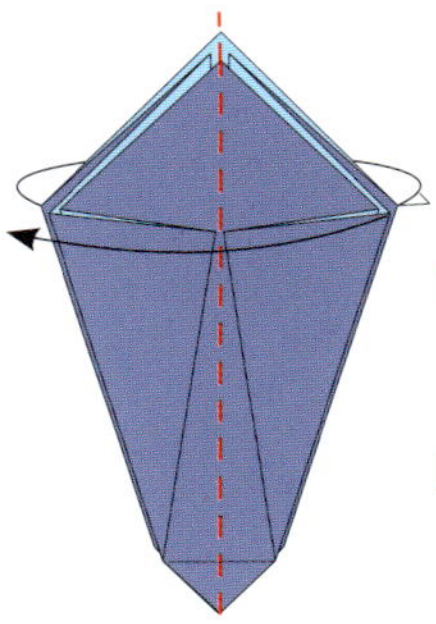

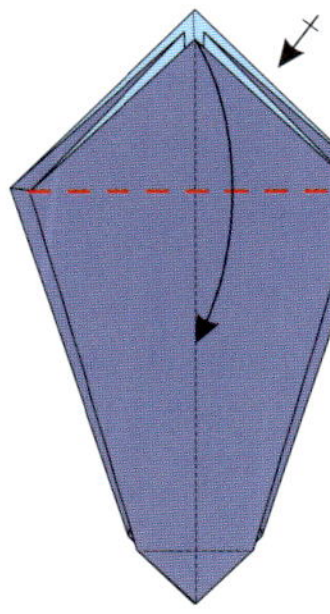

4. Spitze nach unten falten, liegen lassen. Auf der Rückseite wiederholen.
Fold point downwards and leave. Repeat on the back.

5. Nur mit der oberen Papierlage, siehe Pfeil, von rechts nach links falten. Auf der Rückseite wiederholen.
Using only the top layer of paper, see arrow, fold from right to the left. Repeat on the back.

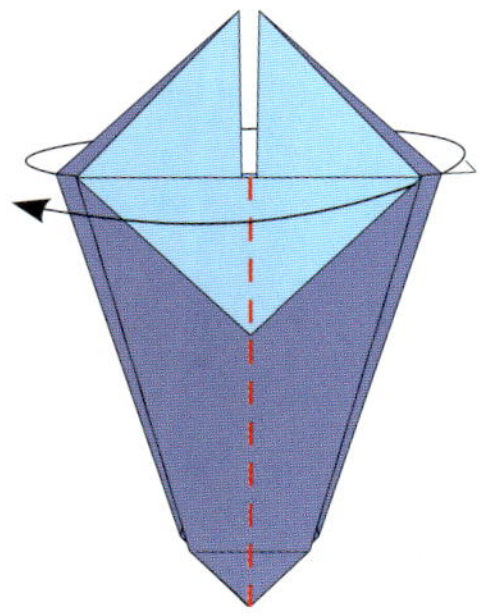

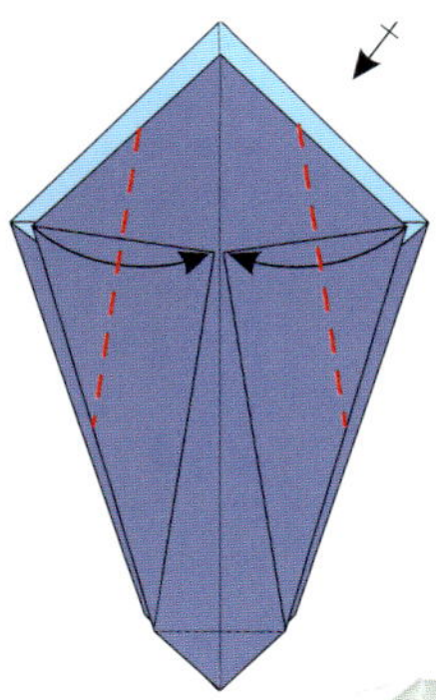

6. Schräge Linien falten, siehe Pfeile, liegen lassen. Auf der Rückseite wiederholen.
Fold oblique lines, see arrows, and leave. Repeat on the back.

11. Viele Varianten sind möglich.
Many variations are possible.

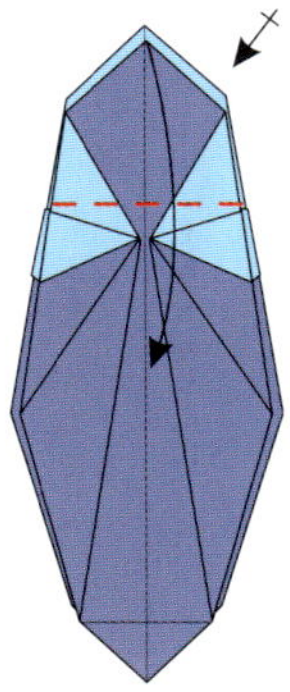

7. Spitze nach unten falten, liegen lassen. Auf der Rückseite wiederholen.
Fold point downwards and leave. Repeat on the back.

8. An der unteren Spitze eine Bergfalte formen, dabei die Spitze eindrücken. Modell von innen auseinanderdrücken, das Modell steht dann flach auf dem Tisch. Die zwei Spitzen waagerecht formen.
Form a mountain-fold on the lower point, at the same time push in the point. Push the model from the inside outwards. Now the model stands flatly on the table. Form the two points horizontally.

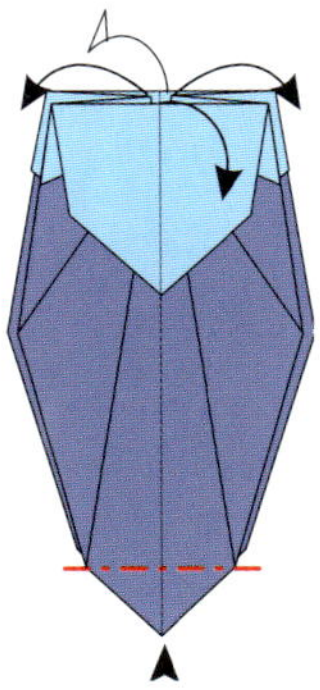

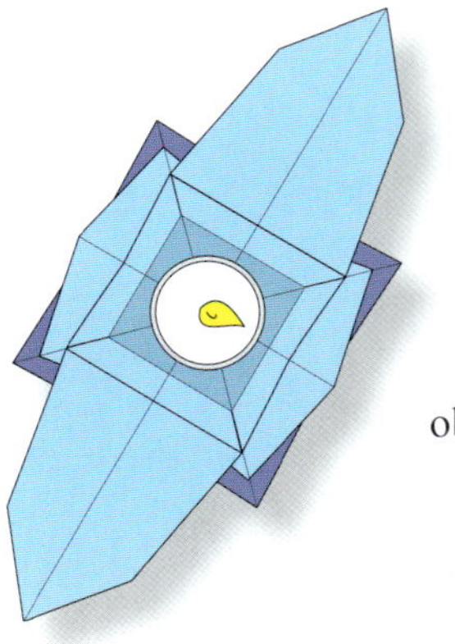

9. Fertiges Modell von oben gesehen.
Finished model seen from above.

10. Fertiges Modell seitlich gesehen.
Finished model seen from the side.

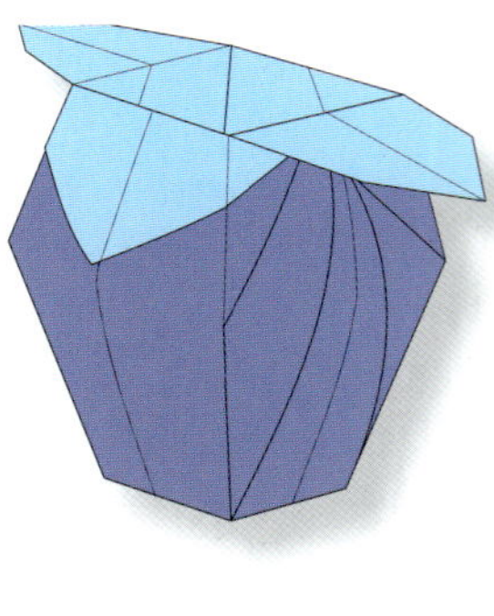

Früchte Fackel

MATERIAL

1 Bogen 30x30 cm flammsicheres Lampenpapier. Bei dem fertigen Modell ist von der Papierrückseite wenig zu sehen. Es kann also durchgefärbtes Papier oder Papier mit einer weißen Rückseite gewählt werden.

One sheet 30x30 cm of not inflammable lamp paper. From the finished model, you won't see much of the back side of the paper. So you can use paper with a coloured or white back side.

Start. Diagramme von Seite 26 bis Nr.5 falten.

Fold charts of page 26 until No.5.

1. Nur mit der oberen Papierlage, siehe Pfeil, von rechts nach links falten. Auf der Rückseite wiederholen.

Using only the top layer of paper, see arrow, fold from the right to the left. Repeat on the back.

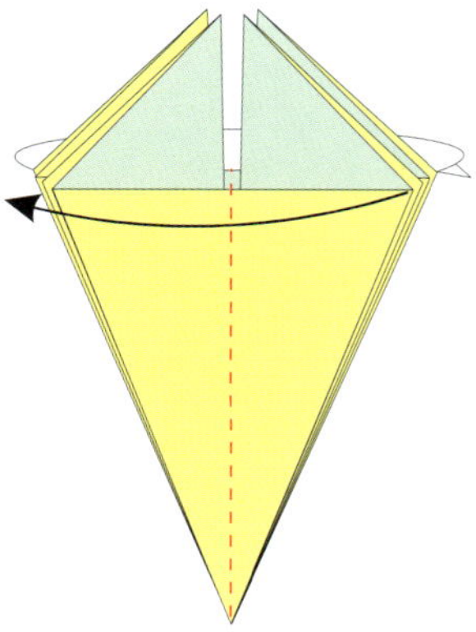

2. Nur mit der oberen Papierlage, siehe Pfeile, schräge Linien falten. Auf der Rückseite wiederholen.

Using only the top layer of paper, see arrow, fold oblique lines. Repeat on the back side.

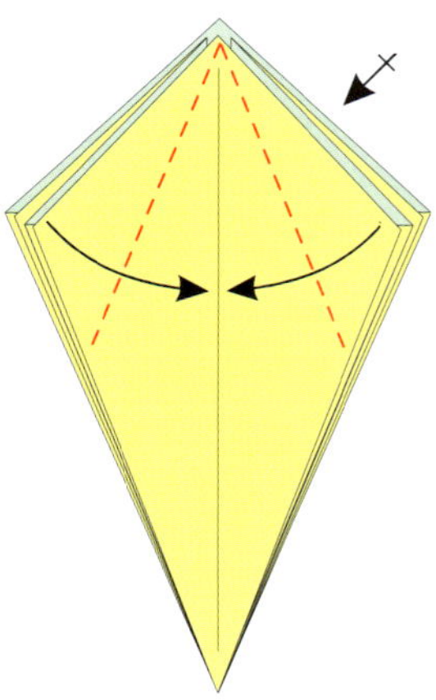

3. Spitze nach unten falten, liegen lassen. Auf der Rückseite wiederholen.

Fold point downwards and leave. Repeat on the back side.

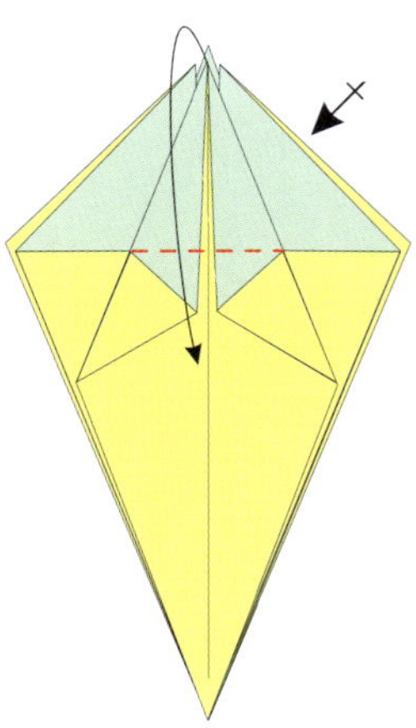

4. Nur mit der oberen Papierlage, siehe Pfeil, von rechts nach links falten. Auf der Rückseite wiederholen.

Using only the top layer of paper, see arrow, fold from the right to the left. Repeat on the back.

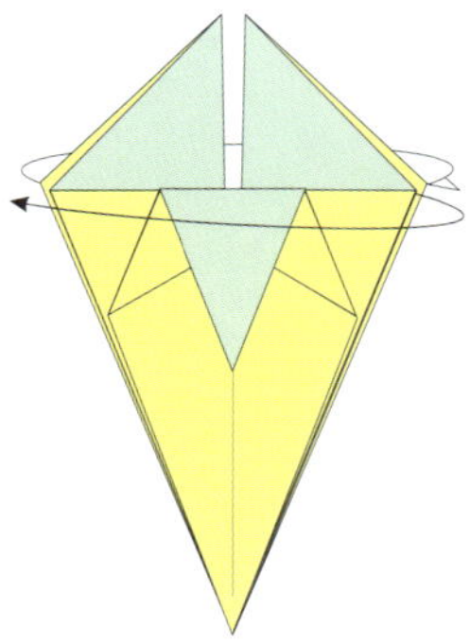

5. Nur mit der oberen Papierlage, siehe Pfeile, schräge Linien falten. Auf der Rückseite wiederholen.

Using only the top layer of paper, see arrow, fold oblique lines. Repeat on the back side.

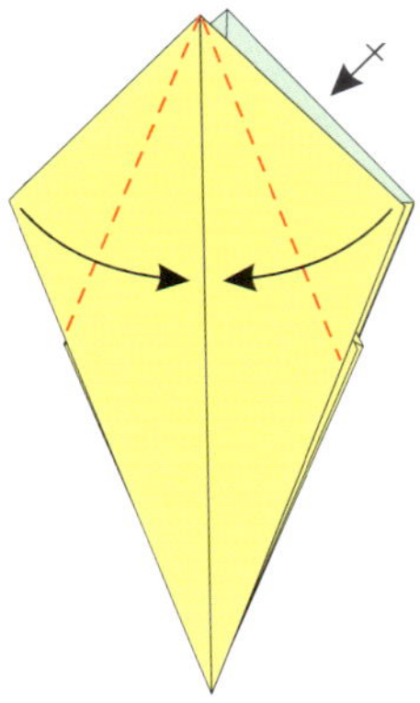

6. Spitze nach unten falten, liegen lassen. Auf der Rückseite wiederholen.

Fold point downwards and leave. Repeat on the back side.

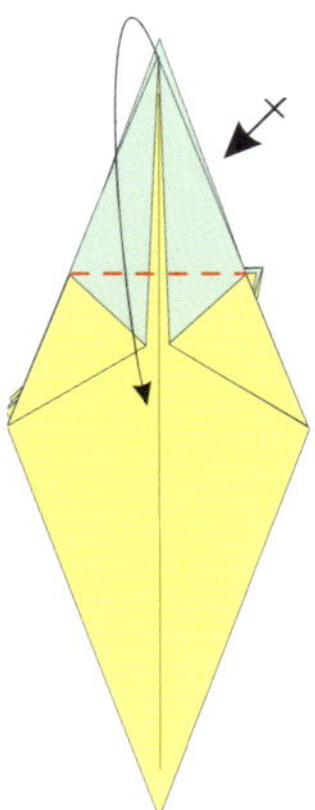

7. An der unteren Spitze Linie falten, wieder öffnen.

Fold the line on the lower point and open up again.

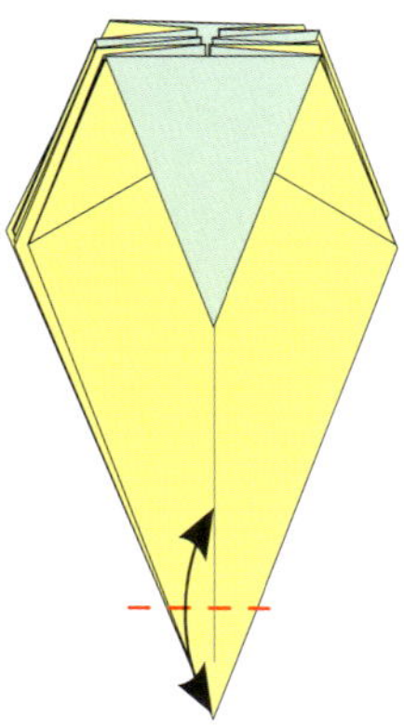

8. Jetzt eine Bergfalte formen, dabei die Spitze eindrücken. Modell von innen auseinanderdrücken, das Papier liegt dann flach auf dem Tisch.

Now form a mountain-fold, at the same time push in the point. Push the model from the inside outwards, so the paper lies flat on the table.

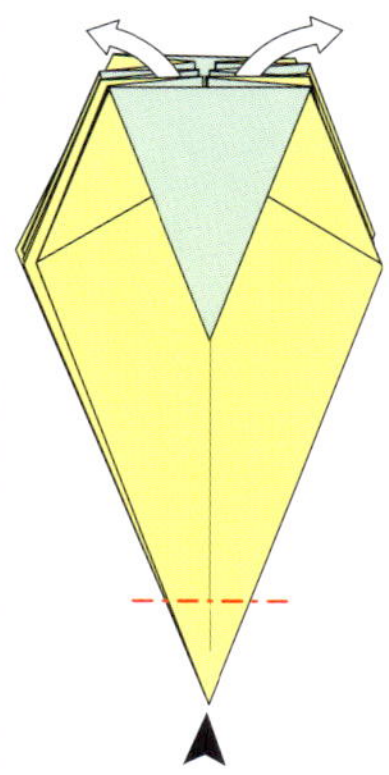

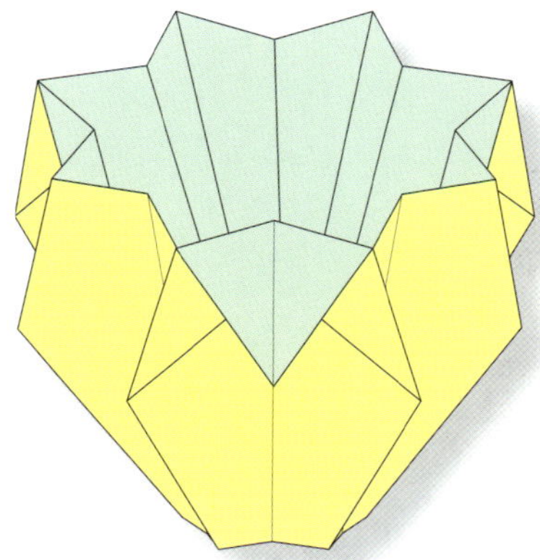

9. Fertiges Modell seitlich gesehen.

Finished model seen from the side.

10. Fertiges Modell von oben gesehen.

Finished model seen from above.

11. Ein weißes und ein rotes Modell ineinander gesetzt.

A white and a red model put in one another.

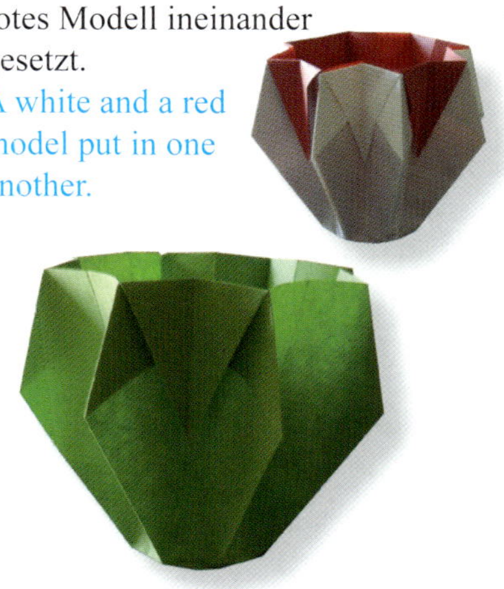

Japanischer Lampion

MATERIAL

2 Bogen 15x15 cm flammsicheres Lampenpapier. Bei dem fertigen Modell ist von der Papierrückseite wenig zu sehen. Es kann also durchgefärbtes Papier oder Papier mit einer weißen Rückseite gewählt werden.

Two sheets 15x15 cm of not inflammable lamp paper. From the finished model, you won't see much of the back side of the paper. So you can use paper with a coloured or white back side.

1. Papier an der senkrechten Linie durchschneiden.
Cut paper on the vertical line.

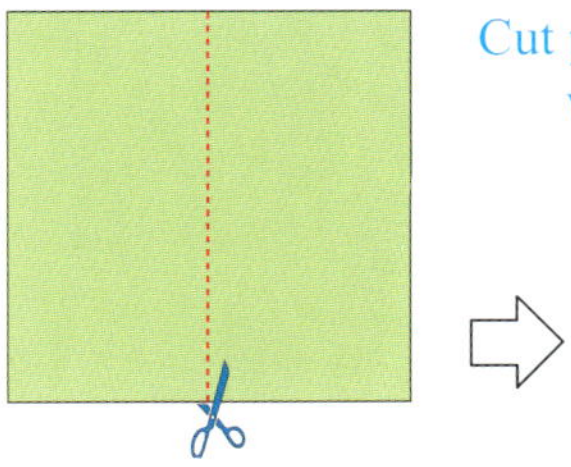

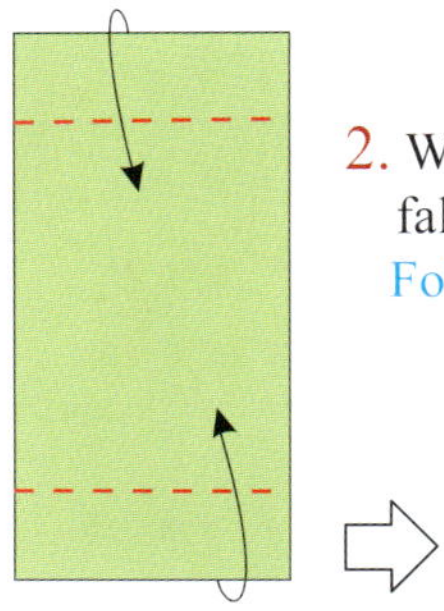

2. Waagerechte Linien falten, liegen lassen.
Fold horizontal lines and leave.

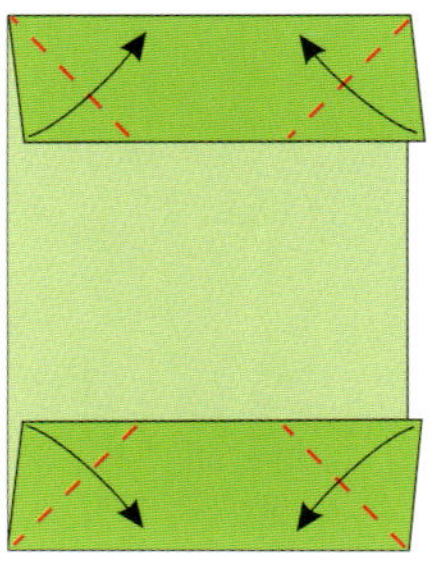

3. Alle vier Ecken falten, siehe Pfeile, liegen lassen.
Fold all four corners, see arrows, and leave.

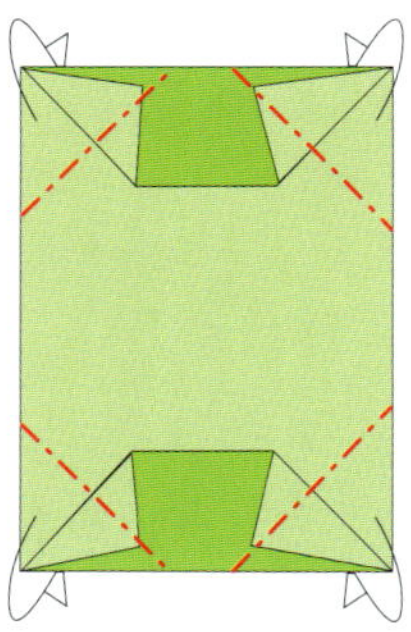

4. Alle vier schrägen Linien zur Rückseite falten (Bergfalte), liegen lassen.
Fold all four oblique lines to the back (mountain-fold) and leave.

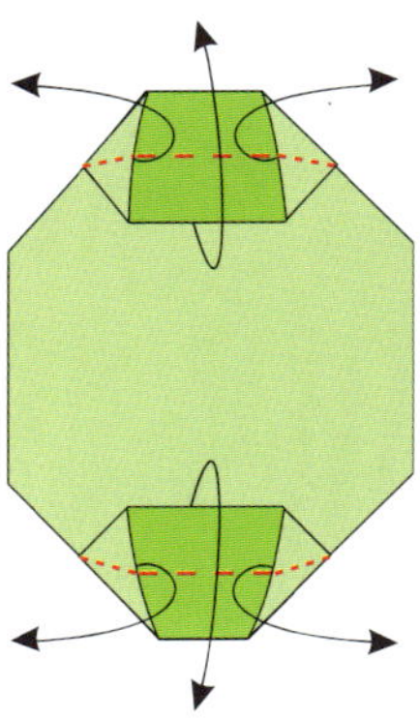

5. Oben und unten waagerechte Linie falten, dabei seitlich auseinanderdrücken (siehe Pfeile).
Fold horizontal line above and below, at the same time push from the side outwards (see arrows).

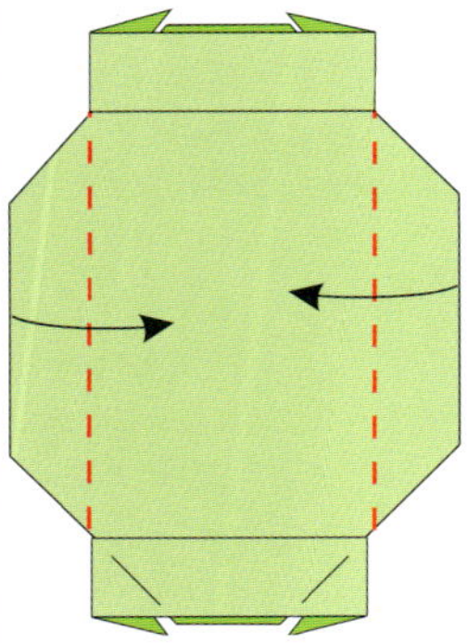

6. Senkrechte Linien falten, liegen lassen.
Fold vertical lines and leave.

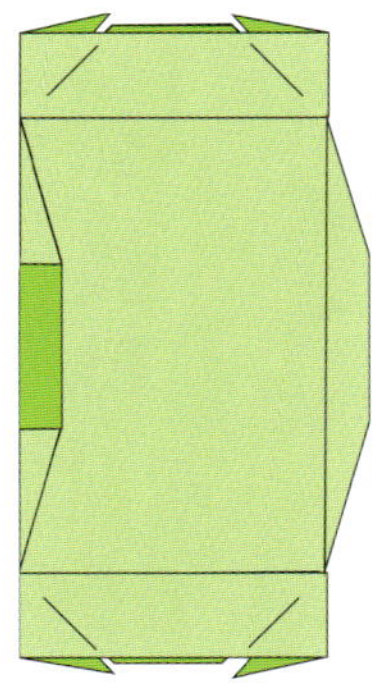

7. Vier Modelle so arbeiten.
Create four models this way.

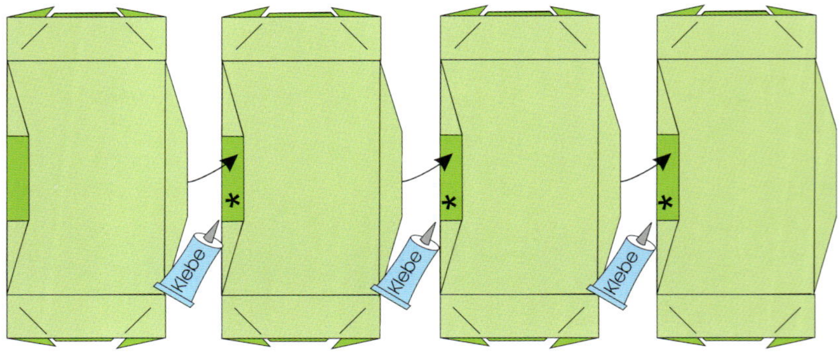

8. Alle vier Teile an den Laschen zusammen kleben. Keinen wasserhaltigen Kleber benutzen.
Glue all four items along the paper flap together. Don't use water based glue.

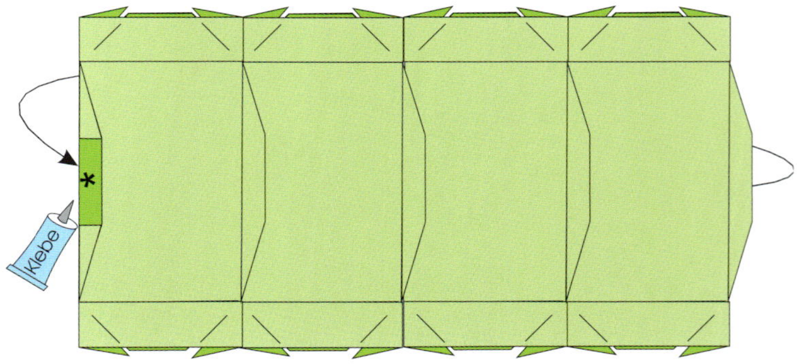

9. Das Ende jetzt an den Beginn kleben. Keinen wasserhaltigen Kleber benutzen.
Now glue the end on the beginning. Don't use water based glue.

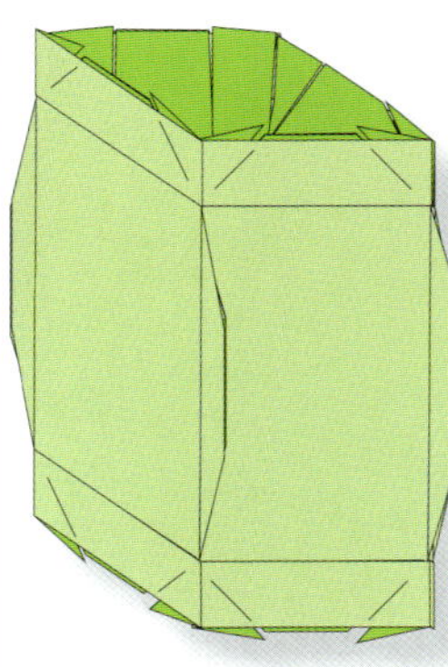

10. Fertiges Modell seitlich gesehen.
Finished model seen from the side.

Lichttüten

MATERIAL

1 Bogen 15x30 cm flammsicheres Lampenpapier. Bei dem fertigen Modell ist von der Papierrückseite wenig zu sehen. Es kann also durchgefärbtes Papier oder Papier mit einer weißen Rückseite gewählt werden.

One sheet 15x30 cm of not inflammable lamp paper. From the finished model, you won't see much of the back side of the paper. So you can choose any design.

1. Senkrechte Linie falten, liegen lassen.

Fold the vertical line and leave.

2. Senkrechte Mitte falten und auf die Papierlasche kleben, siehe Pfeil.

Fold the vertical middle and glue both edges together, see arrow.

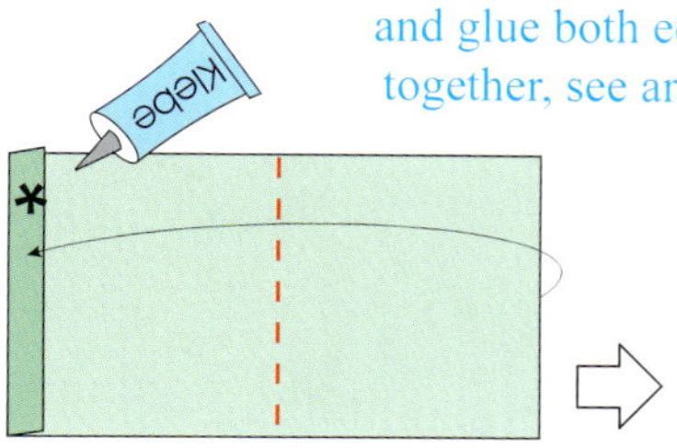

3. Nun die Tiefe der Tüte falten. Bei dieser Papiergröße sollten es 6 cm sein. Also jetzt nur die obere Papierlage um 6 cm nach rechts umlegen bis die rote Linie eine neue Kante rechts bildet und falten. Dabei wird die linke neue Kante automatisch mitgefaltet, siehe auch Pfeile.

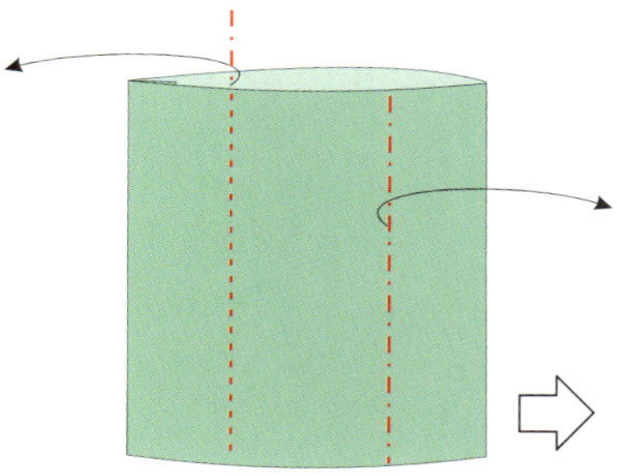

Now fold the depth of the model. Using this size of paper it should be 6 cm. Lay only the top layer of paper 6 cm to the right until the red line becomes the new edge on the right side. At the same time fold the new edge on the left side, see arrows.

4. Für den Tütenfalz auf beiden Seiten senkrechte Linien falten.

Fold the vertical middle on both sides.

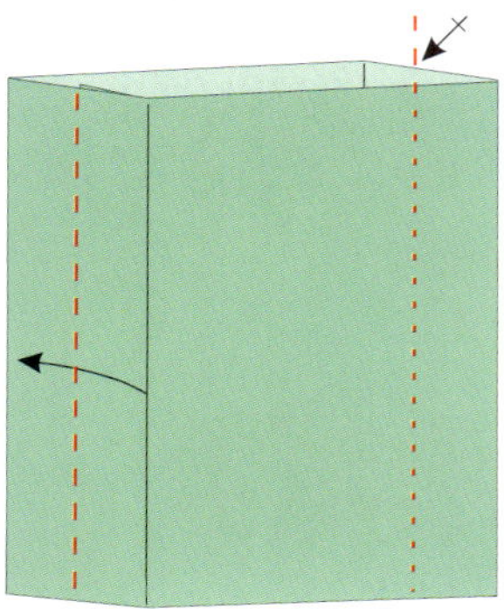

5. Wenn die Tiefe der Tüte 6 cm ist, wird die waagerechte Linie für den Boden auf der Höhe von ca. 4 cm gefaltet. Wieder öffnen. (Also ca. 2/3 der Tiefe)

If the depth of the model is 6 cm, fold the vertical line on the height of 4 cm for the bottom and open up again. (height = 2/3 of the depth)

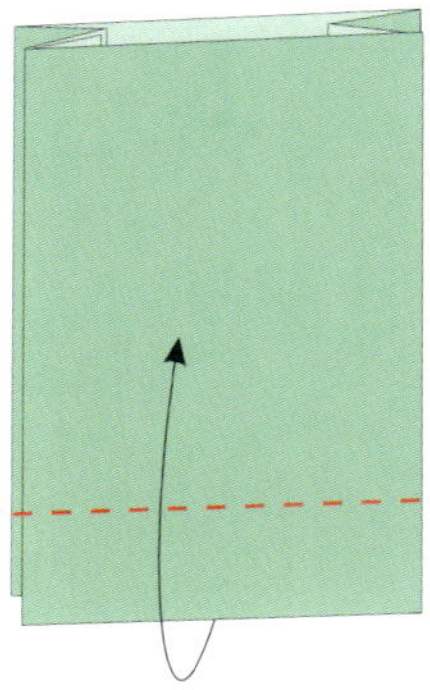

6. Mit beiden Papierlagen, Ecken an die waagerechte Linie falten, wieder öffnen. Modell um 180 Grad drehen.

With both layers of paper, fold corners to the horizontal line and open up again. Turn the model 180 degrees around.

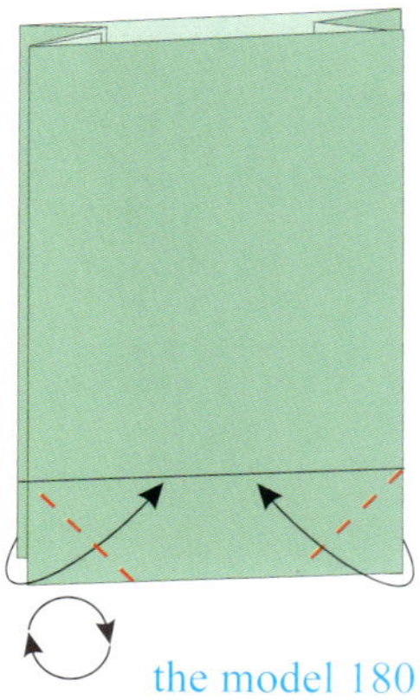

7. Modell von innen auseinander-drücken.

Push the model from the inside outwards.

8. Im Tütenfalz und an den schrägen Linien jetzt Bergfalten formen. Dann Papier seitlich zur Mitte eindrücken.

Fold mountain-folds on the sides and on the oblique lines. Push in the paper from the side to the middle.

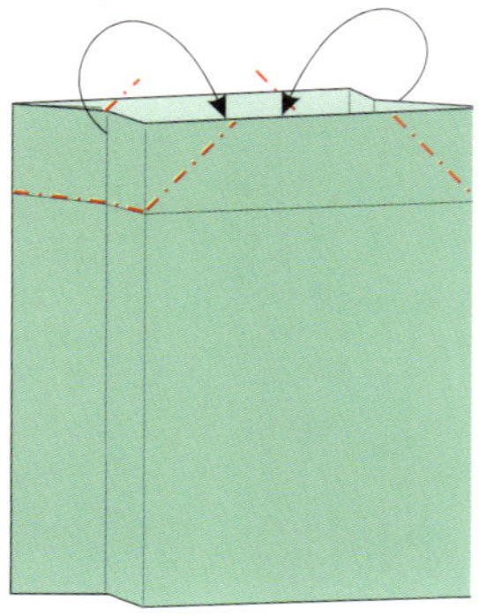

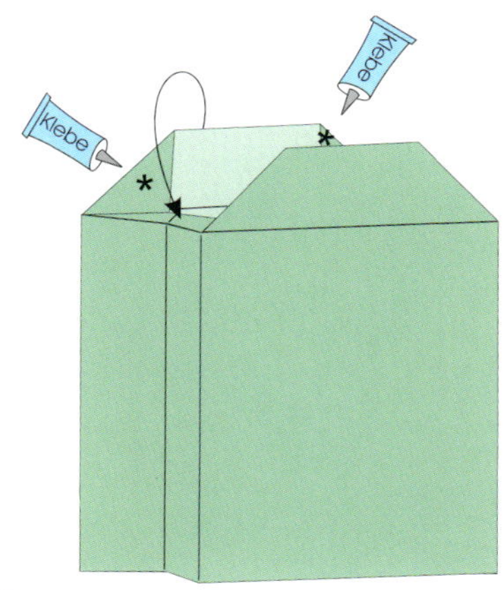

9. Eine Papierlasche zur Mitte legen, siehe Pfeil und festkleben. Keinen wasserhaltigen Kleber benutzen.

Put one paper flap to the middle, see arrow and glue. Don't use water based glue.

10. Jetzt die andere Papierlasche zur Mitte legen und auch festkleben. Keinen wasserhaltigen Kleber benutzen. Modell um 180 Grad drehen.

Now put the other paper flap to the middle and glue. Don't use water based glue. Turn the model 180 degrees around.

11. Fertiges Modell seitlich gesehen.

Finished model seen from the side.

Streifen-Laternen

MATERIAL

2 Bogen 30x30 cm flammsicheres Lampenpapier, 1 Bogen für die äußeren Streifen und 1 Bogen für den inneren Steg. Bei dem fertigen Modell ist von der Papierrückseite wenig zu sehen. Es kann also durchgefärbtes Papier oder Papier mit einer weißen Rückseite gewählt werden.

Two sheets 30x30 cm of not inflammable lamp paper, one for the outer stripes and one for the inner part. From the finished model, you won't see much of the back side of the paper. So you can choose any design.

1. Äußeres Papier, an der senkrechten Linie abschneiden. Rückseite nach oben legen.
Cut off the outer paper along the vertical line. Turn over to the back.

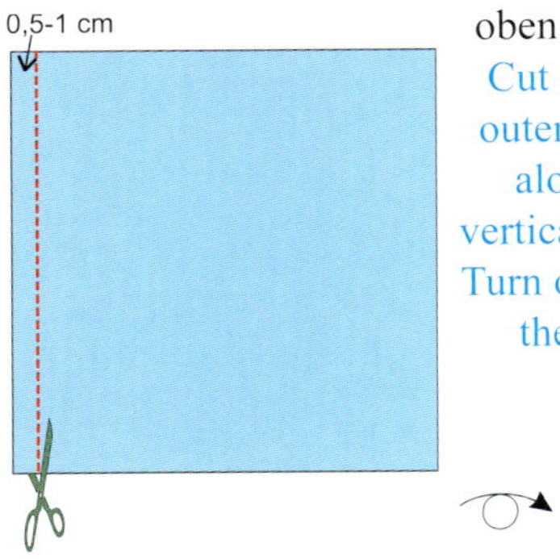

2. Waagerechte Mitte falten, liegen lassen.
Fold vertical middle and leave.

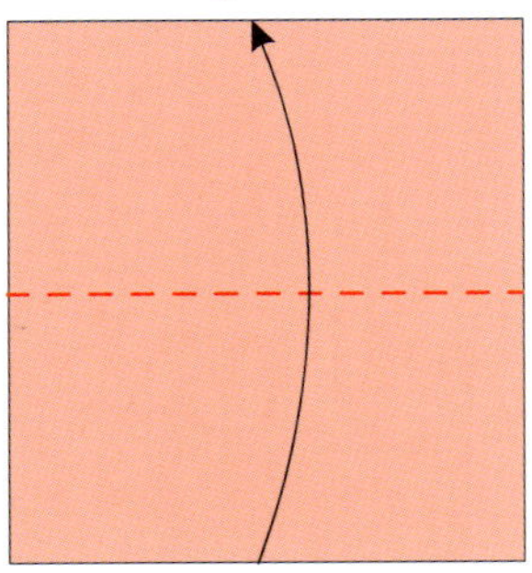

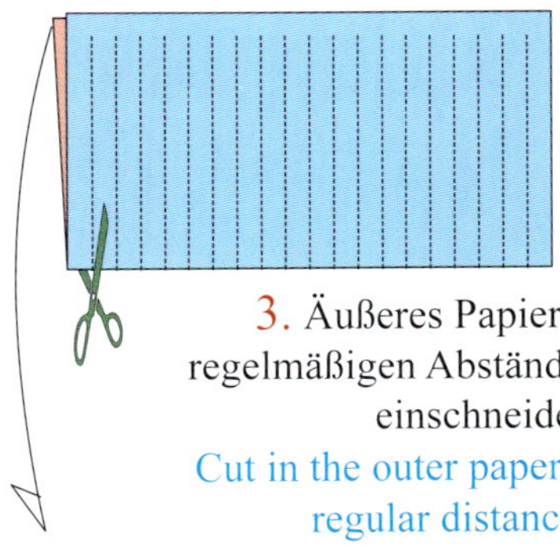

3. Äußeres Papier in regelmäßigen Abständen einschneiden.
Cut in the outer paper in regular distances.

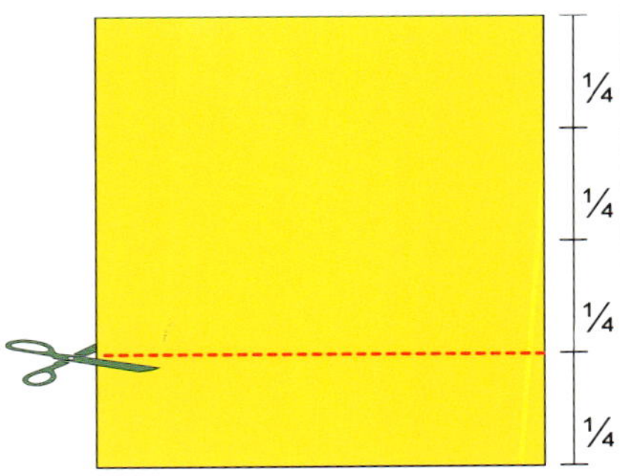

4. Inneres Papier, an der waagerechten Linie abschneiden.
Cut the inner paper along the horizontal line.

5. Nun das äußere Papier auf das innere Papier kleben, siehe Pfeile. Keinen wasserhaltigen Kleber benutzen. Das innere Papier ist etwas länger, daher bleibt ein kleiner Streifen übrig.
Glue the outer paper on the inner paper, see arrows. Don't use a water based glue. The inner paper is a little bit longer, so that a small stripe is left.

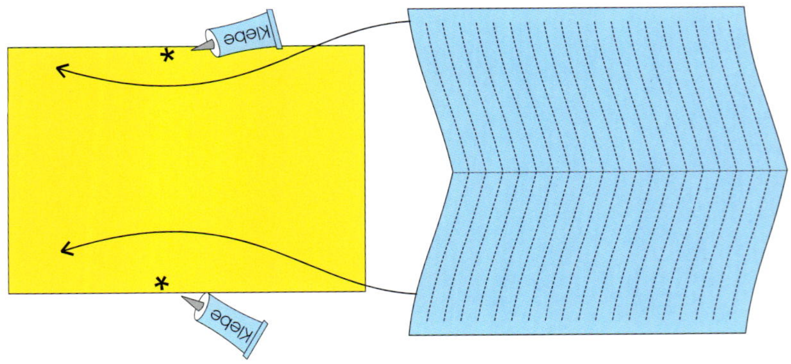

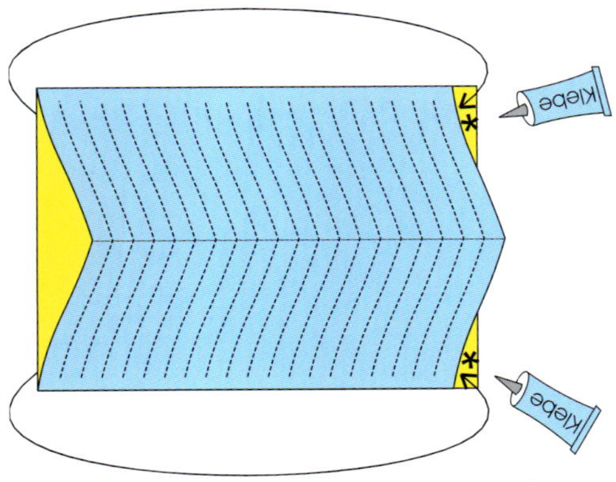

6. Den kleinen Streifen vom inneren Papier an die andere Papierseite kleben, siehe Pfeile. Keinen wasserhaltigen Kleber benutzen. Es ist hilfreich, wenn das Papier vorher zu einer Rundung gedreht wird.
Glue this small stripe of the inner paper on the other edge of the inner paper, see arrows. It is helpful, if the paper got the round form in advance.

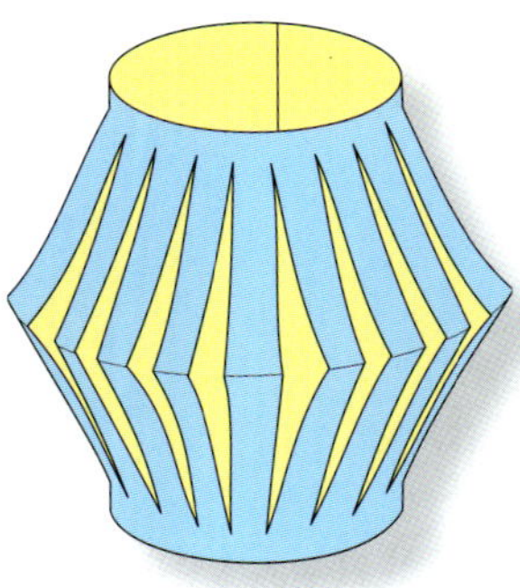

7. Fertiges Modell seitlich gesehen.
Finished model seen from the side.

8. Viele Varianten sind möglich.
Many variations are possible.

MATERIAL

1 Bogen A4 Format flammsicheres Lampenpapier. Bei dem fertigen Modell ist von der Papierrückseite wenig zu sehen. Es kann also durchgefärbtes Papier oder Papier mit einer weißen Rückseite gewählt werden.

One sheet DIN A4 of not inflammable lamp paper. From the finished model, you won't see much of the back side of the paper. So you can choose any design.

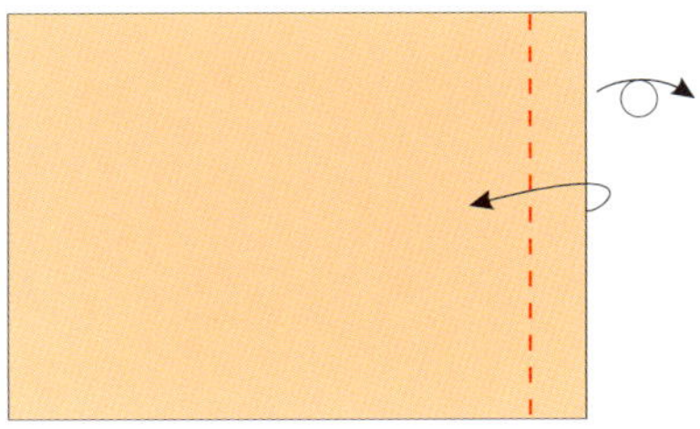

1. Senkrechte Linie falten, liegen lassen. Rückseite nach oben legen.
Fold vertical line and leave. Turn over to the back.

2. Senkrechte Mitte falten und wieder öffnen, siehe Pfeil.

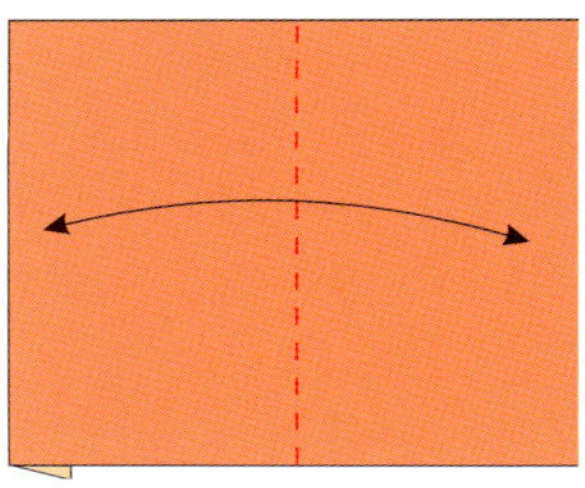

Fold vertical middle and open up again, see arrow.

3. Beide senkrechte Linien falten, wieder öffnen.

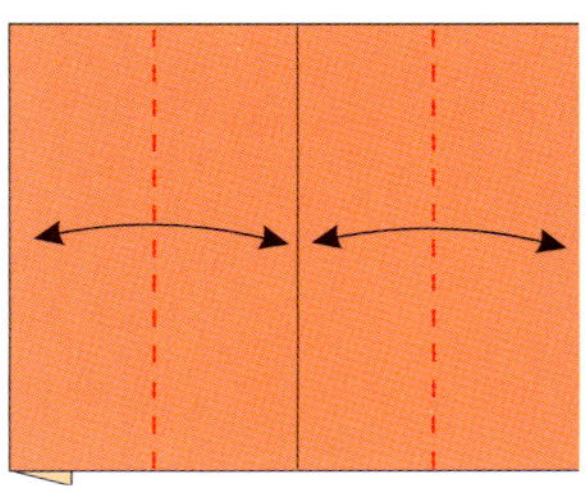

Fold both vertical lines and open up again.

4. Waagerechte Mitte falten, wieder öffnen.

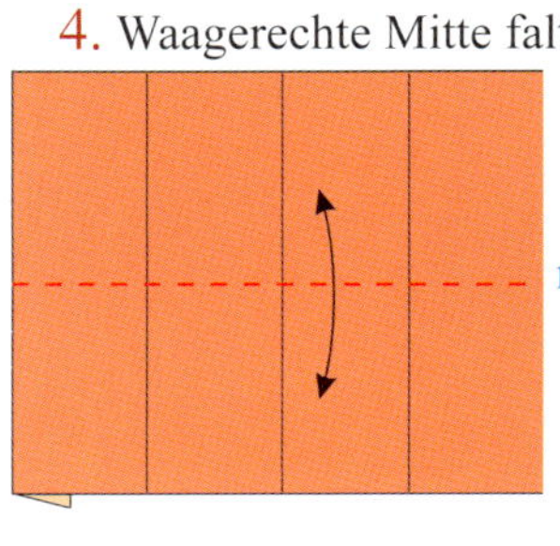

Fold the horizontal middle and open up again.

5. Beide waagerechte Linien falten, wieder öffnen.

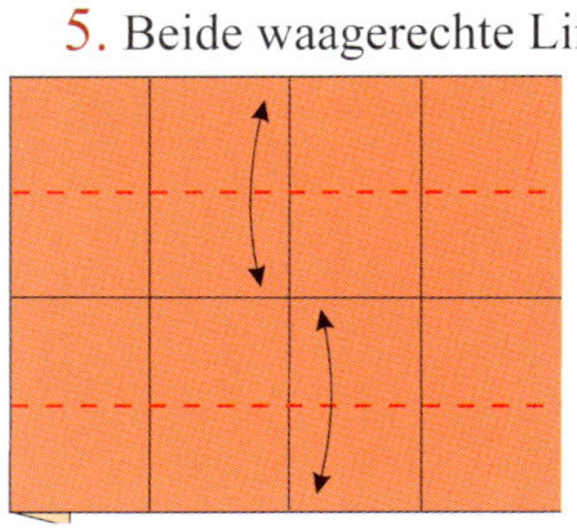

Fold both horizontal lines and open up again.

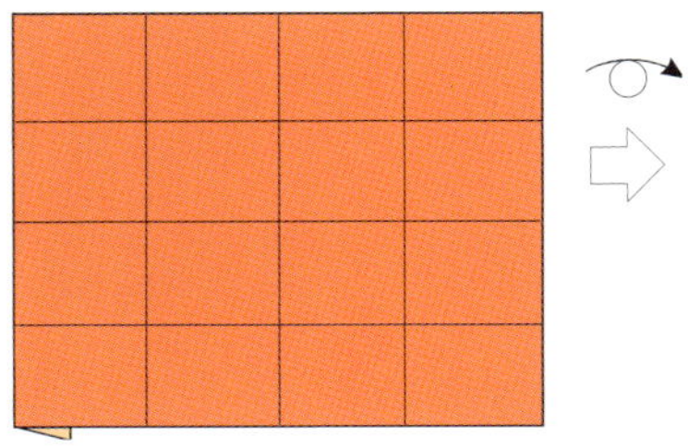

6. Rückseite nach oben legen.
Turn over to the back.

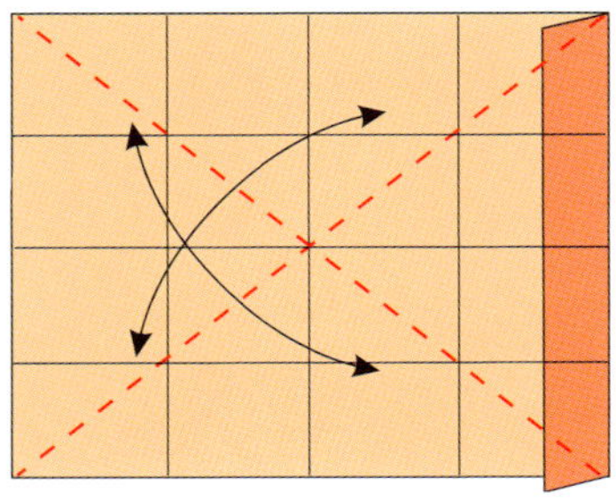

7. Diagonale Linien falten, wieder öffnen.
Fold diagonally lines and open up again.

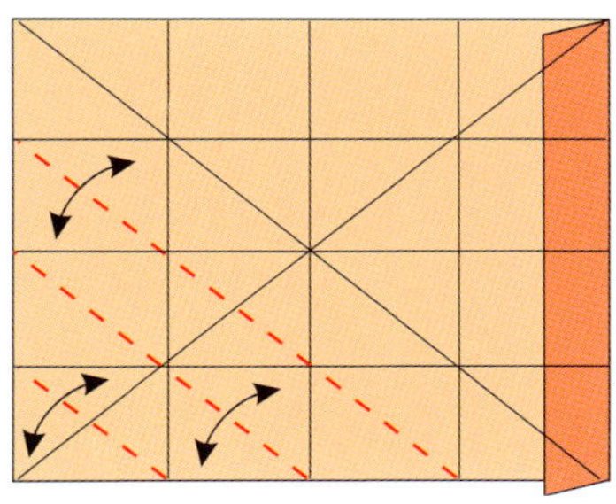

8. Nacheinander die drei diagonalen Linien falten, wieder öffnen.
Fold the three diagonal lines one after the other and open up again.

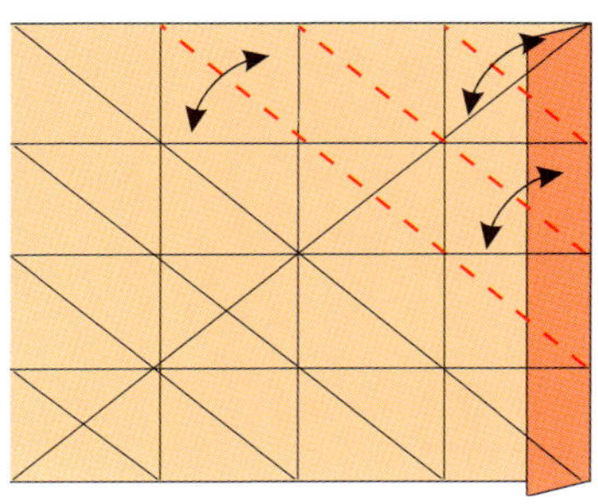

9. Nacheinander die drei diagonalen Linien falten, wieder öffnen.
Fold the three diagonal lines one after the other and open up again.

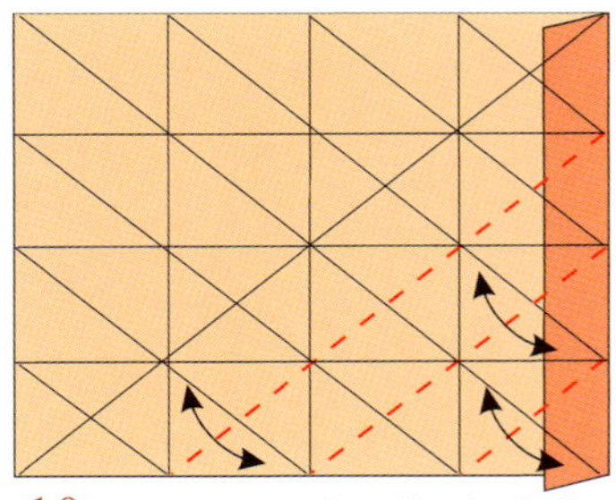

10. Nacheinander die drei diagonalen Linien falten, wieder öffnen.
Fold the three diagonal lines one after the other and open up again.

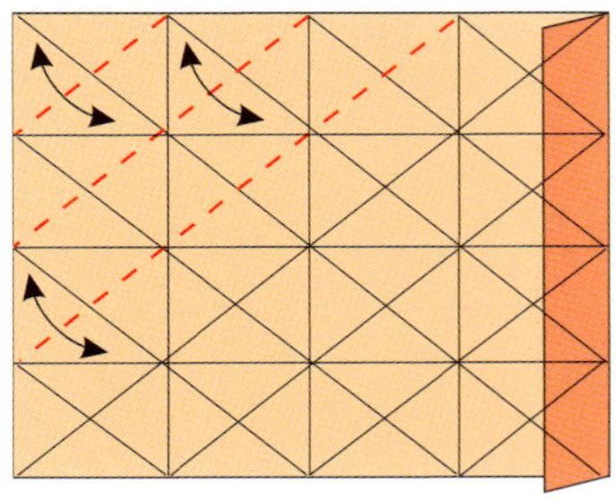

11. Nacheinander die drei diagonalen Linien falten, wieder öffnen.
Fold the three diagonal lines one after the other and open up again.

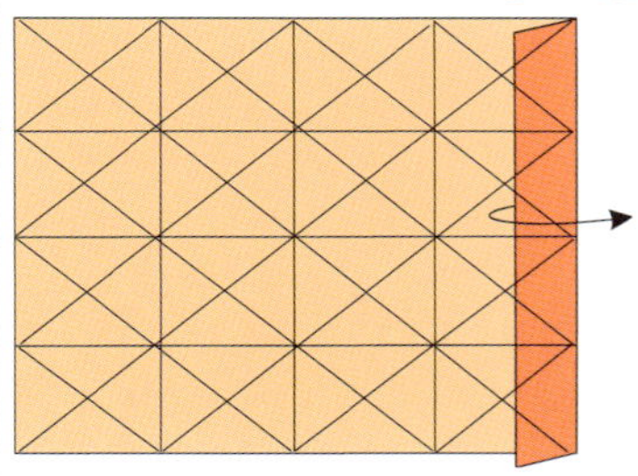

12.
Lasche an der rechten Seite öffnen.
Open flap on the right side.

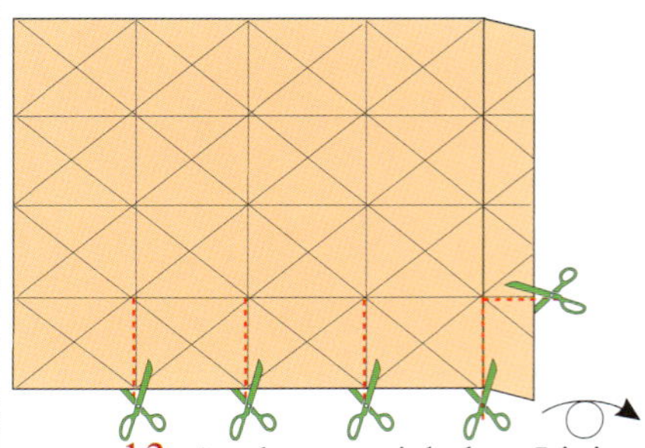

13. An den gestrichelten Linien Papier einschneiden. An der Lasche das Papier abschneiden. Rückseite nach oben legen.
Cut in the paper along the dashed lines and cut off on the flap. Turn over to the back.

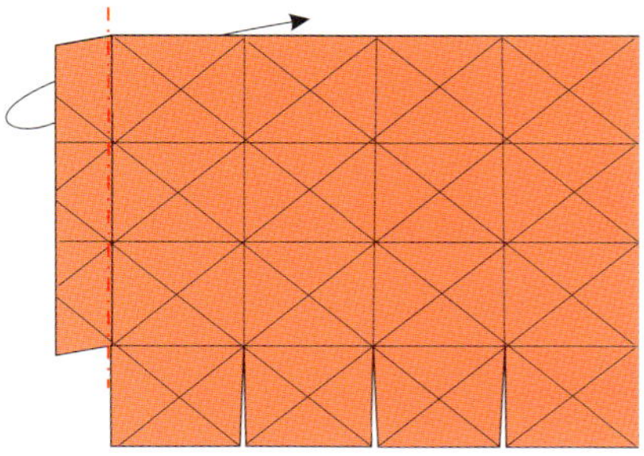

14. An der Lasche eine Bergfalte arbeiten.
Form a mountain-fold on the flap.

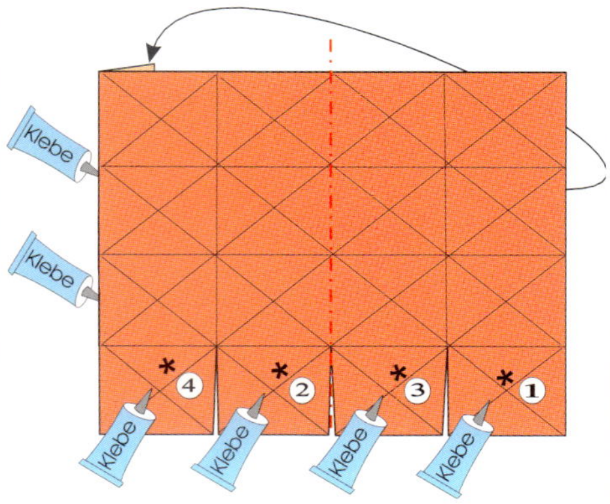

15. Senkrechte Mitte falten und an der Lasche kleben. Danach am Boden die einzelnen Papierlagen aufeinander kleben. Keinen wasserhaltigen Kleber benutzen.
Fold vertical middle and glue on the flap. Then glue the single layers of paper on top of each other. Don't use water based glue.

16. Fertiges Modell seitlich gesehen. In der Mitte der einzelnen gefalteten Rauten eindrücken. Die Rauten bilden sich auch gut, wenn an den Kreuzungspunkten mit beiden Händen die Spitzen etwas geformt werden.
Finished model seen from the side. Push in on the middle of each folded rhombus. Also each rhombus gets in shape well, if you form the points with both hands on the cross-over points.

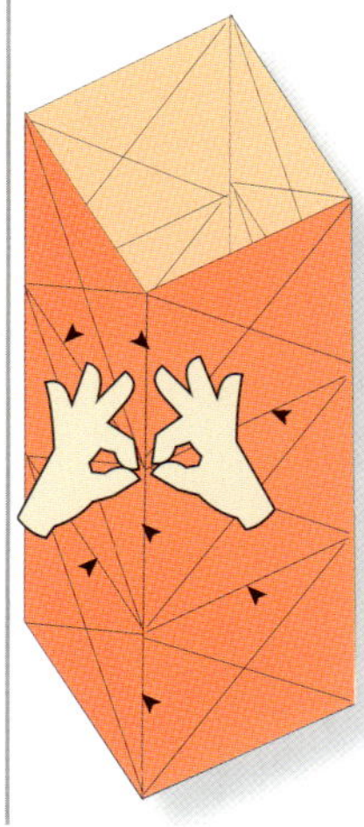

Rautenlichter

aus einem A4-Format
Licht ohne Boden-Raute mittig

MATERIAL
1 Bogen A4 Format flammsicheres Lampenpapier. Bei dem fertigen Modell ist von der Papierrückseite wenig zu sehen. Es kann also durchgefärbtes Papier oder Papier mit einer weißen Rückseite gewählt werden.
One sheet DIN A4 of not inflammable lamp paper. From the finished model, you won't see much of the back side of the paper. So you can choose any design.

Start. Diagramme von Seite 34 bis Nr.6 falten.
Fold charts of page 34 until step No.6.

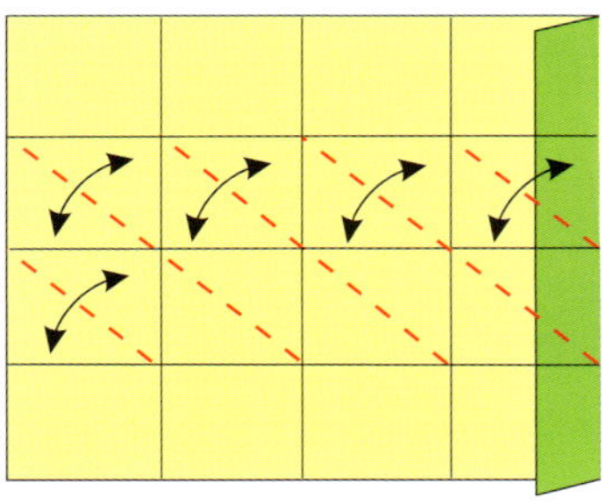

1. Nacheinander alle fünf diagonalen Linien falten, wieder öffnen. Achtung: Die Linien nur in den beiden mittleren Reihen arbeiten.
Fold all five diagonal lines one after the other and open up again. Attention: Form only the lines in both middle rows.

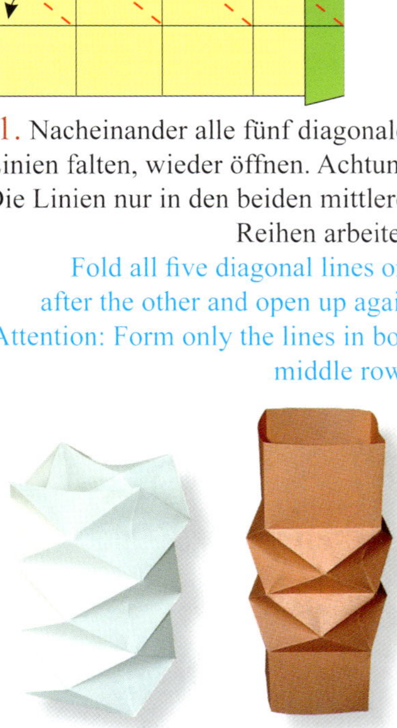

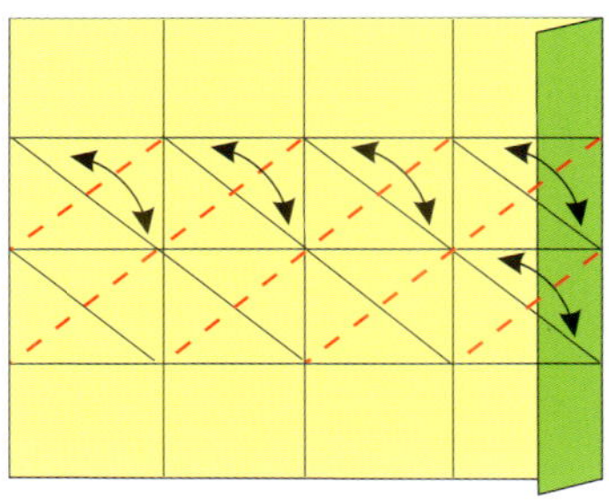

2. Nacheinander die anderen fünf diagonalen Linien falten, wieder öffnen. Achtung: Die Linien nur in den beiden mittleren Reihen arbeiten.
Fold the other five diagonal lines one after the other and open up again. Attention: Form only the lines in both middle rows.

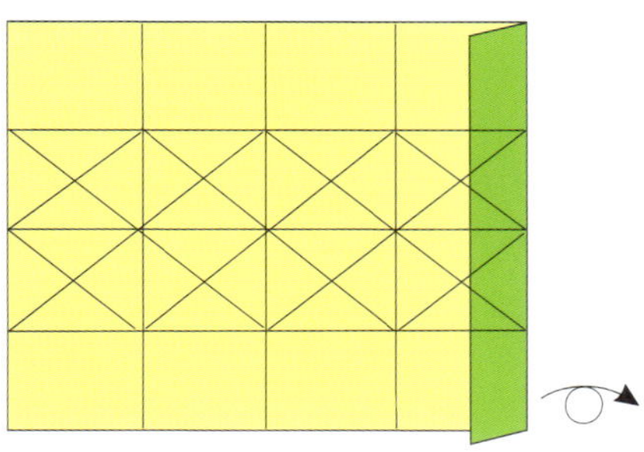

3. Rückseite nach oben legen.
Turn over to the back.

4. Senkrechte Mitte falten und an der Lasche kleben. Keinen wasserhaltigen Kleber benutzen.
Fold vertical middle and glue on the flap. Don't use water based glue.

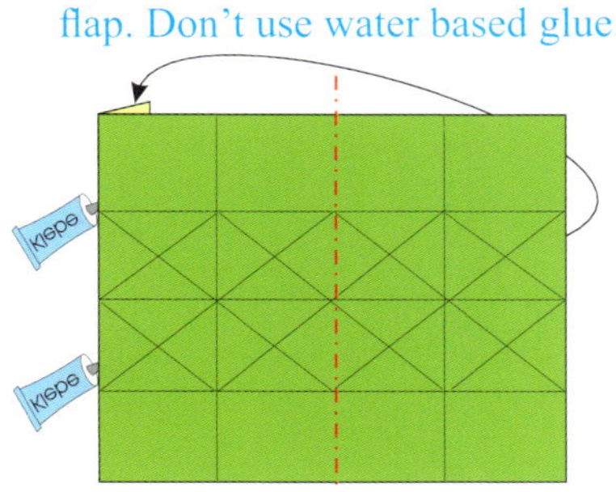

5. Fertiges Modell seitlich gesehen. In der Mitte der einzelnen gefalteten Rauten eindrücken. Die Rauten bilden sich auch gut, wenn an den Kreuzungspunkten mit beiden Händen die Spitzen etwas geformt werden.
Finished model seen from the side. Push in on the middle of each folded rhombus. Also each rhombus gets in shape well, if you form the points with both hands on the cross-over points.

Rautenlichter aus einem A4 Format

Licht ohne Boden-Raute oben

MATERIAL

1 Bogen A4 Format flammsicheres Lampenpapier. Bei dem fertigen Modell ist von der Papierrückseite wenig zu sehen. Es kann also durchgefärbtes Papier oder Papier mit einer weißen Rückseite gewählt werden.

One sheet DIN A4 of not inflammable lamp paper. From the finished model, you won't see much of the back side of the paper. So you can choose any design.

Start. Diagramme von Seite 34 bis Nr.4 falten.

Fold charts of page 34 until step No.4.

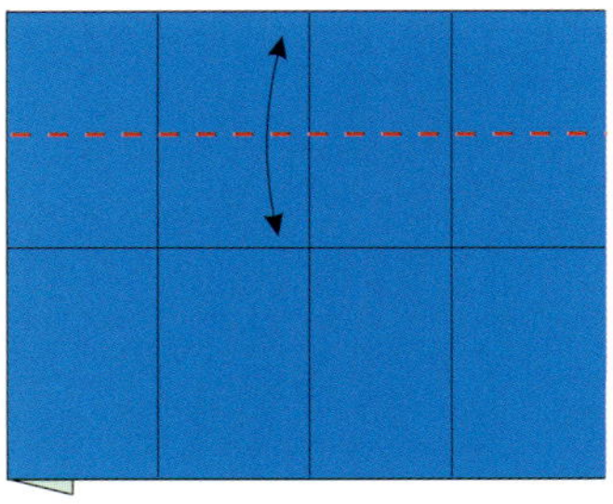

1. Waagerechte Linie falten, wieder öffnen.

Fold the horizontal line and open up again.

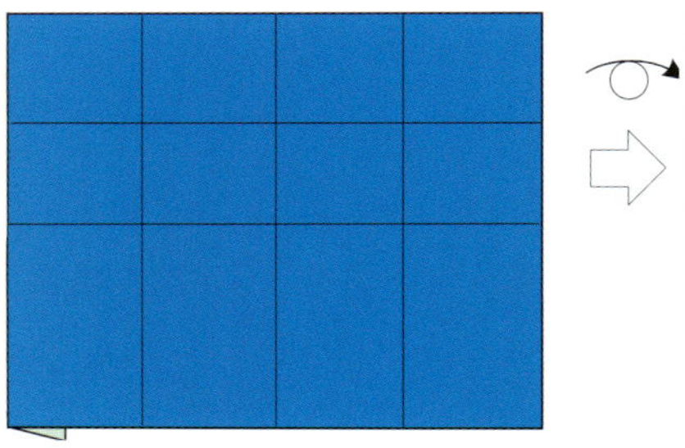

2. Rückseite nach oben legen.

Turn over to the back.

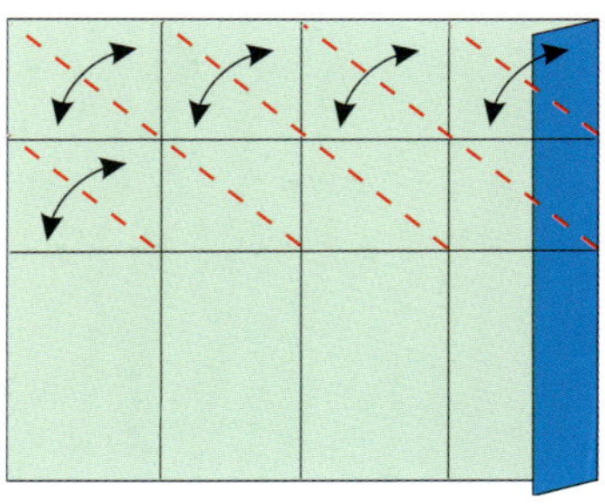

3. Nacheinander alle fünf diagonalen Linien falten, wieder öffnen. Achtung: Die Linien nur in den beiden oberen Reihen arbeiten.

Fold all five diagonal lines one after the other and open up again. Attention: Form only the lines in both upper rows.

Es gibt viele weitere Möglichkeiten, viel Spaß und versucht es!
There are a lot of opportunities, have fun and try it!

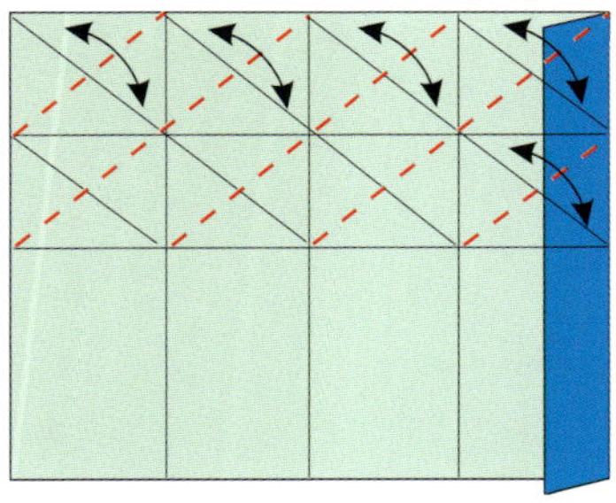

4. Nacheinander die anderen fünf diagonalen Linien falten, wieder öffnen. Achtung: Die Linien nur in den beiden oberen Reihen arbeiten.

Fold the other five diagonal lines one after the other and open up again. Attention: Form only the lines in both upper rows.

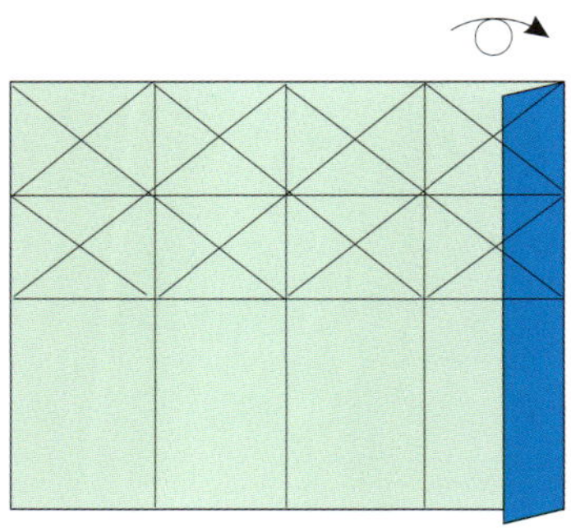

5. Rückseite nach oben legen.

Turn over to the back.

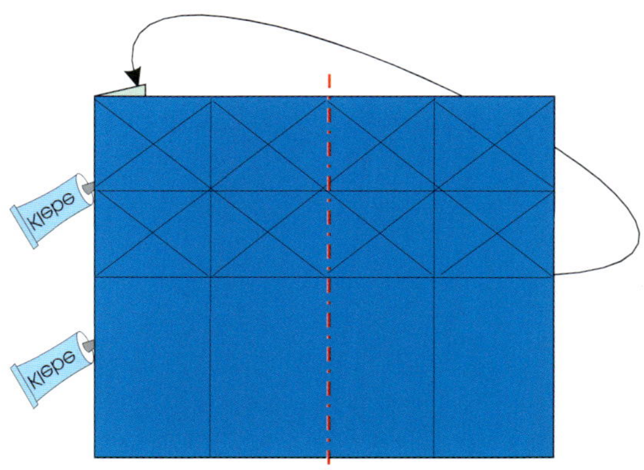

6. Senkrechte Mitte falten und an der Lasche kleben. Keinen wasserhaltigen Kleber benutzen.

Fold vertical middle and glue on the flap. Don't use water based glue.

7. Fertiges Modell seitlich gesehen. In der Mitte der einzelnen gefalteten Rauten eindrücken. Die Rauten bilden sich auch gut, wenn an den Kreuzungspunkten mit beiden Händen die Spitzen etwas geformt werden.

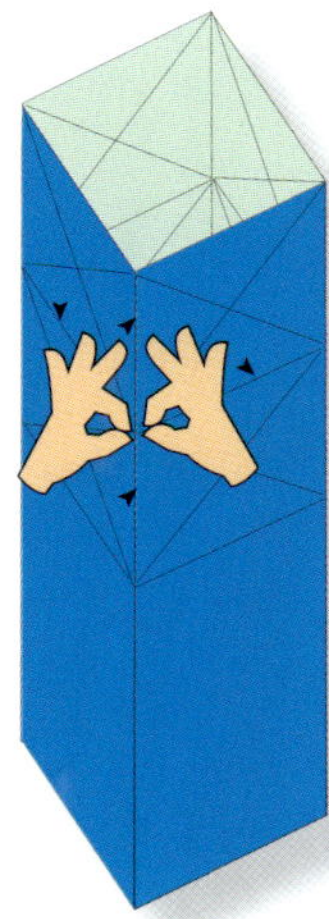

Finished model seen from the side. Push in on the middle of each folded rhombus. Also each rhombus gets in shape well, if you form the points with both hands on the cross-over points.

MATERIAL

1 Bogen 15x30 cm flammsicheres Lampenpapier. Bei dem fertigen Modell ist von der Papierrückseite wenig zu sehen. Es kann also durchgefärbtes Papier oder Papier mit einer weißen Rückseite gewählt werden.

One sheet 15x30 cm of not inflammable lamp paper. From the finished model, you won't see much of the back side of the paper. So you can choose any design.

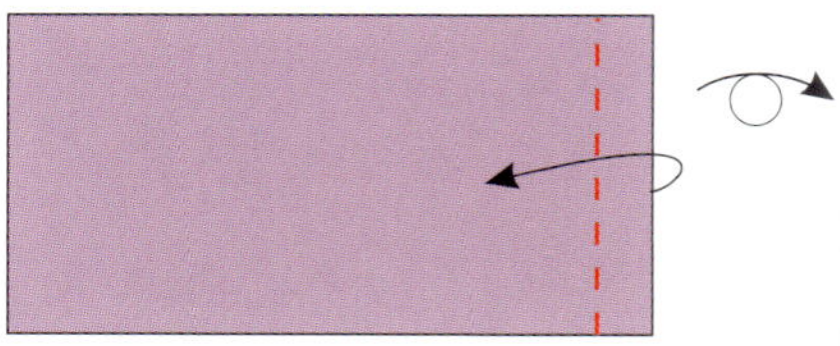

1. Senkrechte Linie falten, liegen lassen. Rückseite nach oben legen.
Fold vertical line and leave. Turn over to the back.

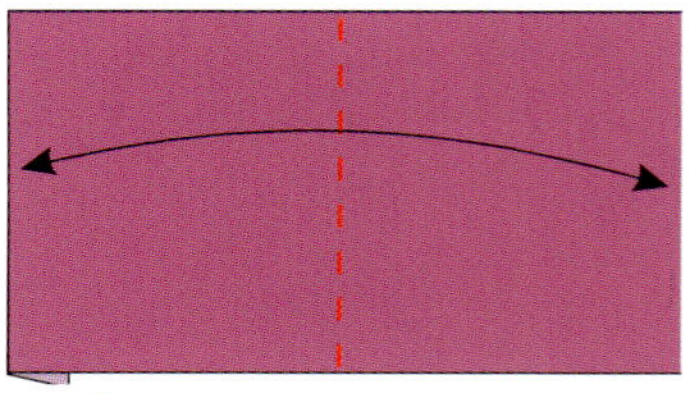

2. Senkrechte Mitte falten, wieder öffnen, siehe Pfeil.
Fold vertical middle and open up again, see arrow.

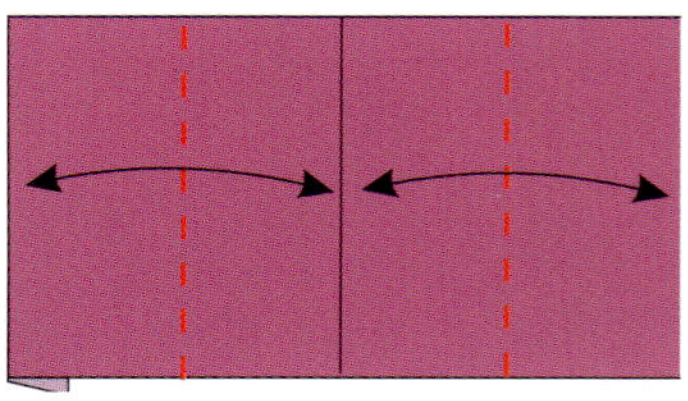

3. Beide senkrechte Linien falten, wieder öffnen.
Fold both vertical lines and open up again.

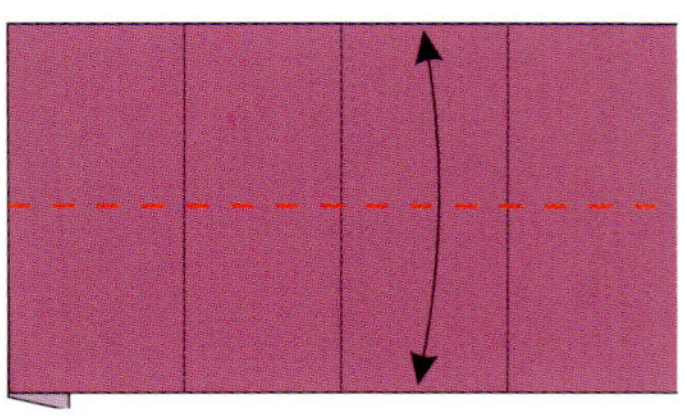

4. Waagerechte Mitte falten, wieder öffnen.
Fold the horizontal middle and open up again.

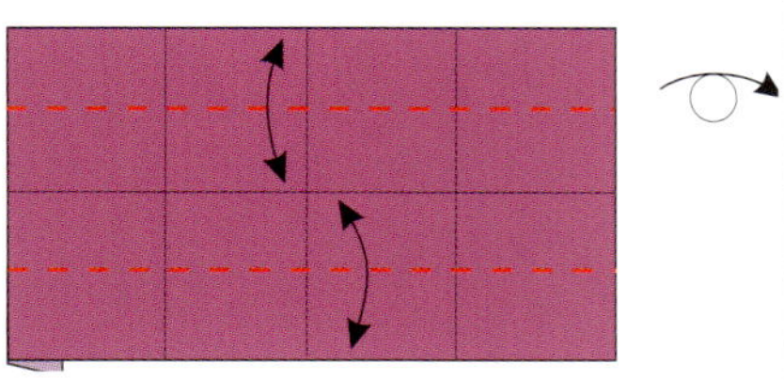

5. Beide waagerechte Linien falten, wieder öffnen. Rückseite nach oben legen.
Fold both horizontal lines and open up again. Turn over to the back.

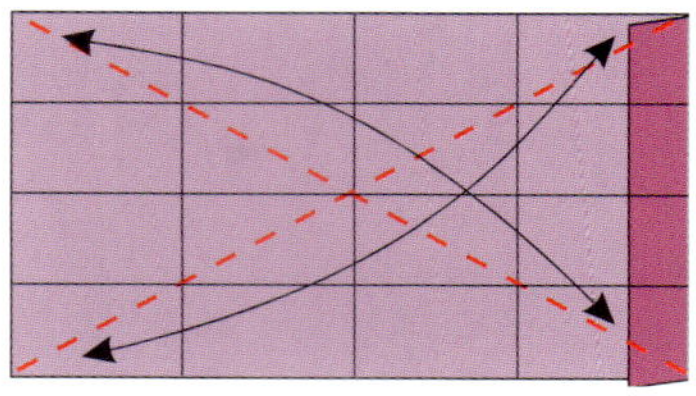

6. Diagonale Linien falten, wieder öffnen.
Fold diagonally lines and open up again.

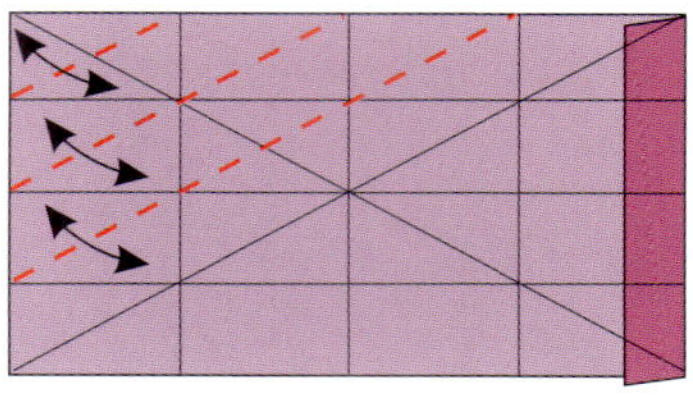

7. Nacheinander die drei diagonalen Linien falten, wieder öffnen.
Fold the three diagonal lines one after the other and open up again.

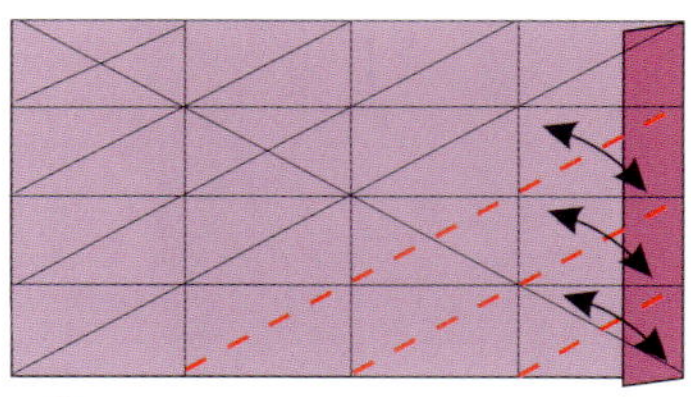

8. Nacheinander die drei diagonalen Linien falten, wieder öffnen.
Fold the three diagonal lines one after the other and open up again.

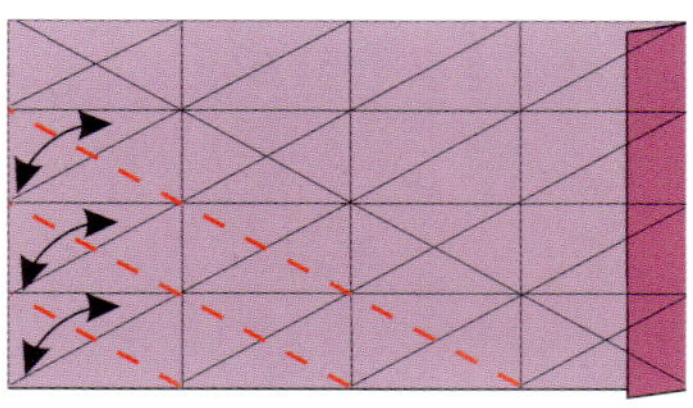

9. Nacheinander die drei diagonalen Linien falten, wieder öffnen.
Fold the three diagonal lines one after the other and open up again.

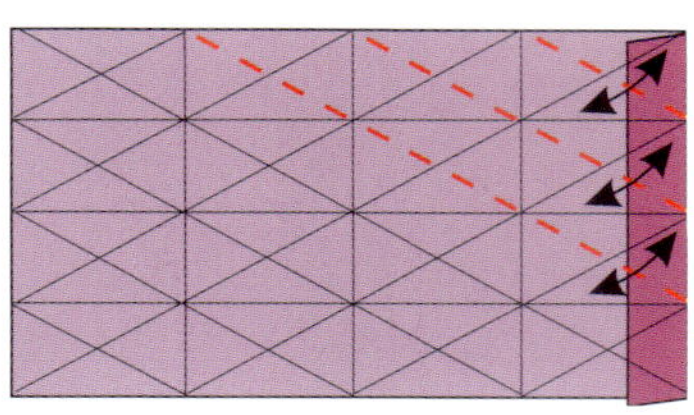

10. Nacheinander die drei diagonalen Linien falten, wieder öffnen.
Fold the three diagonal lines one after the other and open up again.

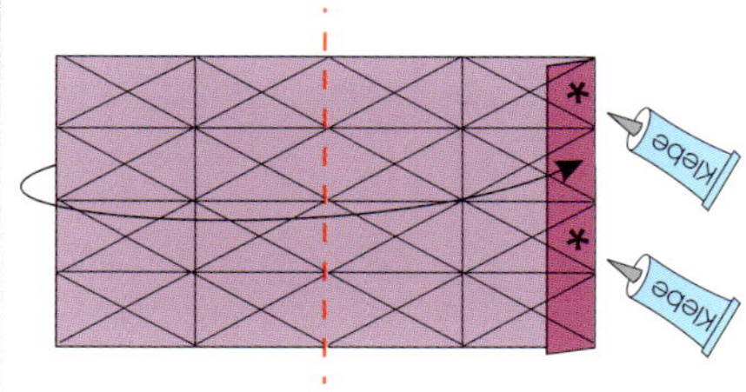

11. Senkrechte Mitte falten und an der Lasche kleben. Keinen wasserhaltigen Kleber benutzen.
Fold vertical middle and glue on the flap. Don't use water based glue.

12. Fertiges Modell seitlich gesehen. In der Mitte der einzelnen gefalteten Rauten eindrücken. Die Rauten bilden sich auch gut, wenn an den Kreuzungspunkten mit beiden Händen die Spitzen etwas geformt werden.
Finished model seen from the side. Push in on the middle of each folded rhombus. Also each rhombus gets in shape well, if you form the points with both hands on the cross-over points.

Rautenlichter aus einem Rechteck

MATERIAL

1 Bogen 15x30 cm flammsicheres Lampenpapier. Bei dem fertigen Modell ist von der Papierrückseite wenig zu sehen. Es kann also durchgefärbtes Papier oder Papier mit einer weißen Rückseite gewählt werden.

One sheet 15x30 cm of not inflammable lamp paper. From the finished model, you won't see much of the back side of the paper. So you can choose any design.

Start. Diagramme von Seite 37 bis Nr.3 falten.

Fold charts of page 37 until step No.3.

1. Zweimal waagerechte Linien falten, wieder öffnen.

Fold twice the horizontal middle and open up again.

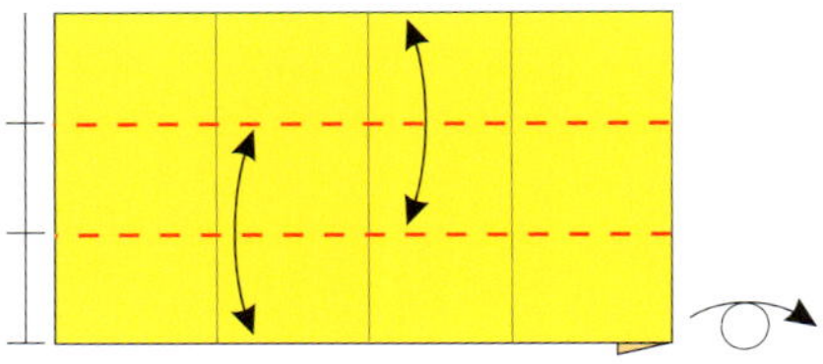

2. Nacheinander alle vier diagonalen Linien falten, wieder öffnen. Achtung: Die Linien nur im mittleren Teil arbeiten.

Fold all four diagonal lines one after the other and open up again. Attention: Form only the lines in the middle row.

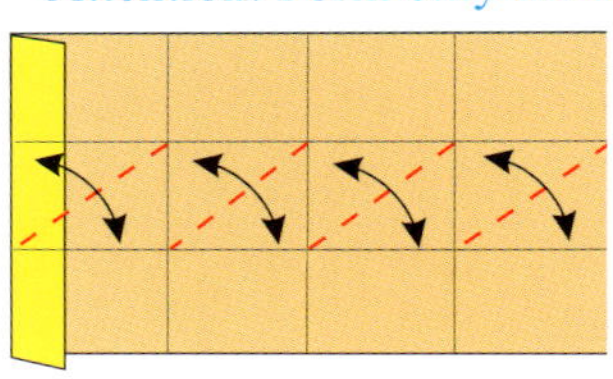

3. Nacheinander alle vier diagonalen Linien falten, wieder öffnen. Achtung: Die Linien nur im mittleren Teil arbeiten.

Fold all four diagonal lines one after the other and open up again. Attention: Form only the lines in the middle row.

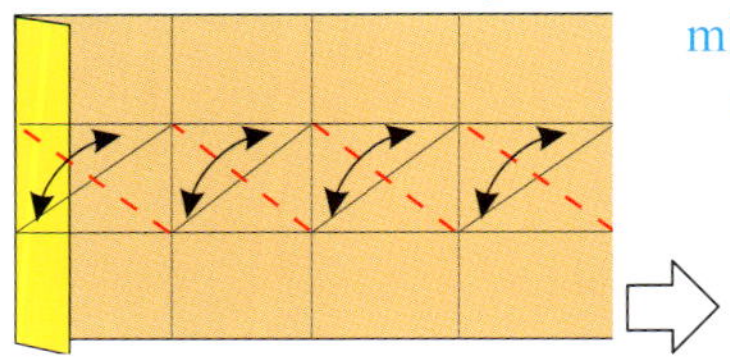

4. Rückseite nach oben legen.

Turn over to the back.

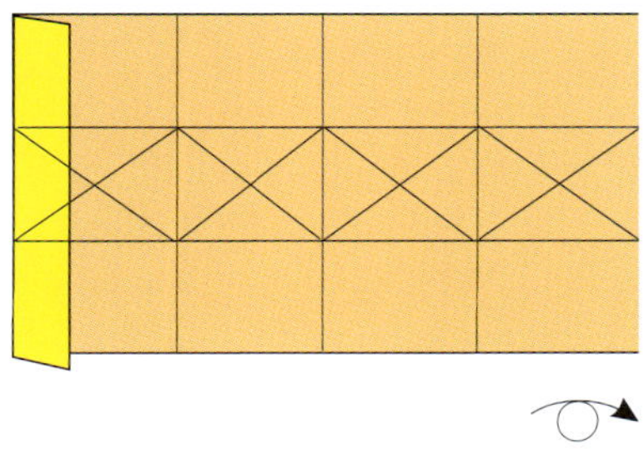

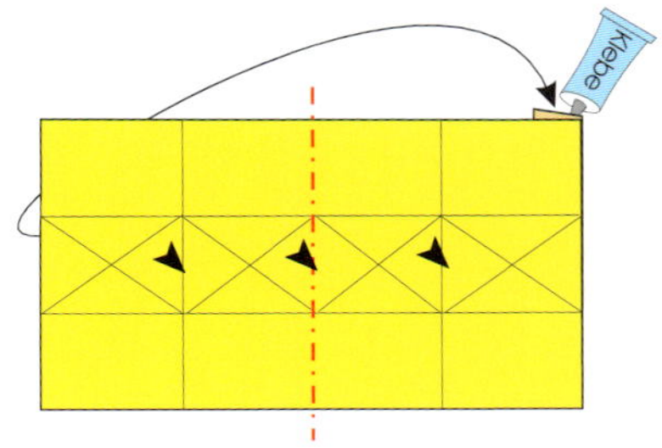

5. Senkrechte Mitte falten und an der Lasche kleben. Keinen wasserhaltigen Kleber benutzen. Rauten eindrücken, dabei an den Kreuzungspunkten mit beiden Händen die Spitzen etwas formen.

Fold vertical middle and glue on the flap. Don't use water based glue. Push in each rhombus, at the same time form the points on the cross-over points with both hands.

Rautenlichter aus einem Rechteck

Licht dreieckige Form

MATERIAL wie oben. Material is the same as above.

Start. Diagramme von Seite 37 bis Nr.1 falten.

Fold charts of page 37 until step No.1.

1. Zweimal senkrechte Linien falten, wieder öffnen.

Fold twice the vertical lines and open up again.

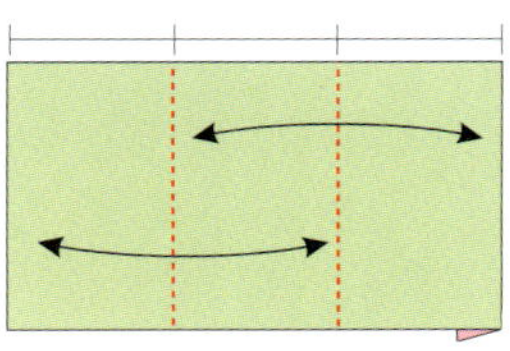

2. Zweimal waagerechte Linien falten, wieder öffnen.

Fold twice the horizontal lines and open up again.

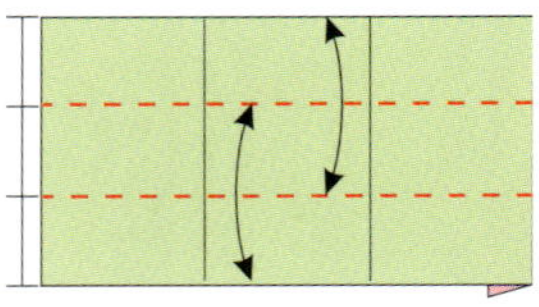

3. Rückseite nach oben legen.

Turn over to the back.

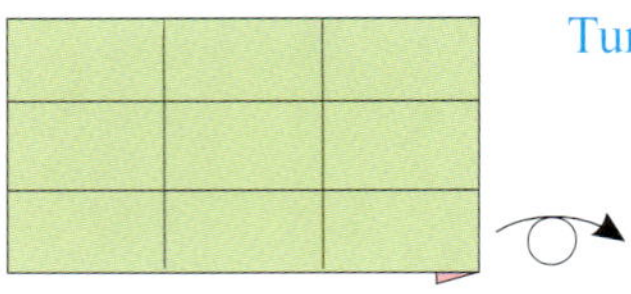

4. Nacheinander alle drei diagonalen Linien falten, wieder öffnen. Achtung: Die Linien nur im mittleren Teil arbeiten.

Fold all three diagonal lines one after the other and open up again. Attention: Form only the lines in the middle row.

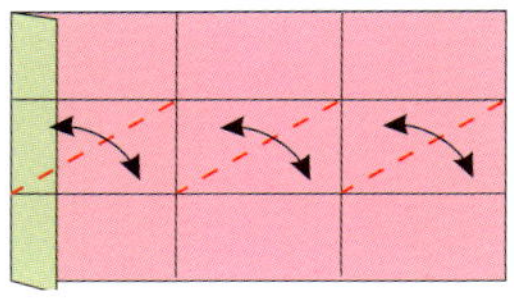

5. Nacheinander alle drei diagonalen Linien falten, wieder öffnen. Achtung: Die Linien nur im mittleren Teil arbeiten.

Fold all three diagonal lines one after the other and open up again. Attention: Form only the lines in the middle row.

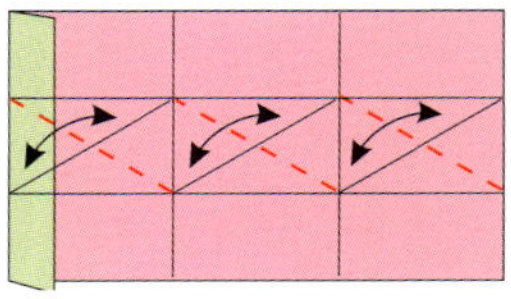

6. Rückseite nach oben legen.

Turn over to the back.

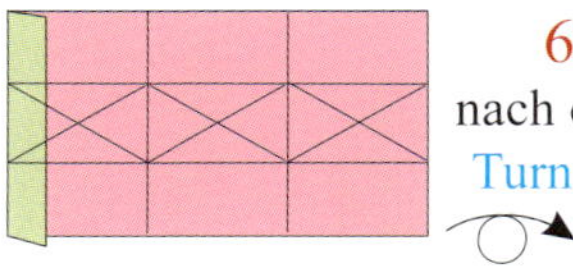

7. Senkrechte Linien als Bergfalte formen. Papier an der Lasche kleben, siehe Pfeil. Keinen wasserhaltigen Kleber benutzen. Rauten eindrücken, dabei an den Kreuzungspunkten mit beiden Händen die Spitzen etwas formen.

Form vertical lines as a mountain-fold and glue on the flap, see arrow. Don't use water based glue. Push in each rhombus, at the same time form the points on the cross-over points with both hands.

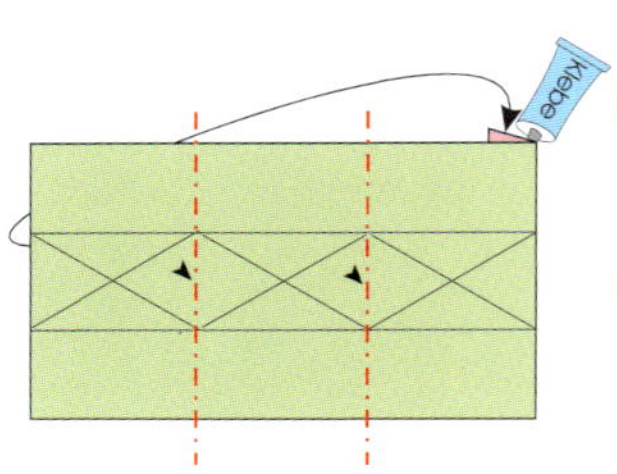

Rautenlichter aus einem Quadrat

MATERIAL

1 Bogen 30x30 cm flammsicheres Lampenpapier. Bei dem fertigen Modell ist von der Papierrückseite wenig zu sehen. Es kann also durchgefärbtes Papier oder Papier mit einer weißen Rückseite gewählt werden.

One sheet 30x30 cm of not inflammable lamp paper. From the finished model, you won't see much of the back side of the paper. So you can choose any design.

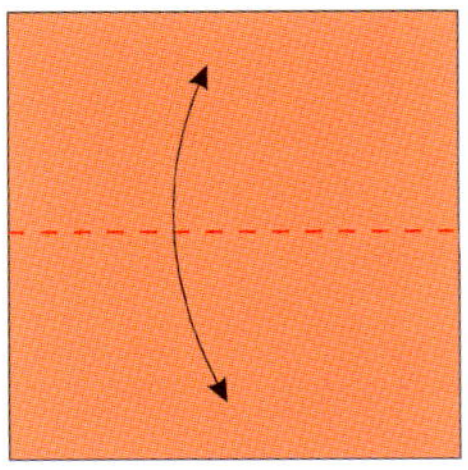

1. Waagerechte Linie falten, wieder öffnen.
Fold horizontal line and open up again.

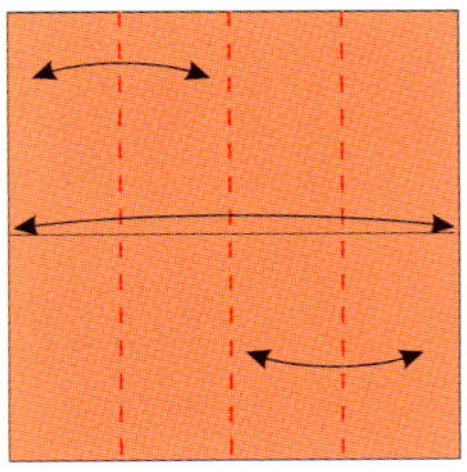

2. Senkrechte Mitte falten, wieder öffnen. Danach die beiden anderen senkrechten Linien falten, wieder öffnen.
Fold vertical middle and open up again. Then fold both other vertical lines and open up again.

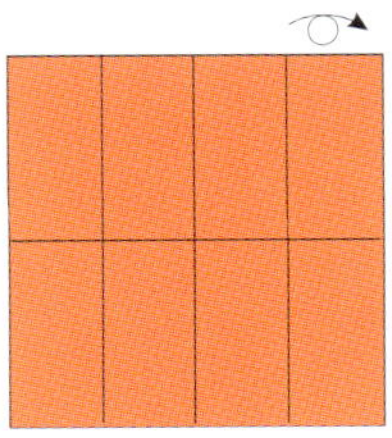

3. Rückseite nach oben legen.
Turn over to the back.

4. Nacheinander die drei diagonalen Linien falten, wieder öffnen. Achtung: Nur in den beiden mittleren Teilen arbeiten.
Fold all three diagonal lines one after the other and open up again. Attention: Work only in both middle rows.

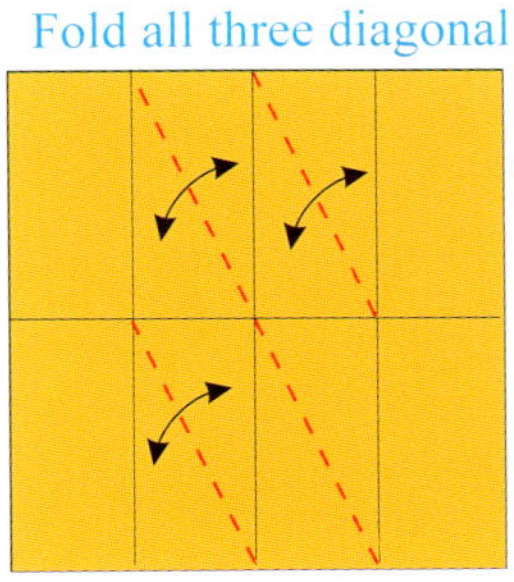

5. Nacheinander die drei diagonalen Linien falten, wieder öffnen. Achtung: Nur in den beiden mittleren Teilen arbeiten.
Fold all three diagonal lines one after the other and open up again. Attention: Work only in both middle rows.

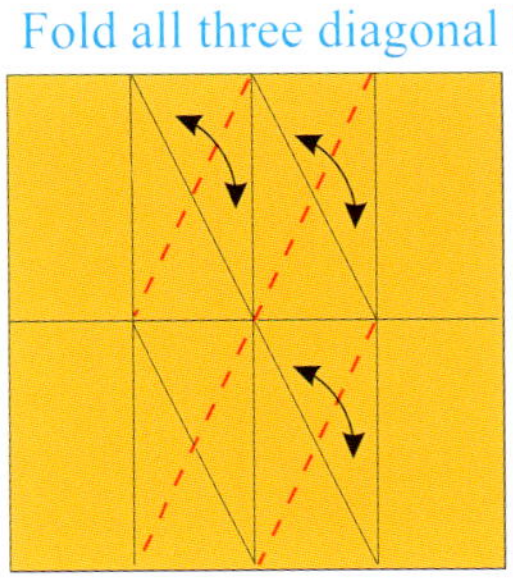

6. An der Mittellinie, zwischen den roten Punkten, mit einem Messer einschneiden. Danach Papier an dieser Linie nach unten legen.
Cut in the middle along the line between the red dots with a knife. Then lay paper along this line downwards.

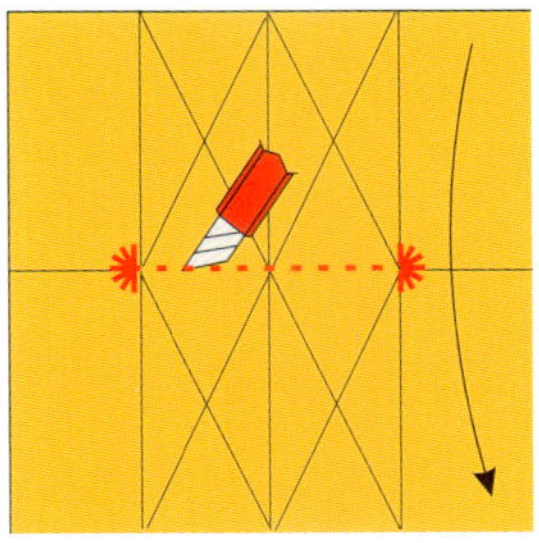

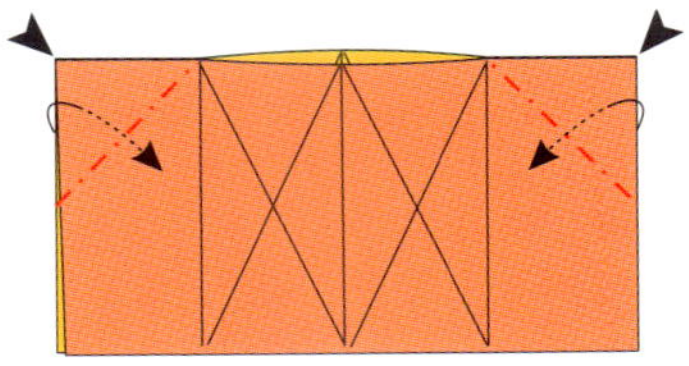

7. An beiden Ecken schräge Linien nach innen falten, liegen lassen.
Fold oblique lines on both corners inwards and leave.

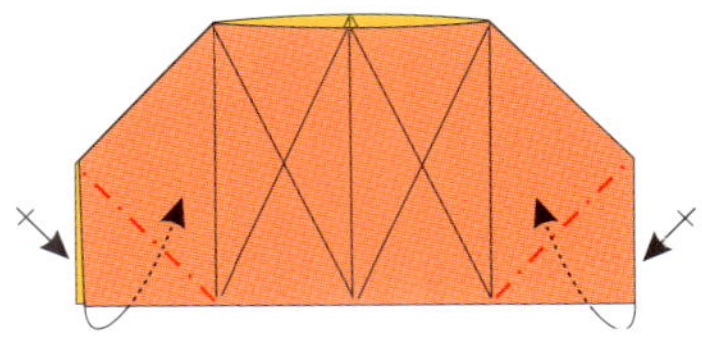

8. An der unteren Ecke schräge Linien nach innen falten, liegen lassen. Auf der Rückseite wiederholen.
Fold oblique lines on the lower corner inwards and leave. Turn over to the back.

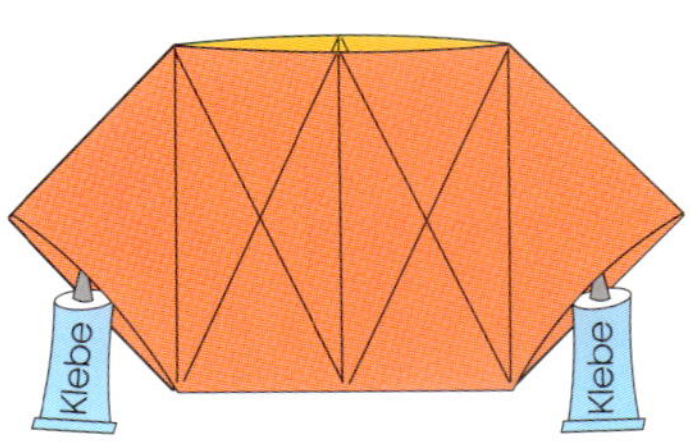

9. Die Papierlagen an der rechten und linken Seite zusammenkleben. Keinen wasserhaltigen Kleber benutzen.
Glue the layers of paper on the right and left side together. Don't use water based glue.

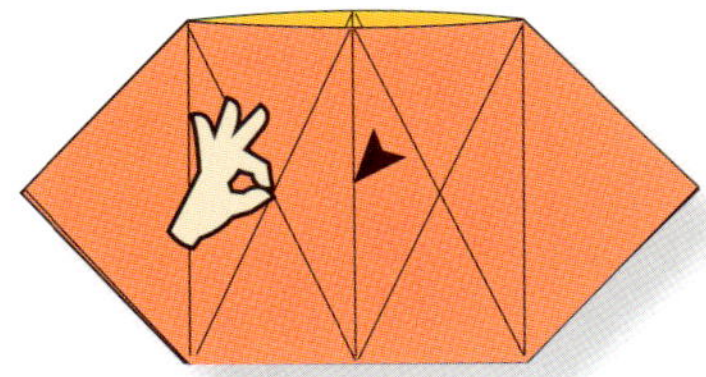

10. Fertiges Modell. In der Mitte der Raute eindrücken. Die Raute bildet sich gut, wenn an den Kreuzungspunkten mit beiden Händen die Spitze etwas geformt wird.
Finished model. Push in on the middle of each rhombus. Also each rhombus gets in shape well, if you form the points with both hands on the cross-over points.

Lichtsäule

Für dieses Modell muss das Papierformat ein Quadrat sein. Die Papiergröße sollte wenigstens 30x30 cm haben. Der Unterschied zu Modell Nr.22 ist, das die Rauten eine quadratische Form haben.

For this model the paper has to be a square. The size should be a minimum of 30x30 cm. The difference to model No.22 is, that each rhombus has got a square form.

Start. Diagramme von Seite 37 bis Nr.12 falten, fertig.
Fold charts of page 37 until step No.12, finished.

Übertopf-Licht

MATERIAL

1 Bogen 30x30 cm flammsicheres Lampenpapier. Bei dem fertigen Modell ist von der Papierrückseite sehr viel zu sehen. Es sollte also nur durchgefärbtes Papier gewählt werden. Allerdings sieht das weiße Papier auch sehr schön aus.

One sheet 30x30 cm of not inflammable lamp paper. From the finished model, you will see much of the back side of the paper. So you should choose paper with a coloured back. It also will look very lovely, using white paper only.

1. Zweimal waagerecht die Mitte falten, wieder öffnen. Rückseite nach oben legen.
Fold twice the horizontal middle and open up again. Turn over to the back.

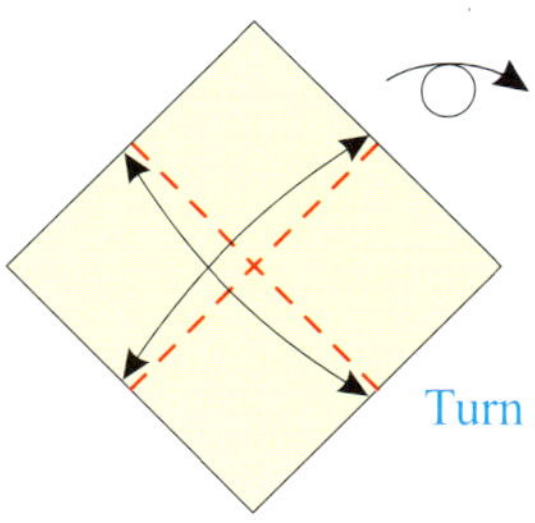

2. Zweimal diagonal die Mitte falten, wieder öffnen. Rückseite nach oben legen.
Fold twice the middle diagonally and open up again. Turn over to the back.

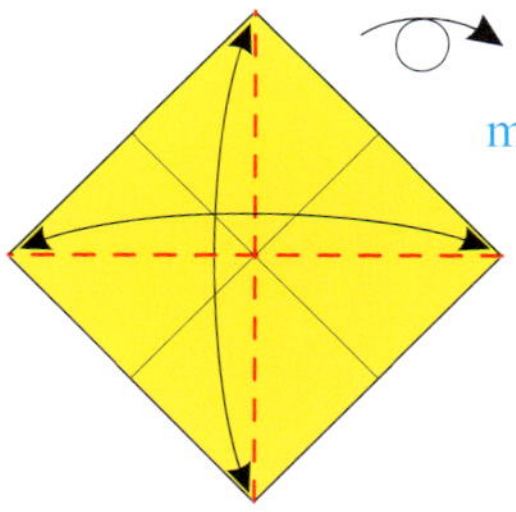

3. Von der waagerechten Mitte (Bergfalte), die seitlichen Ecken zur oberen Ecke legen. Die untere Ecke dann ebenfalls nach oben legen, siehe Pfeile.
From the horizontal middle (mountain-fold), lay the corners from the side to the upper corner. Also lay the lower corner to the upper corner, see arrows.

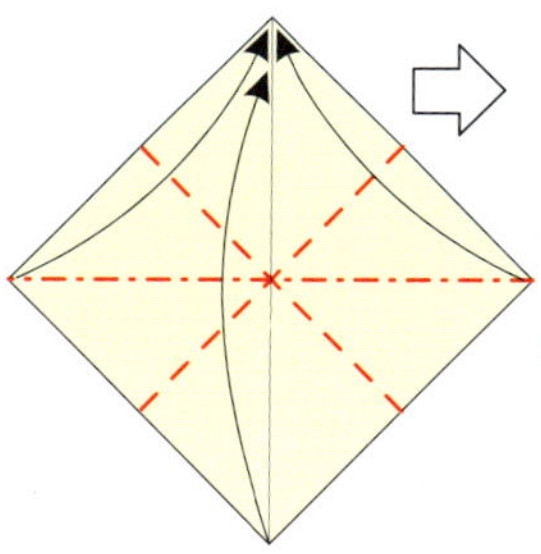

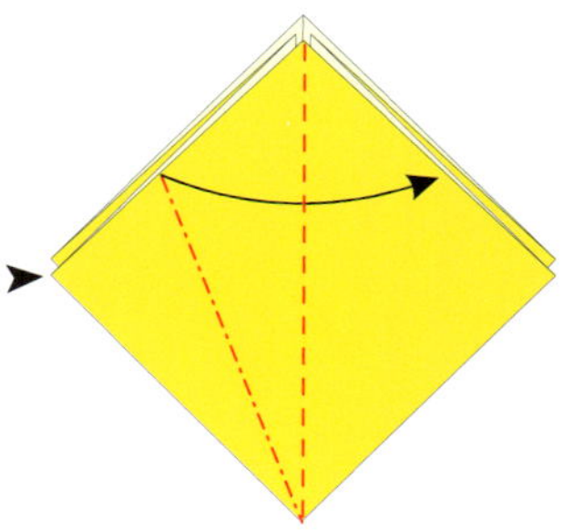

4. Bergfalte nach rechts falten, dabei die Ecke flach drücken.
Fold mountain-fold to the right and push the corner flat.

5. Mit den anderen drei Ecken den Arbeitsschritt Nr.4 wiederholen.
Repeat working step No.4 with the other three corners.

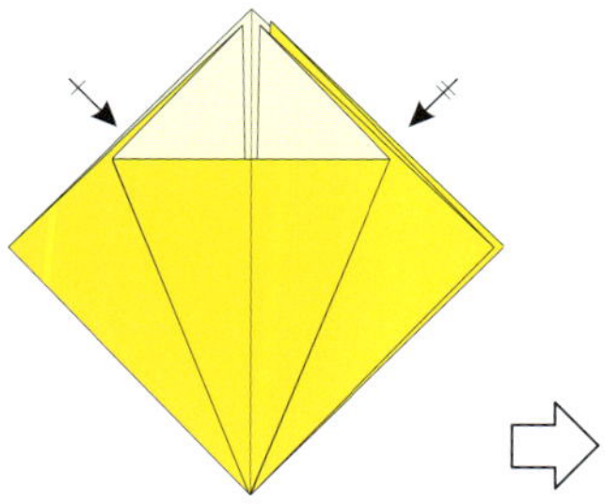

6. Spitzen an der Linie abschneiden.
Cut off the points along the line.

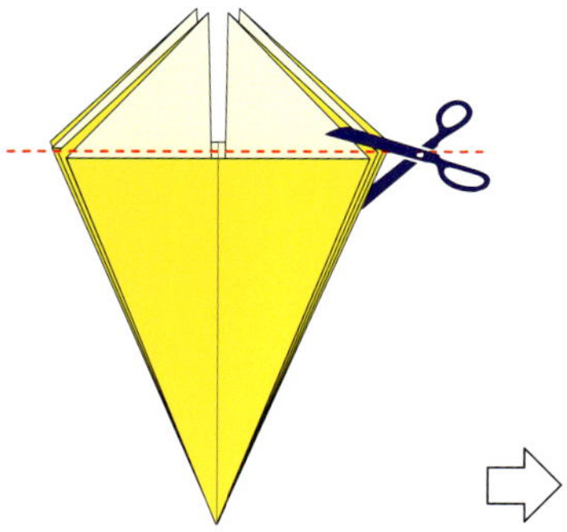

7. Nur mit der oberen Papierlage, siehe Pfeil, schräge Linien zur Mitte falten. Auf der Rückseite wiederholen.
Using only the top layer of paper, see arrow, fold oblique lines to the middle. Repeat on the back.

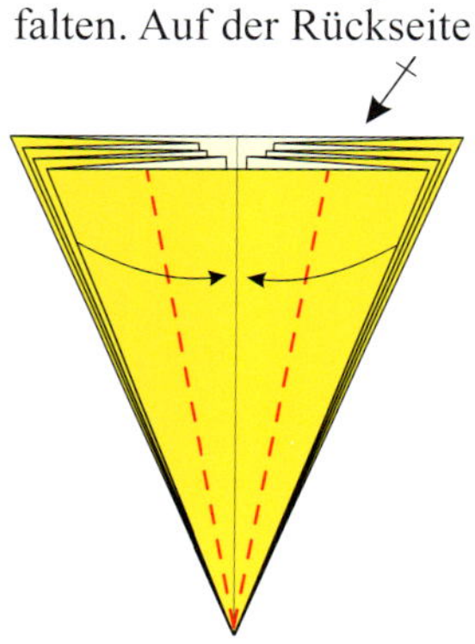

8. Nur mit der oberen Papierlage, siehe Pfeil, von links nach rechts falten. Auf der Rückseite wiederholen.
Using only the top layer of paper, see arrow, fold from left to the right. Repeat on the back.

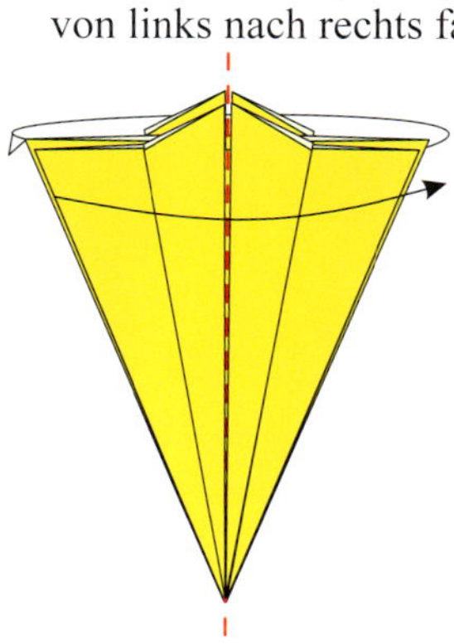

9. Schräge Linien zur Mitte falten, liegen lassen. Auf der Rückseite wiederholen.
Fold oblique lines to the middle and leave. Repeat on the back.

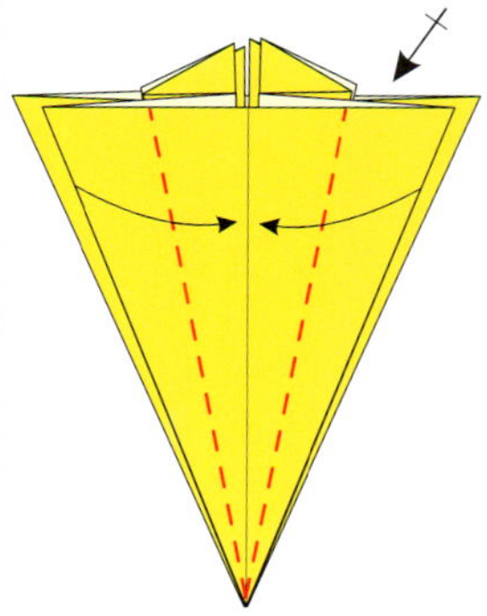

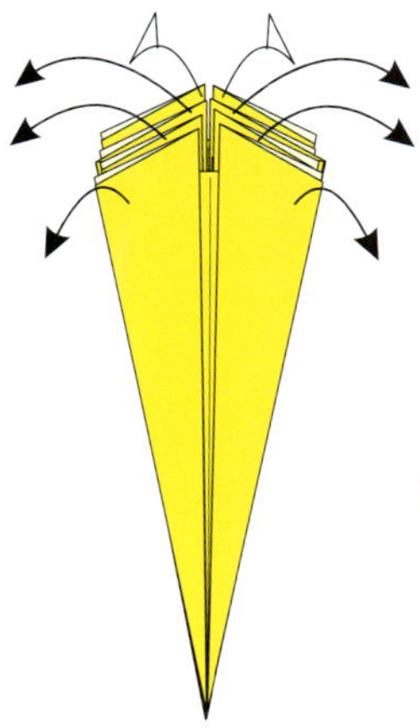

10. Arbeitsschritte von Nr.7 und Nr.9 wieder öffnen, siehe Pfeile.
Open up working steps No.7 and No.9, see arrows.

11. Alle schrägen Linien von Nr.7 und Nr.9 zur Bergfalte formen und dann nach innen legen.
Form all oblique lines from No.7 and No.9 as a mountain-fold and lay inwards.

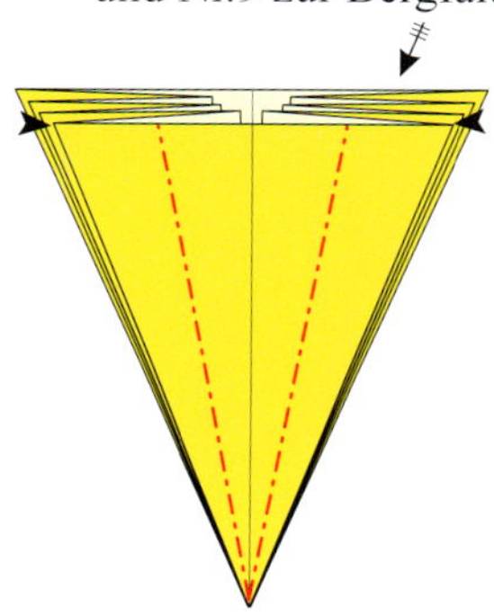

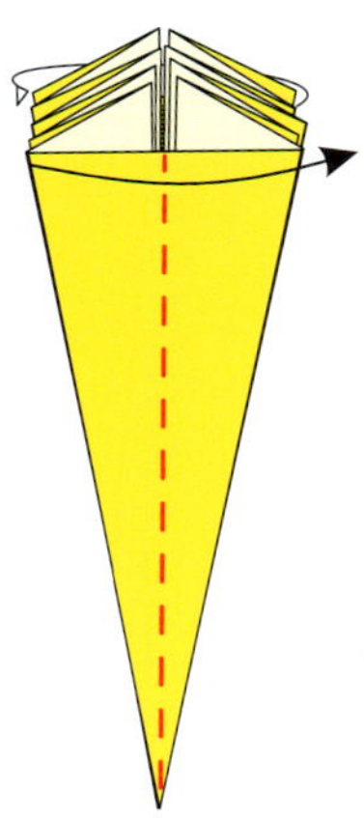

12. Nur mit der oberen Papierlage, siehe Pfeil, von links nach rechts falten. Auf der Rückseite wiederholen.
Using only the top layer of paper, see arrow, fold from left to the right. Repeat on the back.

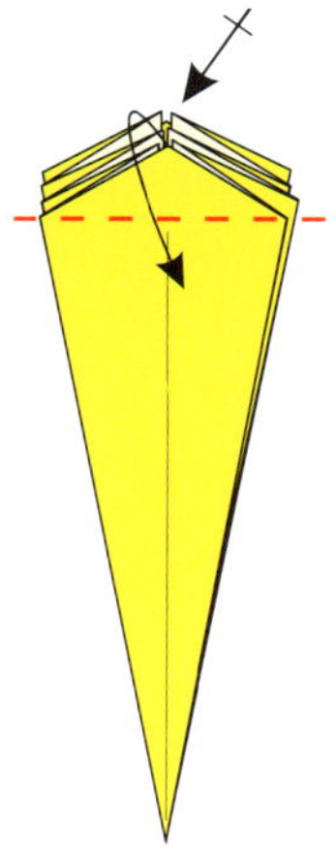

13. Spitze nach unten falten, liegen lassen. Auf der Rückseite wiederholen.
Fold point downwards and leave. Repeat on the back.

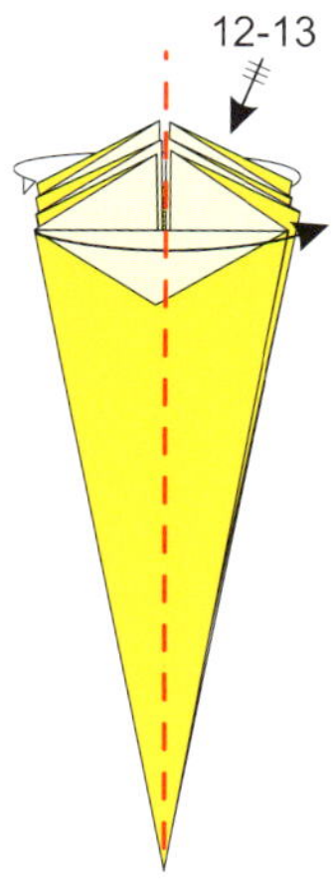

14. Arbeitsschritte Nr.12 und Nr.13 mit allen Spitzen wiederholen.
Repeat working steps No.12 and No.13 with all points.

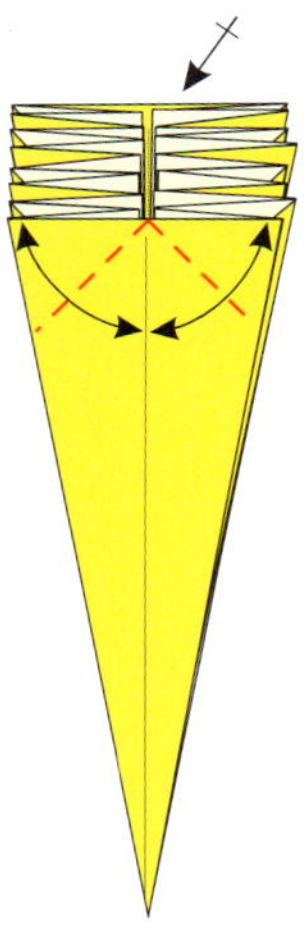

15. Schräge Linien zur Mitte falten, wieder öffnen. Auf der Rückseite wiederholen.
Fold oblique lines to the middle and open up again. Repeat on the back.

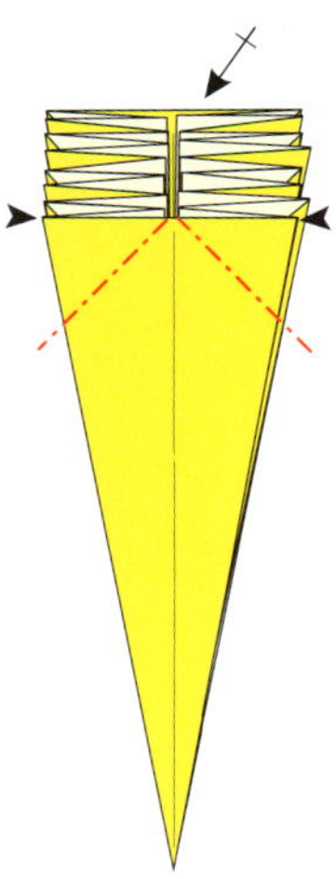

16. Linien zur Bergfalte formen, die Ecken dann nach innen legen. Auf der Rückseite wiederholen.
Form lines as a mountain-fold and lay corners inwards. Repeat on the back.

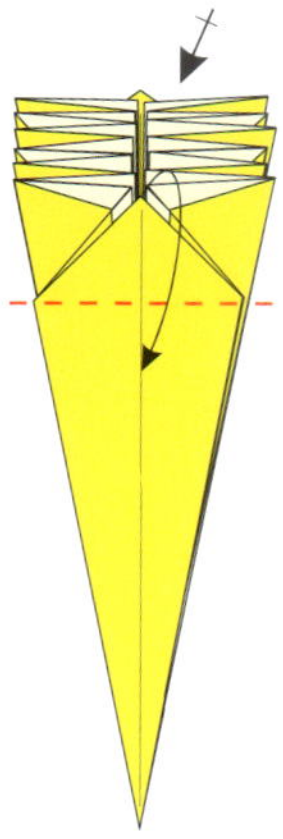

17. Spitze nach unten falten, liegen lassen. Auf der Rückseite wiederholen.
Fold point downwards and leave. Repeat on the back.

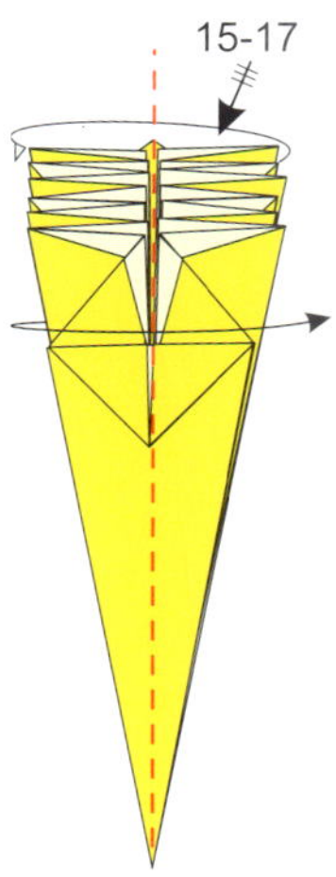

18. Nur mit der oberen Papierlage, siehe Pfeil, von links nach rechts falten. Auf der Rückseite wiederholen. Dann Arbeitsschritte von Nr.15 bis Nr.17 mit allen Ecken wiederholen.
Using only the top layer of paper, see arrow, fold from left to the right. Repeat on the back. Then repeat working steps from No.15 to No.17 with all corners.

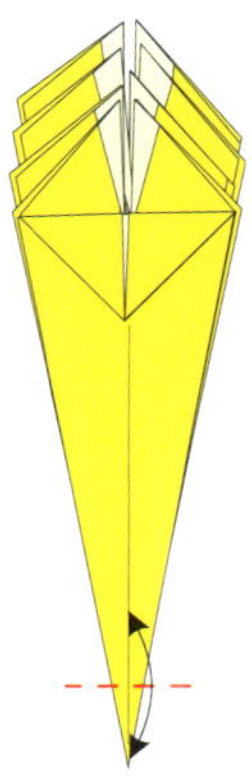

19. An der unteren Spitze, waagerechte Linie falten, wieder öffnen.
Fold horizontal line on the lower point and open up again.

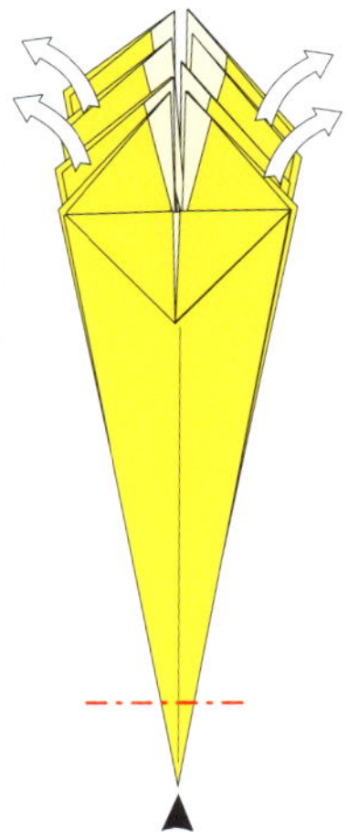

20. Jetzt eine Bergfalte formen, dabei die Spitze eindrücken. Modell von innen auseinanderdrücken, das Modell steht dann flach auf dem Tisch.
Form a mountain-fold and push in the point. Push the model from the inside outwards. Now the model stands flatly on the table.

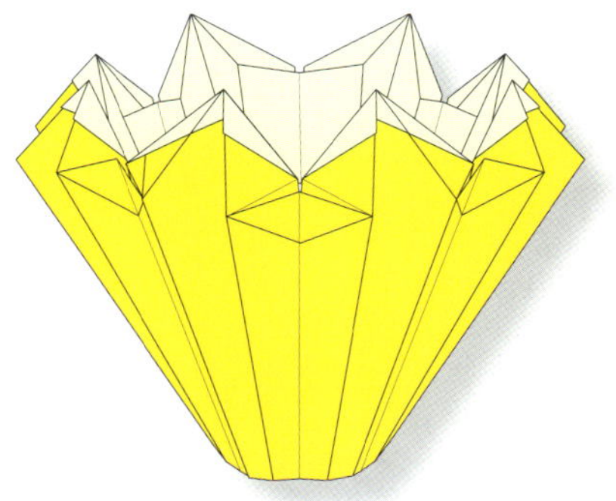

21. Fertiges Modell seitlich gesehen.
Finished model seen from the side.

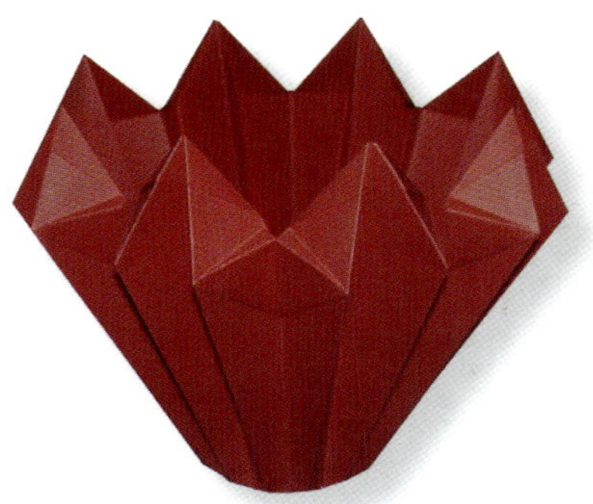

Eiszapfen Licht

Modell von Jannie van Schuylenburg

MATERIAL

1 Bogen 30x30 cm flammsicheres Lampenpapier. Bei dem fertigen Modell ist von der Papierrückseite wenig zu sehen. Es kann also jedes Papier ausgewählt werden. Allerdings sieht es mit dem weißen Papier besonderst schön aus.

One sheet 30x30 cm of not inflammable lamp paper. From the finished model, you won't see much of the back side of the paper. So you can choose any design. It will look very lovely using white paper.

Start. Diagramme von Seite 40 bis Nr.3 falten.

Fold charts of page 40 until step No.3.

1. Nur mit der oberen Papierlage, siehe Pfeil, schräge Linien zur Mitte falten. Auf der Rückseite wiederholen.

Using only the top layer of paper, see arrow, fold oblique lines to the middle. Repeat on the back side.

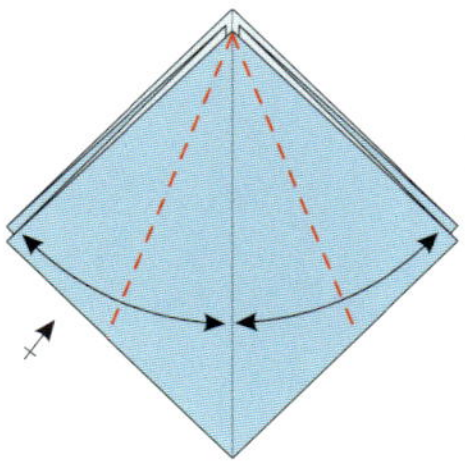

2. An der unteren Spitze die waagerechte Linie falten, wieder öffnen. Achtung: Auf die seitliche Höheneinteilung achten.

On the lower point fold the horizontal middle and open up again. Attention: Note the heights arrangement on the side.

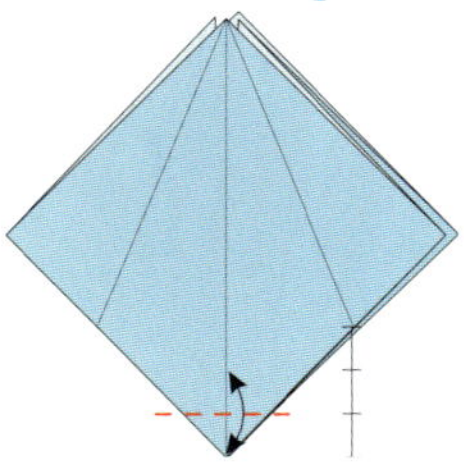

3. Nur mit der oberen Papierlage, rechte schräge Linie wieder zur Mitte legen, liegen lassen.

Using only the top layer of paper, lay the right oblique line to the middle and leave.

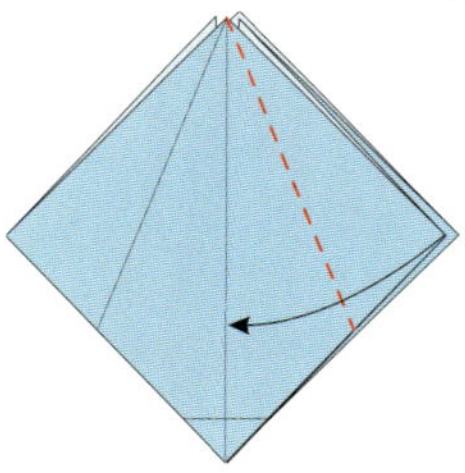

4. Nur mit der oberen Papierlage, an der rechten Seite schräge Linie falten, Falzbein benutzen. Die Arbeitsschritte Nr.3 und Nr.4 wieder öffnen.

Using only the top layer of paper, fold on the right side the oblique line, using a bonefolder. Working steps No.3 and No.4 open up again.

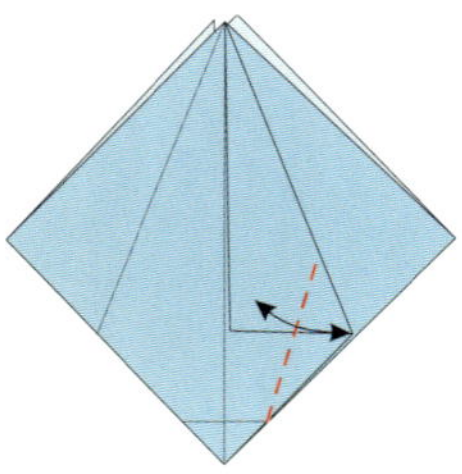

5. Nur mit der oberen Papierlage, rechte schräge Linie, siehe Pfeil, zur Linie falten, wieder öffnen.

Using only the top layer of paper, right oblique line, see arrow, fold to the line and open up again.

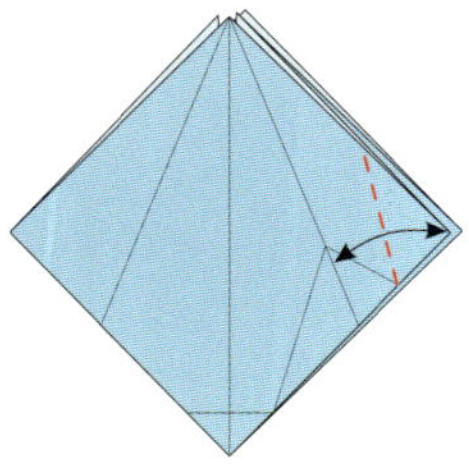

6. Nur mit der oberen Papierlage, siehe Pfeil, von links nach rechts falten. Auf der Rückseite wiederholen.

Using only the top layer of paper, see arrow, fold from the left to the right. Repeat on the back.

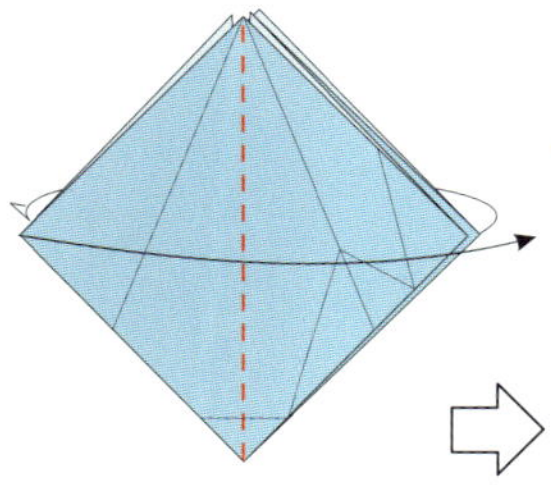

7. Mit den anderen drei Ecken, die Arbeitsschritte von Nr.3 bis Nr.6 wiederholen.

With the other three corners, repeat working steps from No.3 until No.6.

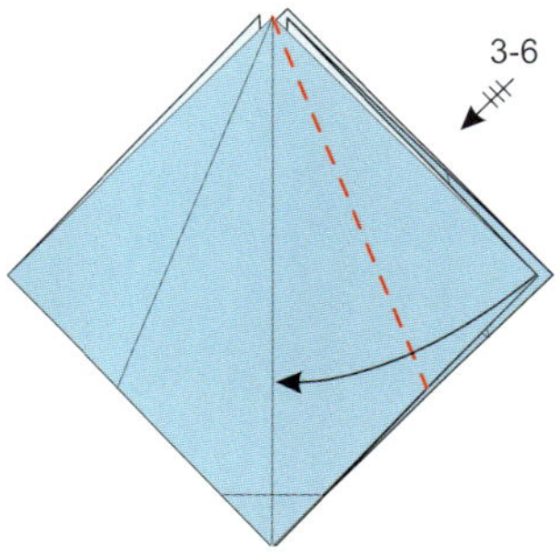

8. An den schrägen Linien Bergfalten formen und nach innen legen. Auf der Rückseite wiederholen.

Form mountain-folds along the oblique lines and lay inwards. Repeat on the back.

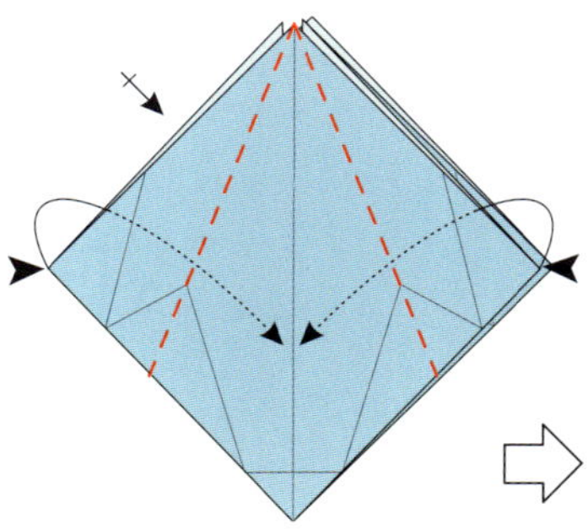

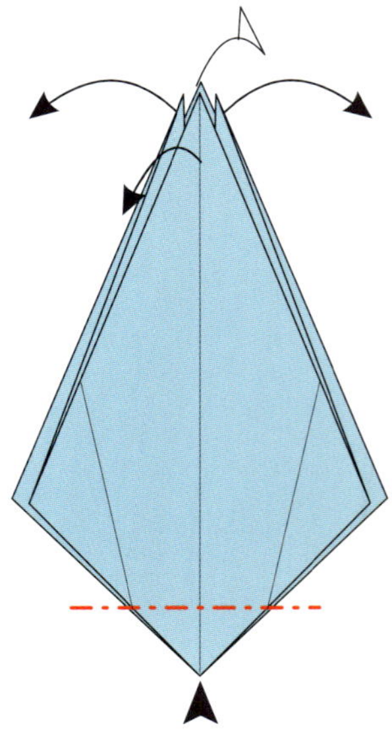

9. Modell von innen auseinanderdrücken. An der unteren Spitze Bergfalte formen und die Spitze eindrücken, das Papier liegt dann flach auf dem Tisch.

Push the model from the inside outwards. On the lower point form a mountain-fold and push in the point. Now the paper lies flatly on the table.

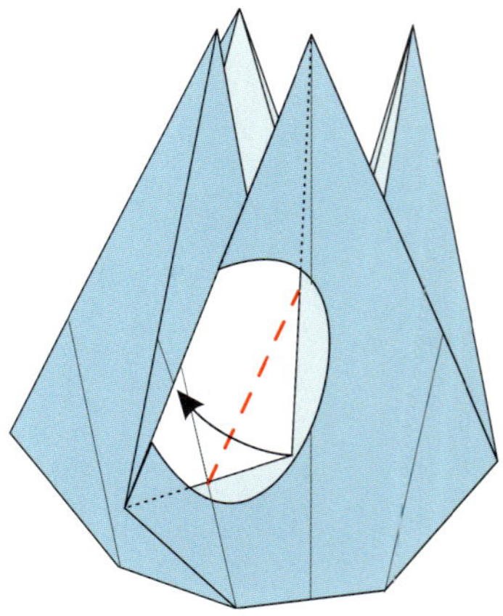

10. Achtung: Im weißen Oval sind die inneren Papierlagen zu sehen. Damit die Eiszapfen eng zusammenbleiben, Spitze nach links legen, liegen lassen. Es kann auch ein Falzbein zu Hilfe genommen werden.

Attention: On the white oval you can see the internal paper layers. In order to keep the icicle tight together, lay the point to the left and leave. You can use a bonefolder.

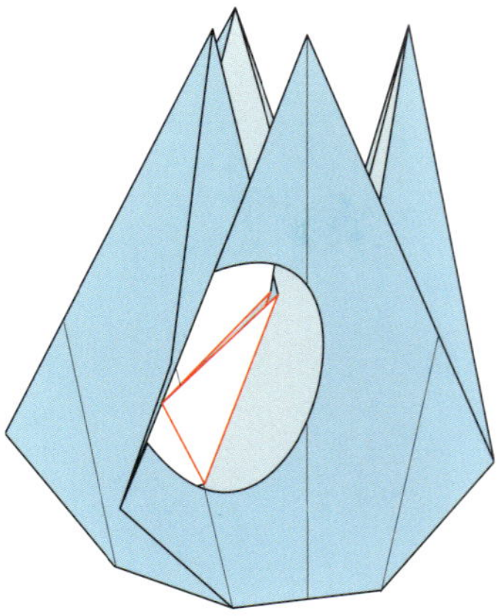

11. Sollte es nicht gut halten, kann auch geklebt werden. Keinen wasserhaltigen Kleber benutzen.
If it is not firm, you can glue it. Do not use a water based glue.

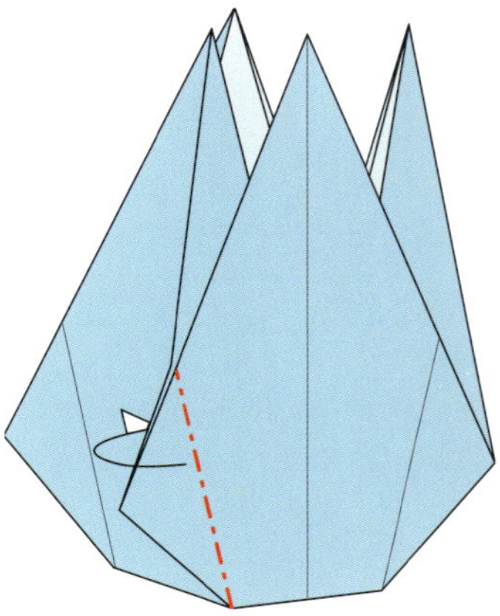

12. An der Ecke eine Bergfalte arbeiten, liegen lassen.
Form a mountain-fold on the corner and leave.

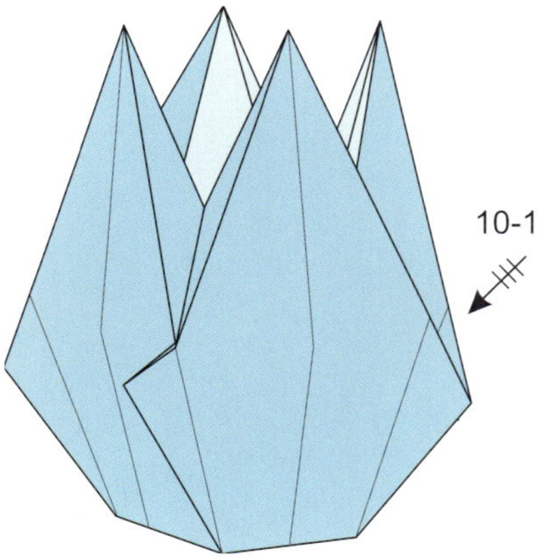

13. Die Arbeitsschritte von Nr.10 bis Nr.12 mit den drei anderen Ecken wiederholen.
Repeat working steps No.10 until No.12 with the other three corners.

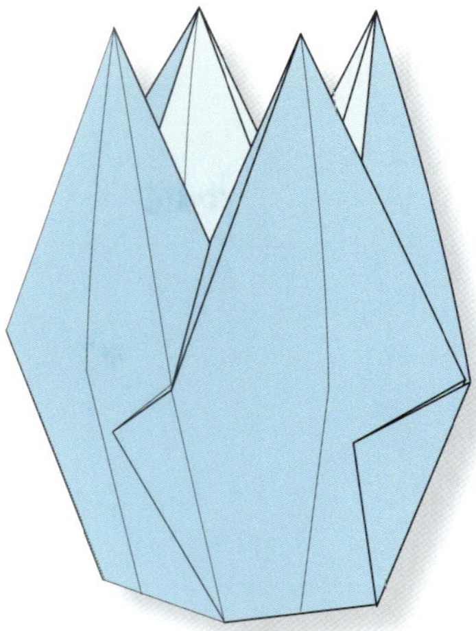

14. Fertiges Modell seitlich gesehen.
Finished model seen from the side.

Hohes Stern-Dosen Licht

MATERIAL

1 Bogen 30x30 cm flammsicheres Lampenpapier. Bei dem fertigen Modell ist von der Papierrückseite sehr viel zu sehen. Es sollte also durchgefärbtes Papier ausgewählt werden. Allerdings sieht es mit dem weißen Papier auch sehr schön aus.

One sheet 30x30 cm of not inflammable lamp paper. From the finished model, you won't see much of the back side of the paper. So you can use paper with a coloured back side. It will also look lovely with white paper.

Start. Diagramme von Seite 40 bis Nr.3 falten.
Fold charts of page 40 until No.3.

1. Nur mit der oberen Papierlage, siehe Pfeil, schräge Linien zur Mitte falten, liegen lassen. Auf der Rückseite wiederholen.
Using only the top layer of paper, see arrow, fold oblique lines to the middle and leave. Repeat on the back side.

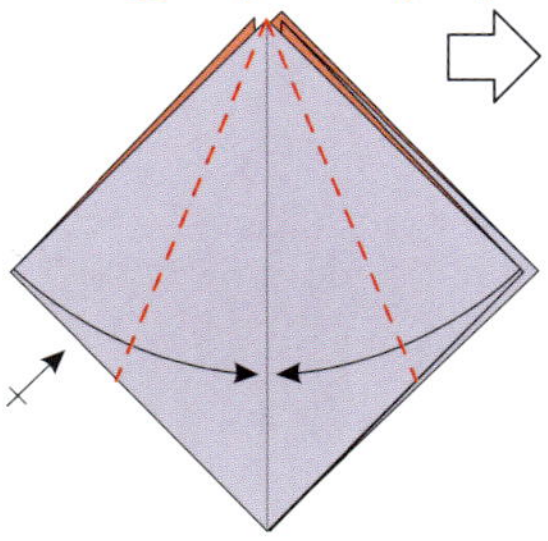

2. Nur mit der oberen Papierlage, schräge Linien als Bergfalte arbeiten und dann nach außen legen. Auf der Rückseite wiederholen.
Using only the top layer of paper, form oblique lines as a mountain-fold and lay outwards. Repeat on the back side.

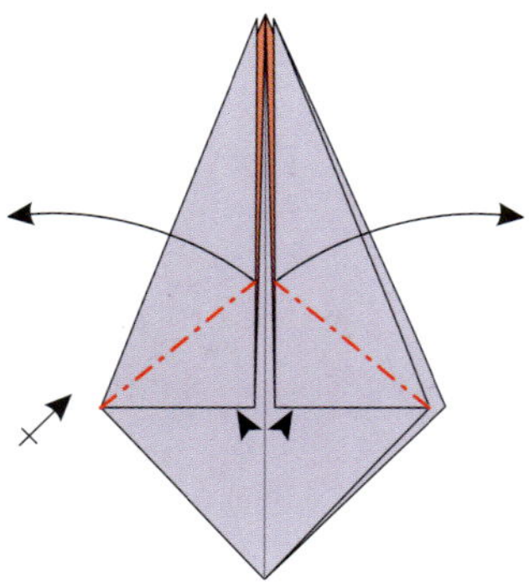

3. Nur mit der oberen Papierlage, siehe Pfeil, von links nach rechts falten. Auf der Rückseite wiederholen.
Using only the top layer of paper, see arrow, fold from the left to the right. Repeat on the back.

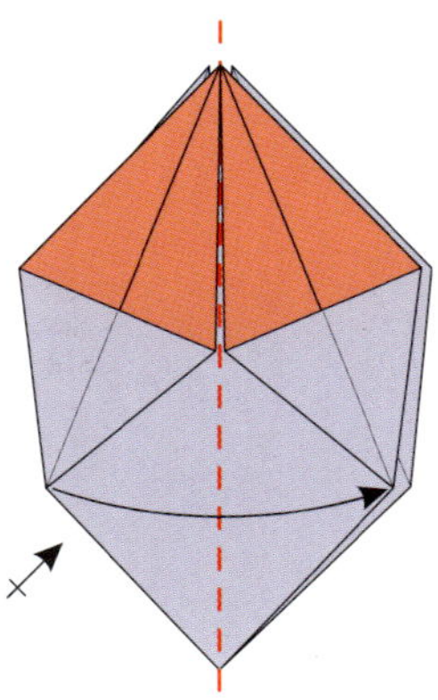

4. Nur mit der oberen Papierlage, siehe Pfeil, schräge Linien zur Mitte falten, liegen lassen. Auf der Rückseite wiederholen.
Using only the top layer of paper, see arrow, fold oblique lines to the middle and leave. Repeat on the back side.

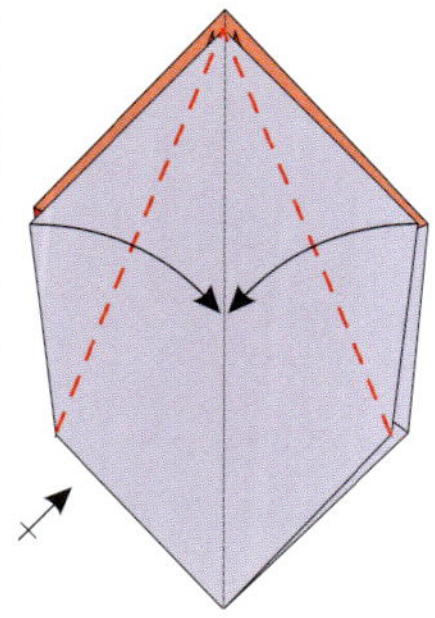

5. An der unteren Spitze die waagerechte Linie falten, wieder öffnen. Achtung: Auf die seitliche Höheneinteilung achten.
On the lower point fold the horizontal line and open up again. Attention: Note the heights arrangement on the side.

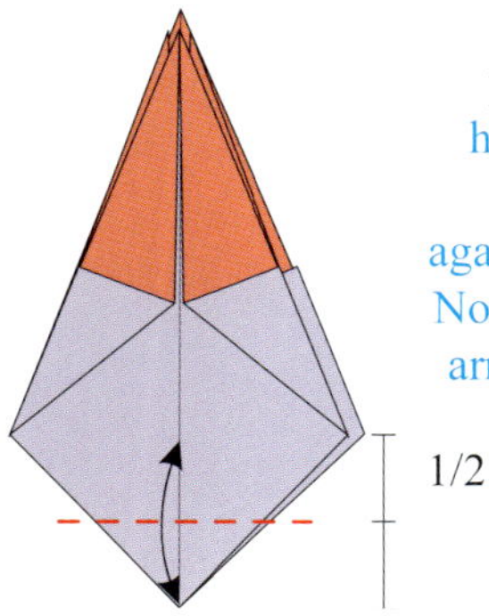

6. Modell von innen auseinanderdrücken, dabei an allen vier Spitzen waagerechte Linie falten. An der unteren Spitze Bergfalte formen und die Spitze eindrücken, das Modell steht dann flach auf dem Tisch.
Push the model from the inside outwards, at the same time fold a horizontal line on all four points. On the lower point form a mountain-fold and push in the point. Now the model stands flatly on the table.

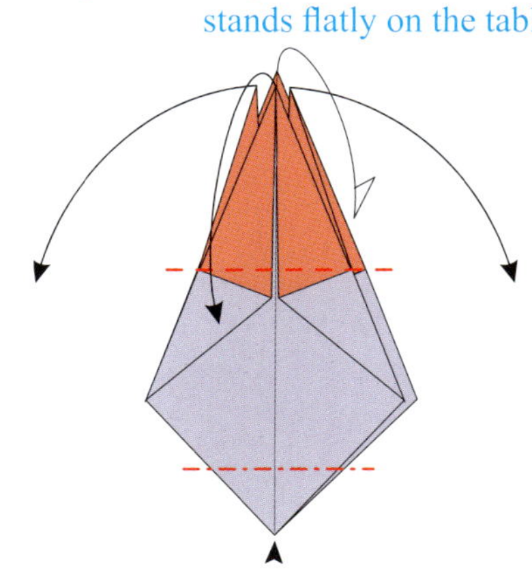

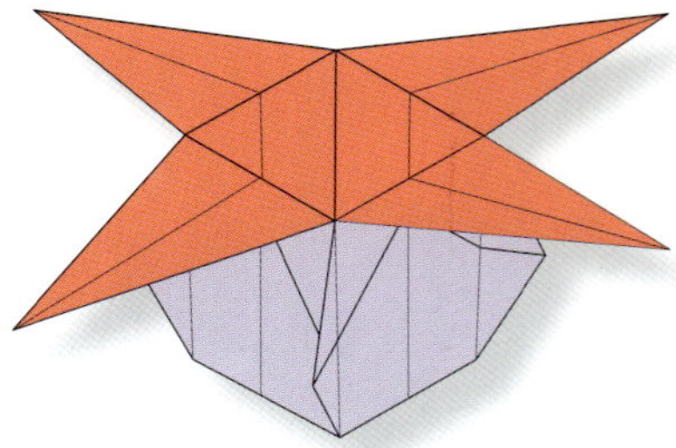

7. Fertiges Modell seitlich gesehen.
Finished model seen from the side.

8. Fertiges Modell von oben gesehen.
Finished model seen from above.

9. Die waagerechten Spitzen nach unten falten. Es entsteht dadurch ein anderer Lichteffekt.
Fold the horizontal points downwards. Now there is another light-effect.

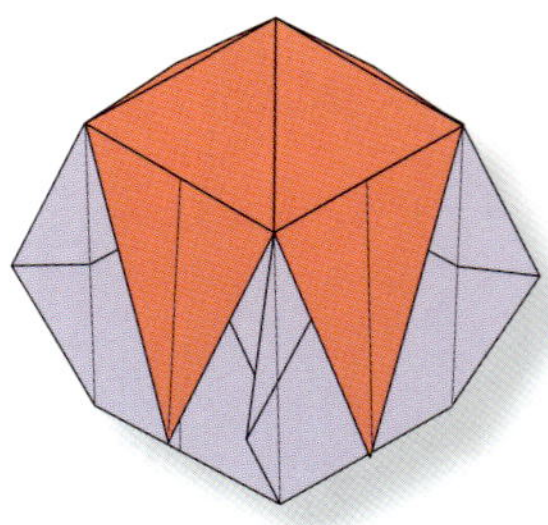

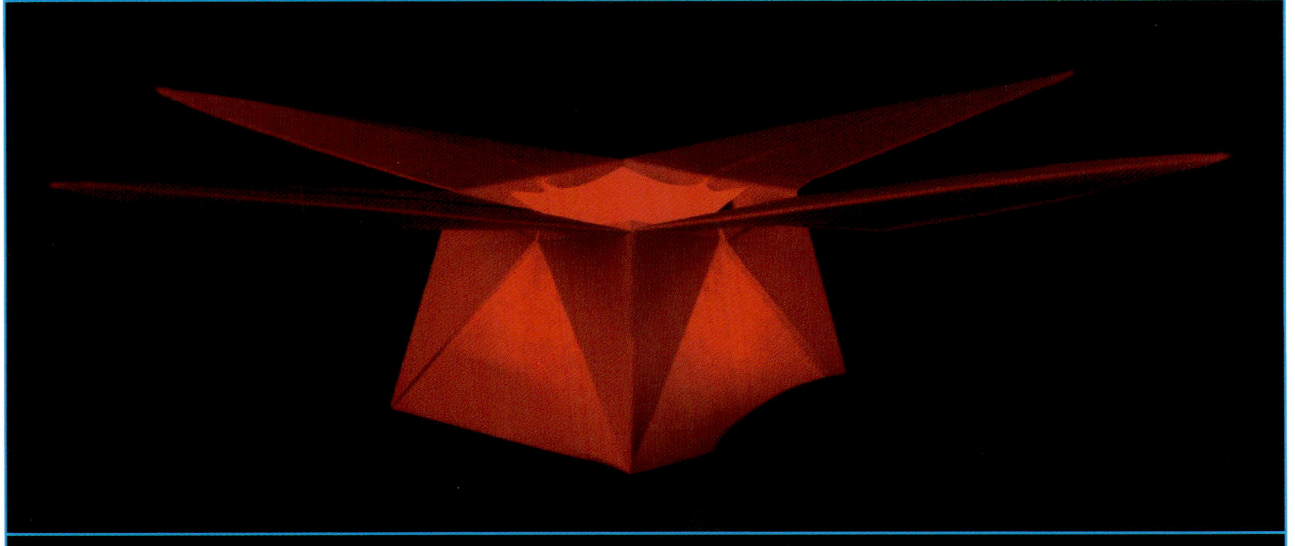

Kleines Stern-Dosen Licht

Modell von Jannie van Schuylenburg

MATERIAL

1 Bogen 30x30 cm flammsicheres Lampenpapier. Bei dem fertigen Modell ist von der Papierrückseite wenig zu sehen. Es kann also jedes Design ausgewählt werden.

One sheet 30x30 cm of not inflammable lamp paper. From the finished model, you won't see much of the back side of the paper. So you can choose any design.

Start. Diagramme von Seite 40 bis Nr.3 falten.

Fold charts of page 40 until step No.3.

1. Nur mit der oberen Papierlage, siehe Pfeil, schräge Linien zur Mitte falten, wieder öffnen. Auf der Rückseite wiederholen.

Using only the top layer of paper, see arrow, fold oblique lines to the middle and open up again. Repeat on the back.

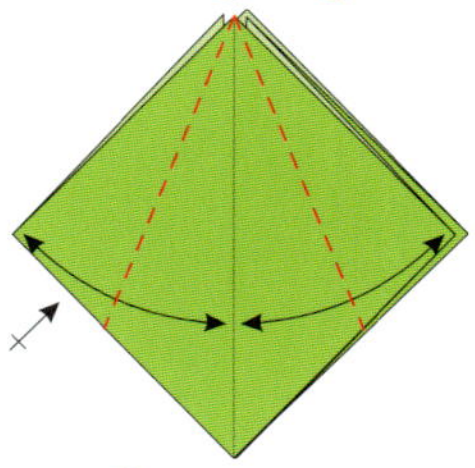

2. Nur mit der oberen Papierlage, schräge Linien als Bergfalte formen und dann nach innen legen. Auf der Rückseite wiederholen.

Using only the top layer of paper, form oblique lines as a mountain-fold and lay inwards. Repeat on the back.

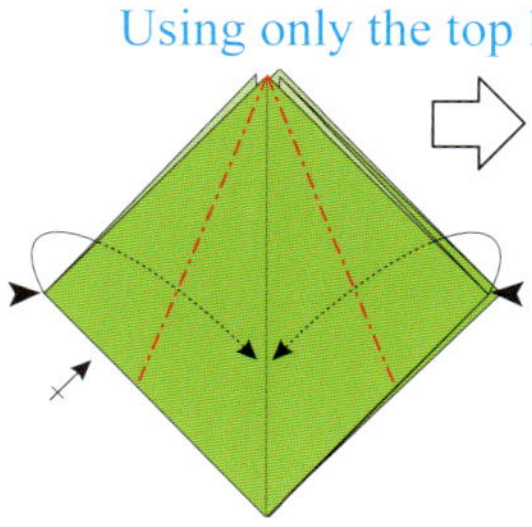

3. Nur mit der oberen Papierlage, siehe Pfeil, schräge Linien zur Mitte falten, wieder öffnen. Auf der Rückseite wiederholen.

Using only the top layer of paper, see arrow, fold oblique lines to the middle and open up again. Repeat on the back.

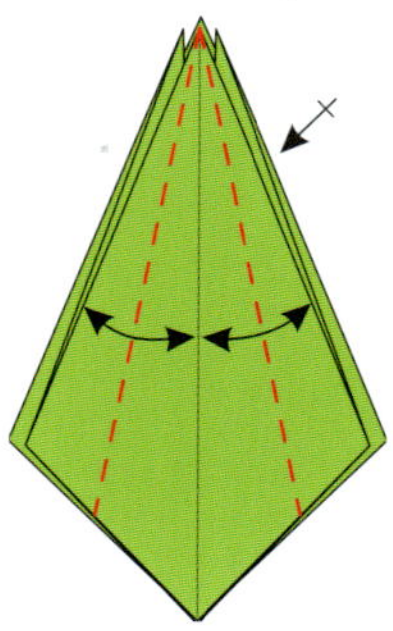

4. Nur mit der oberen Papierlage, siehe Pfeile, schräge Linien falten, wieder öffnen. Auf der Rückseite wiederholen.

Using only the top layer of paper, see arrows, fold oblique lines and open up again. Repeat on the back.

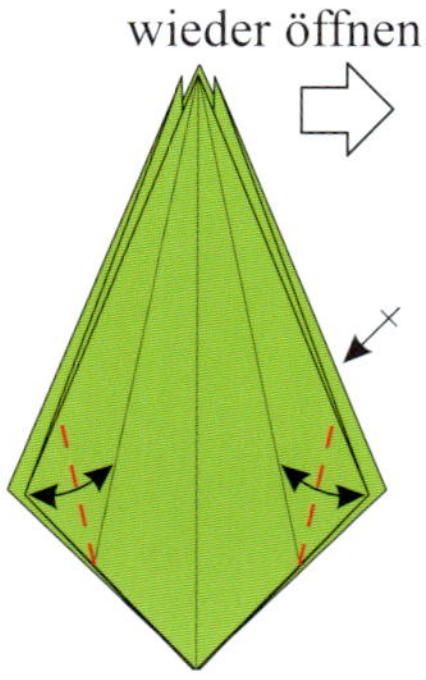

5. Schräge Linien von Arbeitsschritt Nr.4 als Bergfalte formen. Linien von Nr.3 wieder zur Mitte legen, dabei an den seitlichen Ecken flachdrücken. Auf der Rückseite wiederholen.

Form oblique lines from working step No.4 as a mountain-fold. Lay lines from No.3 back to the middle and push the corners on the side flat. Repeat on the back.

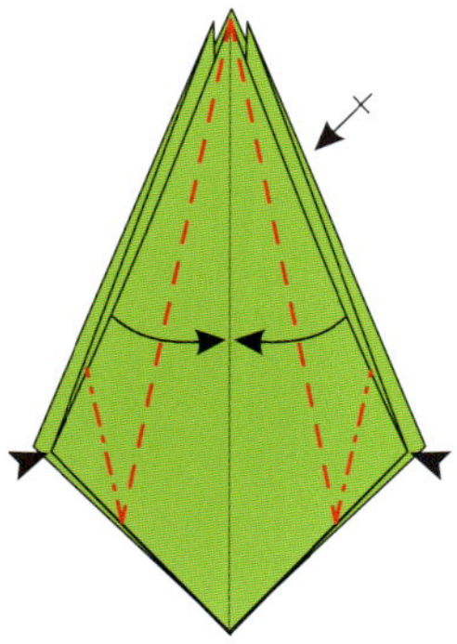

6. Nur mit der oberen Papierlage, siehe Pfeile, Bergfalte formen und nach innen legen. Auf der Rückseite wiederholen.

Using only the top layer of paper, see arrows, form a mountain-fold and lay inwards. Repeat on the back.

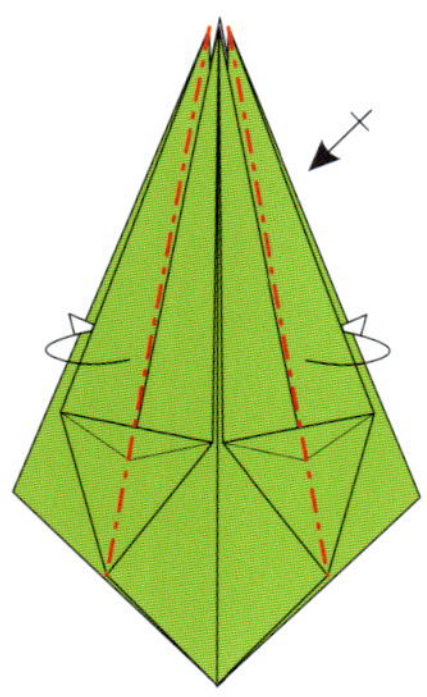

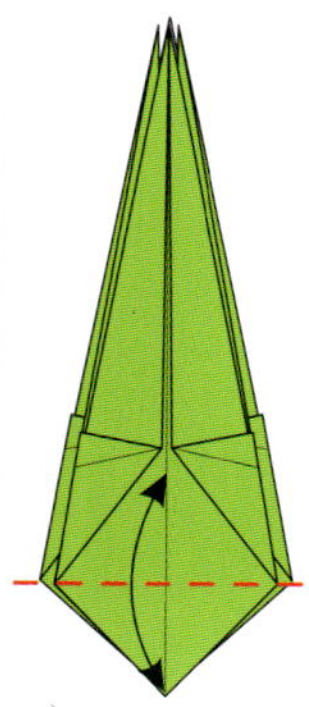

7. An der unteren Spitze die waagerechte Linie falten, wieder öffnen.

Fold the horizontal line on the lower point and open up again.

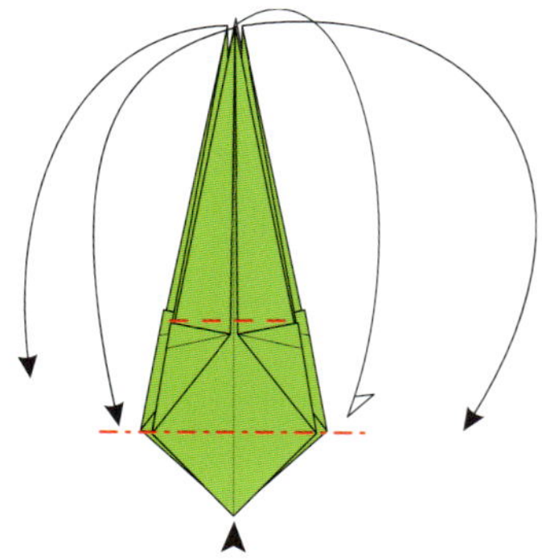

8. Modell von innen auseinanderdrücken, dabei an allen vier Spitzen waagerechte Linie falten. An der unteren Spitze Bergfalte formen und die Spitze eindrücken, das Modell steht dann flach auf dem Tisch.

Push the model from the inside outwards, at the same time fold the horizontal line on all four points. On the lower point form a mountain-fold and push in the point. Now the model stands flatly on the table.

9. An den inneren Dreiecken waagerechte Linien falten, liegen lassen.

On the inner triangles fold horizontal lines and leave.

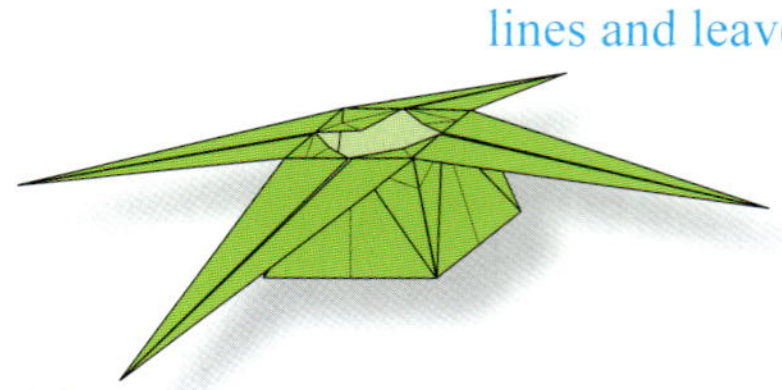

10. Fertiges Modell seitlich gesehen.

Finished model seen from the side.

11. Fertiges Modell von oben gesehen.

Finished model seen from above.

Kranich Dosen Licht

Modell von Jannie van Schuylenburg

MATERIAL

1 Bogen 30x30 cm flammsicheres Lampenpapier. Bei dem fertigen Modell ist von der Papierrückseite wenig zu sehen. Es kann also jedes Papier ausgewählt werden. Allerdings sieht es mit dem weißen Papier besonderst schön aus.

One sheet 30x30 cm of not inflammable lamp paper. From the finished model, you won't see much of the back side of the paper. So you can choose any design. It will look very lovely using white paper.

Start. Diagramme von Seite 46 bis Nr.9 falten.

Fold charts of page 46 until step No.9.

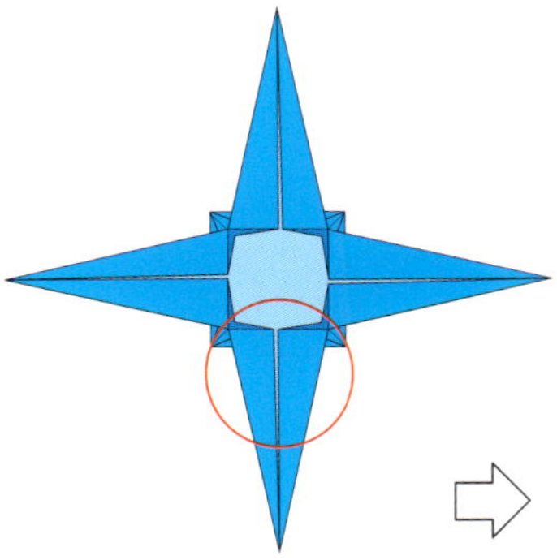

1. Die folgenden Diagramme beziehen sich nur auf den kleinen Ausschnitt, siehe Kreis.

The following charts are only related to the small part, see circle.

2. Schräge Linie falten, siehe Pfeil, wieder öffnen.

Fold oblique lines, see arrow, and open up again.

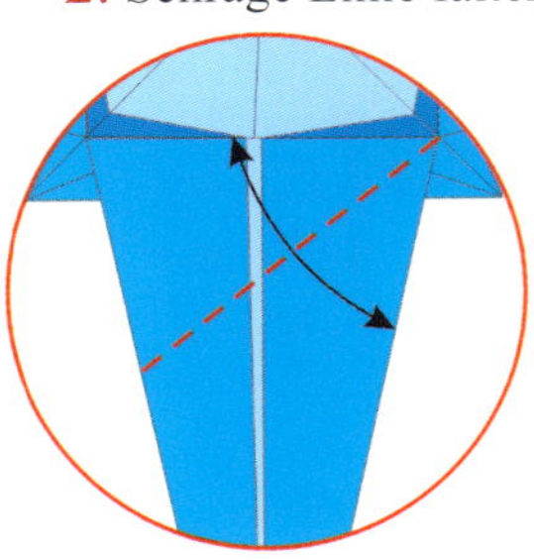

3. Schräge Linie falten, siehe Pfeil, wieder öffnen.

Fold oblique lines, see arrow, and open up again.

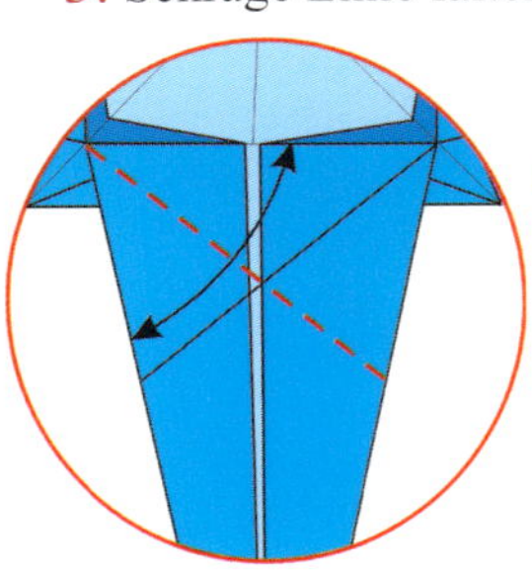

4. Waagerechte Linie falten, siehe Pfeil, wieder öffnen.

Fold horizontal lines, see arrow, and open up again.

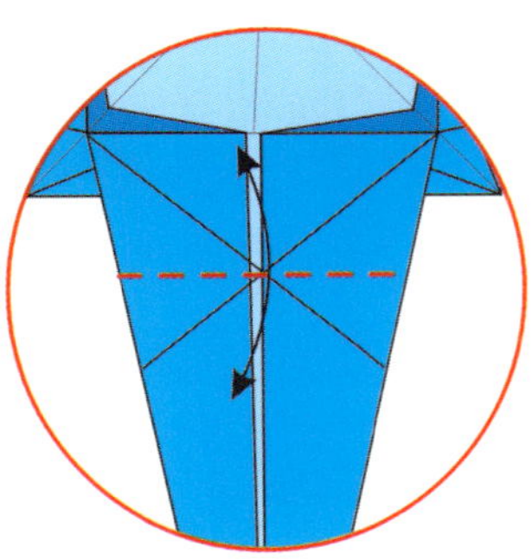

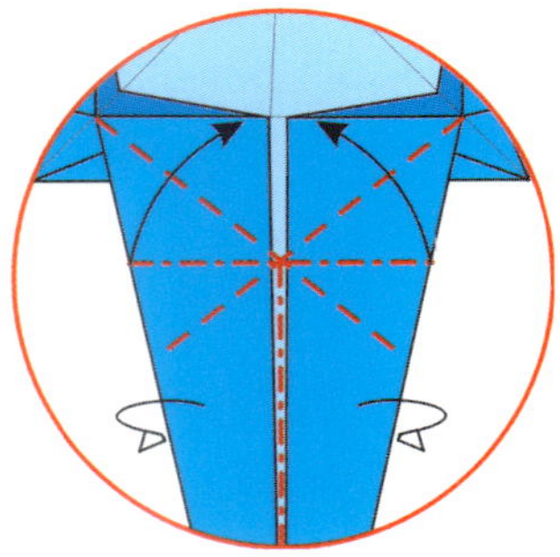

5. Waagerechte Linie zur Bergfalte formen. Senkrechte Mitte bis zur waagerechten Linie auch zur Bergfalte formen. Dann von beiden Seiten zur Mitte die waagerechte Linie eindrücken, siehe Pfeile.

Form horizontal line as a mountain-fold. Also form vertical middle as a mountain-fold until the horizontal line. Then push in the horizontal line from both sides to the middle, see arrows.

6. Für den Schnabel, siehe Pfeil, eine schräge Linie falten und dann die Spitze nach innen versenken.

For the beak, see arrow, fold a oblique line and push the point inwards.

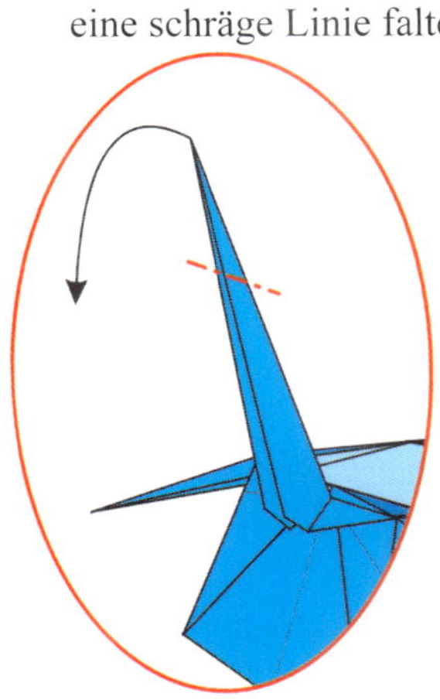

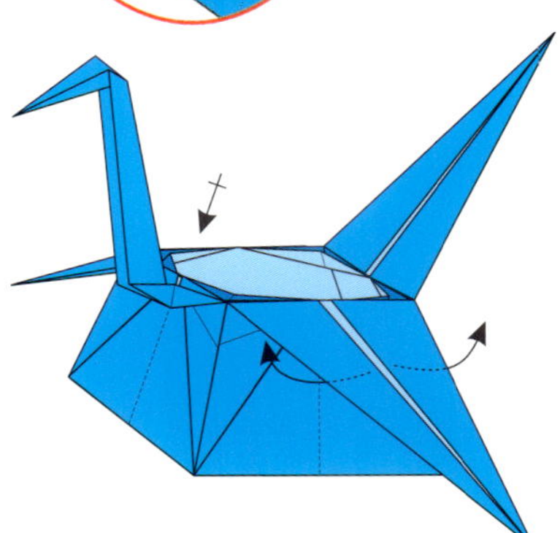

7. An den seitlichen Flügeln das Papier von der Unterseite schräg nach außen falten.

Fold paper from the bottom of the wings slanting to the outside.

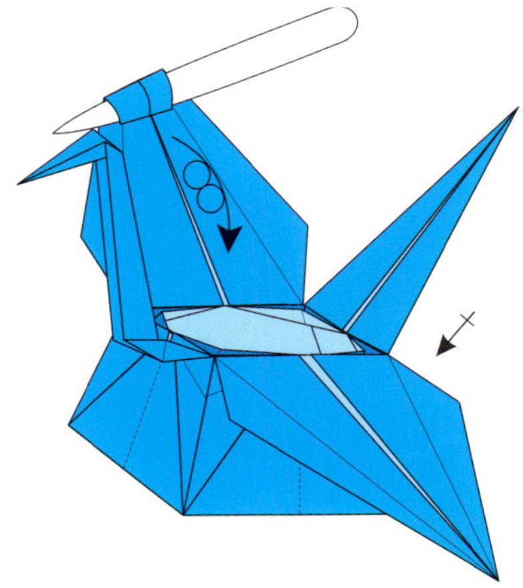

8. Die seitlichen Spitzen über ein Falzbein rollen, dadurch wird das Papier rund und die Flügelform entsteht.

Roll the points from the side over a bonefolder, so that the paper becomes round and the wing form arises.

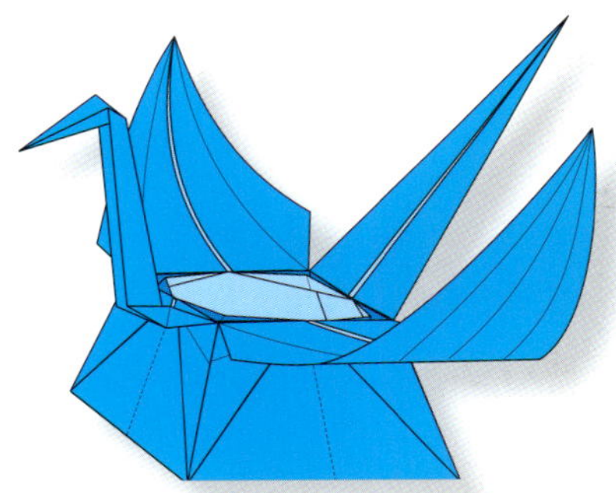

9. Fertiges Modell seitlich gesehen.

Finished model seen from the side.

10. Fertiges Modell von oben gesehen.

Finished model seen from above.

Flacher Lichtstern

MATERIAL

1 Blatt 15x15 cm flammsicheres Lampenpapier. Bei dem fertigen Modell ist von der Papierrückseite nichts zu sehen. Es kann also durchgefärbtes Papier oder Papier mit einer weißen Rückseite gewählt werden.

One sheet 15x15 cm of not inflammable lamp paper. From the finished model, you won't see much of the back side of the paper. So you can use paper with a coloured or white back side.

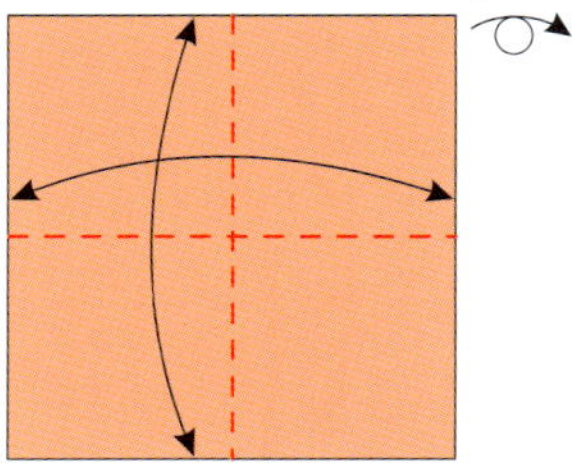

1. Zweimal waagerecht die Mitte falten, wieder öffnen. Rückseite nach oben legen.
Fold twice the middle horizontally and open up again. Turn over to the back.

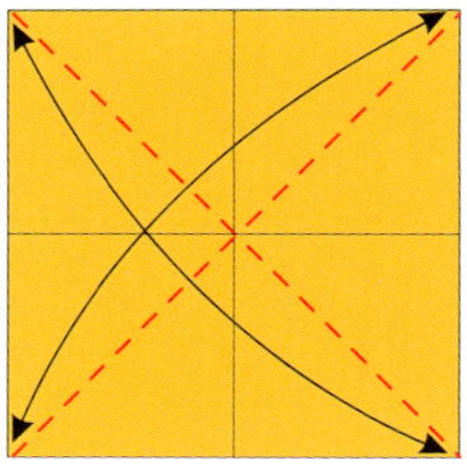

2. Zweimal diagonal die Mitte falten, wieder öffnen.
Fold twice the middle diagonally and open up again.

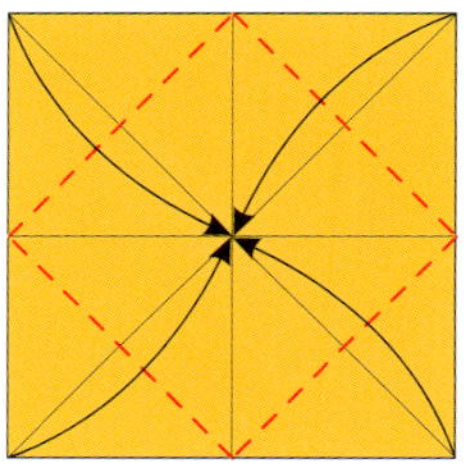

3. Alle vier Ecken zur Mitte falten, liegen lassen.
Fold all four corners towards the middle and leave.

4. Modell drehen und die Rückseite nach oben legen.
Turn the model around. Turn over to the back.

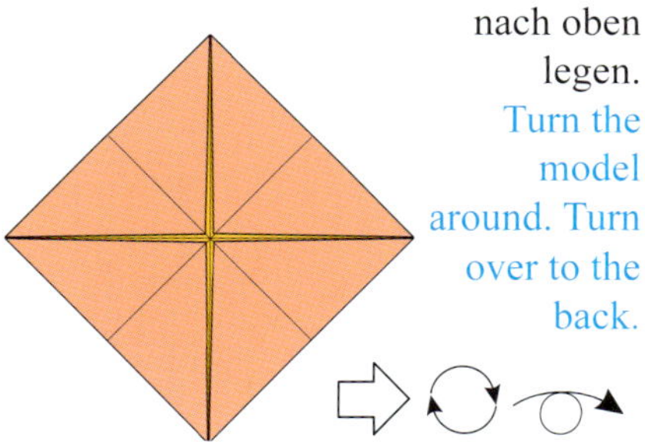

5. Von der waagerechten Mitte (Bergfalte), seitlich zur unteren Mitte legen. Die obere Mitte dann ebenfalls nach unten legen, siehe Pfeile.
From the horizontal middle (mountain-fold), put sidewards to the lower middle. Now put the upper middle also below, see arrows.

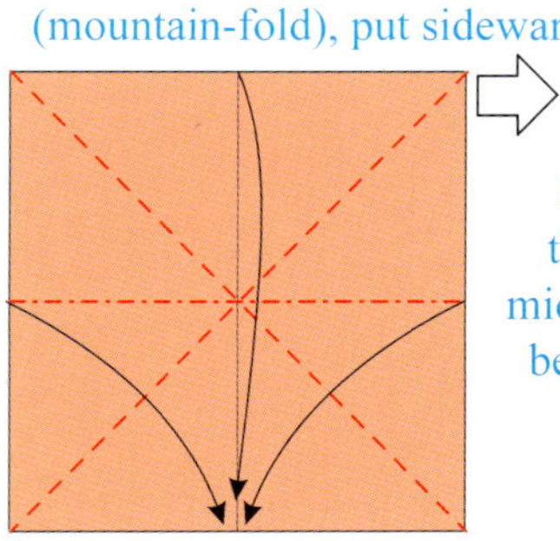

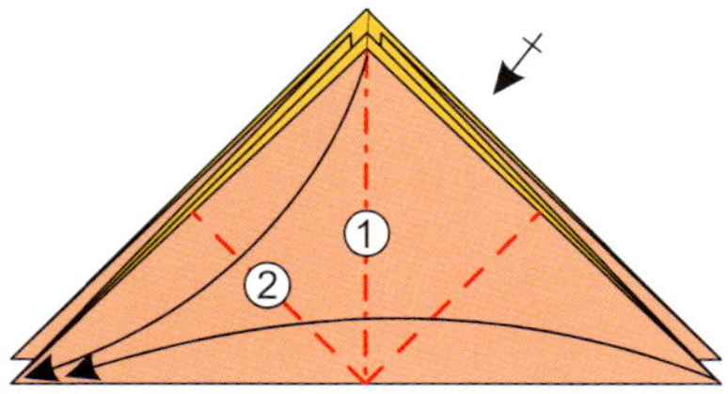

6. Nur mit der oberen Papierlage, Linie Nr.1 als Bergfalte an die untere Papierkante falten, liegen lassen. Die Talfalte Nr.2 wird dabei automatisch mitgefaltet. Die rechte Ecke nach links legen, dabei die schräge Linie falten, liegen lassen. Auf der Rückseite wiederholen.
Using only the top layer of paper, fold line No.1 as a mountain-fold to the lower paper edge and leave. The valley-fold No.2 will be folded at the same time automatically. Put the right corner to the left and fold the oblique line. Keep folded. Repeat on the back side.

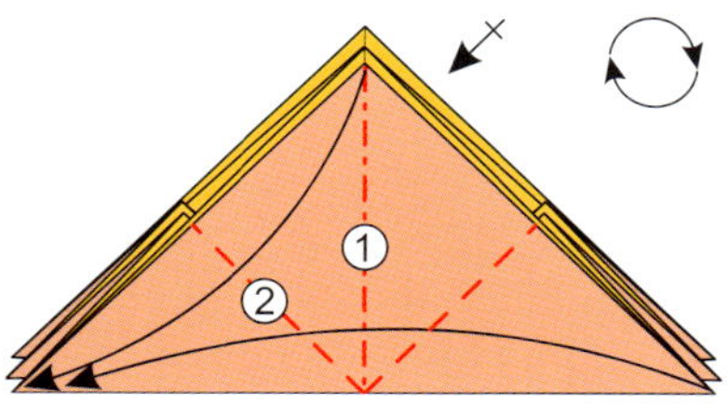

7. Die Arbeitsschritte von Nr.6 alle wiederholen. Modell um 180 Grad drehen.
Repeat all working steps from No.6. Turn model 180 degrees around.

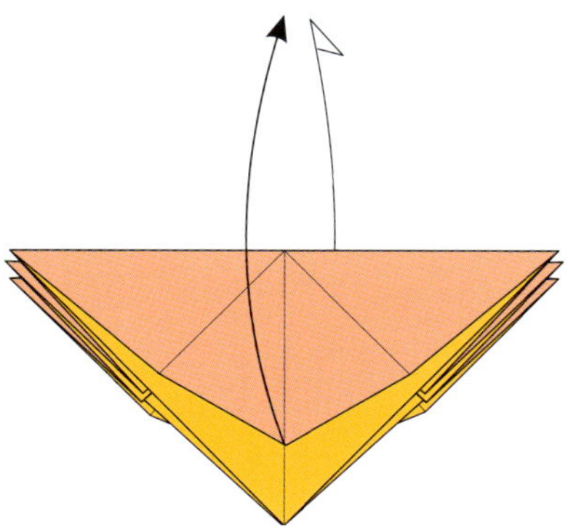

8. Beide Spitzen nach oben legen, liegen lassen.
Put both points to the top and leave.

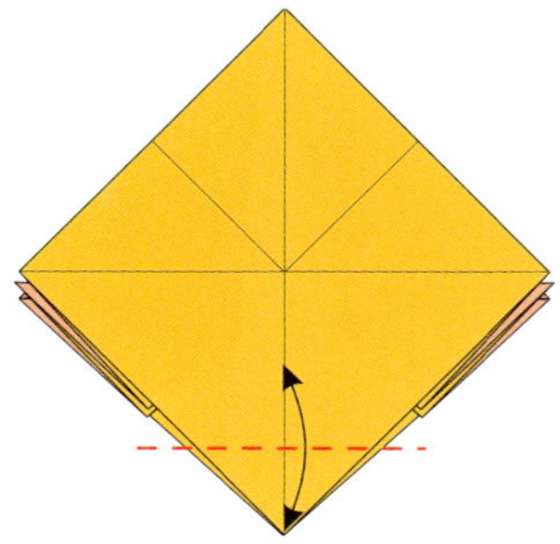

9. An der unteren Spitze waagerechte Linie falten, wieder öffnen.
Fold horizontal line on the lower point and open up again.

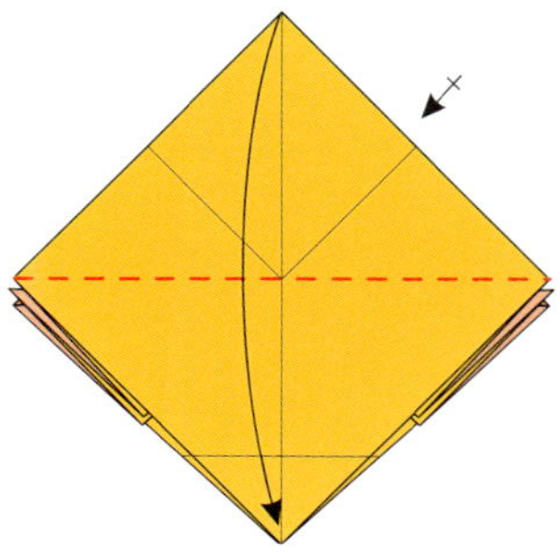

10. Spitze wieder nach unten falten, liegen lassen. Auf der Rückseite wiederholen.
Fold point downwards and leave. Repeat on the back side.

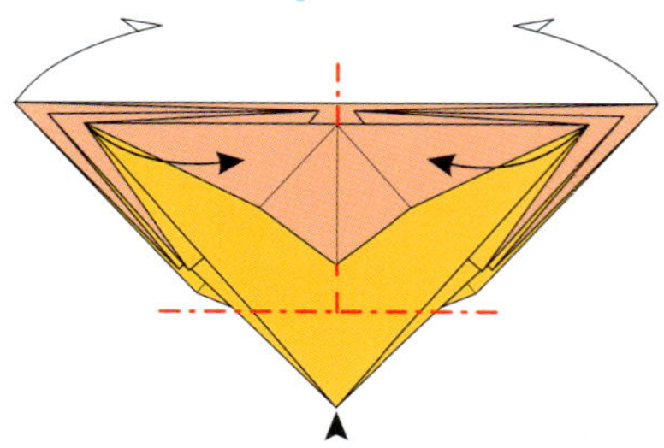

11. An der waagerechten Linie Bergfalte formen, danach auf der Vorder- und Rückseite die senkrechte Linie auch zur Bergfalte formen. Von innen auseinanderdrücken, dadurch wird aus dem flachen Papier die aufgestellte Form. Alle acht Spitzen können noch etwas geformt werden.
Form a mountain-fold along the horizontal line. Then form a mountain-fold along the vertical line on the front and back side. Push the model from the inside outwards, thus it becomes the set up form out of the flat paper. All eight points can be formed a little bit.

12. Fertiges Modell von oben gesehen.
Finished model seen from above.

13. Fertiges Modell seitlich gesehen.
Finished model seen from the side.

Hoher Lichtstern

MATERIAL

1 Blatt 30x30 cm flammsicheres Lampenpapier. Bei dem fertigen Modell ist von der Papierrückseite nichts zu sehen. Es kann also durchgefärbtes Papier oder Papier mit einer weißen Rückseite gewählt werden.

One sheet 30x30 cm of not inflammable lamp paper. From the finished model, you won't see much of the back side of the paper. So you can use paper with a coloured or white back side.

Start. Diagramme von Seite 48 bis Nr.10 falten.
Fold charts of page 48 until No.10.

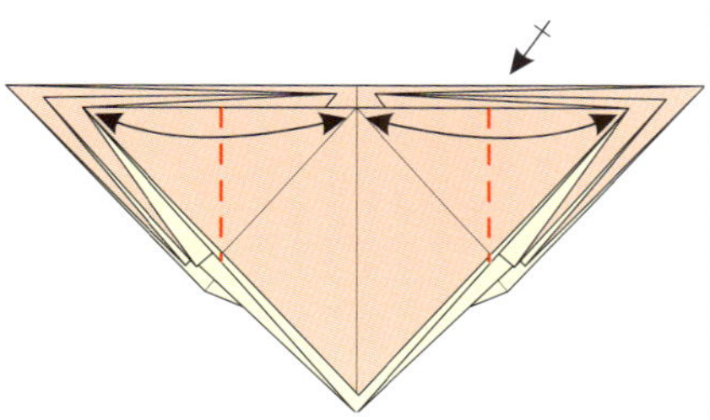

1. Senkrechte Linien falten, wieder öffnen. Auf der Rückseite wiederholen.
Fold the vertical line and open up again. Repeat on the back side.

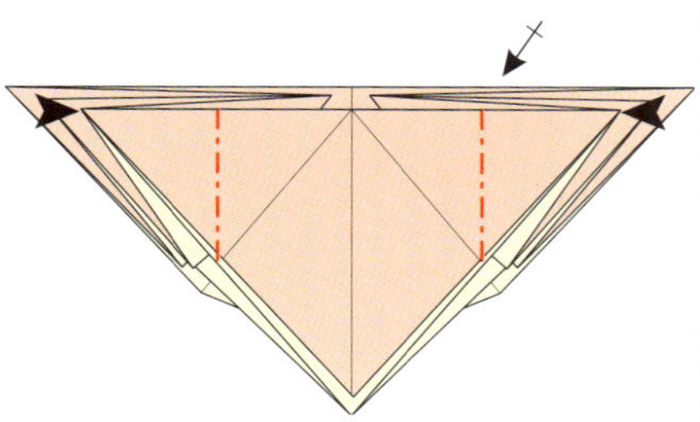

2. Linien als Bergfalten formen, dann nach innen legen, dabei von der Ecke her eindrücken. Auf der Rückseite wiederholen.
Form lines as mountain-folds, then lay inwards, at the same time push in from the corner. Repeat on the back side.

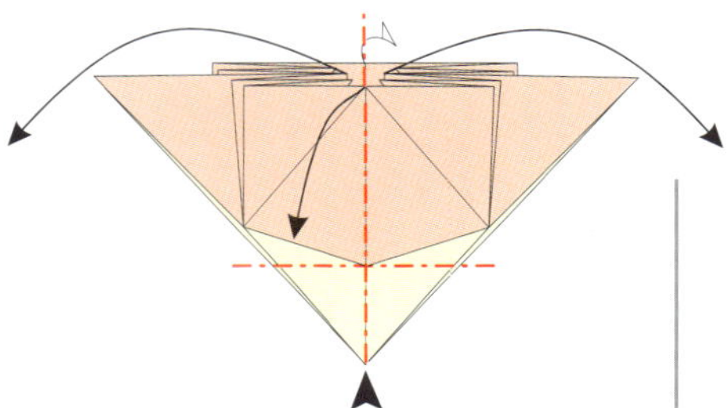

3. An der waagerechten Linie Bergfalte formen, danach auf der Vorder- und Rückseite die senkrechte Linie auch zur Bergfalte formen. Von innen auseinanderdrücken, dadurch wird aus dem flachen Papier die aufgestellte Form. Alle acht Spitzen können noch etwas geformt werden.
Form a mountain-fold along the horizontal line. Then form a mountain-fold along the vertical line on the front and back side. Push the model from the inside outwards, thus it becomes the set up form out of the flat paper. All eight points can be formed a little bit.

4. Fertiges Modell von oben gesehen.
Finished model seen from above.

5. Fertiges Modell seitlich gesehen.
Finished model seen from the side.

Paper Frog Lampenpapier
Farbe: Weiß

Paper Frog Lampenpapier
Dekor: Vierfarben

Der Klassiker-Standard

MATERIAL

1 Bogen 30x30 cm flammsicheres Lampenpapier. Bei dem fertigen Modell ist von der Papierrückseite wenig zu sehen. Es sollte also durchgefärbtes Papier oder Papier mit einer weißen Rückseite gewählt werden.

One sheet 30x30 cm of not inflammable lamp paper. From the finished model, you won't see much of the back side of the paper. So you can choose any design.

1. Zweimal waagerecht die Mitte falten, wieder öffnen. Rückseite nach oben legen.

Fold twice the horizontal middle and open up again. Turn over to the back.

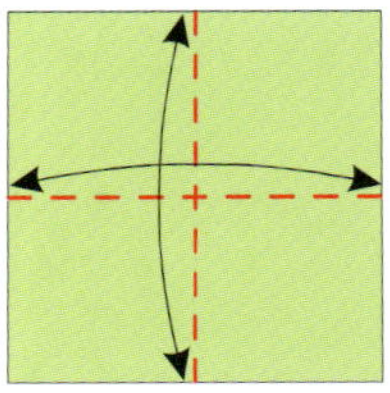

2. Zweimal diagonal die Mitte falten, wieder öffnen. Rückseite nach oben legen.

Fold twice the middle diagonally and open up again. Turn over to the back.

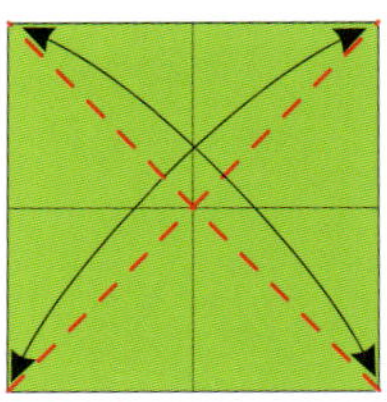

3. Von der waagerechten Mitte (Bergfalte), die seitlichen Ecken zur oberen Ecke legen. Die untere Ecke dann ebenfalls nach oben legen, siehe Pfeile.

From the horizontal middle (mountain-fold), lay the corners from the side to the upper corner. Also lay the lower corner to the upper corner, see arrows.

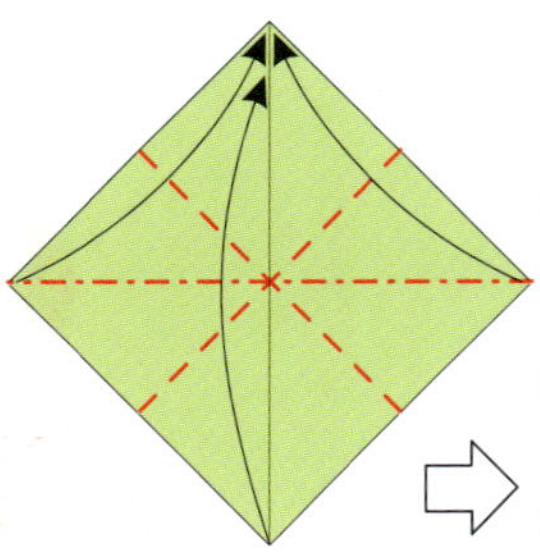

4. Bergfalte nach rechts falten, dabei die Ecke flach drücken.

Fold mountain-fold to the right and push the corner flat.

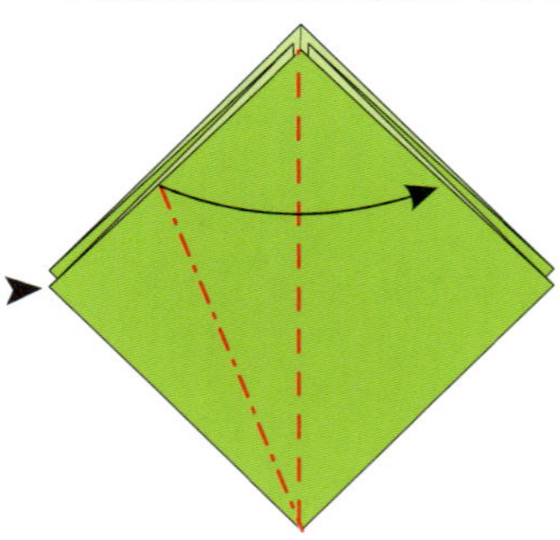

5. Mit den anderen drei Ecken den Arbeitsschritt Nr.4 wiederholen.

Repeat working step No.4 with the other three corners.

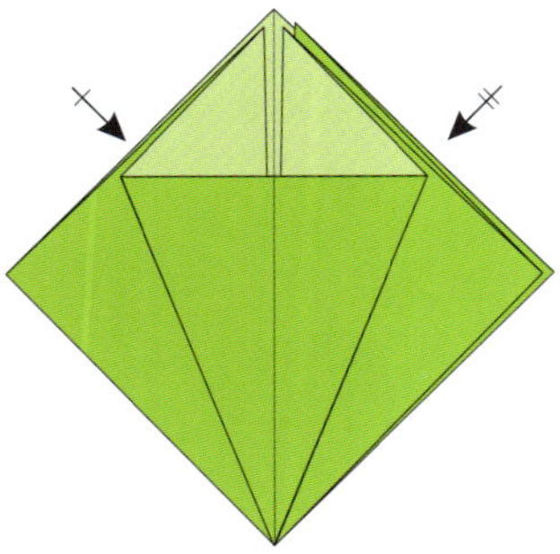

6. Spitzen an der Linie abschneiden.

Cut off points along the line.

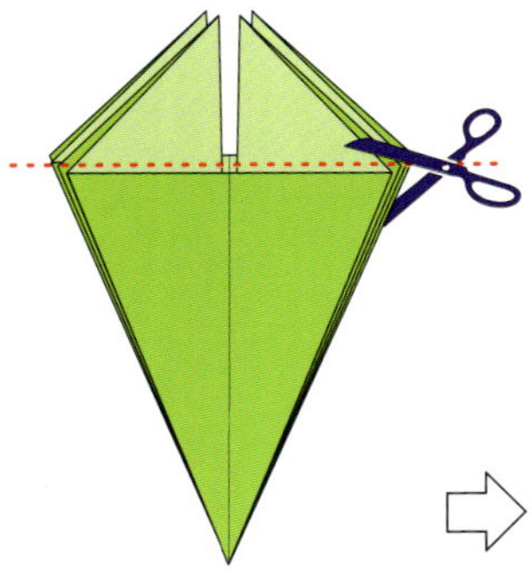

7. Nur mit der oberen Papierlage, siehe Pfeil, schräge Linien zur Mitte falten. Auf der Rückseite wiederholen.

Using only the top layer of paper, see arrow, fold oblique lines to the middle. Repeat on the back.

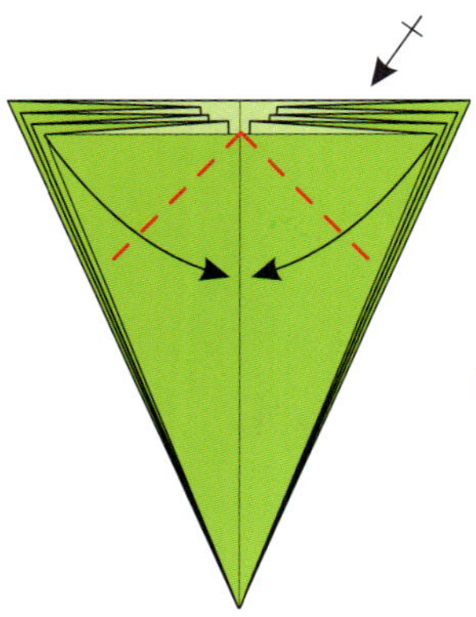

8. Nur mit der oberen Papierlage, siehe Pfeil, von rechts nach links falten. Auf der Rückseite wiederholen.

Using only the top layer of paper, see arrow, fold from right to the left. Repeat on the back.

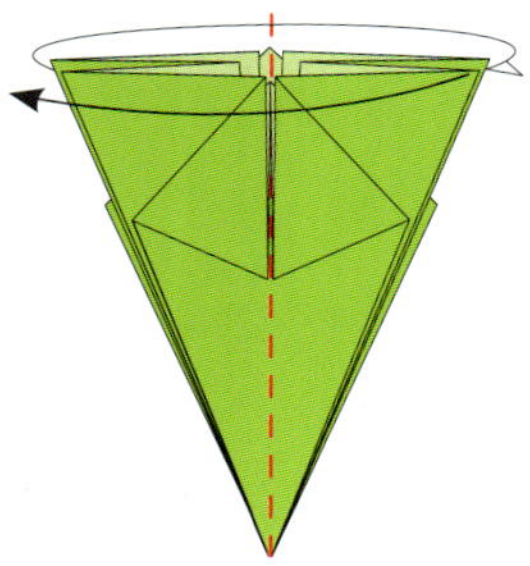

9. Schräge Linien zur Mitte falten, liegen lassen. Auf der Rückseite wiederholen.

Fold oblique lines to the middle and leave. Repeat on the back.

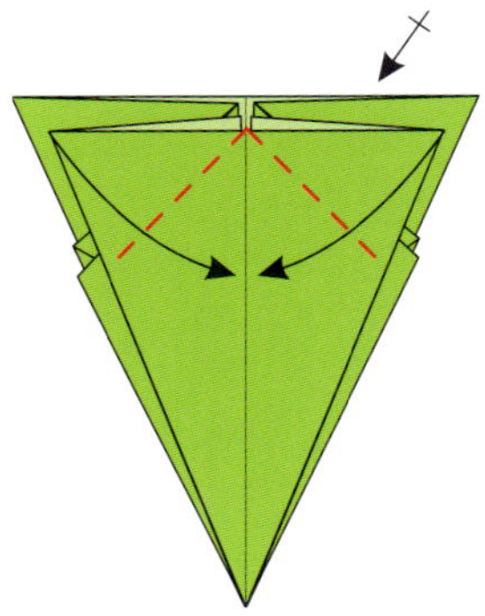

10. Arbeitsschritte von Nr.7 und Nr.9 wieder öffnen, siehe Pfeile.

Repeat working steps No.7 and No.9 and open up again, see arrows.

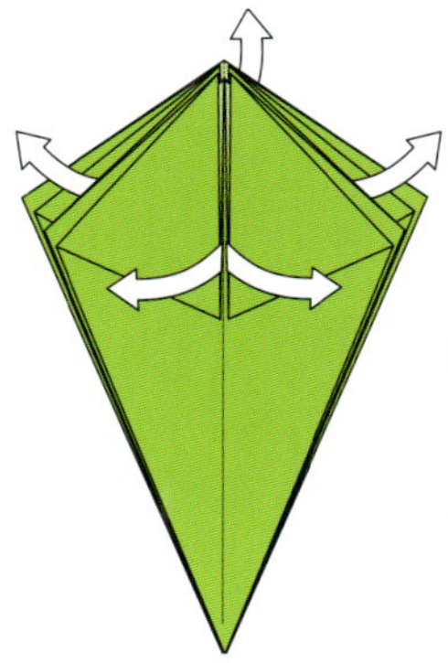

11. Alle schrägen Linien von Nr.7 und Nr.9 zur Bergfalte formen und dann nach innen legen.

Fold all oblique lines from No.7 and No.9 as a mountain-fold und lay inwards.

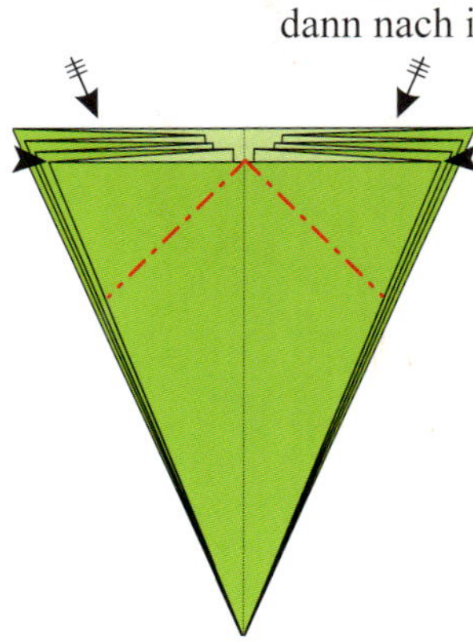

12. Nur mit der oberen Papierlage Spitze nach unten falten, liegen lassen.

Using only the top layer of paper fold point downwards and leave.

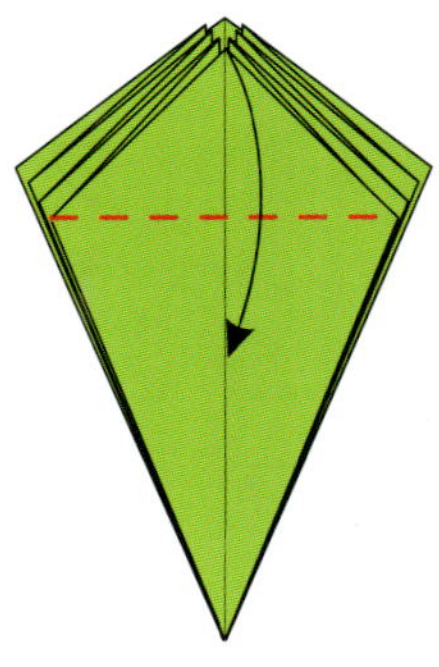

13. Nur mit der oberen Papierlage von links nach rechts falten, liegen lassen. Arbeitsschritte Nr.12 und Nr.13 mit allen Spitzen wiederholen.

Using only the top layer of paper fold from left to the right and leave. Repeat working steps No.12 and No.13 with all points.

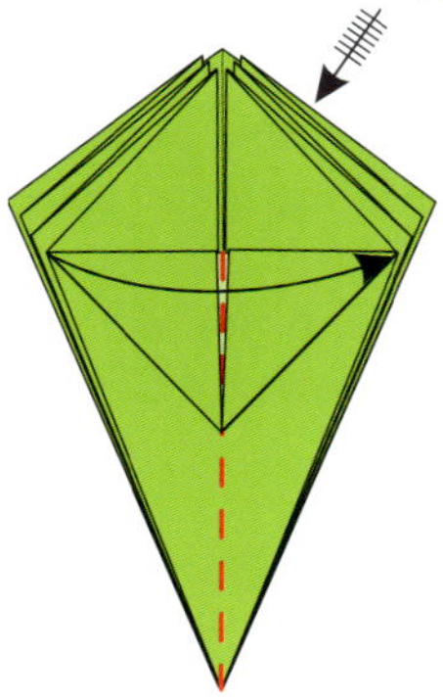

14. An der unteren Spitze waagerechte Linie falten, wieder öffnen.

Fold horizontal line on the lower point and open up again.

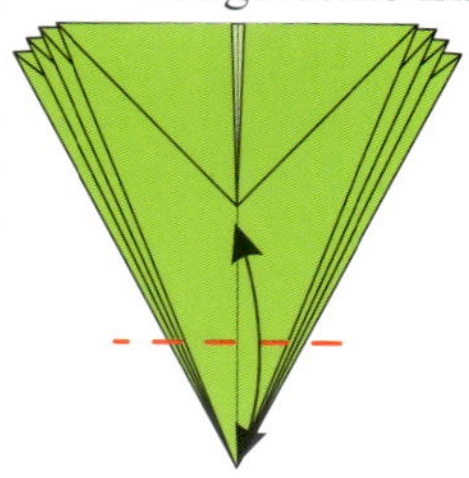

15. Jetzt eine Bergfalte an der unteren Spitze formen, dabei die Spitze eindrücken. Modell von innen auseinanderdrücken, das Modell steht dann flach auf dem Tisch.

Form a mountain-fold on the lower point and push in the point. Push the model from the inside outwards. Now the model stands flatly on the table.

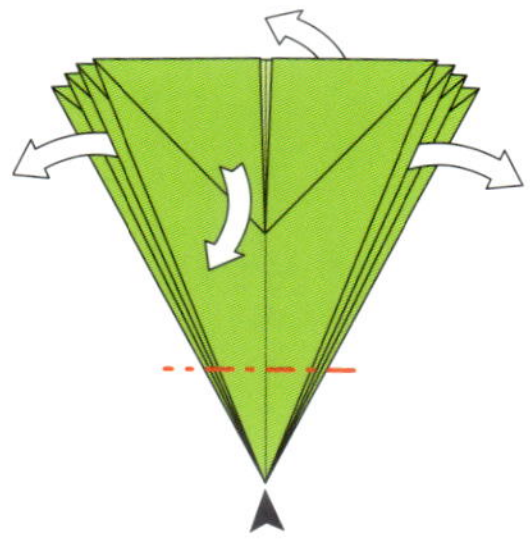

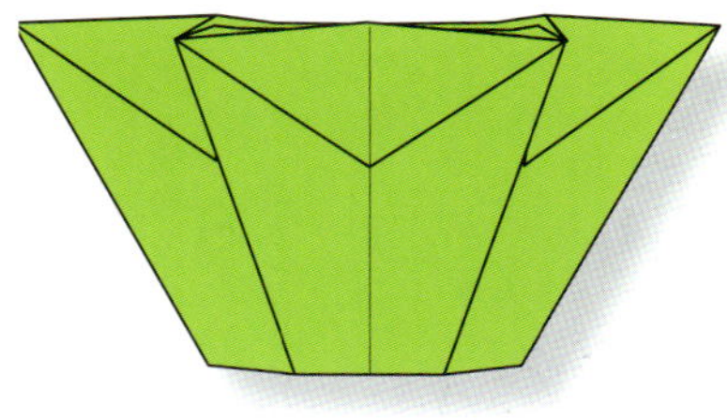

16. Fertiges Modell seitlich gesehen.

Finished model seen from the side.

17. Fertiges Modell von oben gesehen.

Finished model seen from above.

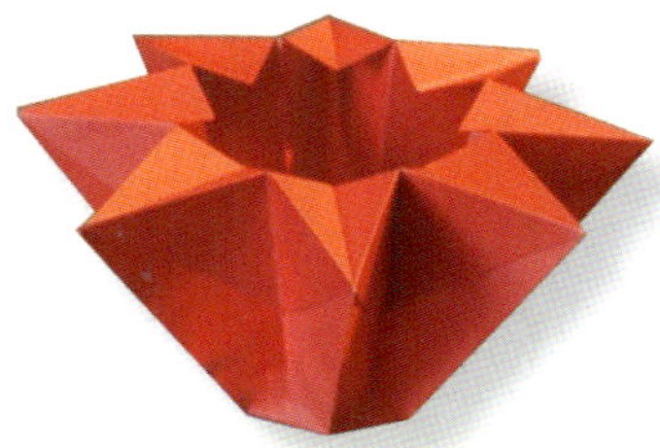

Der Klassiker Variante 1

MATERIAL

1 Bogen 30x30 cm flammsicheres Lampenpapier. Bei dem fertigen Modell ist von der Papierrückseite wenig zu sehen. Es sollte also durchgefärbtes Papier oder Papier mit einer weißen Rückseite gewählt werden.

One sheet 30x30 cm of not inflammable lamp paper. From the finished model, you won't see much of the back side of the paper. So you can choose any design.

Start. Diagramme von Seite 52 bis Nr.14 falten.

Fold charts of page 52 until step No.14.

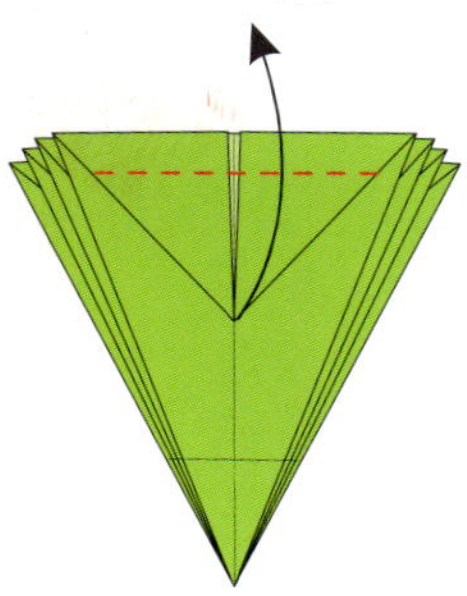

1. Waagerechte Linie falten, liegen lassen.

Fold horizontal line and leave.

4. Fertiges Modell von oben gesehen.

Finished model seen from above.

2. Nur mit der oberen Papierlage von links nach rechts falten, liegen lassen. Arbeitsschritte Nr.1 und Nr.2 mit allen Spitzen wiederholen.

Using only the top layer of paper fold from left to the right and leave. Repeat working steps No.1 and No.2 with all points.

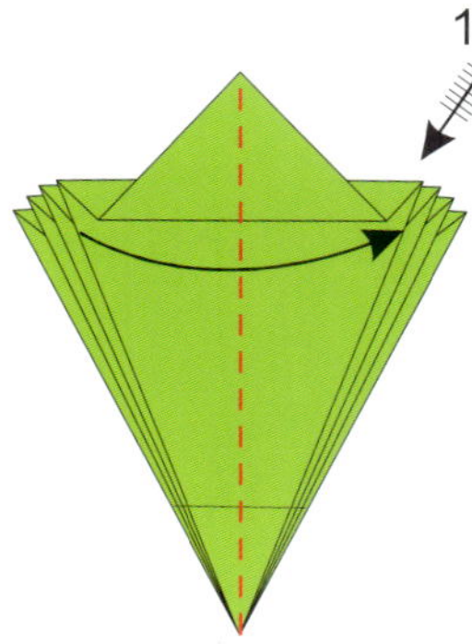

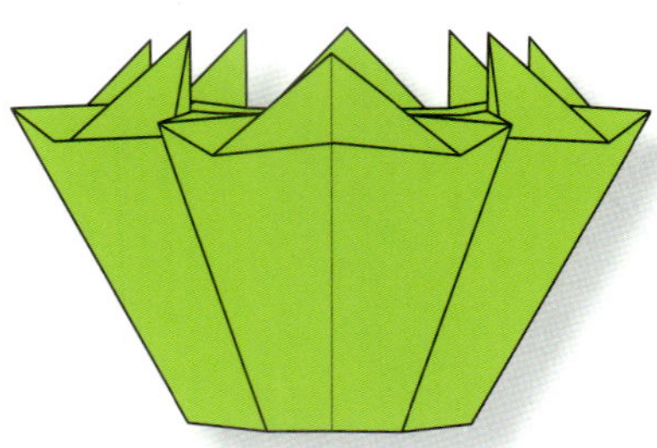

5. Fertiges Modell seitlich gesehen.

Finished model seen from the side.

3. Jetzt eine Bergfalte an der unteren Spitze formen, dabei die Spitze eindrücken. Modell von innen auseinanderdrücken, das Modell steht dann flach auf dem Tisch.

Form a mountain-fold on the lower point and push in the point. Push the model from the inside outwards. Now the model stands flatly on the table.

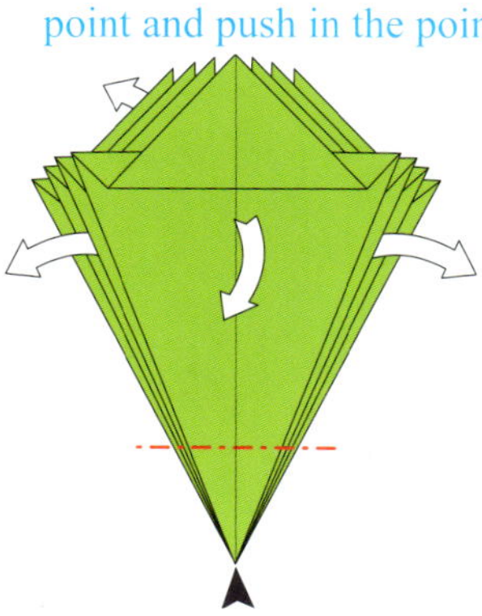

Der Klassiker Variante 2

MATERIAL

1 Bogen 30x30 cm flammsicheres Lampenpapier. Bei dem fertigen Modell ist von der Papierrückseite wenig zu sehen. Es kann also durchgefärbtes Papier oder Papier mit einer weißen Rückseite gewählt werden.

One sheet 30x30 cm of not inflammable lamp paper. From the finished model, you won't see much of the back side of the paper. So you can choose any design.

Start. Diagramme von Seite 52 bis Nr.14, dann Variante 1 bis Nr.2 falten.

Fold charts of page 52 until step No.14. Then fold variation 1 until No.2.

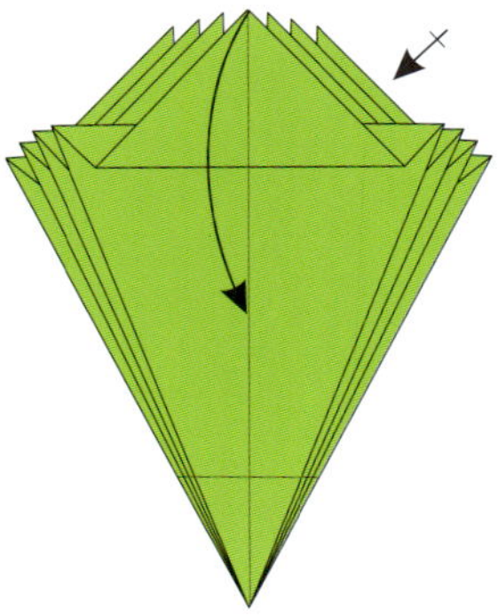

1. Spitze nach unten legen, liegen lassen. Auf der Rückseite wiederholen.

Lay point downwards and leave. Repeat on the back.

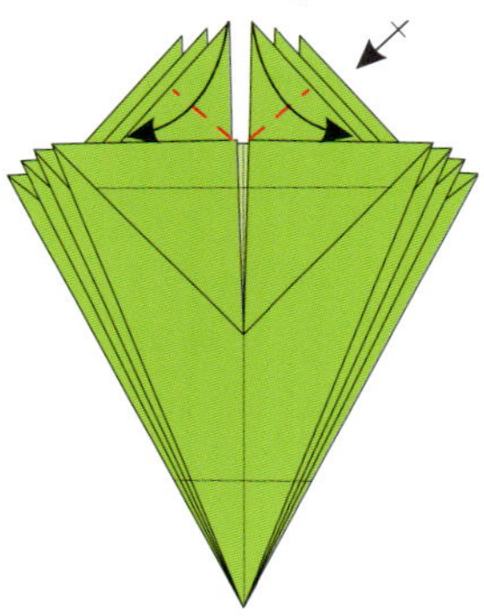

2. Schräge Linien falten, liegen lassen. Auf der Rückseite wiederholen.

Fold oblique lines and leave. Repeat on the back.

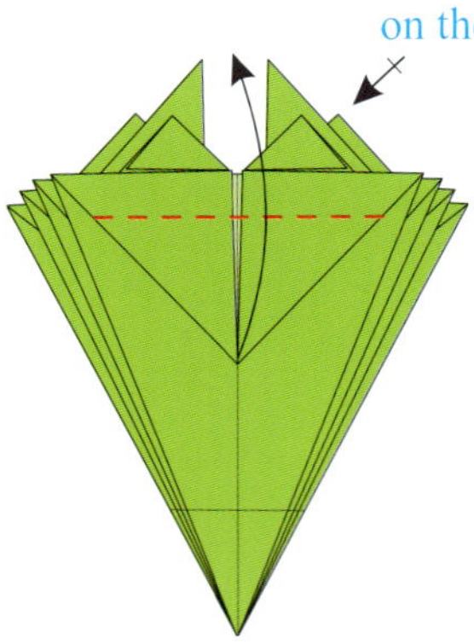

3. Spitze wieder nach oben falten, liegen lassen. Auf der Rückseite wiederholen.

Fold point upwards and leave. Repeat on the back.

4. Nur mit der oberen Papierlage von links nach rechts falten, liegen lassen. Auf der Rückseite wiederholen.

Using only the top layer of paper fold from left to the right and leave. Repeat on the back.

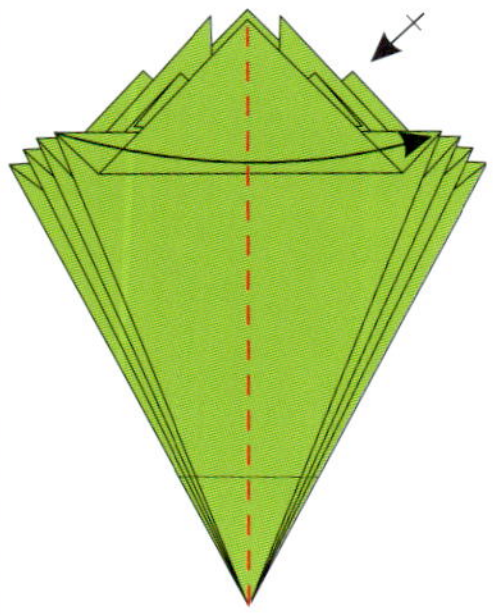

5. Waagerechte Linie nach unten falten, liegen lassen. Auf der Rückseite wiederholen.

Fold horizontal line downwards and leave. Repeat on the back.

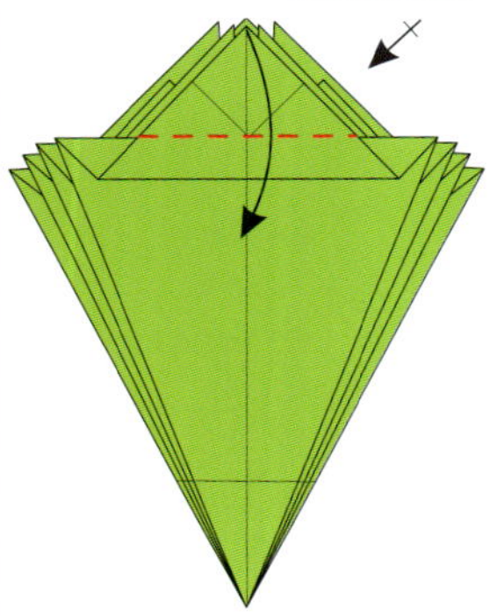

6. Schräge Linien falten, liegen lassen. Auf der Rückseite wiederholen.

Fold oblique lines and leave. Repeat on the back.

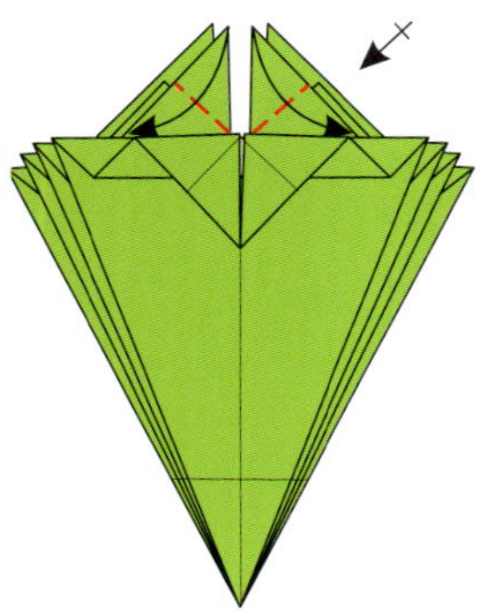

7. Arbeitsschritt Nr.5 mit den restlichen Spitzen wiederholen.

Repeat working step No.5 with the remaining points.

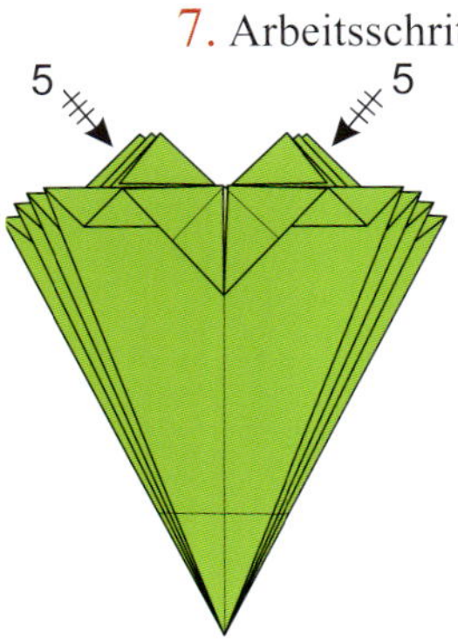

8. An der kleinen Spitze schräge Bergfalten formen und senkrecht eine Talfalte arbeiten. Mit den restlichen sieben Spitzen diesen Arbeitsgang wiederholen. Jetzt eine Bergfalte an der unteren Spitze formen, dabei die Spitze eindrücken. Modell von innen auseinanderdrücken, das Modell steht dann flach auf dem Tisch.

Form a oblique mountain-fold and a vertical valley-fold on the small point. Repeat this working step with the remaining seven points. Form a mountain-fold on the lower point and push in the point. Push the model from the inside outwards. Now the model stands flatly on the table.

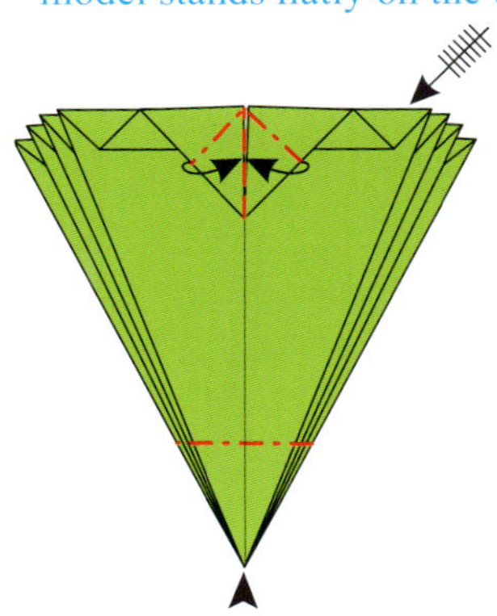

9. Fertiges Modell seitlich gesehen.

Finished model seen from the side.

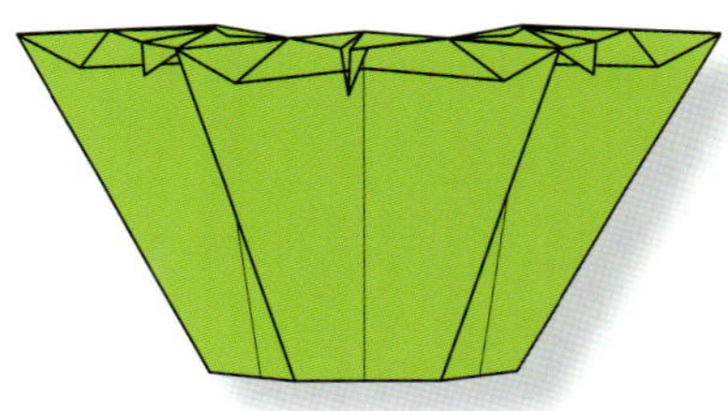

10. Fertiges Modell von oben gesehen.

Finished model seen from above.

Der Klassiker Variante 3

MATERIAL

1 Bogen 30x30 cm flammsicheres Lampenpapier. Bei dem fertigen Modell ist von der Papierrückseite wenig zu sehen. Es sollte also durchgefärbtes Papier oder Papier mit einer weißen Rückseite gewählt werden.

One sheet 30x30 cm of not inflammable lamp paper. From the finished model, you won't see much of the back side of the paper. So you can choose any design.

Start. Diagramme von Seite 52 bis Nr.14 falten.
Fold charts of page 52 until step No.14.

1. Schräge Linie an der linken Seite der Spitze bis zur Mitte falten, wieder öffnen.
Fold oblique line on the left side of the point to the middle and open up again.

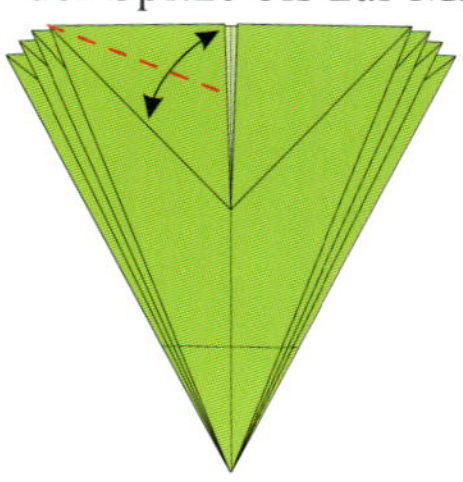

2. Schräge Linie an der rechten Seite der Spitze bis zur Mitte falten, wieder öffnen.
Fold oblique line on the right side of the point to the middle and open up again.

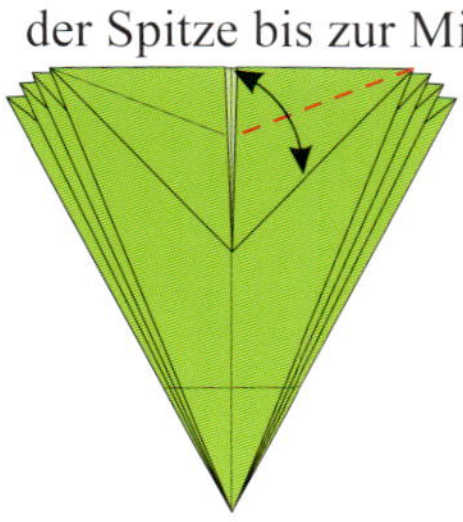

3. Die Spitze nun von rechts und links an den Linien nach oben legen. In der Mitte bildet sich eine Spitze.
Lay the point from the right and the left along the lines upwards. A point arises in the middle.

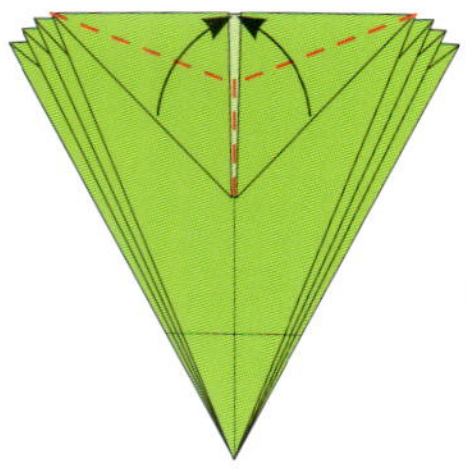

4. Senkrechte Linie an der neu entstandenen Spitze falten.
Fold vertical line along the new point.

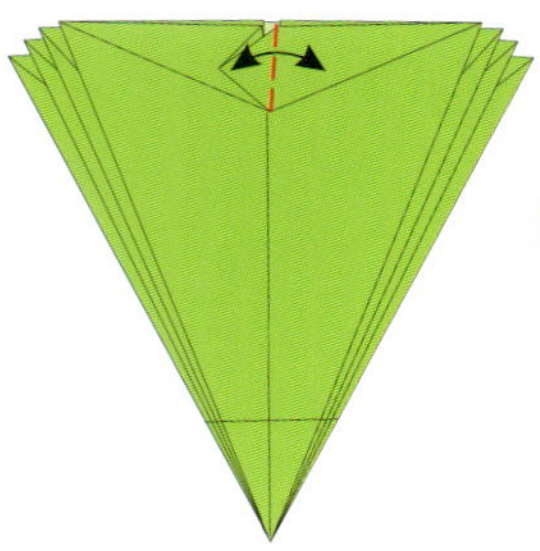

5. Nur mit der oberen Papierlage von links nach rechts falten, liegen lassen.
Using only the top layer of paper fold from left to the right and leave.

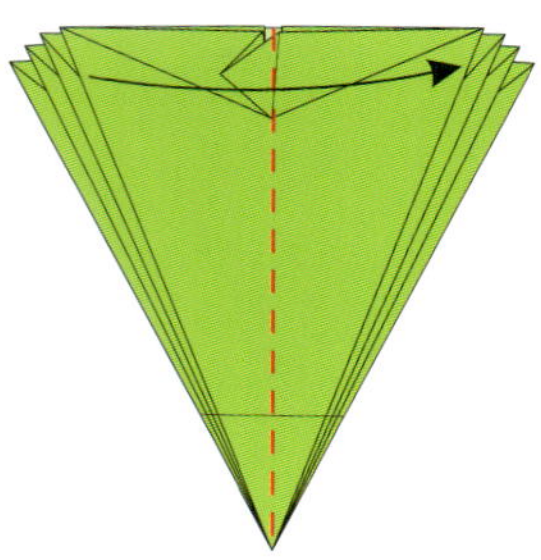

6. Arbeitsschritte von Nr.1 bis Nr.5 mit den anderen Spitzen wiederholen. Danach an der unteren Spitze eine Bergfalte formen, dabei die Spitze eindrücken. Modell von innen auseinanderdrücken, das Papier liegt dann flach auf dem Tisch.
Repeat working steps from No.1 to No.5 with the other points. Form a mountain-fold on the lower point and push in the point. Push the model from the inside outwards. Now the model stands flatly on the table.

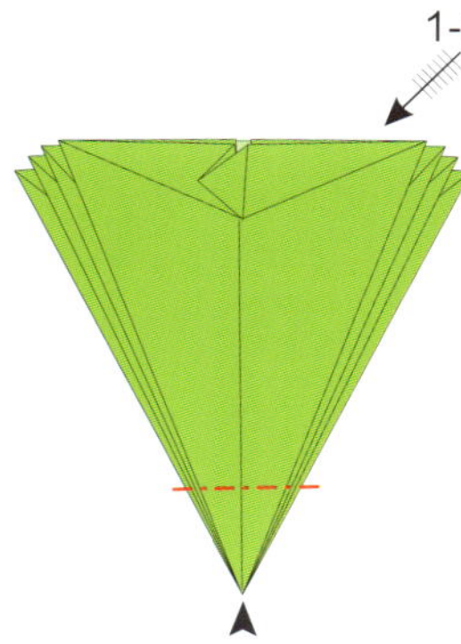

7. Fertiges Modell seitlich gesehen.
Finished model seen from the side.

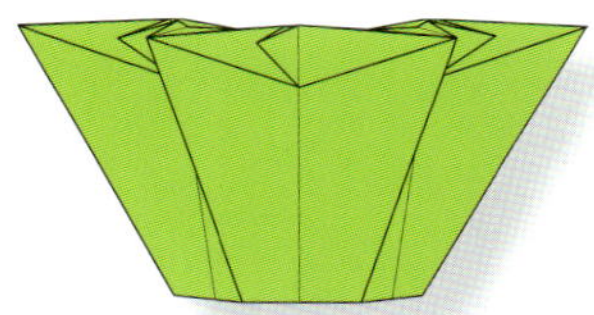

8. Fertiges Modell von oben gesehen.
Finished model seen from above.

Der Klassiker Variante 4

MATERIAL

1 Bogen 30x30 cm flammsicheres Lampenpapier. Bei dem fertigen Modell ist von der Papierrückseite wenig zu sehen. Es kann also durchgefärbtes Papier oder Papier mit einer weißen Rückseite gewählt werden.

One sheet 30x30 cm of not inflammable lamp paper. From the finished model, you won't see much of the back side of the paper. So you can choose any design.

Start. Diagramme von Seite 52 bis Nr.14, dann Variante 3 bis Nr.6 falten.
Fold charts of page 52 until step No.14. Then fold variation 3 until No.6.

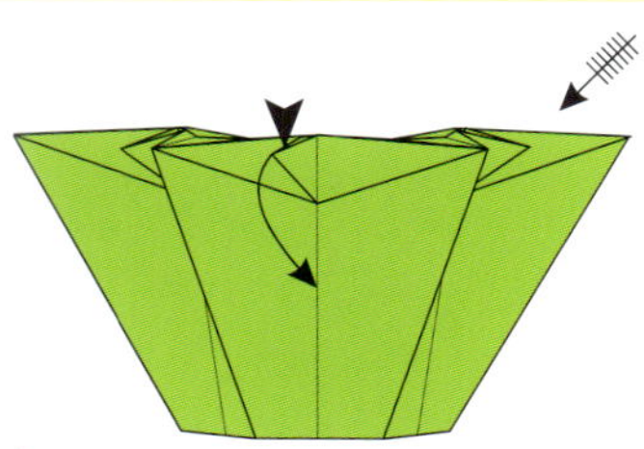

1. Spitze nach unten ziehen, liegen lassen. Mit allen anderen Spitzen wiederholen.
Pull point downwards and leave. Repeat with all other points.

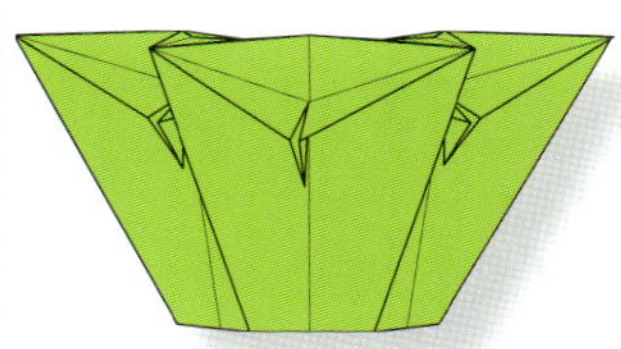

2. Fertiges Modell seitlich gesehen.
Finished model seen from the side.

3. Fertiges Modell von oben gesehen.
Finished model seen from above.

Der Klassiker Variante 5

MATERIAL

1 Bogen 30x30 cm flammsicheres Lampenpapier. Bei dem fertigen Modell ist von der Papierrückseite wenig zu sehen. Es sollte also durchgefärbtes Papier oder Papier mit einer weißen Rückseite gewählt werden.

One sheet 30x30 cm of not inflammable lamp paper. From the finished model, you won't see much of the back side of the paper. So you can choose any design.

Start. Diagramme von Seite 52 bis Nr.11 falten.

Fold charts of page 52 until step No.11.

1. Spitze nach unten falten, wieder öffnen. Mit allen anderen Spitzen wiederholen. An der unteren Spitze waagerechte Linie falten, wieder öffnen.

Fold point downwards and open up again. Repeat with all other points. Fold horizontal line on the lower point and open up again.

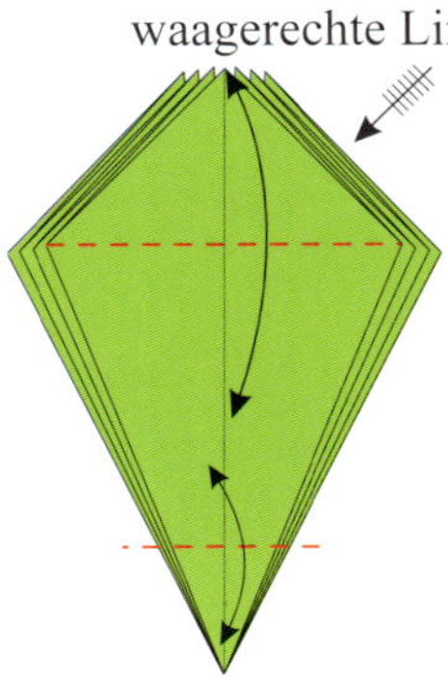

2. Spitze nach unten legen, liegen lassen. Auf der Rückseite wiederholen.

Lay point downwards and open up again. Repeat on the back.

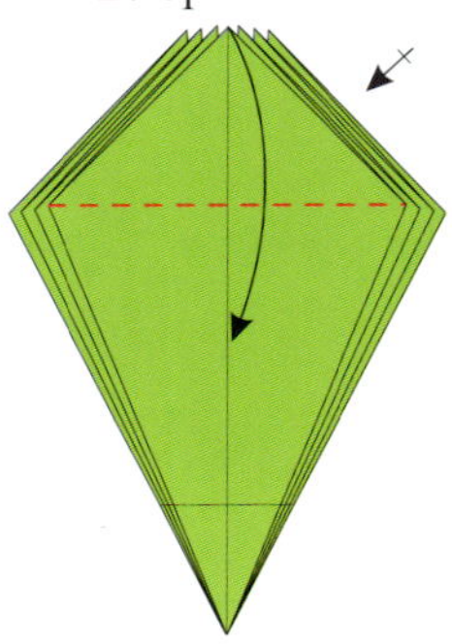

3. Schräge Linien falten, liegen lassen. Auf der Rückseite wiederholen.

Fold oblique lines and leave. Repeat on the back.

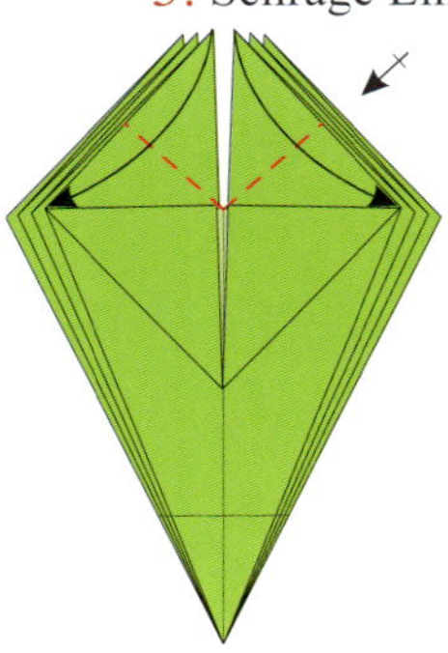

4. Spitze nach oben legen, siehe Pfeil, liegen lassen. Auf der Rückseite wiederholen.

Lay point upwards, see arrow, and leave. Repeat on the back.

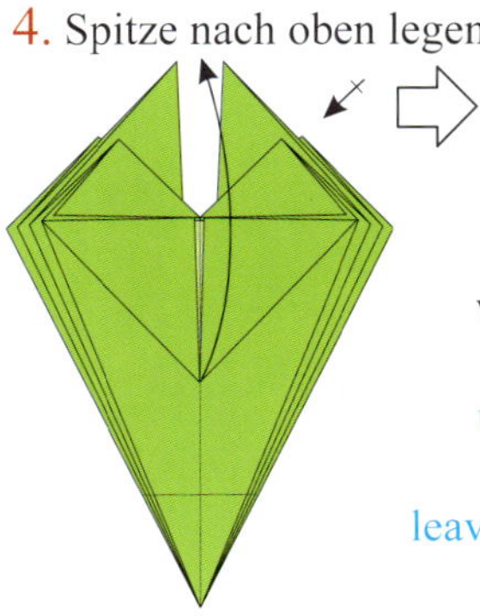

5. Nur mit der oberen Papierlage von links nach rechts falten, liegen lassen. Auf der Rückseite wiederholen.

Using only the top layer of paper fold from left to the right and leave. Repeat on the back.

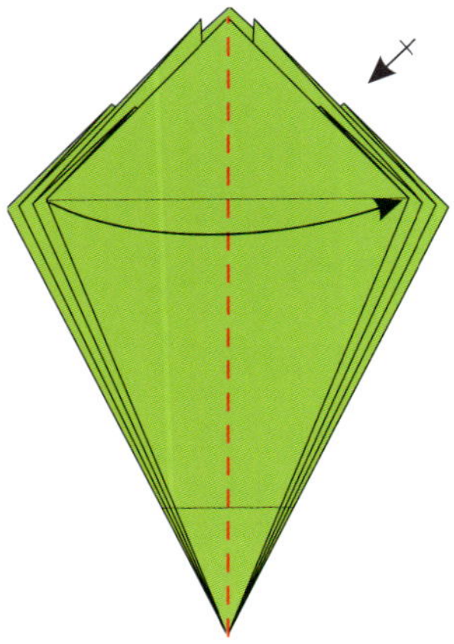

6. Spitze nach unten legen, liegen lassen. Auf der Rückseite wiederholen.

Lay point downwards and leave. Repeat on the back.

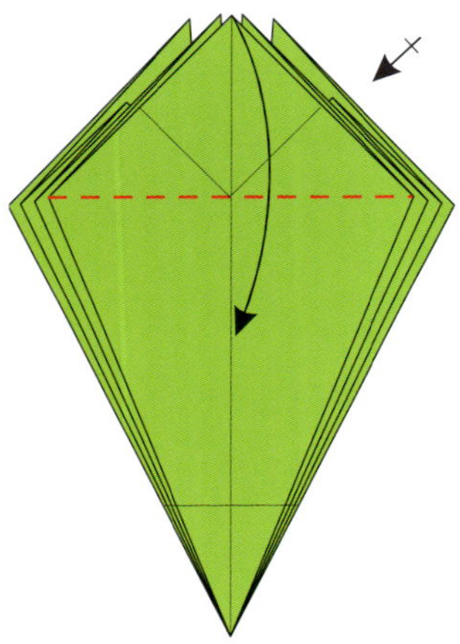

7. Schräge Linien falten, liegen lassen. Auf der Rückseite wiederholen.

Fold oblique lines and leave. Repeat on the back.

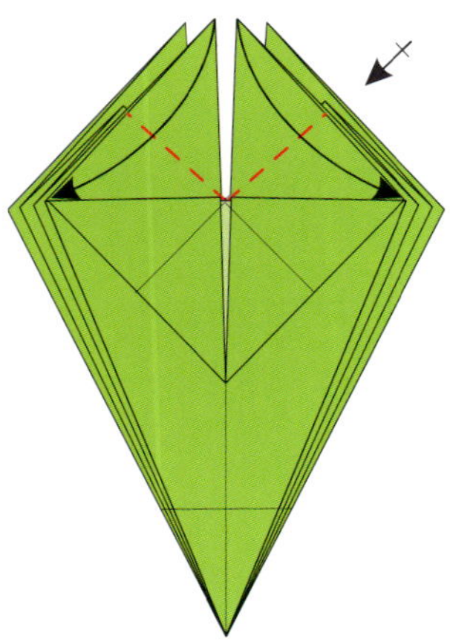

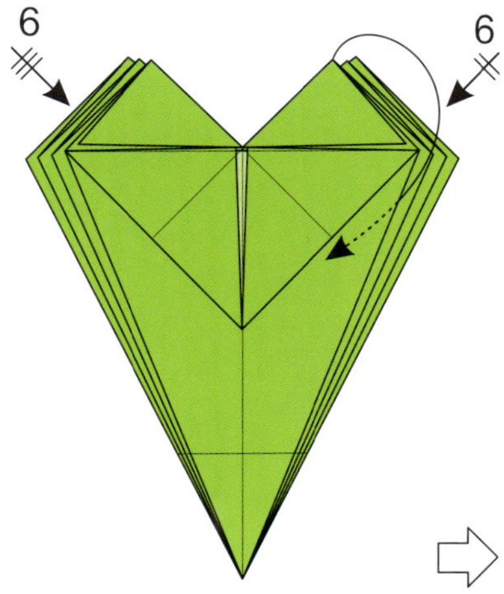

8. Mit allen Spitzen Arbeitsgang Nr.6 wiederholen.

Repeat working step No.6 with all points.

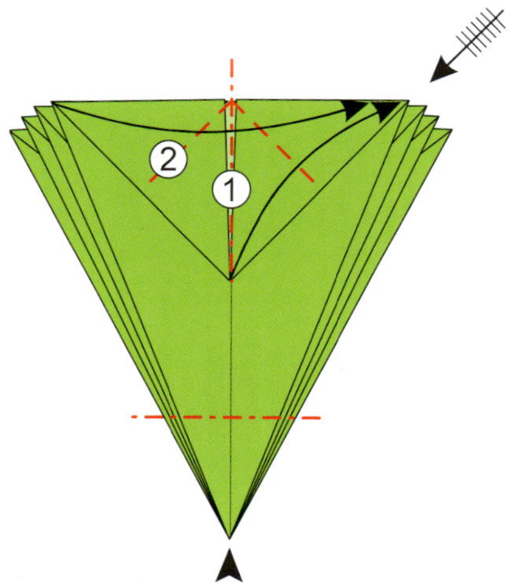

9. An der Spitze schräge Talfalten formen und senkrecht eine Bergfalte arbeiten. Mit den restlichen sieben Spitzen diesen Arbeitsgang wiederholen. Jetzt an der unteren Spitze eine Bergfalte formen, dabei die Spitze eindrücken. Modell von innen auseinanderdrücken, das Modell steht dann flach auf dem Tisch.

Form oblique valley-folds and a vertical mountain-fold on the point. Repeat this working step with the remaining seven points. Form a mountain-fold on the lower point and push in the point. Push the model from the inside outwards. Now the model stands flatly on the table.

10. Fertiges Modell von oben gesehen.
Finished model seen from above.

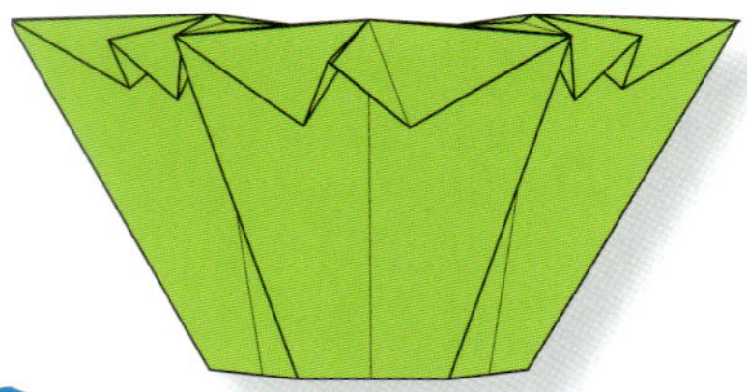

11. Fertiges Modell seitlich gesehen.
Finished model seen from the side.

Der Klassiker Variante 6

MATERIAL

1 Bogen 30x30 cm flammsicheres Lampenpapier. Bei dem fertigen Modell ist von der Papierrückseite wenig zu sehen. Es kann also durchgefärbtes Papier oder Papier mit einer weißen Rückseite gewählt werden.
One sheet 30x30 cm of not inflammable lamp paper. From the finished model, you won't see much of the back side of the paper. So you can choose any design.

Start. Diagramme von Seite 52 bis Nr.11, dann Variante 5 bis Nr.8 falten.
Fold charts of page 52 until step No.11. Then fold variation 5 until No.8.

1. Die inneren schrägen Linien zur Bergfalte formen und die äußeren schrägen Linien als Talfalte arbeiten. Die Talfalten dann nach unten zusammenführen, siehe Pfeile. Mit den restlichen sieben Spitzen diesen Arbeitsgang wiederholen. Jetzt eine Bergfalte an der unteren Spitze formen, dabei die Spitze eindrücken. Modell von innen auseinanderdrücken, das Modell steht dann flach auf dem Tisch.
Form the inner oblique lines as a mountain-fold and the outer oblique lines as a valley-fold. Then meet the valley-folds downwards, see arrows. Repeat this working step with the remaining seven points. Form a mountain-fold on the lower point and push in the point. Push the model from the inside outwards. Now the model stands flatly on the table.

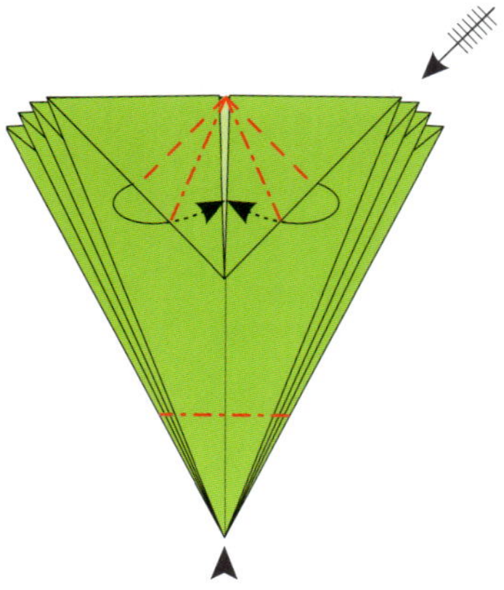

2. Fertiges Modell von oben gesehen.
Finished model seen from above.

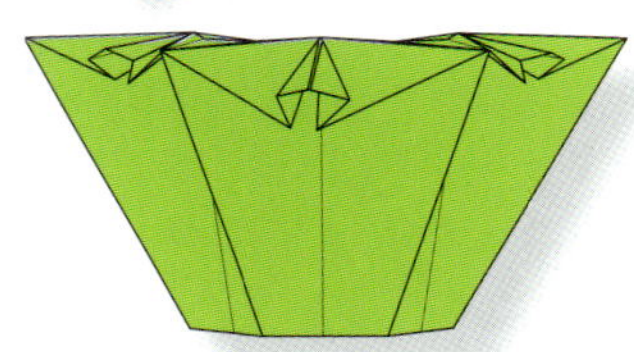

3. Fertiges Modell seitlich gesehen.
Finished model seen from the side.

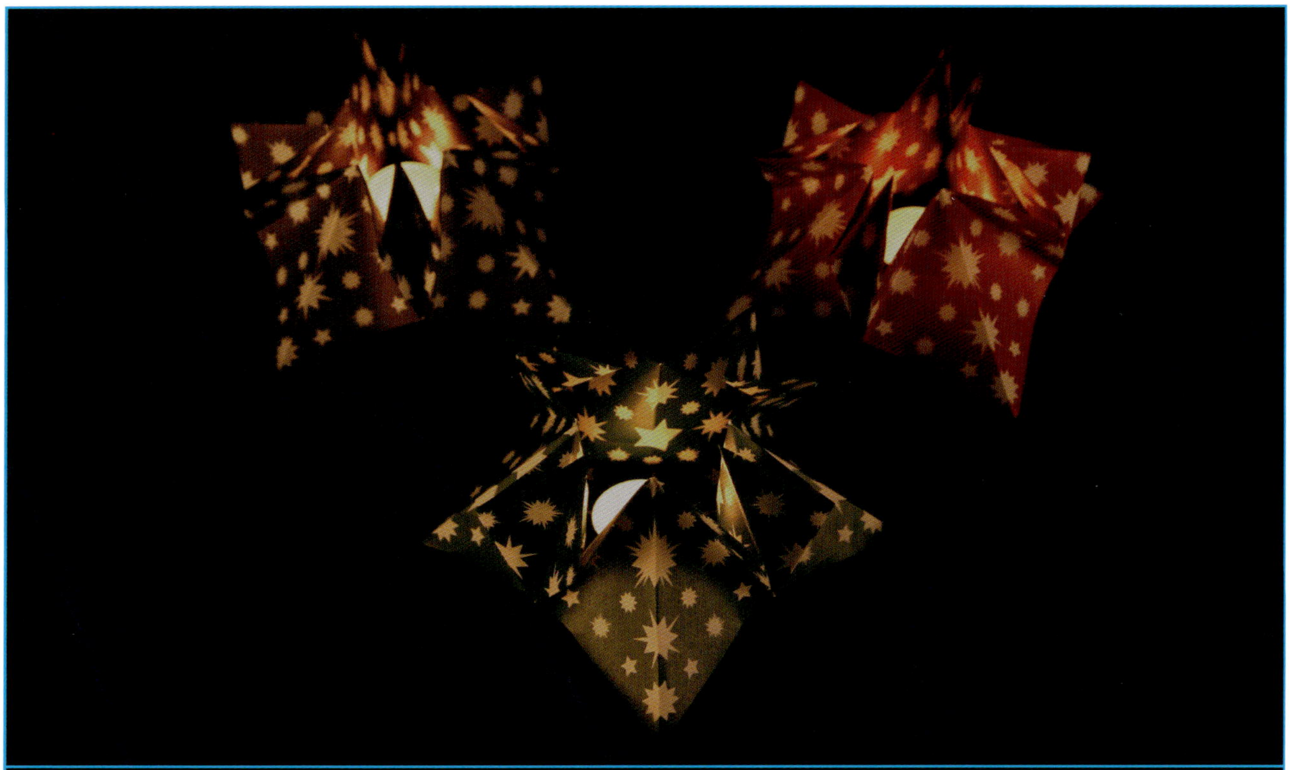

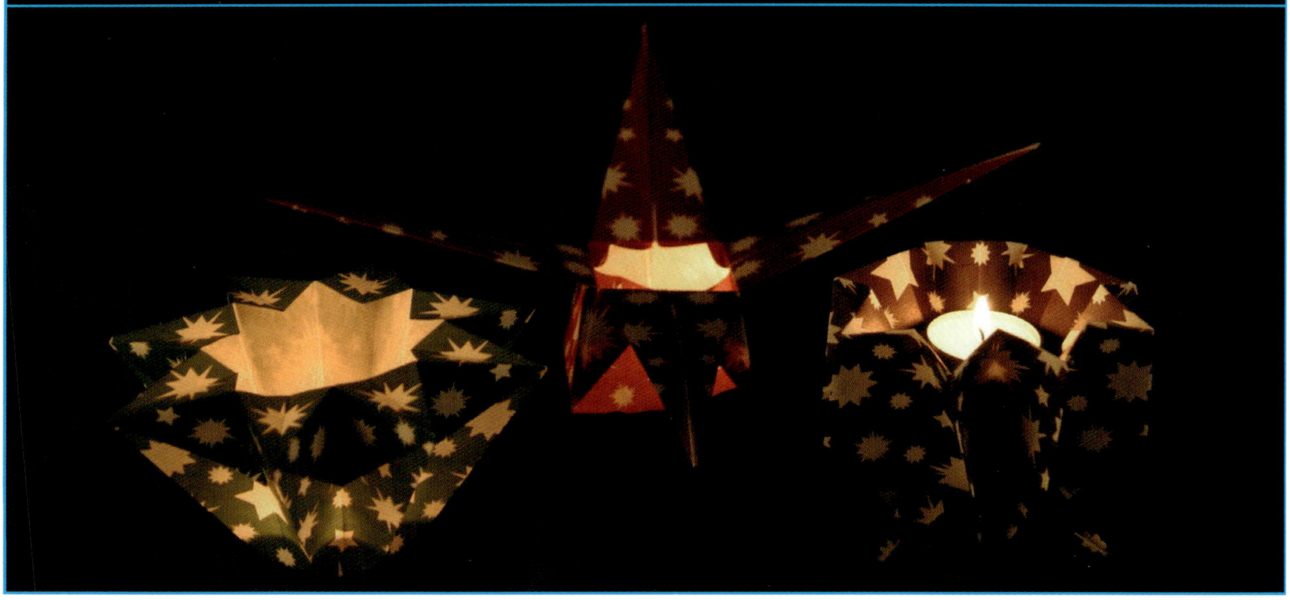

Das weiße Lampenpapier kann auch bemalt werden, vor oder nach dem Falten, wie auf dem Foto unten angedeutet.
The white lamp paper can be painted, before or after the folding, as suggested on the picture below.

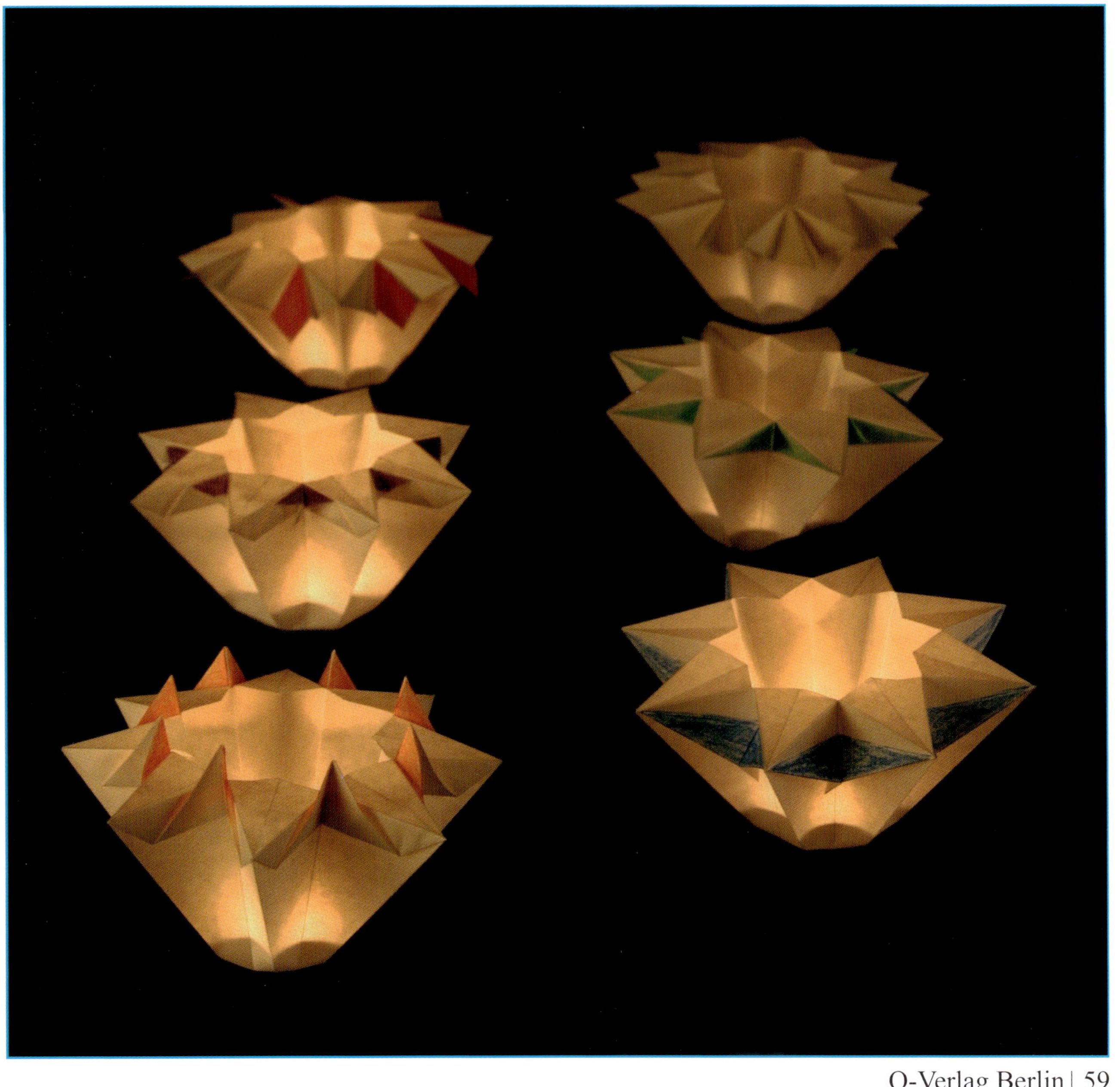

Kelch Licht

Modell von Jannie van Schuylenburg

MATERIAL

1 Bogen 30x30 cm flammsicheres Lampenpapier. Bei dem fertigen Modell ist von der Papierrückseite nichts zu sehen. Es kann also jedes Papier ausgewählt werden.

One sheet 30x30 cm of not inflammable lamp paper. From the finished model, you won't see much of the back side of the paper. So you can choose any design.

Start. Diagramme von Seite 52 bis Nr.3 falten.

Fold charts of page 52 until step No.3.

1. Bergfalte nach rechts falten, dabei die Ecke flach drücken.

Fold mountain-fold to the right, at the same time push the corner flat.

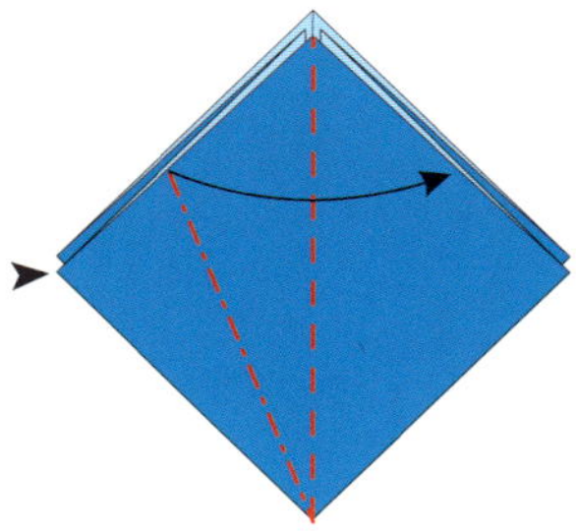

2. Mit den anderen drei Ecken den Arbeitsschritt Nr.1 wiederholen.

Repeat working step No.1 with the other three corners.

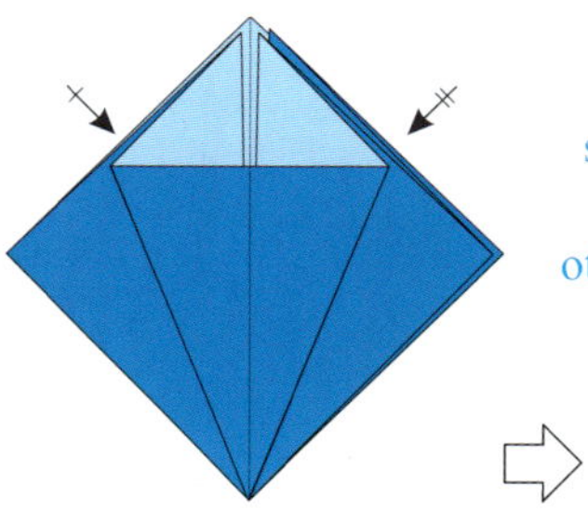

3. Nur mit der oberen Papierlage, schräge Linien zur Mitte falten, liegen lassen. Mit allen anderen Spitzen wiederholen.

Using only the top layer of paper, fold oblique lines to the middle and leave. Repeat with all other points.

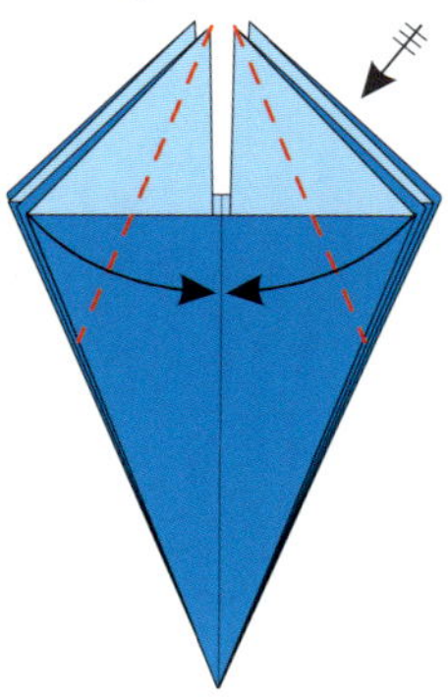

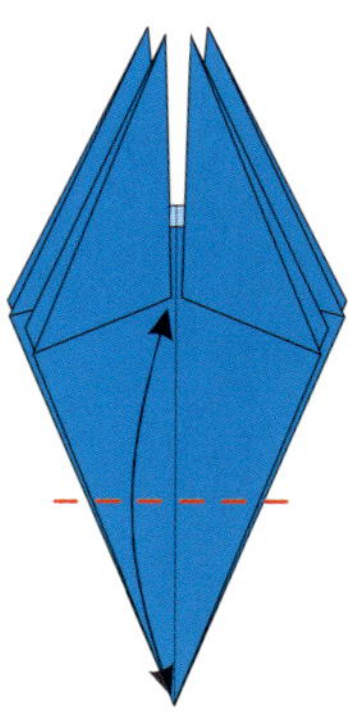

4. Untere Spitze nach oben falten, siehe Pfeil, wieder öffnen.

Fold lower point upwards, see arrow, and open up again.

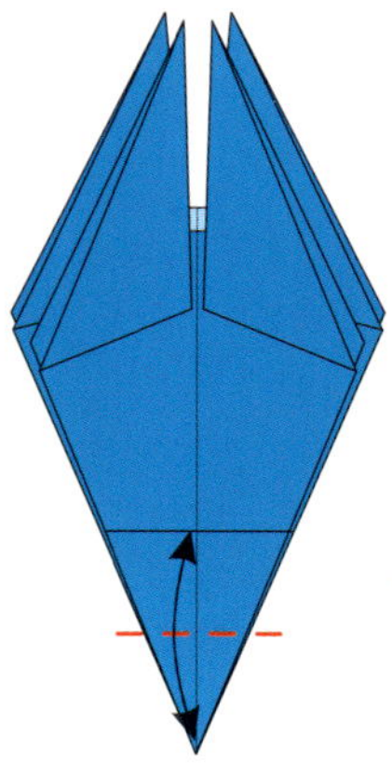

5. Untere Spitze nach oben an die Linie falten, siehe Pfeil, wieder öffnen.

Fold lower point upwards to the line, see arrow, and open up again.

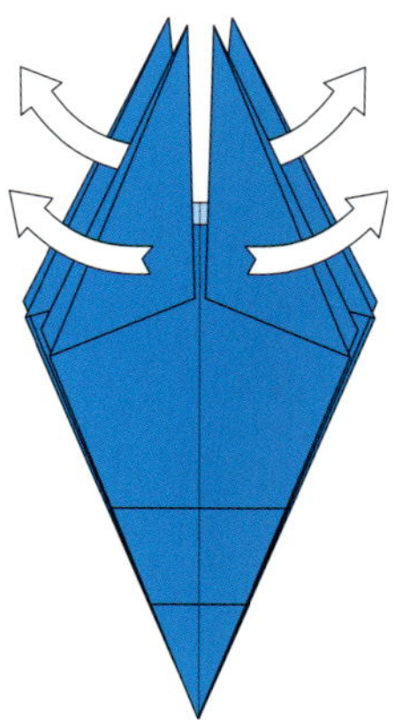

6. Arbeitsschritte von Nr.3 wieder öffnen.

Open up again working step No.3.

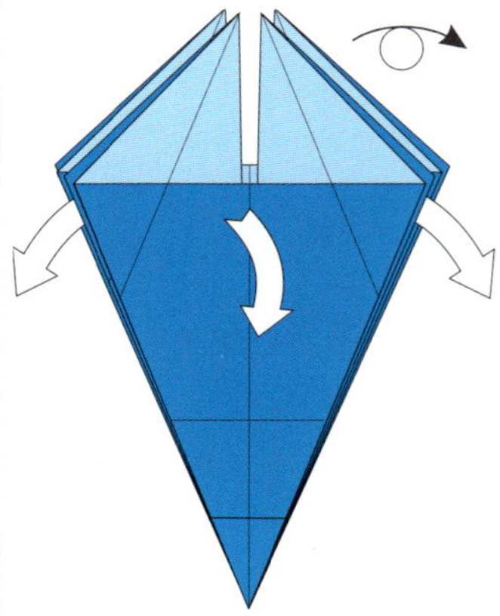

7. Modell von innen auseinanderdrücken, das Papier liegt dann flach auf dem Tisch.

Push the model from the inside outwards, so the paper lies flatly on the table.

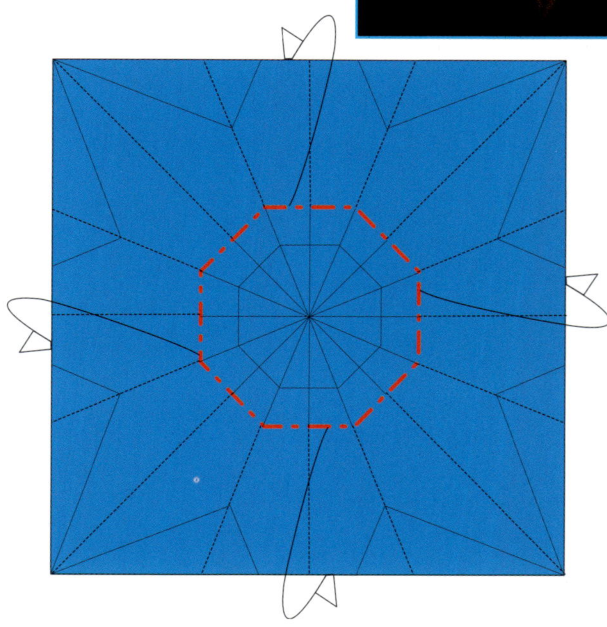

8. An der roten Linie eine Bergfalte formen, dabei die Papierecken nach unten halten. Siehe auch Diagramm Nr.9.

Form a mountain-fold along the red line, at the same time hold the corners down. See chart No.9.

9. Seitlich die acht Ecken eindrücken. Die Papiermitte wird von innen nach oben gedrückt, dabei bleibt die rote Linie als Talfalte liegen. Dieser Arbeitsgang wird benötigt, damit das Papier wieder flach auf dem Tisch liegen kann. Das Modell um 180 Grad drehen.

Push in the eight corners from the side. Push the middle of the paper from the inside to the top, at the same time leave the red line as a valley-fold. This working step is needed, in order to lie the paper flatly on the table. Turn model 180 degrees around.

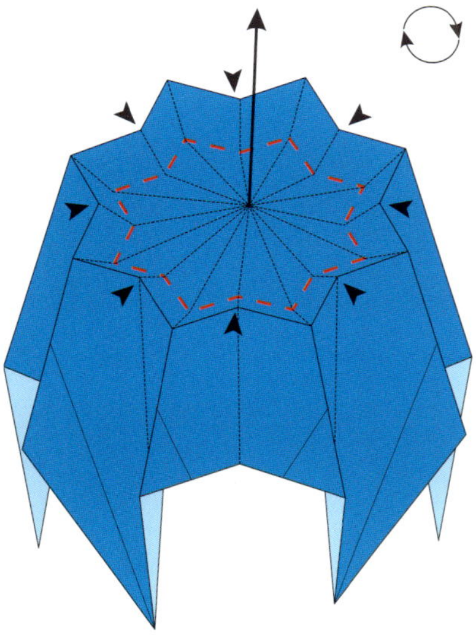

10. Nur mit der oberen Papierlage schräge Linien zur Mitte falten, liegen lassen. Mit allen anderen Spitzen wiederholen.

Using only the top layer of paper, fold oblique lines to the middle and leave. Repeat with all other points.

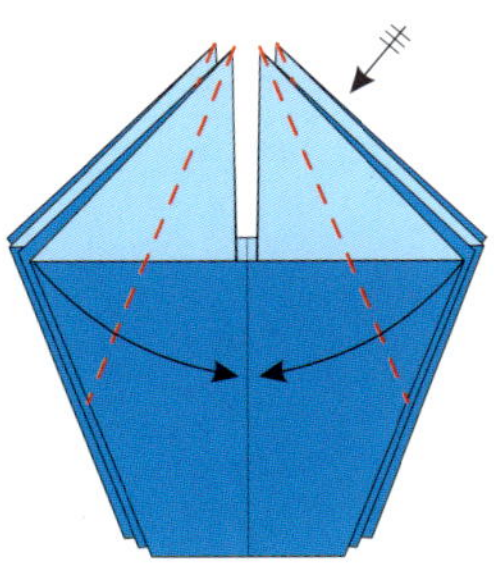

11. Nur mit der oberen Papierlage von rechts nach links falten, liegen lassen. Auf der Rückseite wiederholen.

Using only the top layer of paper, fold from the right to the left. Repeat on the back.

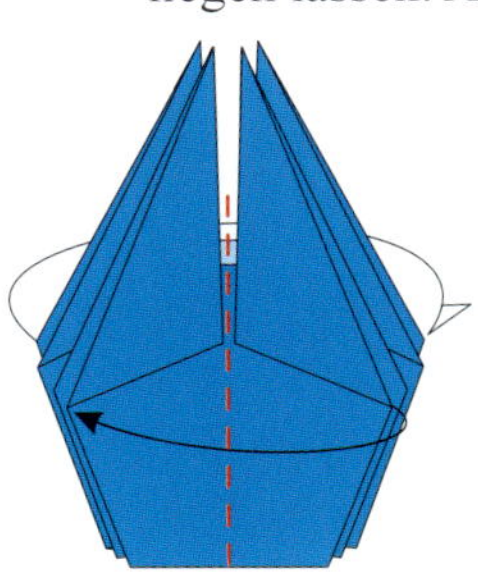

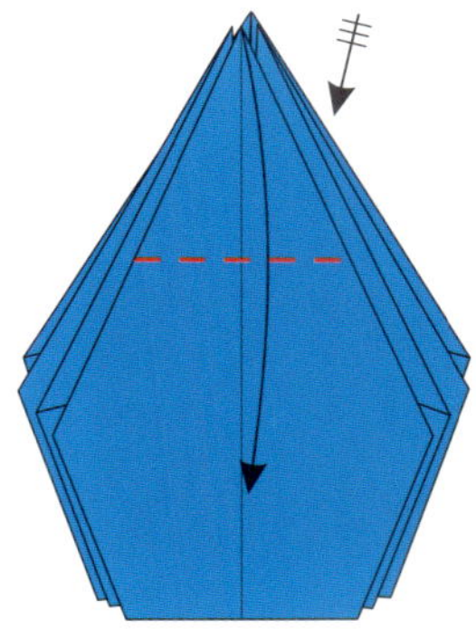

12. Spitze nach unten falten, liegen lassen. Mit allen anderen Spitzen wiederholen.

Fold point downwards and leave. Repeat with all other points.

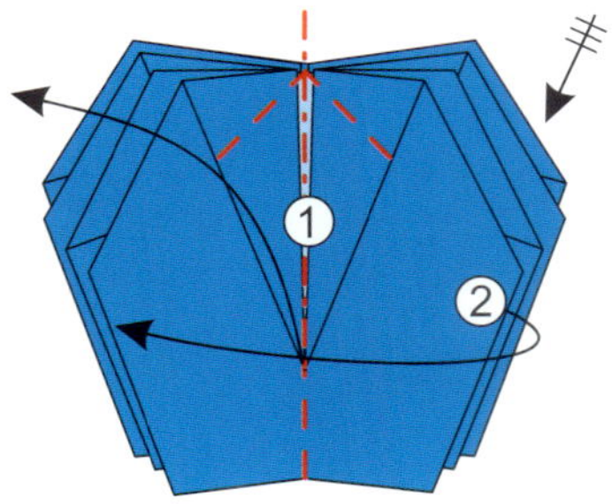

13. An der Spitze Linie Nr.1 zur Bergfalte formen und dann nach links legen, dadurch werden die schrägen Linien gefaltet. Jetzt nur obere Papierlage von rechts nach links legen, siehe Pfeil (2), liegen lassen. Diese beiden Arbeitsschritte mit den anderen drei Spitzen wiederholen. So entstehen die Füße auf denen das Modell dann steht.

On the point form line No.1 as a mountain-fold and put it to the left, so the oblique lines will be folded. Using only the top layer of paper, fold from the right to the left, see arrow (2), and leave. Repeat these two working steps with the other three points. This way the feet arise on which the model can stand.

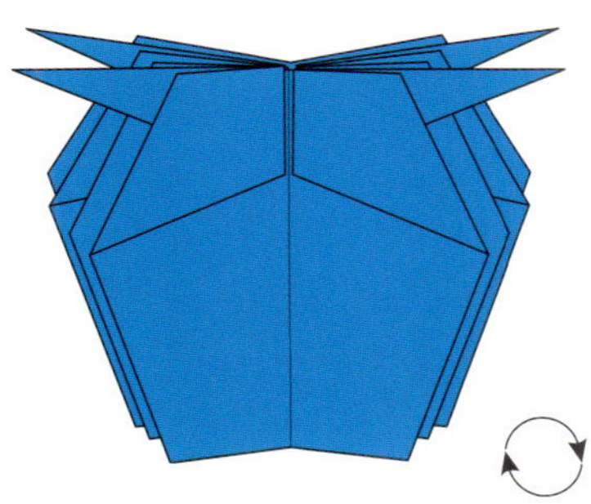

14. Modell um 180 Grad drehen.

Turn model 180 degrees around.

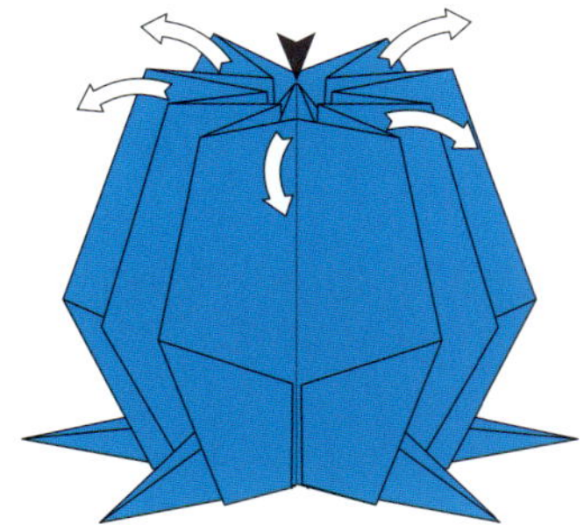

15. Modell von innen auseinanderdrücken, die innere Spitze liegt dann flach, aber nicht auf dem Tisch. Die Besonderheit dieses Lichtes ist, dass die Flamme auf halber Höhe ist und somit besondere Lichteffekte entstehen.

Push the model from the inside outwards, so the internal point lies flatly, but not on the table. The speciality of this light is that the flame is on half of the height, so that special light-effects arise.

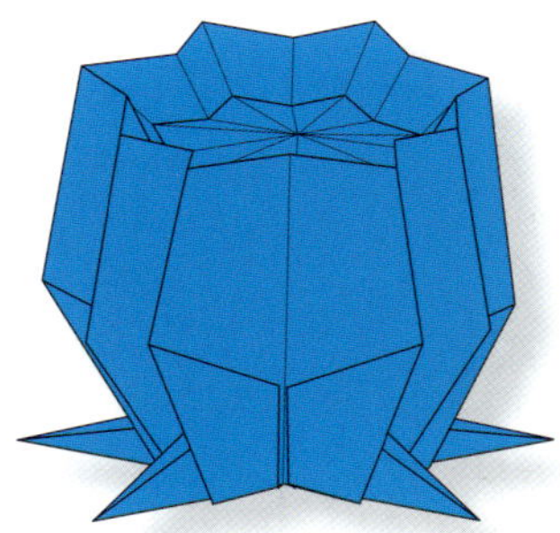

16. Fertiges Modell seitlich gesehen.

Finished model seen from the side.

17. Fertiges Modell mit Licht seitlich gesehen.

Finished model with light seen from the side.

Lichterketten Übersicht

mit Lichterketten durchs Jahr

Seite 63

Seite 67

Seite 71

Seite 65

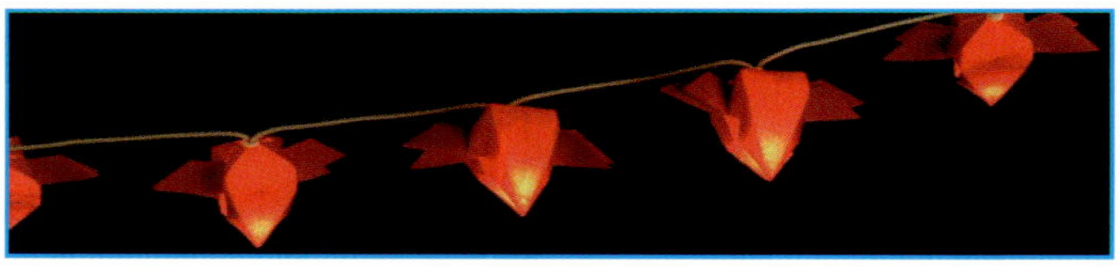

Seite 66

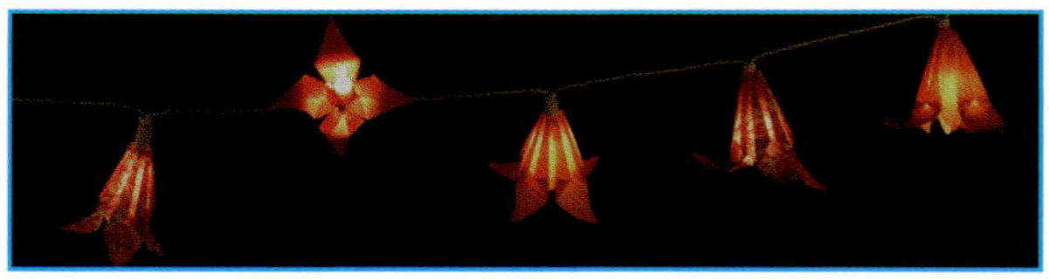

Seite 69

Seite 70

Seite 73

Seite 75

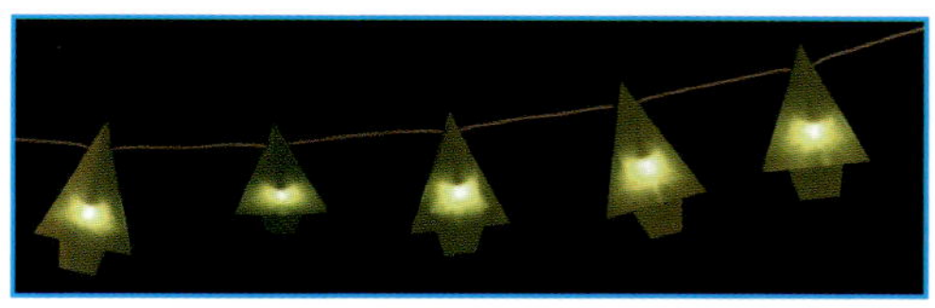

Seite 77

Seite 64

Seite 72

Seite 78

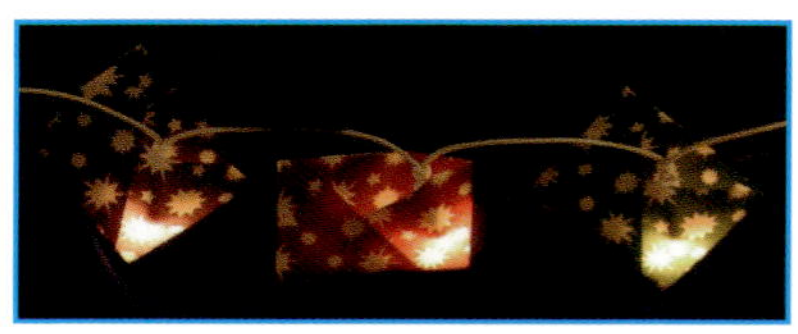

Seite 76

Tulpen Lichterkette

MATERIAL

1 Bogen 15x15 cm Papier für 1 Licht. Es kann jedes Papier gewählt werden.

One sheet 15x15 cm paper for one light. You can choose any design.

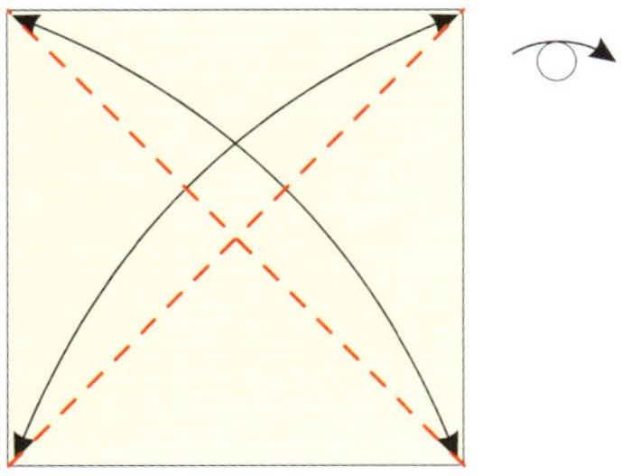

1. Zweimal diagonal die Mitte falten, wieder öffnen. Rückseite nach oben legen.

Fold twice the middle diagonally and open up again. Turn over to the back.

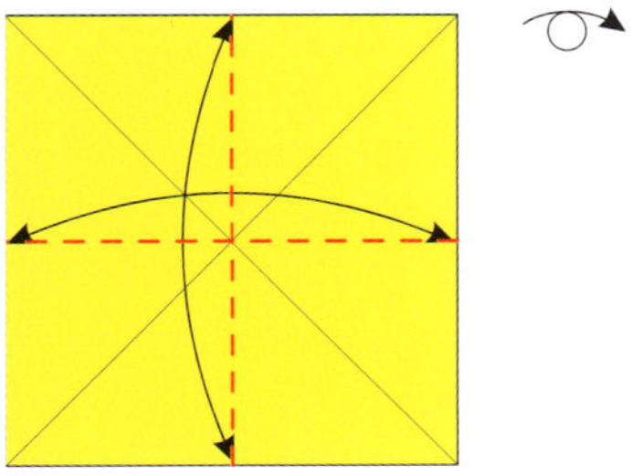

2. Zweimal waagerecht die Mitte falten, wieder öffnen. Rückseite nach oben legen.

Fold twice the middle horizontally and open up again. Turn over to the back.

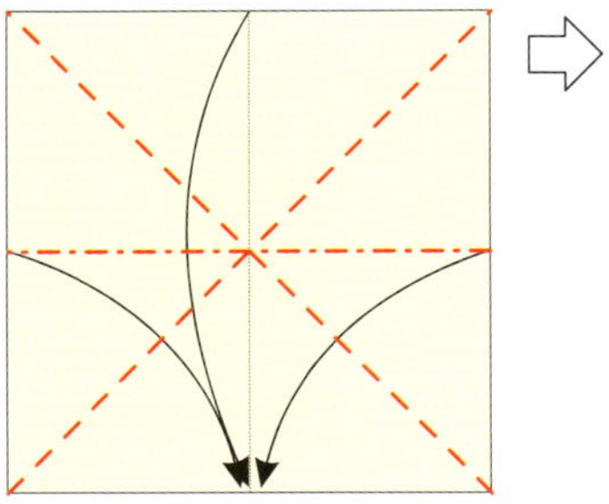

3. Von der waagerechten Mitte (Bergfalte), Papier seitlich zum unteren Mittelpunkt legen, siehe Pfeile. Es entsteht ein Dreieck.

From the horizontal middle (mountain-fold), lay paper from the side to the lower centre. A triangle arises.

4. Spitzen zur oberen Mitte falten, liegen lassen. Auf der Rückseite wiederholen.

Fold points to the upper middle and leave. Repeat on the back.

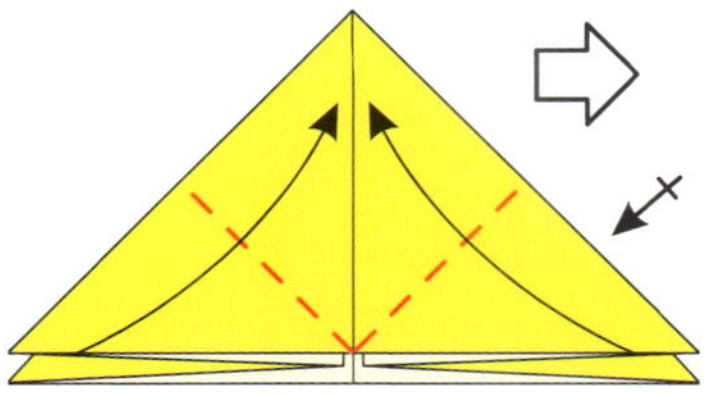

5. Nur mit der oberen Papierlage, siehe Pfeil, von rechts nach links falten. Auf der Rückseite wiederholen.

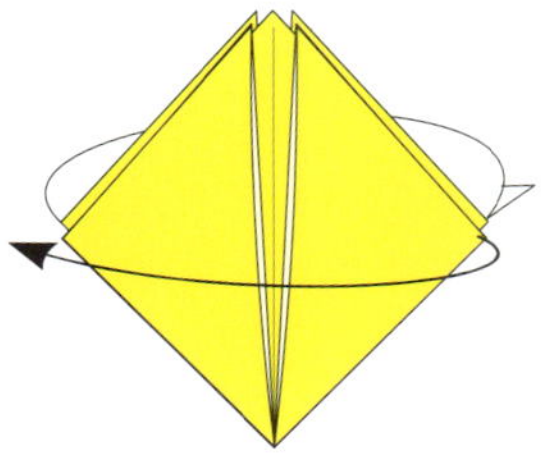

Using only the top layer of paper, see arrow, fold from right to the left. Repeat on the back.

6. Nur mit der oberen Papierlage, siehe Pfeil, schräge Linie zur Mitte falten.

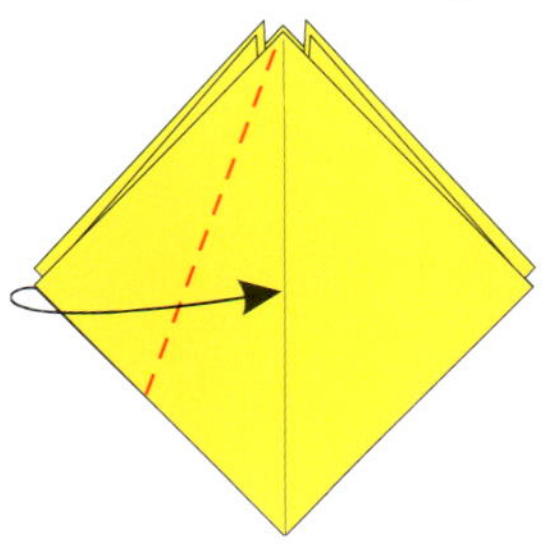

Using only the top layer of paper, see arrow, fold oblique line to the middle.

7. Nur mit der oberen Papierlage, siehe Pfeil, schräge Linie zur Mitte falten. Spitze, siehe Pfeil, in die linke Papiertüte schieben.

Using only the top layer of paper, see arrow, fold oblique line to the middle. Slide point, see arrow, into the left paper bag.

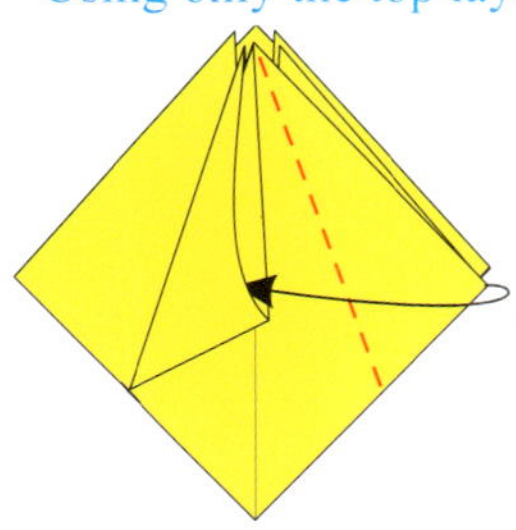

8. Arbeitsschritte von Nr.6 und Nr.7 auf der Rückseite wiederholen.

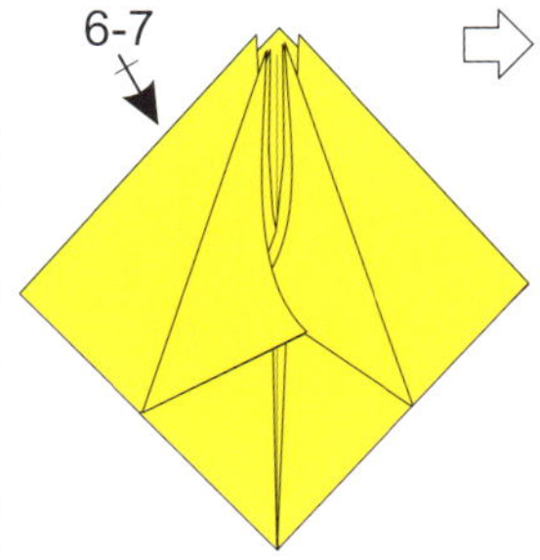

Repeat working steps No.6 and No.7 on the back.

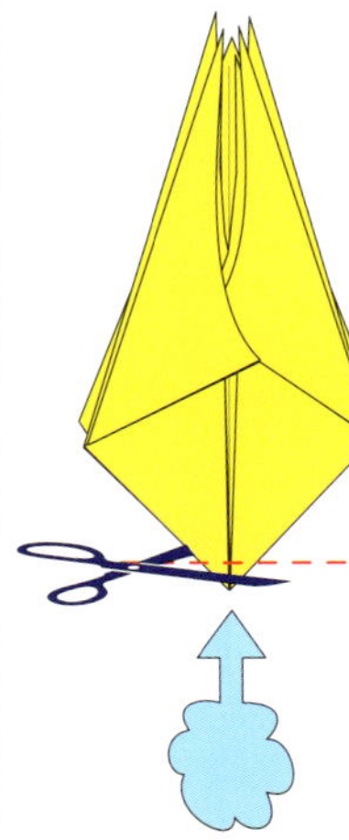

9. Untere Spitze etwas abschneiden. Jetzt kräftig hineinblasen, damit die 3D Form entsteht.

Cut off the lower point a little bit. Now strongly inflate, so that the 3D form arises.

10. Die vier äußeren Spitzen jetzt vorsichtig von oben nach unten formen. So entstehen die Blütenblätter.

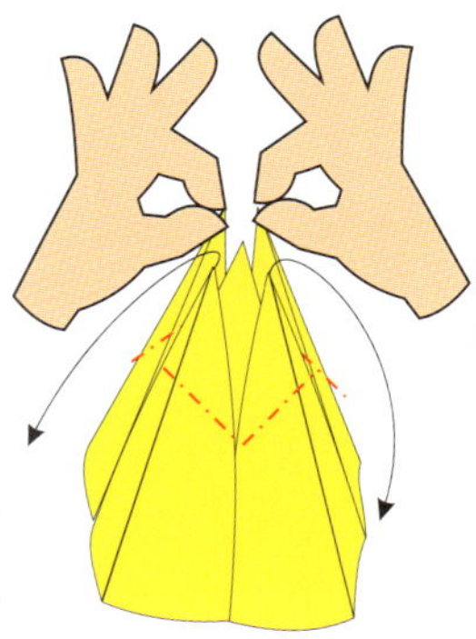

Form the four outer points carefully from top to bottom, so that the petal arises.

11. Fertiges Modell seitlich gesehen. Das Loch nach oben halten und über den Leuchtkörper schieben.

Finished model seen from the side. Hold the hole upwards and slide it over the light bulb.

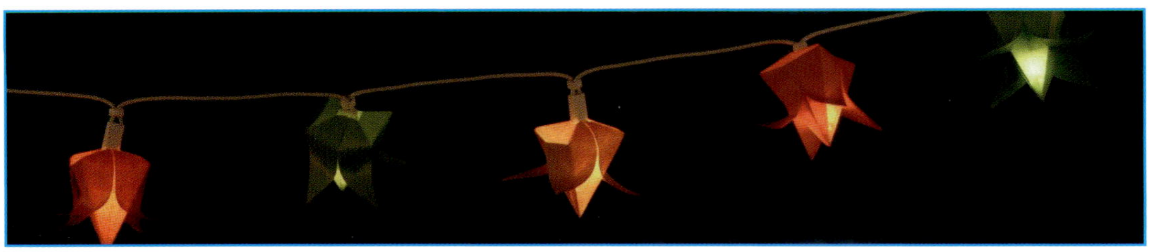

Lichttütenkette

MATERIAL

1 Bogen 7,5x15 cm Papier für 1 Licht. Es kann jedes Papier gewählt werden.

One sheet 7,5x15 cm paper for one light. You can choose any design.

1. Senkrechte Linie falten, liegen lassen.
Fold the vertical line and leave.

2. Senkrechte Mitte falten und auf die Papierlasche kleben, siehe Pfeil.
Fold the vertical middle and glue both edges together, see arrow.

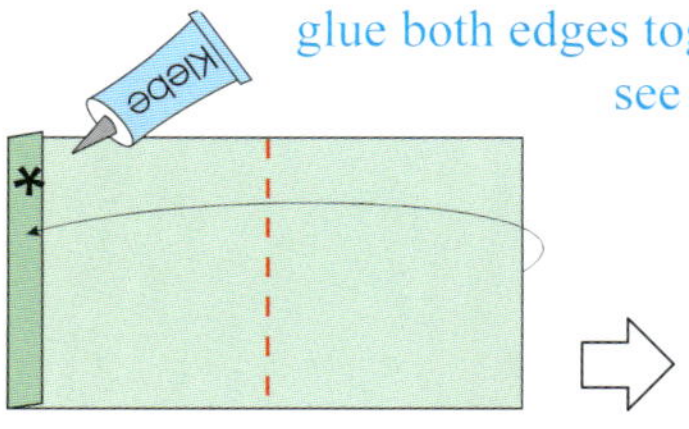

3. Nun die Tiefe der Tüte falten. Bei dieser Papiergröße sollten es 2 cm sein. Also jetzt nur die obere Papierlage um 2 cm nach rechts umlegen bis die rote Linie eine neue Kante rechts bildet und falten. Dabei wird die linke neue Kante automatisch mitgefaltet, siehe auch Pfeile.

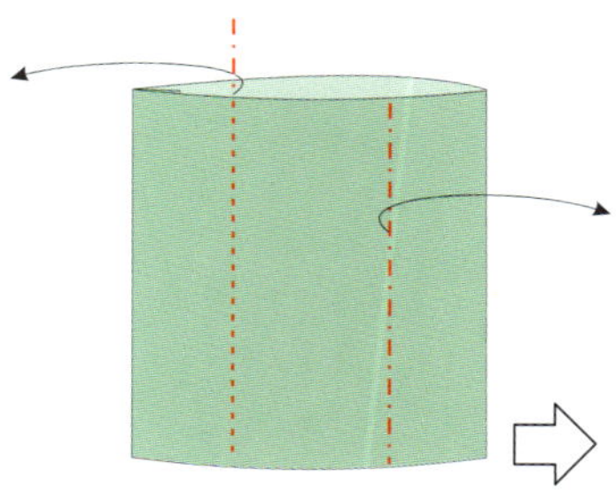

Now fold the depth of the model. Using this size of paper it should be 6 cm. Lay only the top layer of paper 6 cm to the right until the red line becomes the new edge on the right side. At the same time fold the new edge on the left side, see arrows.

4. Für den Tütenfalz auf beiden Seiten senkrechte Linien falten.
Fold the vertical lines on both sides.

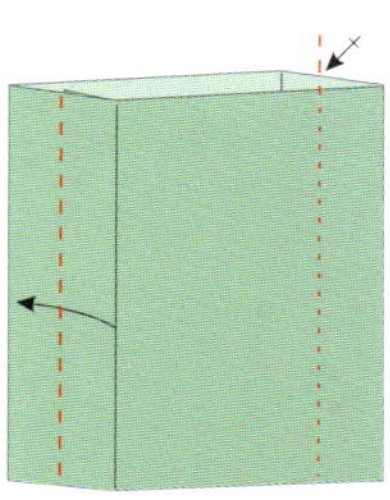

5. Wenn die Tiefe der Tüte 2 cm ist, wird die waagerechte Linie für den Boden auf der Höhe von ca. 1,3 cm gefaltet, wieder öffnen. (Also ca. 2/3 der Tiefe)
If the depth of the model is 6 cm, fold the horizontal line on the height of 4 cm for the bottom and open up again. (height = 2/3 of the depth)

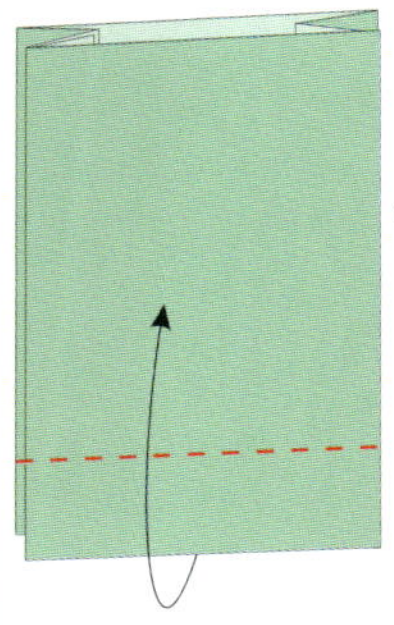

6. Mit beiden Papierlagen, Ecken an die waagerechte Linie falten, wieder öffnen. Modell um 180 Grad drehen.
With both layers of paper, fold corners to the horizontal line and open up again. Turn the model 180 degrees around.

7. Modell von innen auseinanderdrücken.
Push the model from the inside outwards.

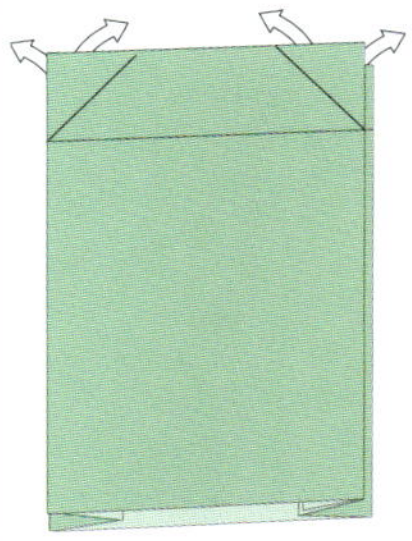

8. Im Tütenfalz und an den schrägen Linien jetzt Bergfalten formen. Dann Papier seitlich zur Mitte eindrücken.
Fold mountain-folds on the sides and on the oblique lines. Push in the paper from the side to the middle.

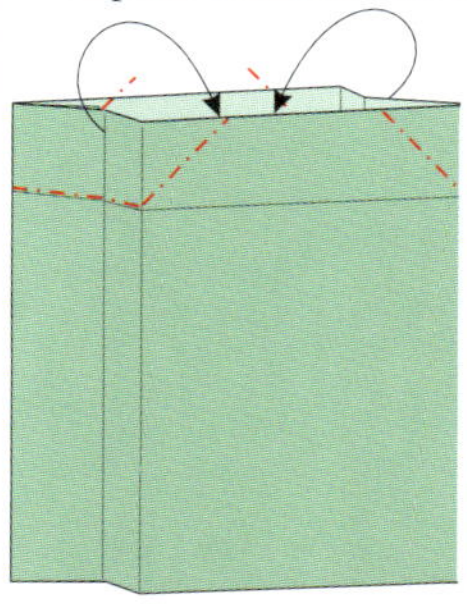

9. Eine Papierlasche zur Mitte legen, siehe Pfeil und festkleben. Keinen wasserhaltigen Kleber benutzen.
Put one paper flap to the middle, see arrow and glue. Don't use water based glue.

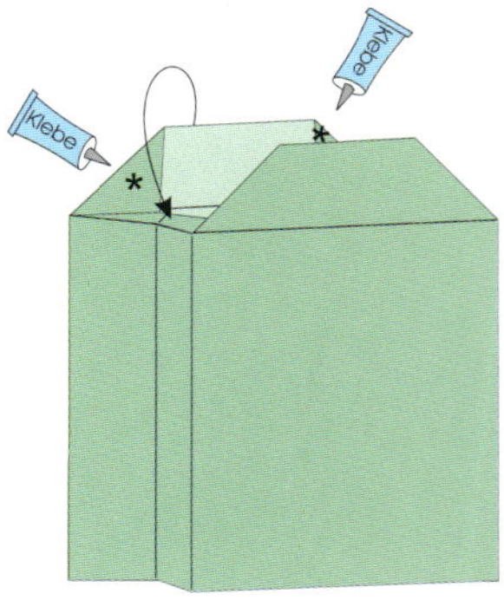

10. Jetzt die andere Papierlasche zur Mitte legen und auch festkleben. Keinen wasserhaltigen Kleber benutzen. Modell um 180 Grad drehen.
Now put the other paper flap to the middle and glue. Don't use water based glue. Turn the model 180 degrees around.

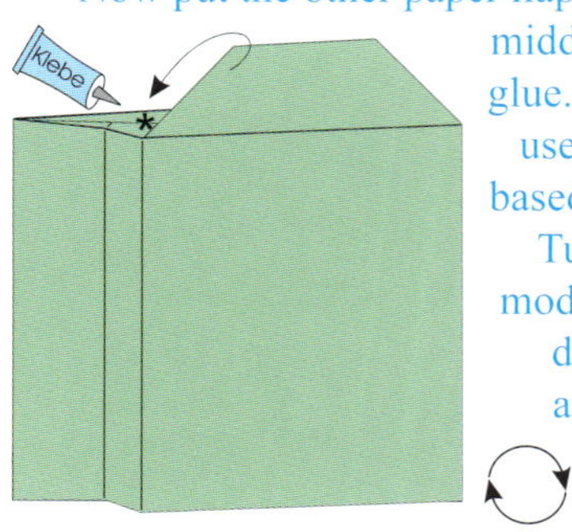

11. Fertiges Modell seitlich gesehen.
Finished model seen from the side.

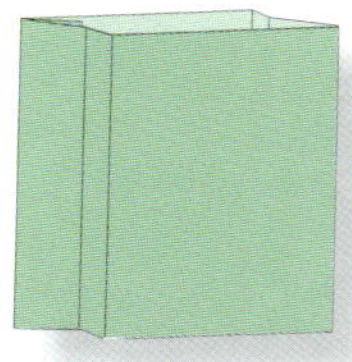

12. Am offenen Rand in der Mitte ein Loch durch beide Papierlagen arbeiten.
Ein Band durchziehen und die Tüte dann über ein Licht stülpen. Zum Halt über dem Kabel eine Schleife binden.
Make a hole in the middle of the open edge through both layers of paper. Pull a ribbon through the hole and slide the model over a light bulb. Then make a bow over the wire in order to fix it.

Würfel Lichterkette

MATERIAL

1 Bogen 15x15 cm Papier für 1 Licht. Es kann jedes Papier gewählt werden.
One sheet 15x15 cm paper for one light. You can choose any design.

1. Zweimal diagonal die Mitte falten, wieder öffnen. Rückseite nach oben legen.
Fold twice the middle diagonally and open up again. Turn over to the back.

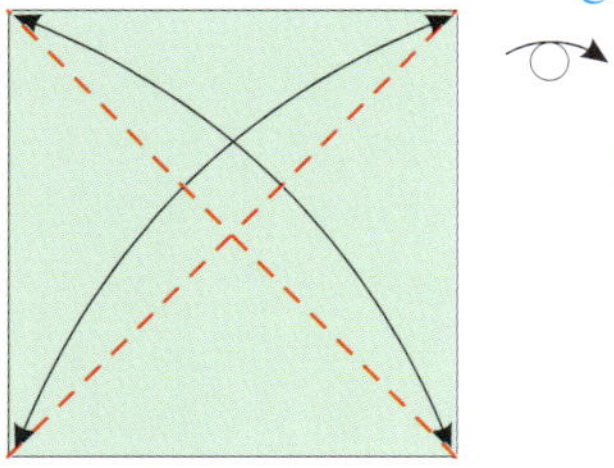

2. Zweimal waagerecht die Mitte falten, wieder öffnen. Rückseite nach oben legen.
Fold twice the middle horizontally and open up again. Turn over to the back.

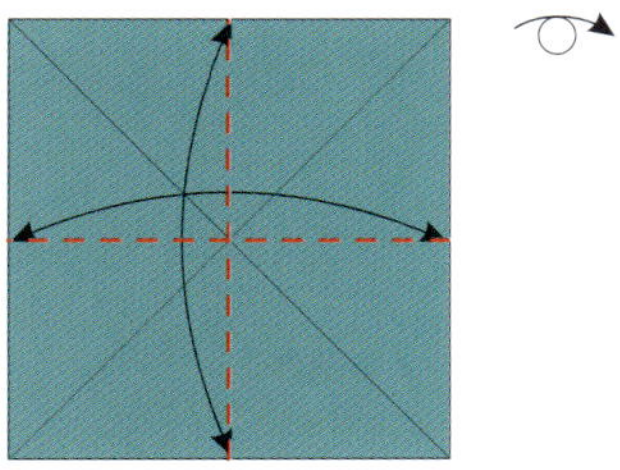

3. Von der waagerechten Mitte (Bergfalte), Papier seitlich zum unteren Mittelpunkt legen, siehe Pfeile. Es entsteht ein Dreieck.
From the horizontal middle (mountain-fold), lay paper from the side to the lower centre. A triangle arises.

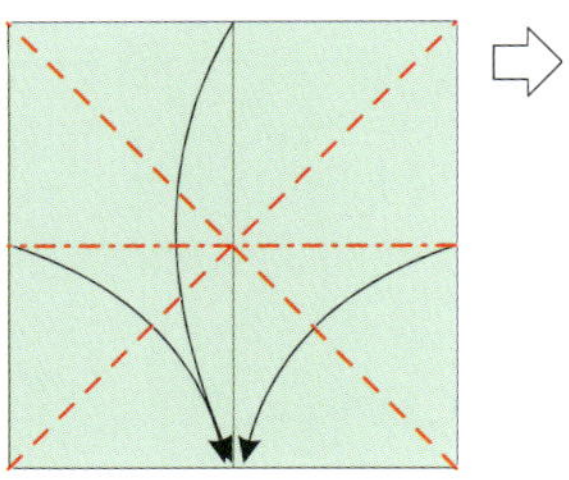

4. Spitzen zur oberen Mitte falten, liegen lassen. Auf der Rückseite wiederholen.
Fold points to the upper middle and leave. Repeat on the back.

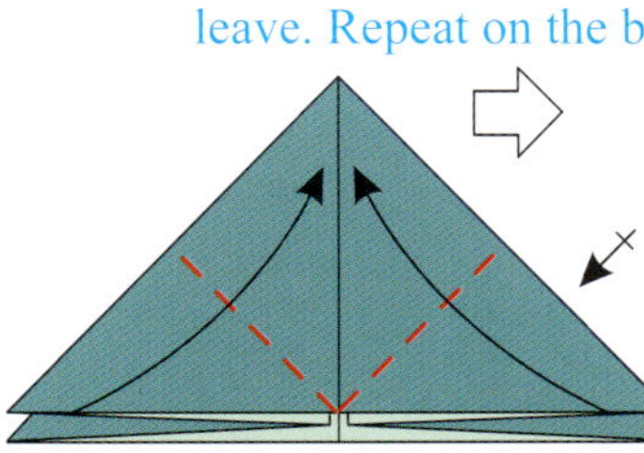

5. Nur mit der oberen Papierlage, siehe Pfeile, senkrechte Linien falten, wieder öffnen. Auf der Rückseite wiederholen.
Using only the top layer of paper, see arrow, fold vertical lines and open up again. Repeat on the back.

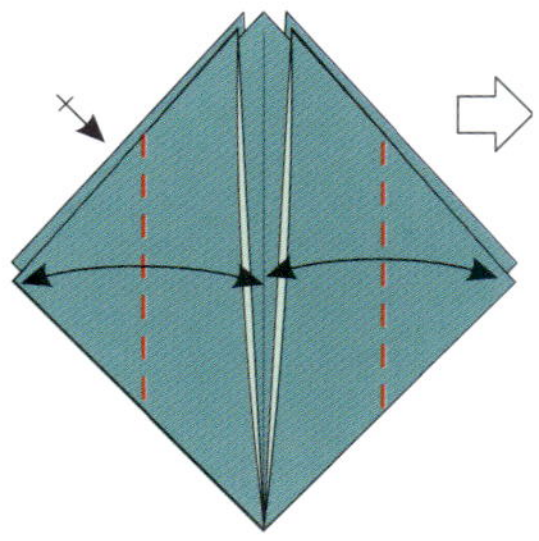

6. Nur mit der oberen Papierlage, siehe Pfeile, Spitzen nach unten falten, liegen lassen. Auf der Rückseite wiederholen.
Using only the top layer of paper, see arrow, fold points downwards and leave. Repeat on the back.

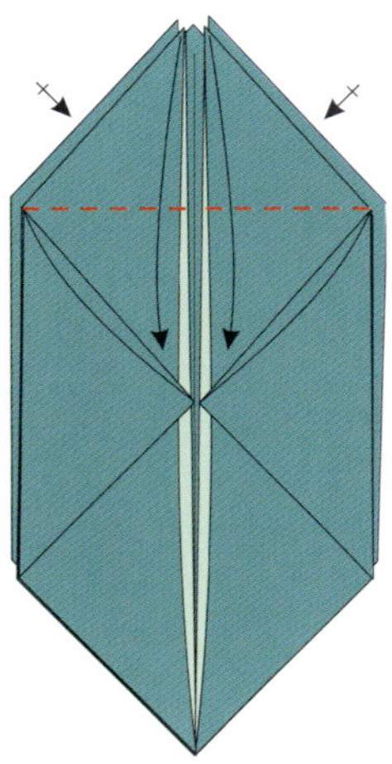

7. Nur mit der oberen Papierlage, siehe Pfeile, schräge Linien falten, Ecken dann in die Papiertüten schieben. Auf der Rückseite wiederholen.
Using only the top layer of paper, see arrow, fold oblique lines and slide corners into the paper bags. Repeat on the back.

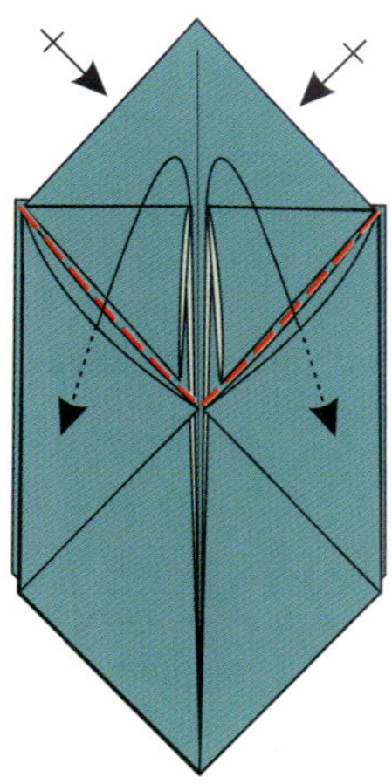

8. Waagerechte Linie an der oberen und unteren Spitze falten, wieder öffnen.
Fold horizontal line on the upper and lower point and open up again.

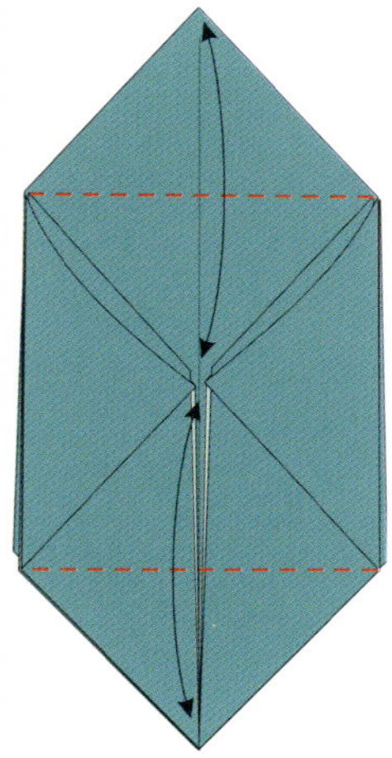

9. Untere Spitze etwas abschneiden. Jetzt kräftig hineinblasen, damit die 3D Form entsteht.
Cut off the lower point a little bit. Now strongly inflate, so that the 3D form arises.

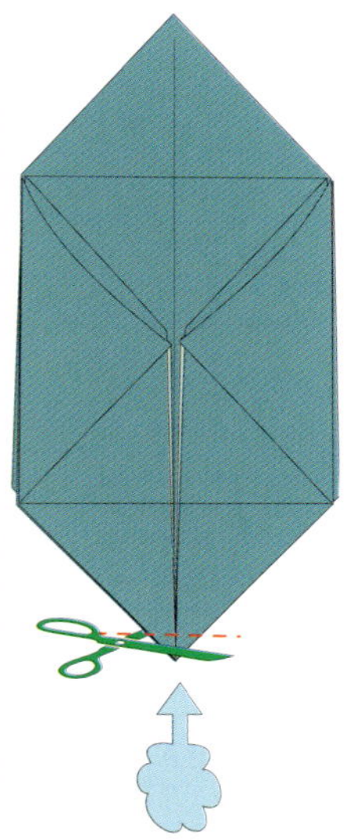

10. Fertiges Modell seitlich gesehen. Das Loch nach oben halten und über den Leuchtkörper schieben.
Finished model seen from the side. Hold the hole upwards and slide it over the light bulb.

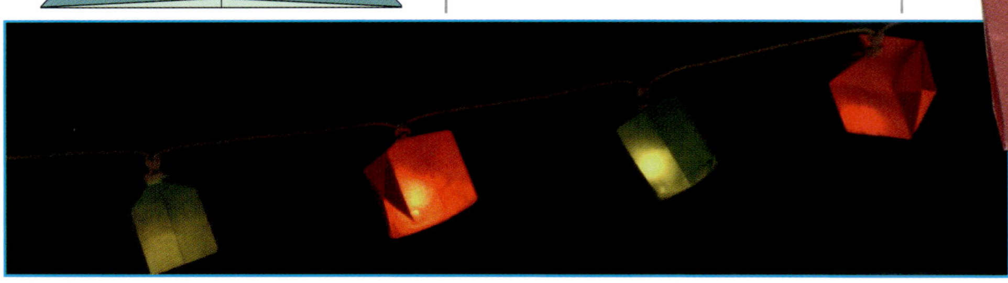

Lichterketten mit 3D Herzen

MATERIAL

1 Bogen 15x15 cm Papier für 1 Licht. Es kann also jedes Papier gewählt werden, es sollte aber rot sein, oder rote Muster haben.

One sheet 15x15 cm paper for one light. You can choose any paper, but it should be red or with a red pattern.

Start. Diagramme von Seite 65 bis Nr.3 falten. Modell um 180 Grad drehen.

Fold charts of page 65 until step No.3. Turn model 180 degrees around.

1. Spitzen zur unteren Mitte falten, liegen lassen. Auf der Rückseite wiederholen.

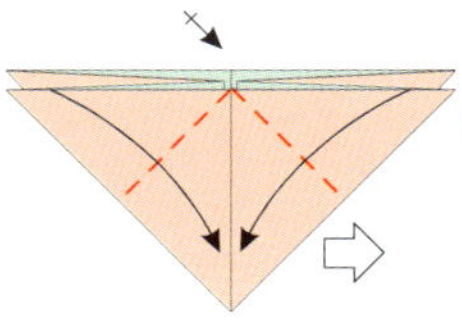

Fold points to the lower middle and leave. Repeat on the back.

2. Nur mit der oberen Papierlage, siehe Pfeile, senkrechte Linien falten, wieder öffnen. Auf der Rückseite wiederholen.

Using only the top layer of paper, see arrows, fold vertical lines and open up again. Repeat on the back.

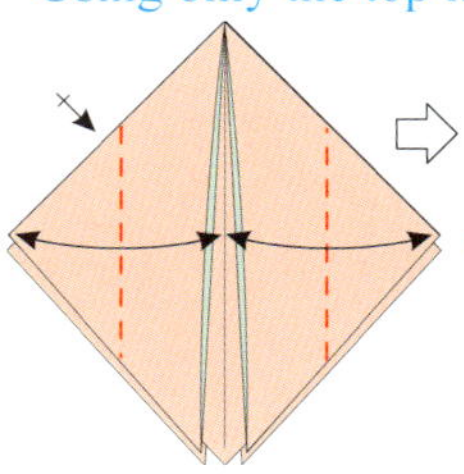

3. Nur mit der oberen Papierlage, siehe Pfeil, Spitze nach rechts oben legen.

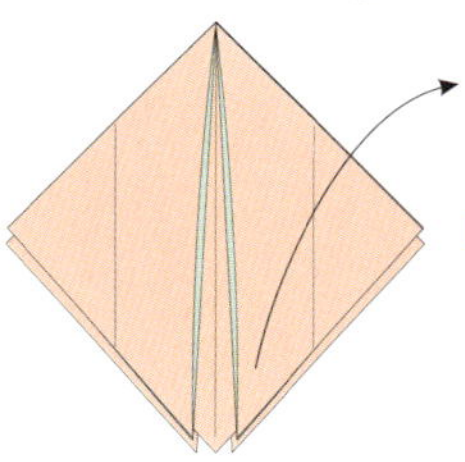

Using only the top layer of paper, see arrow, lay the point upwards to the right.

4. Nur mit der oberen Papierlage, siehe Pfeil, senkrechte Linie falten, liegen lassen.

Using only the top layer of paper, see arrow, fold vertical line and leave.

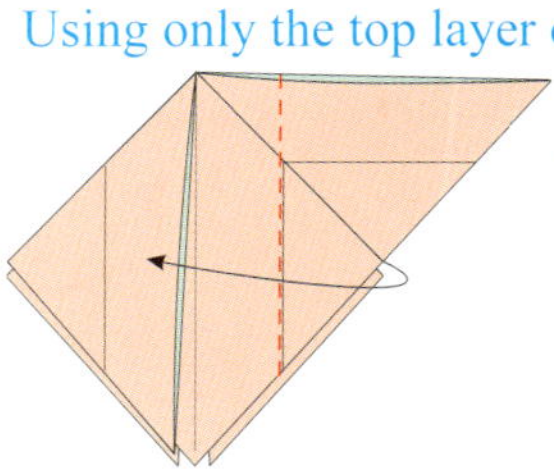

5. Ecke an die Linie falten, wieder öffnen.

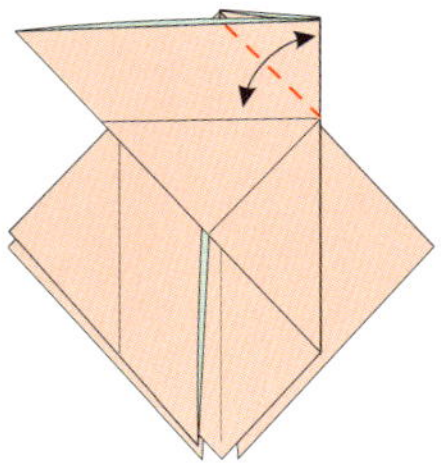

Fold corner to the line and open up again.

6. Schräge Linie zur Bergfalte formen, siehe Pfeil, Papierlage nach unten legen.

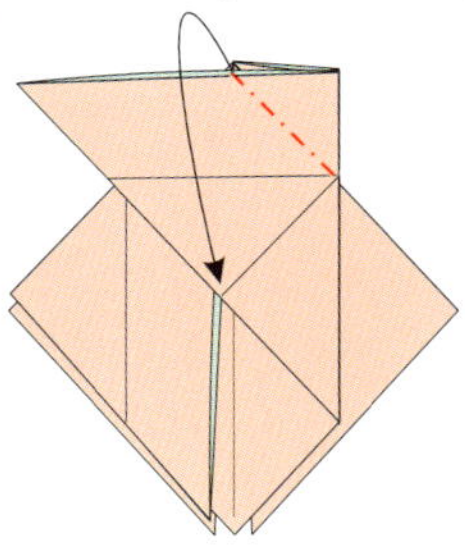

Form oblique line as a mountain-fold, see arrow and lay the layer of paper downwards.

7. Den entstandenen Papierstreifen nach rechts falten, liegen lassen.

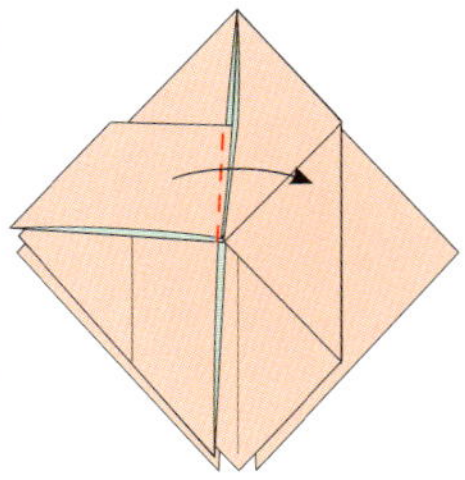

Fold the arised paper stripe to the right and leave.

8. Arbeitsschritte von Nr.3 bis Nr.7 an der linken Seite wiederholen.

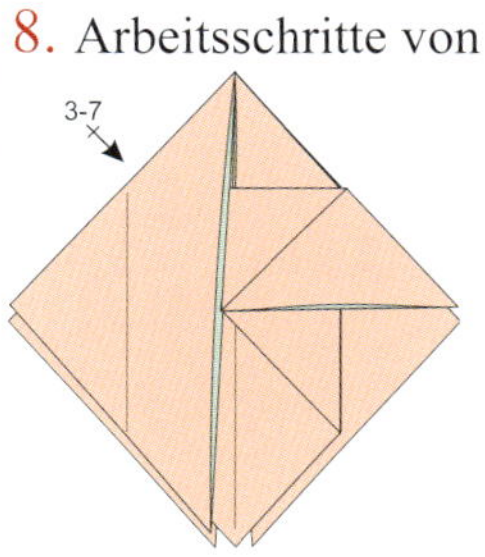

Repeat working steps from No.3 to No.7 on the left side.

9. Arbeitsschritte von Nr.3 bis Nr.7 an beiden Seiten der Rückseite wiederholen.

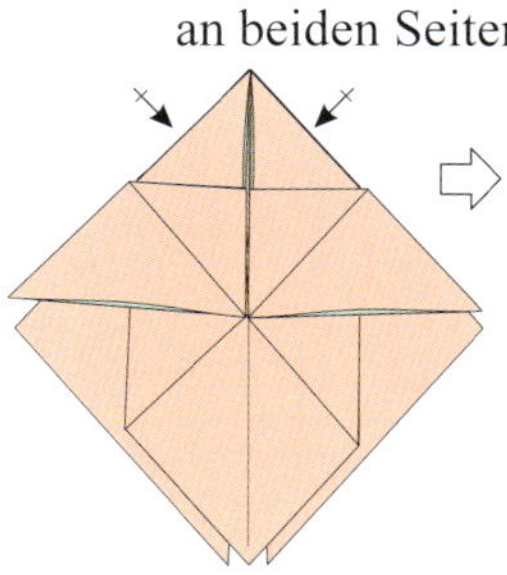

Repeat working steps from No.3 to No.7 both sides of the back.

10. Nur mit der oberen Papierlage, siehe Pfeile, Papierkanten zur senkrechten Mitte falten, liegen lassen. Achtung: Die Talfalte geht unter den seitlichen Flügeln weiter. Auf der Rückseite wiederholen.

Using only the top layer of paper, see arrows, fold edges to the vertical middle and leave. Attention: The valley-fold continues below the wings. Repeat on the back.

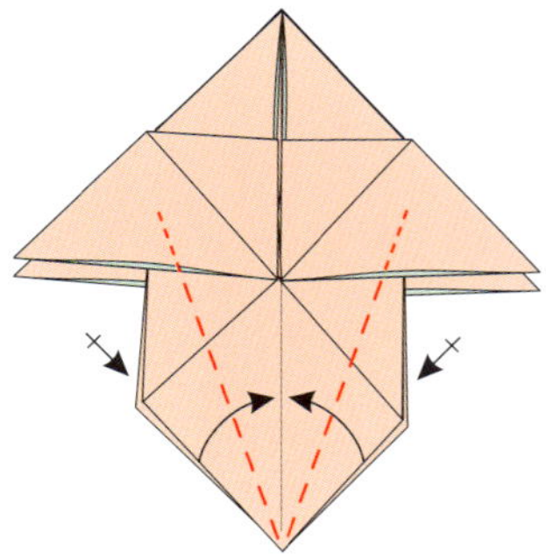

11. Obere Spitze etwas abschneiden. Jetzt kräftig hineinblasen, damit die 3D Form entsteht. Die Flügel der Vorderseite dabei von rechts und links zusammen drücken. Auf der Rückseite wiederholen.

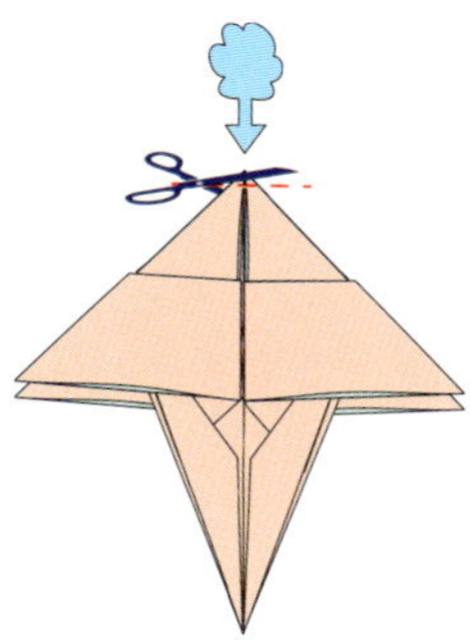

Cut off the upper point a little bit. Now strongly inflate, so that the 3D form arises. Also push in the wings of the front from the right and the left. Repeat on the back.

12. Fertiges Modell seitlich gesehen. Das Loch nach oben halten und über den Leuchtkörper schieben.

Finished model seen from the side. Hold the hole upwards and slide it over the light bulb.

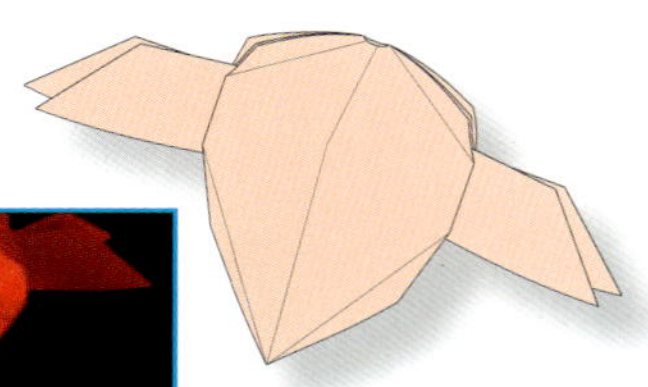

Lichtkugeln

MATERIAL

6 Bogen 5x5 cm Papier für 1 Licht. Bei dem fertigen Modell ist die Papierrückseite zu sehen. Es sollte also durchgefärbtes Papier gewählt werden.

Six sheets 5x5 cm paper for one light. From the finished model, you will see much of the back side of the paper. So you should choose paper with a coloured back.

1. Die sechs Arbeitspapiere in der gewünschten Größe zuschneiden. Die ersten vier Bogen, siehe Zeichnung, zusammen kleben. Keinen wasserhaltigen Kleber benutzen.

Cut paper, so that you get the six sheets. Glue the first four sheets together, see chart. Don't use water based glue.

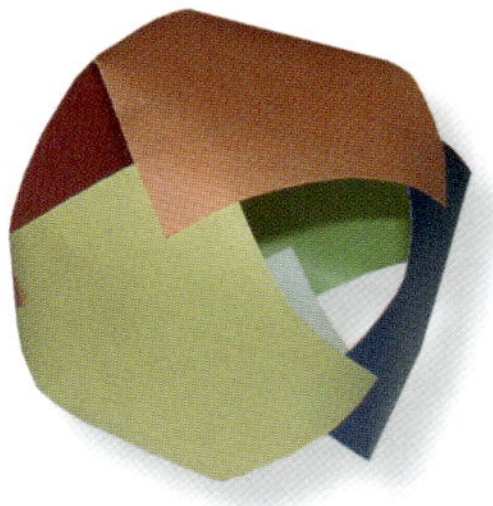

2. Die letzten zwei Bogen, siehe Zeichnung, auf das zweite Arbeitspapier kleben. Keinen wasserhaltigen Kleber benutzen.

The last two sheets, see chart, glue on the second sheet. Don't use water based glue.

4. Fertiges Modell seitlich gesehen. Eines der Löcher nach oben halten und über den Leuchtkörper schieben.

Finished model seen from the side. Hold the hole upwards and slide it over the light bulb.

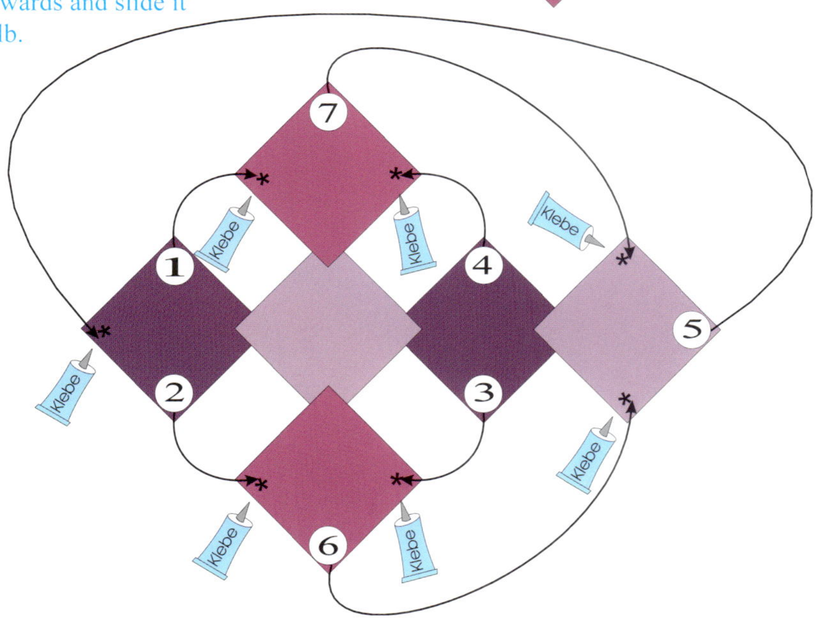

3. Nun alle Arbeitspapiere zu einer Kugel zusammen kleben, dabei unbedingt auf die Reihenfolge der Nummern achten. Keinen wasserhaltigen Kleber benutzen.

Now glue all sheets together as a ball. Please note the order of the numbers. Don't use water based glue.

Lilienkette

MATERIAL

1 Bogen 15x15 cm Papier für 1 Licht. Es kann jedes Papier gewählt werden.

One sheet 15x15 cm paper for one light. You can choose any design.

1. Zweimal waagerecht die Mitte falten, wieder öffnen. Rückseite nach oben legen.

Fold twice the horizontal middle and open up again. Turn over to the back.

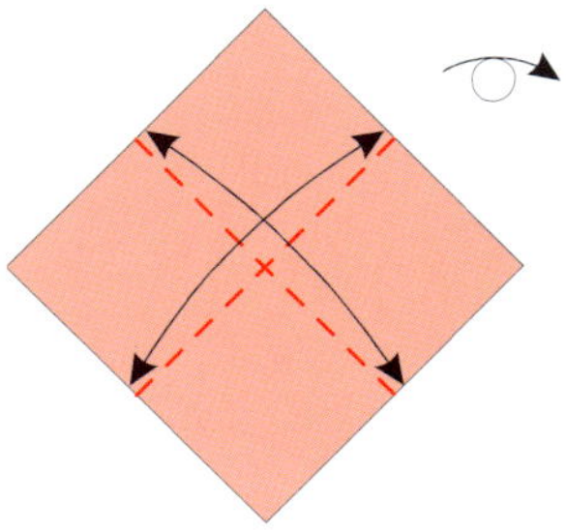

2. Zweimal diagonal die Mitte falten, wieder öffnen. Rückseite nach oben legen.

Fold twice the middle diagonally and open up again. Turn over to the back.

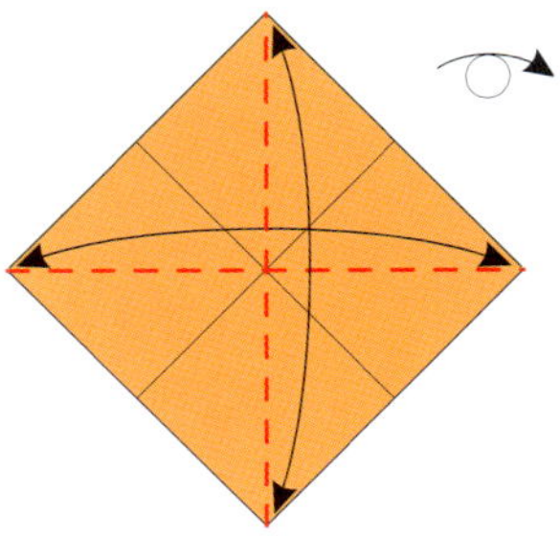

3. Von der waagerechten Mitte (Bergfalte), die seitlichen Ecken zur oberen Ecke legen. Die untere Ecke dann ebenfalls nach oben legen, siehe Pfeile.

From the horizontal middle (mountain-fold), lay the corners from the side to the upper corner. Also lay the lower corner to the upwards, see arrows.

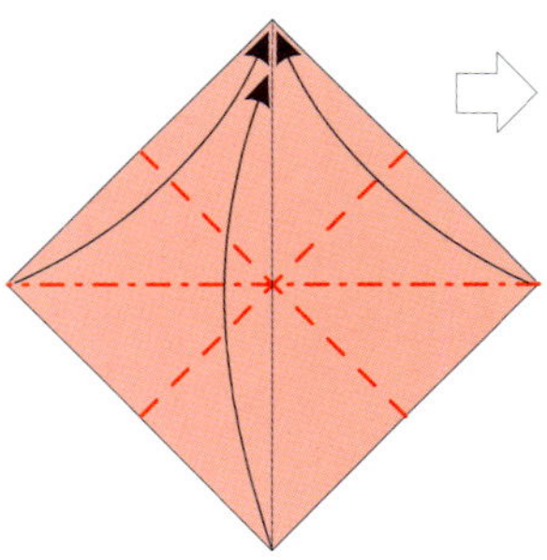

4. Bergfalte nach rechts falten, dabei die Ecke flach drücken.

Fold a mountain-fold to the right and push in the corner.

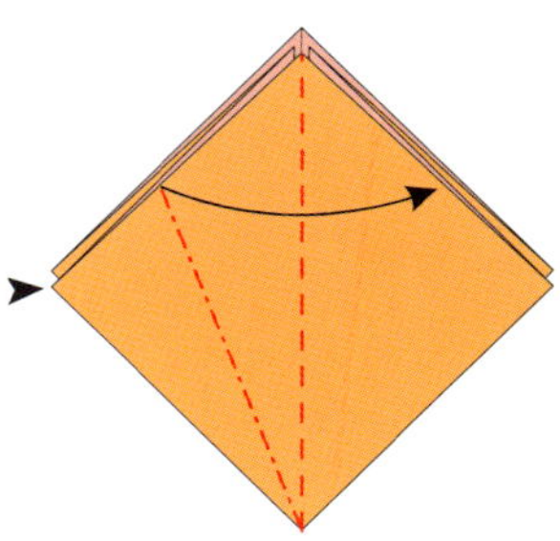

5. Mit den anderen drei Ecken den Arbeitsschritt Nr.4 wiederholen.

Repeat working step No.4 with the other three corners.

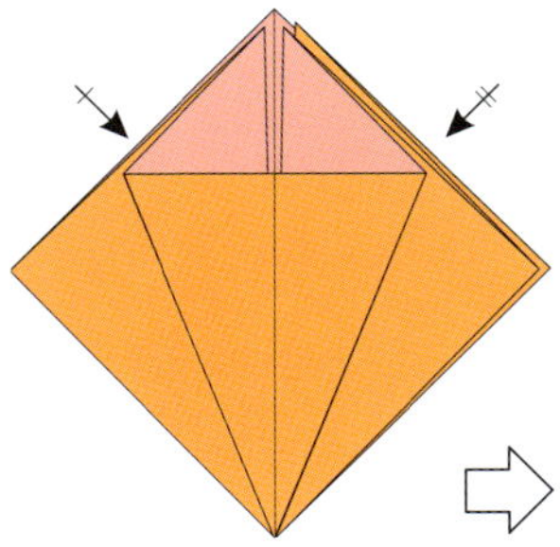

6. Nur mit der oberen Papierlage, schräge Linien zur Mitte falten, liegen lassen. Mit allen anderen Spitzen wiederholen.

Using only the top layer of paper, fold oblique lines to the middle and leave. Repeat with all other points.

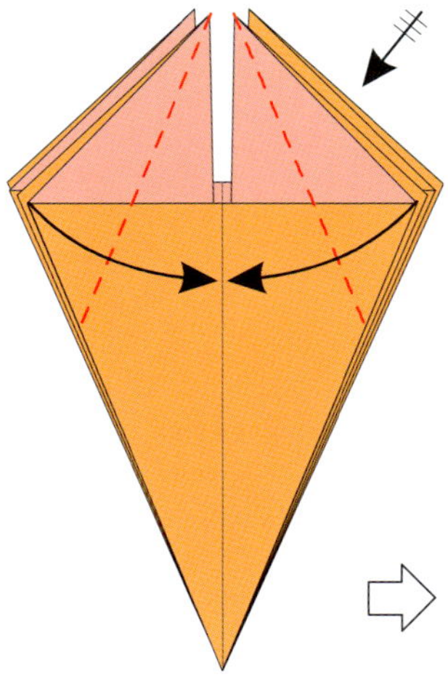

7. Untere Spitze nach oben falten, siehe Pfeil, wieder öffnen.

Fold lower point upwards, see arrow and open up again.

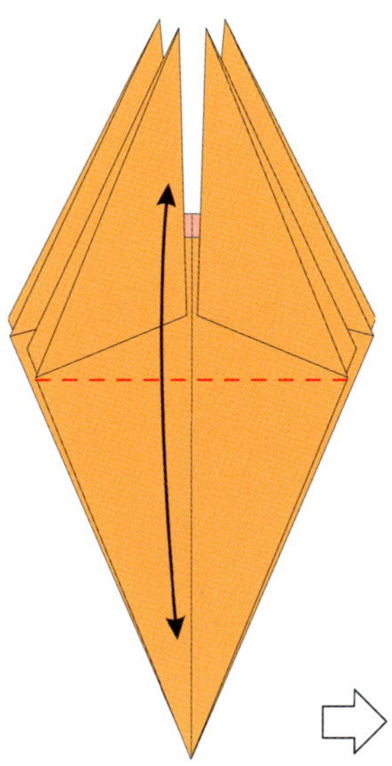

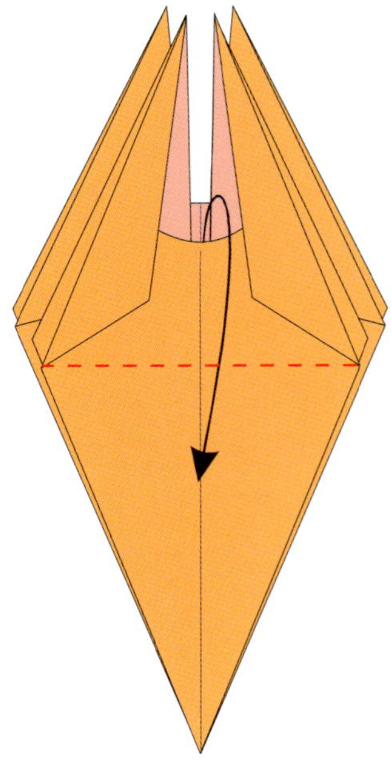

8. Nur mit der oberen Papierlage von der Mitte aus, an der waagerechten Linie, nach unten formen, siehe Pfeil. Es entsteht eine Spitze, siehe auch Diagramm Nr.9.

Using only the top layer of paper, form paper from the middle downwards along the horizontal line, see arrow. A point arises, see chart No.9.

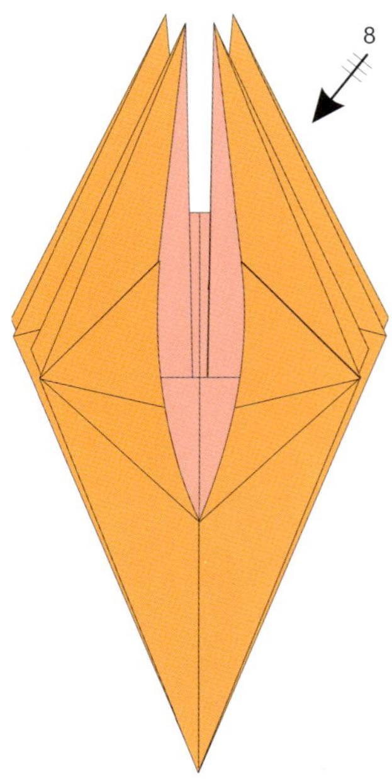

9. Arbeitsschritte von Nr.8 mit allen anderen Spitzen wiederholen.

Repeat working step No.8 with all other points.

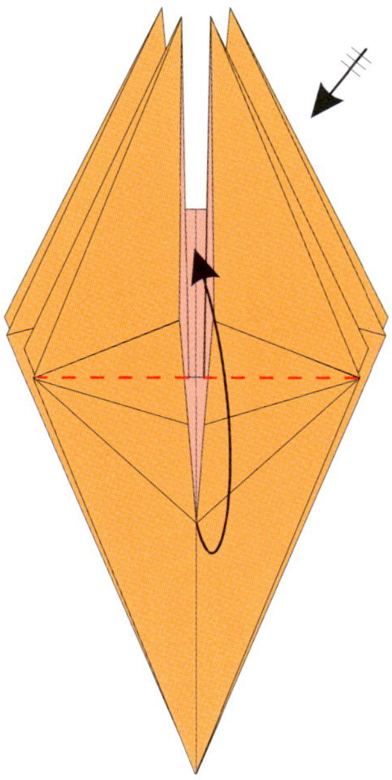

10. Die neu entstandene Spitze nach oben falten, liegen lassen. Mit allen anderen Spitzen wiederholen.
Fold the new point upwards and leave. Repeat with all other points.

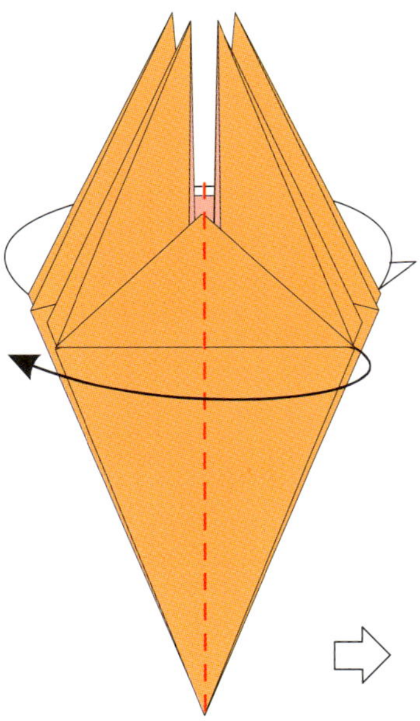

11. Nur mit der oberen Papierlage von rechts nach links falten, liegen lassen. Auf der Rückseite wiederholen.
Using only the top layer of paper, fold from right to the left and leave. Repeat on the back.

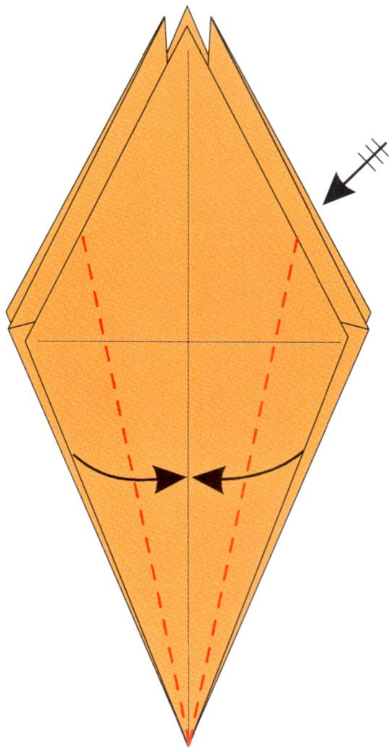

12. Nur mit der oberen Papierlage schräge Linien zur Mitte falten, liegen lassen. Mit den anderen drei Papierlagen wiederholen.
Using only the top layer of paper, fold oblique lines to the middle and leave. Repeat with the other three layers of paper.

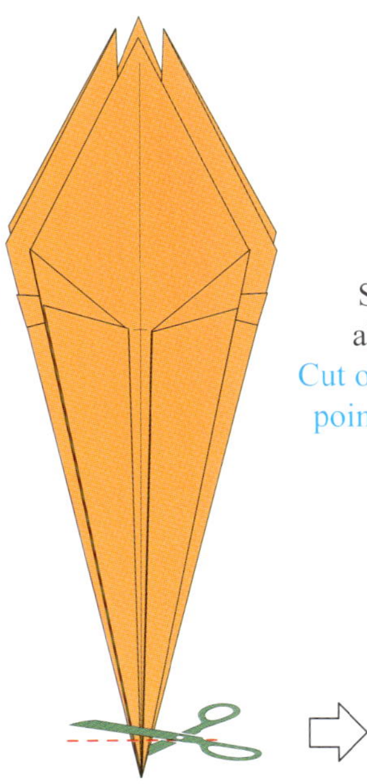

13. Untere Spitze etwas abschneiden.
Cut off the lower point a little bit.

14. Alle vier Spitzen über ein Falzbein rollen, dadurch wird das Papier rund und die Blütenform entsteht. Modell von unten etwas auseinander drücken.
Roll all four points over a bonefolder, so that the paper becomes round and the petal form arises. Push the model from the bottom outwards.

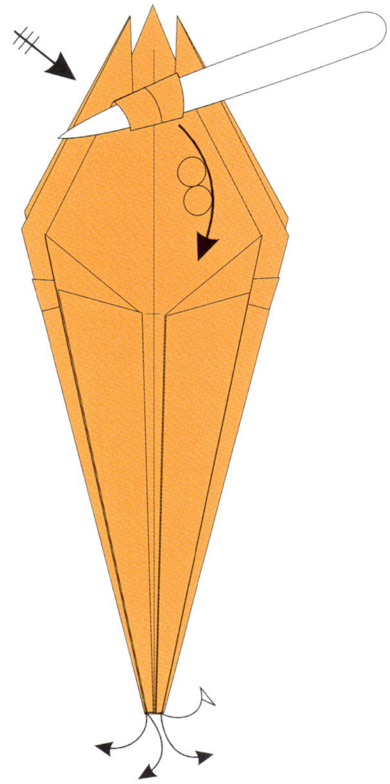

15. Fertiges Modell seitlich gesehen. Das Loch nach oben halten und über den Leuchtkörper schieben.
Finished model seen from the side. Hold the hole upwards and slide it over the light bulb.

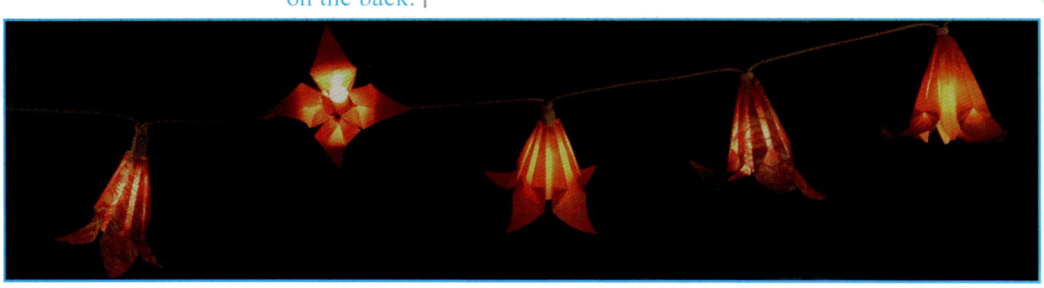

Leuchtfrösche

MATERIAL

1 Bogen 15x15 cm Papier für 1 Licht. Es kann jedes Papier ausgewählt werden, aber grün sollte es sein.

One sheet 15x15 cm paper for one light. You can choose any paper, but it should be green.

Start. Diagramme von Seite 68 bis Nr.9 falten.

Fold charts of page 68 until step No.9.

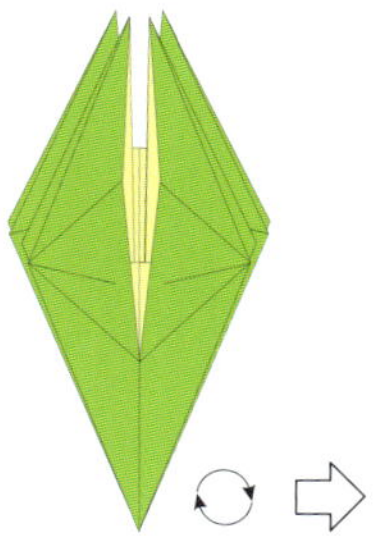

1. Modell um 180 Grad drehen.

Turn model 180 degrees around.

2. Nur mit der oberen Papierlage von rechts nach links falten, liegen lassen. Auf der Rückseite wiederholen.

Using only the top layer of paper, fold from right to the left and leave. Repeat on the back.

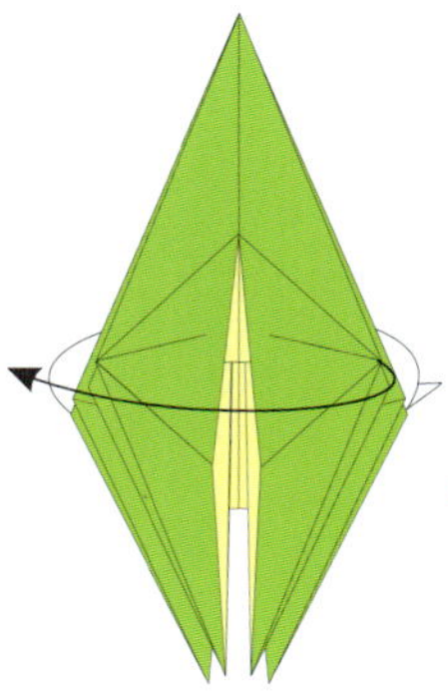

3. Nur mit der oberen Papierlage schräge Linien zur Mitte falten, liegen lassen. Mit den anderen drei Papierlagen wiederholen.

Using only the top layer of paper, fold oblique lines to the middle and leave. Repeat with the other three layers of paper.

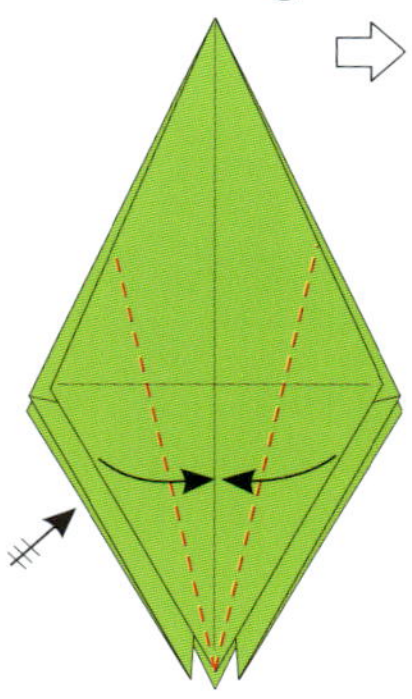

4. Nur mit der oberen Papierlage von rechts nach links falten, liegen lassen. Auf der Rückseite wiederholen.

Using only the top layer of paper, fold from right to the left and leave. Repeat on the back.

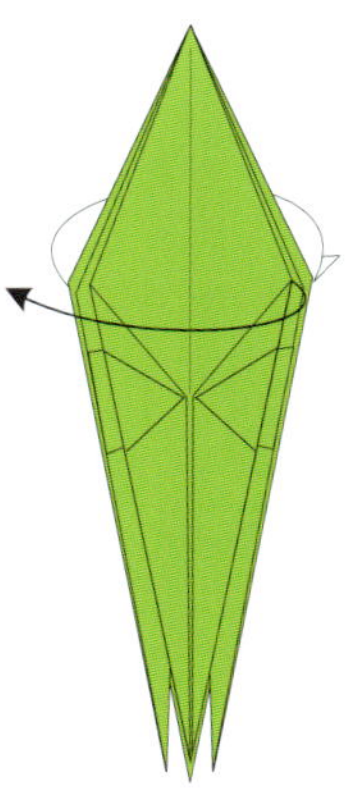

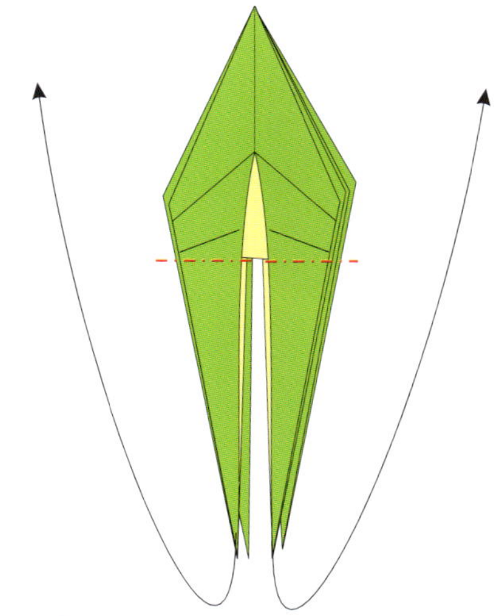

5. An den beiden vorderen Spitzen, waagerechte Bergfalte arbeiten und die Spitzen dann nach innen, soweit wie möglich nach oben legen, siehe auch Diagramm Nr.6.

Form a mountain-fold on the two upper points and lay them to the top and inwards, see also chart No.6.

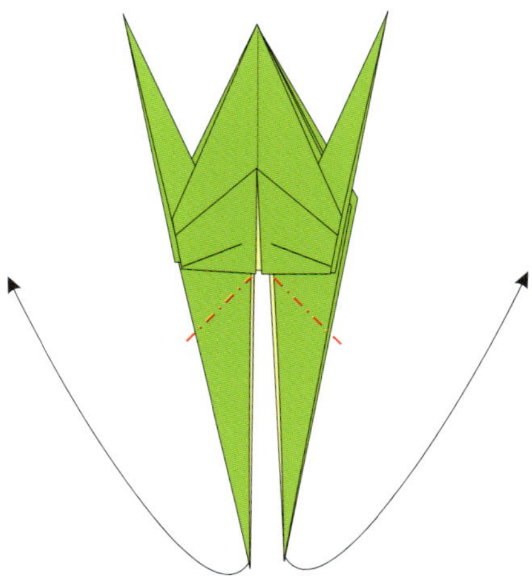

6. An den beiden hinteren Spitzen, schräge Bergfalte arbeiten und die Spitzen dann nach innen, soweit wie möglich seitlich legen, siehe auch Diagramm Nr.7.

Form a oblique mountain-fold on the two lower points and lay them inwards and to the side, see also chart No.7.

7. An allen vier Spitzen schräg nach hinten falten.

Fold all four points slanting to the back.

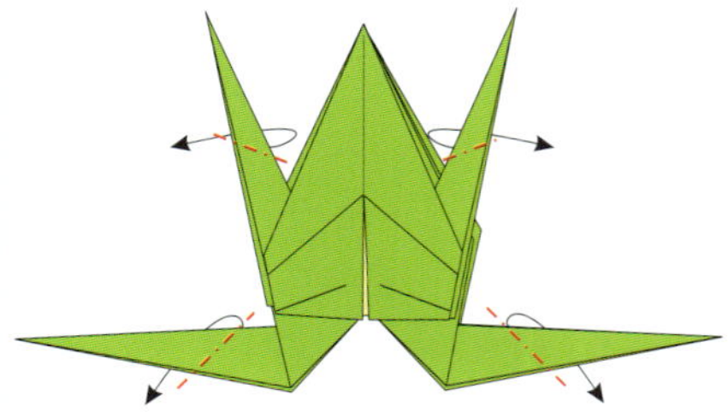

8. Nochmals alle vier Spitzen schräg nach oben falten.

Again fold all four points slanting upwards.

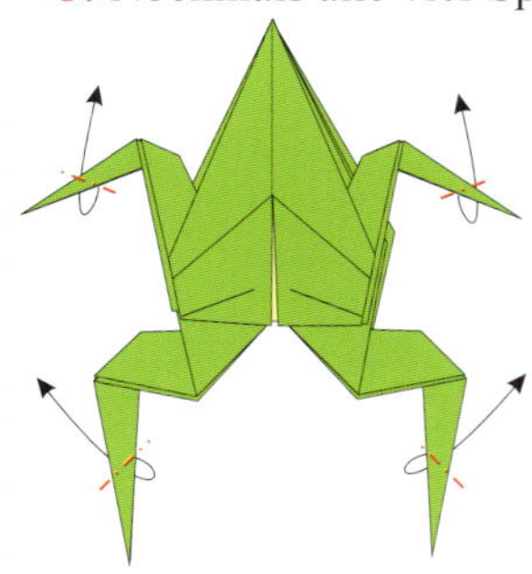

9. Das untere Loch etwas vergrößern. Jetzt kräftig hineinblasen, damit die 3D Form entsteht.

Expand the lower hole a little bit. Now strongly inflate, so that the 3D form arises.

10. Fertiges Modell seitlich gesehen. Das Loch nach oben halten und über den Leuchtkörper schieben.

Finished model seen from the side. Hold the hole upwards and slide it over the light bulb.

Oktoberfest-Lichterkette

MATERIAL

1 Bogen 15x15 cm Papier für 2 Lichter. Papier muss mit bayerischen Motiven bedruckt sein.

One sheet 15x15 cm paper for two lights. The paper has to have Bavarian patterns.

1. Papier an der diagonalen Linie durchschneiden.
Cut paper along the diagonal line.

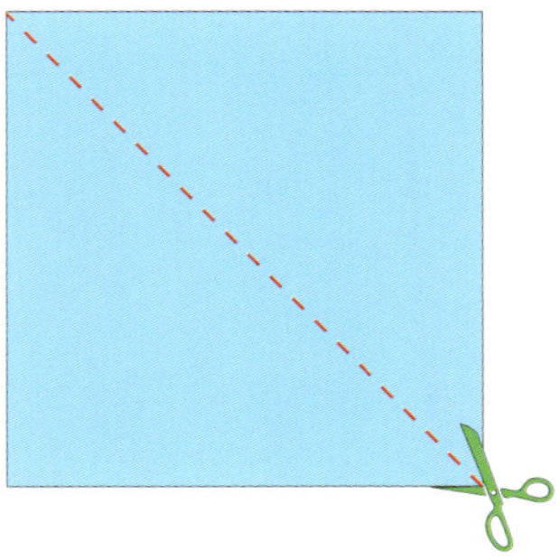

2. Mit nur einer Papierhälfte, diagonale Linie falten, liegen lassen.
Using only one half of paper, fold the diagonal line and leave.

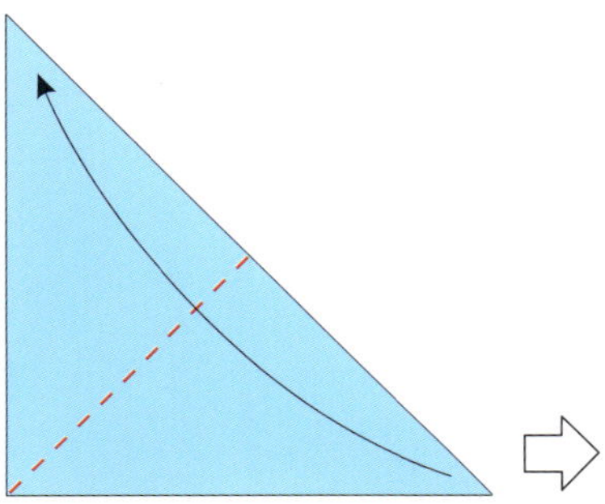

3. An der rechten Spitze das Papier in einem runden Bogen abschneiden.
Cut off the paper on the right point in a round curve.

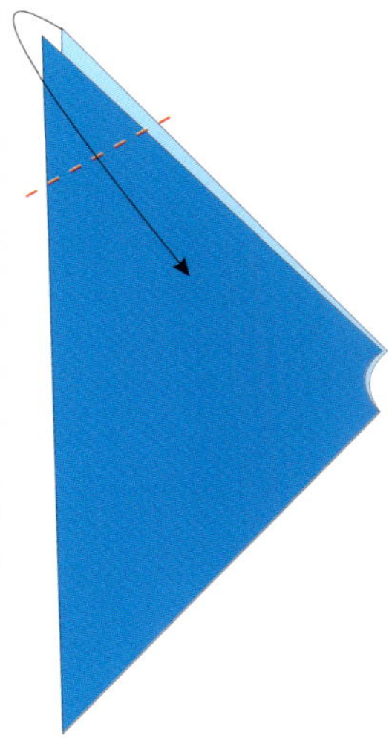

4. An der oberen Spitze schräge Linie nach unten falten.
Fold oblique line on the upper point downwards.

5. Modell nach beiden Seiten öffnen.
Open model to both sides.

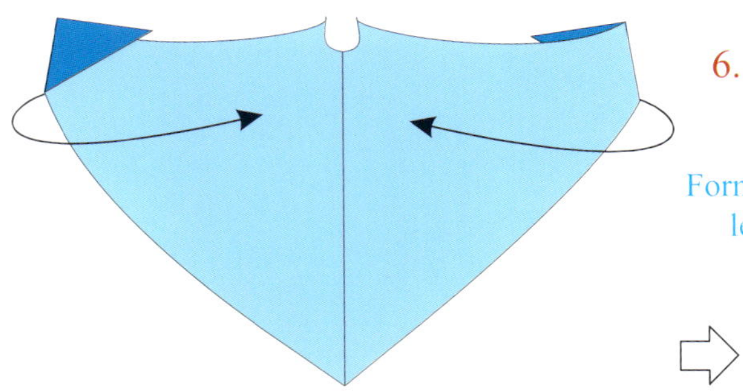

6. Papier von rechts und links zur Mitte in eine Rundung bringen.
Form paper from right and left to the middle into a curve.

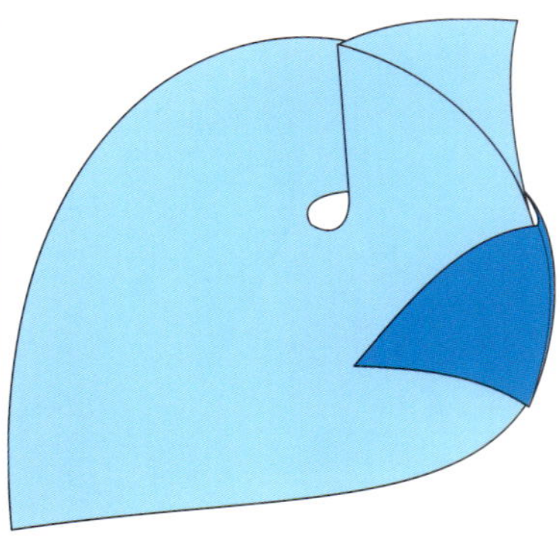

7. Ecken an den Knicken einmal nach innen und einmal nach außen legen, dadurch bekommt die Tüte den Halt. Es kann auch noch geklebt werden, keinen wasserhaltigen Kleber benutzen.
Lay corners along the folds once inwards and once outwards, so that the model gets hold. You can glue it, as well. Don't use water based glue.

8. Fertiges Modell seitlich gesehen. Das Loch nach oben halten und über den Leuchtkörper schieben.
Finished model seen from the side. Hold the hole upwards and slide it over the light bulb.

Sonnenlichtkette

MATERIAL

2 Bogen 15x30 cm Papier für 1 Licht. Bei dem fertigen Modell ist die Papierrückseite zu sehen. Es sollte also durchgefärbtes Papier gewählt werden.

Two sheets 15x30 cm paper for one light. From the finished model, you will see the back side of the paper. So you should choose paper with a coloured back.

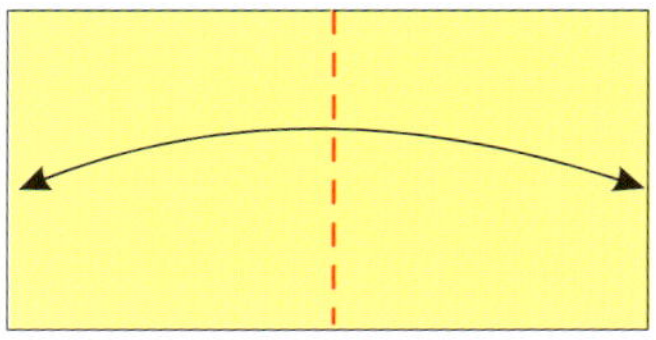

1. Senkrechte Mitte falten, wieder öffnen.

Fold the vertical middle and open up again.

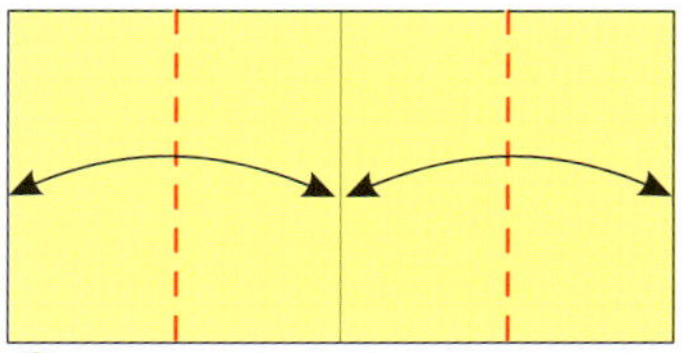

2. Senkrechte Linien zur Mitte falten, wieder öffnen.

Fold the vertical lines to the middle and open up again.

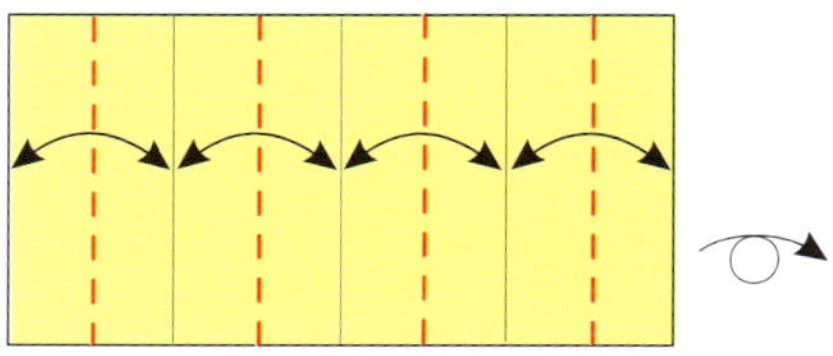

3. In allen vier Teilen jeweils die Mitte falten, wieder öffnen. Rückseite nach oben legen.

Fold on all four parts the middle and open up again. Turn over to the back.

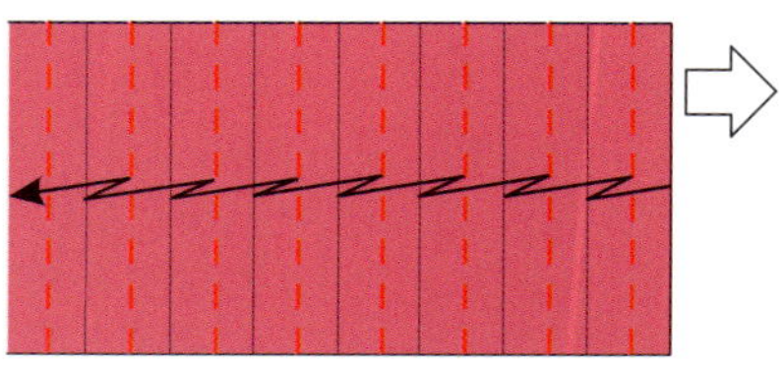

4. In allen acht Teilen wieder jeweils die Mitte falten, liegen lassen. Dadurch ist jetzt die Zickzackfaltung entstanden.

Fold on all eight parts the middle and leave. Now you got the zigzag fold.

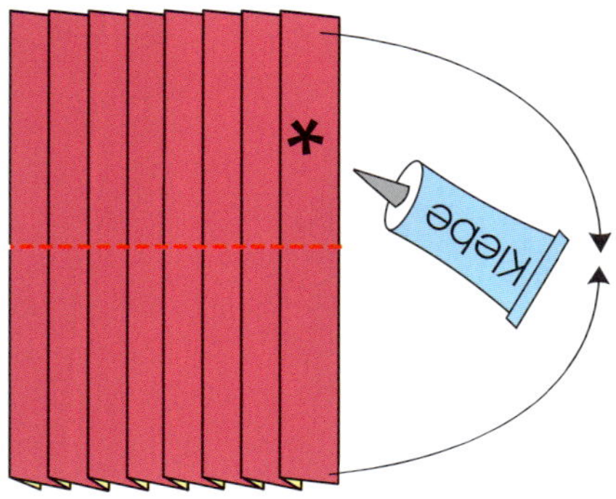

5. Waagerechte Mitte falten, wieder öffnen. Obere Hälfte an die untere Hälfte kleben, siehe Pfeile, damit ein Rundbogen entsteht. Keinen wasserhaltigen Kleber benutzen.

Fold the horizontal middle and open up again. Glue the upper on the lower part, see arrow, so that an arch arises. Do not use water based glue.

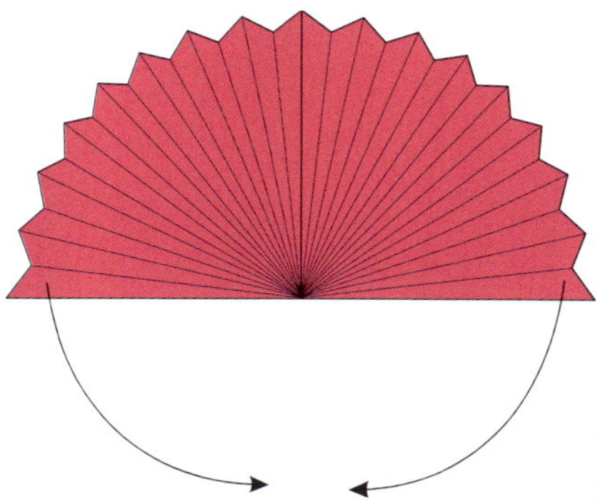

6. Wenn der Kleber getrocknet ist, von rechts und links zur unteren Mitte biegen.

After the glue did dry, bend from the right and the left to the lower middle.

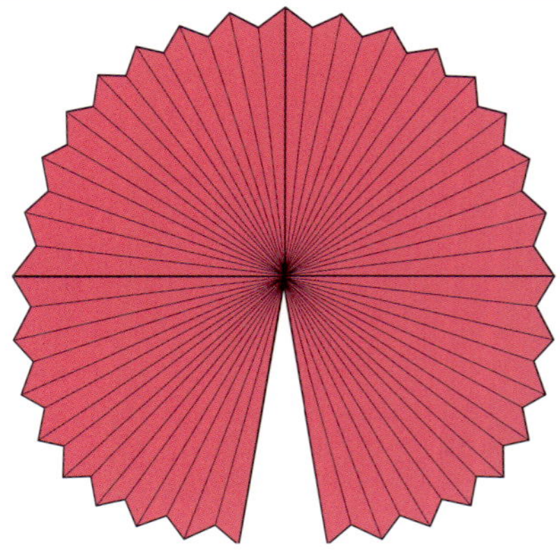

7. So muss das Modell jetzt aussehen. Es werden zwei gleiche Teile benötigt.

Now the model has to look like this. A second equal model is needed.

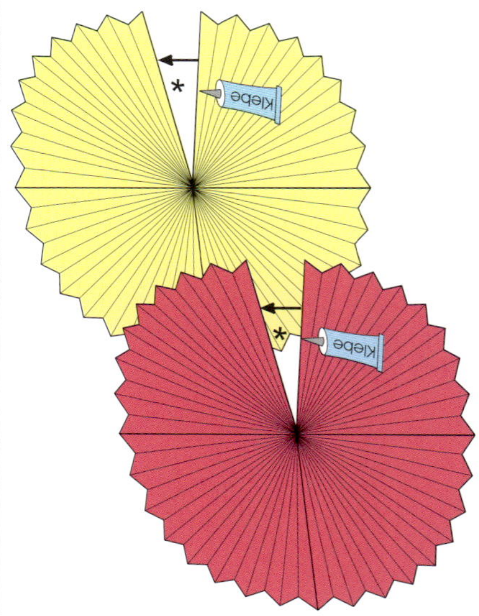

8. Erstes Modell vor einem Leuchtkörper. Öffnung nach oben über das Kabel schieben, Papierlagen zusammenkleben. Zweites Modell hinter einem Leuchtkörper. Öffnung nach oben über das Kabel schieben, Papierlagen zusammenkleben.

First model in front of a light bulb. Slide opening upwards over the wire and glue the layers of paper together. Second model behind a light bulb. Slide opening upwards over the wire and glue the layers of paper together.

Kette mit Friedenstauben

MATERIAL

1 Bogen 15x15 cm Papier für 1 Licht. Es wurde weißes Kristall-Papier mit Prägung ausgewählt.

One sheet 15x15 cm paper for one light. We used embossed crystal paper.

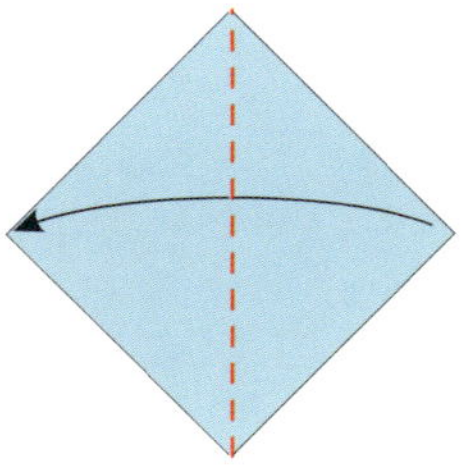

1. Diagonal die Mitte falten, liegen lassen.
Fold the middle diagonally and leave.

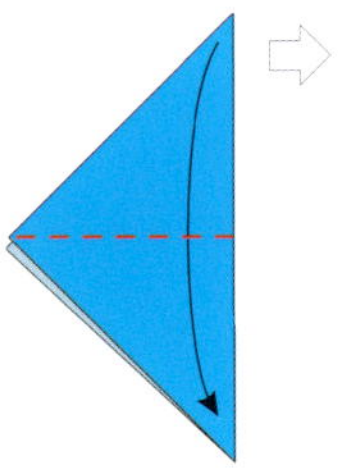

2. Von oben nach unten waagerechte Linie falten, liegen lassen.
Fold the horizontal line from top to bottom and leave.

3. Nur mit der oberen Papierlage, schräge Linien nach oben falten, liegen lassen. Auf der Rückseite wiederholen.

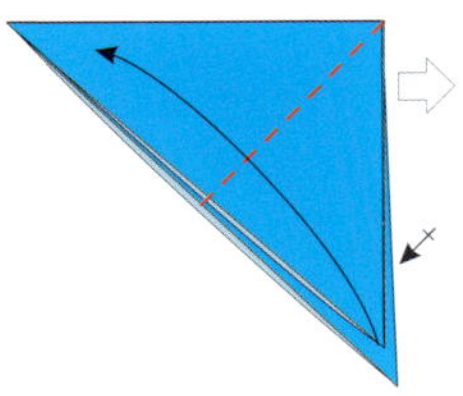

Using only the top layer of paper, fold oblique line upwards and leave. Repeat on the back.

4. Nur mit der oberen Papierlage, Spitze nach oben falten, wieder öffnen.

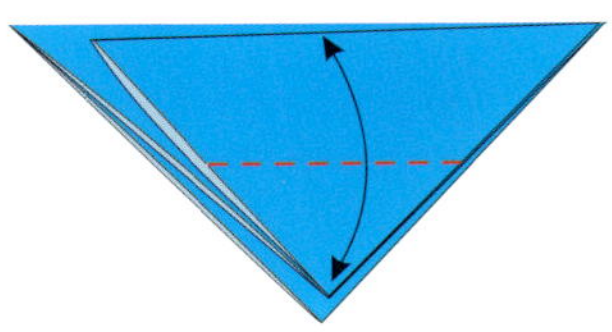

Using only the top layer of paper, fold point upwards and open up again.

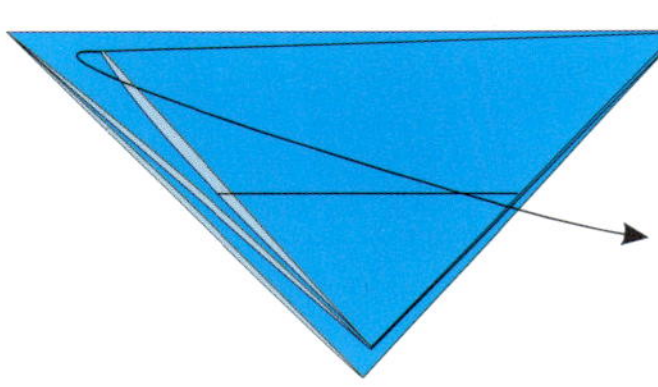

5. Nur mit der oberen Papierlage, linke Spitze nach rechts legen.
Using only the top layer of paper, lay the left point to the right.

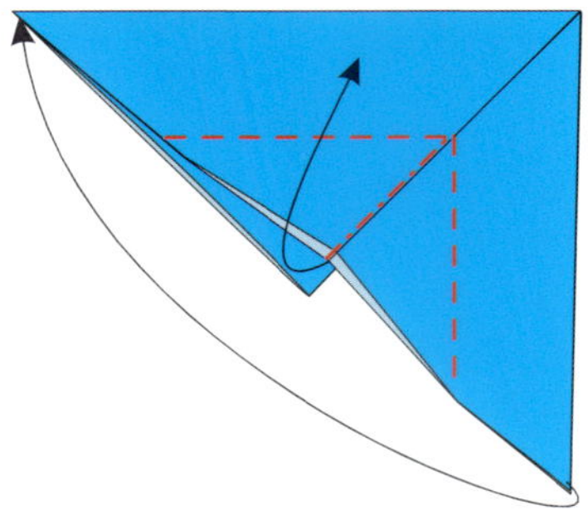

6. Nur mit der oberen Papierlage, rechte untere Spitze nach links oben legen, dabei schräge Linie in der Mitte zur Bergfalte formen, und auch nach oben legen.
Using only the top layer of paper, lay right lower point to the upper left, at the same time form oblique line in the middle as a mountain-fold and lay it upwards, as well.

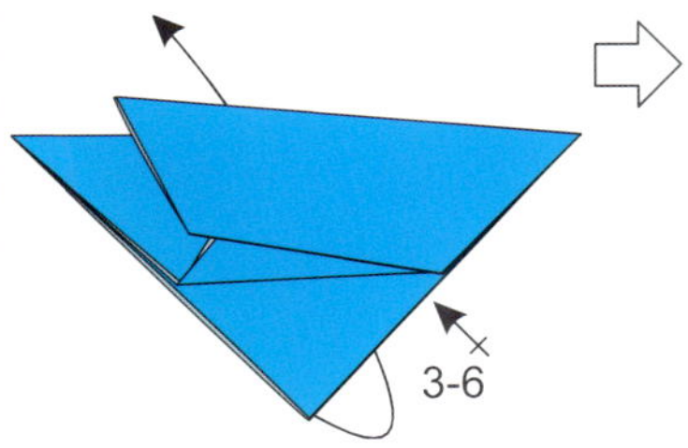

7. Arbeitsschritte Nr.3 bis Nr.6 auf der Rückseite wiederholen.
Repeat working steps from No.3 to No.6 on the back.

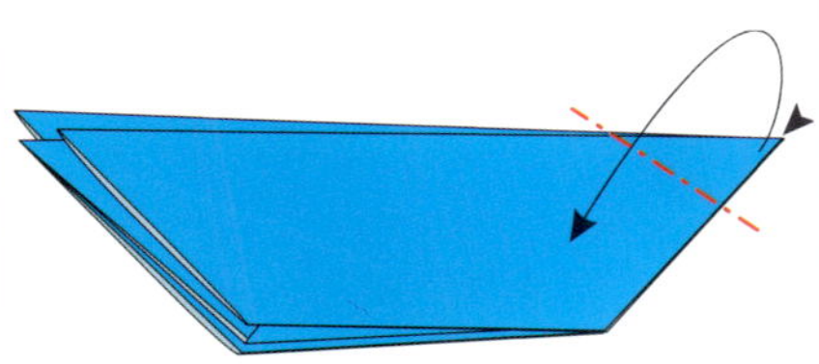

8. Für den Schnabel, siehe Pfeil, eine schräge Linie falten und dann die Spitze nach innen versenken.
For the beak, see arrow, fold a oblique line and push the point inwards.

9. Nur mit der oberen Papierlage von links nach rechts oben schräge Linie falten, liegen lassen. Auf der Rückseite wiederholen.
Using only the top layer of paper, fold oblique line from the left to the right and leave. Repeat on the back.

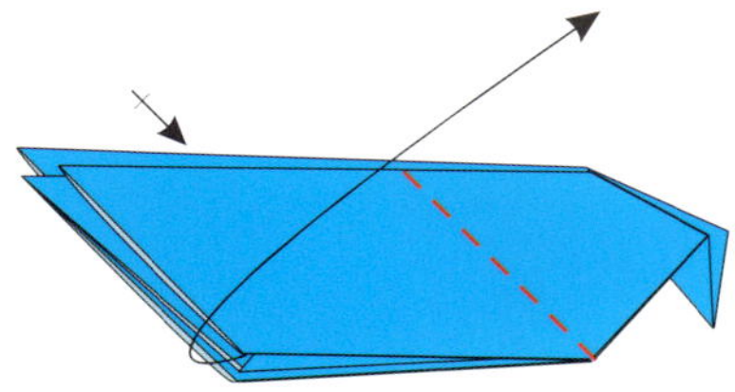

10. Spitze nach unten falten, wieder öffnen.
Fold point downwards and open up again.

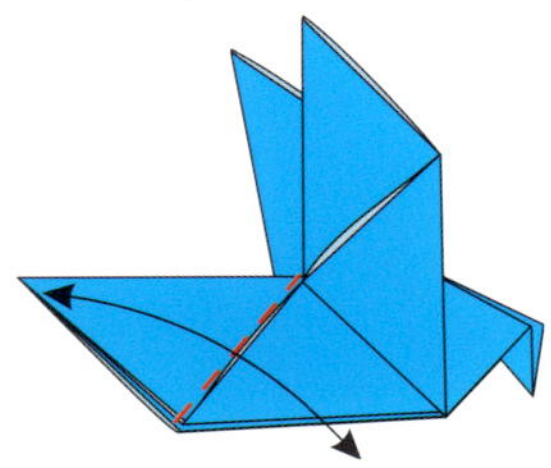

11. Schräge Linie an die neue Linie falten, wieder öffnen.
Fold oblique line to the new line and open up again.

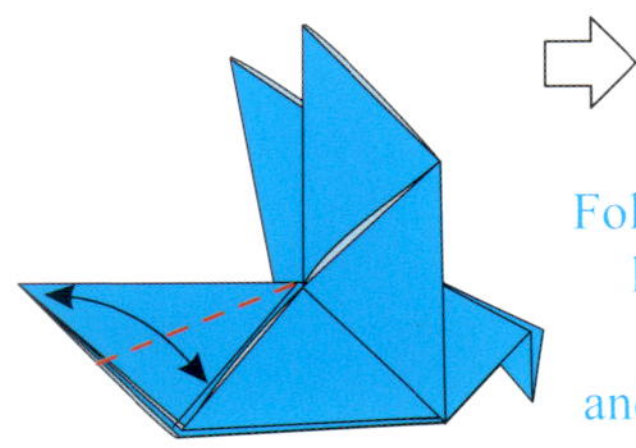

12. Linie von Nr.11 zur Bergfalte formen und nach unten legen, dabei in der Mitte eindrücken.
Form line from No.11 as a mountain-fold and lay it downwards, at the same time push in the middle.

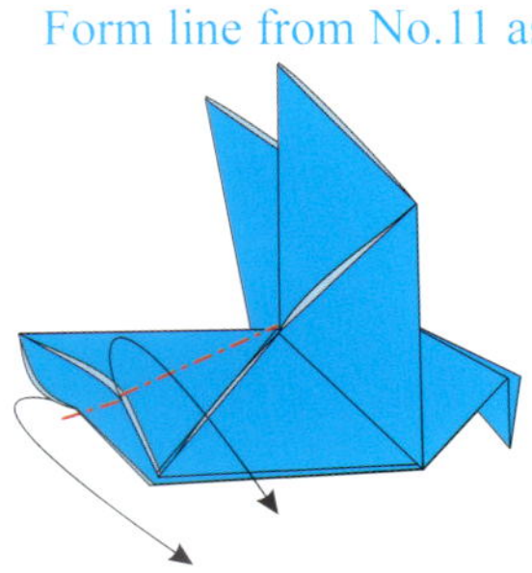

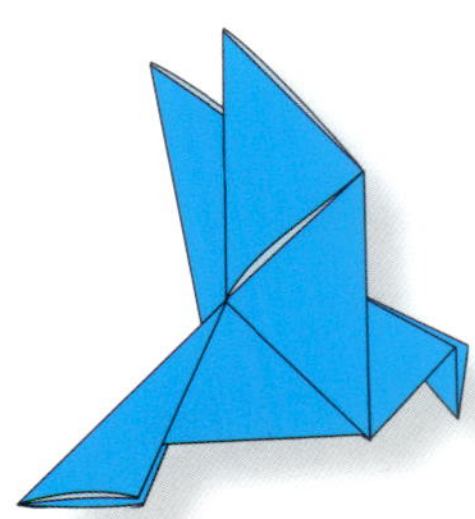

13. Fertiges Modell seitlich gesehen. Den Leuchtkörper in die obere Mitte schieben.
Finished model seen from the side. Slide the light bulb into the upper middle.

Lichterengelkette

Modell von Jannie van Schuylenburg

MATERIAL

1 Bogen 15x15 cm Papier für 1 Licht. Es kann jedes Papier ausgewählt werden.

One sheet 15x15 cm paper for one light. You can choose any design.

Start. Diagramme von Seite 68 bis Nr.3 falten. Modell um 180 Grad drehen.

Fold charts of page 68 until step No.3. Turn model 180 degrees around.

1. Bergfalte nach rechts falten, dabei die Ecke flach drücken.

Fold mountain-fold to the right and push the corner flat.

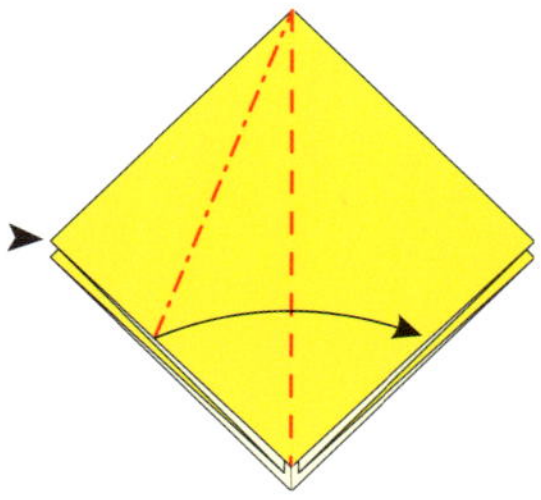

2. Rückseite nach oben legen.

Turn over to the back.

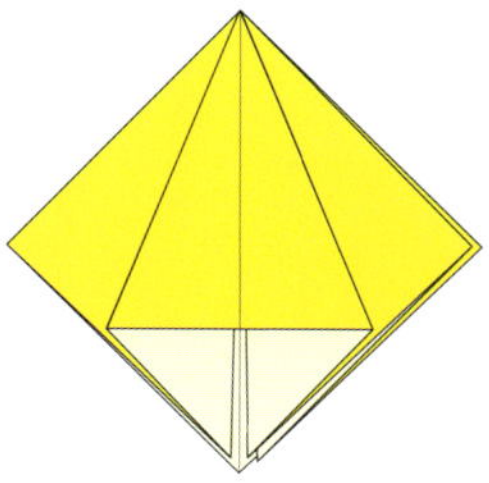

3. Schräge Linien an die Mitte falten, wieder öffnen. An der linken Seite der Rückseite wiederholen.

Fold oblique lines to the middle and open up again. Repeat on the left side of the back.

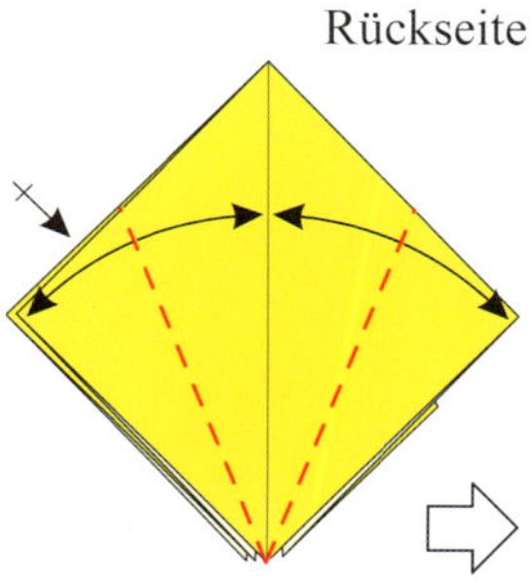

4. Bergfalten formen und nach innen legen, dabei die Ecke flach drücken. An der linken Seite der Rückseite wiederholen.

Form a mountain-fold and lay it inwards. At the same time push the corner flat. Repeat on the left side of the back.

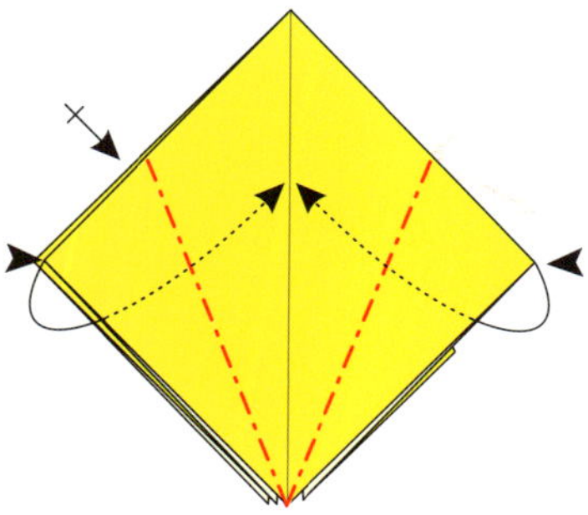

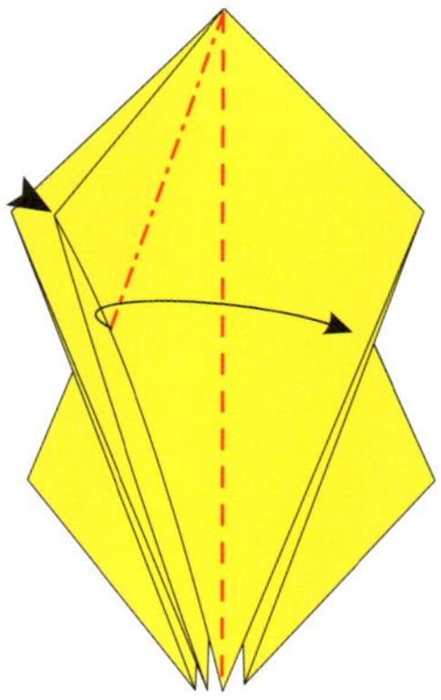

5. Nur mit der oberen Papierlage, schräge Linie nach rechts falten, dabei die Ecke flach drücken. Achtung: Langsam arbeiten, damit das Papier nicht einreißt.

Using only the top layer of paper, fold oblique line to the right and push the corner flat. Attention: Work slowly, so that the paper doesn't tear.

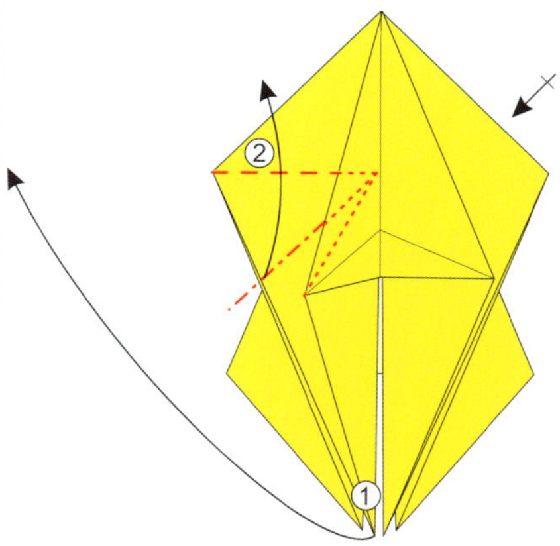

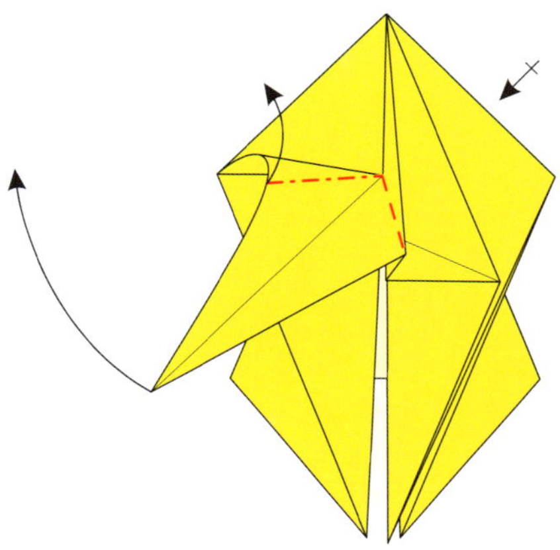

6. + 7. Linke untere Spitze Nr.1 öffnen, zur linken Seite drehen und so weit wie möglich nach oben schieben. Die eingezeichnete Berg- und Talfalte Nr.2 bilden sich dann automatisch. Achtung: Langsam arbeiten, damit das Papier nicht einreißt. Diesen Arbeitsgang dann auch auf der rechten Seite wiederholen.

Open lower left point No.1, turn it to the left and slide it upwards as far as possible. The mountain and valley fold No.2 arises automatically. Attention: Work slowly, so that the paper doesn't tear. Repeat this working step on the right side.

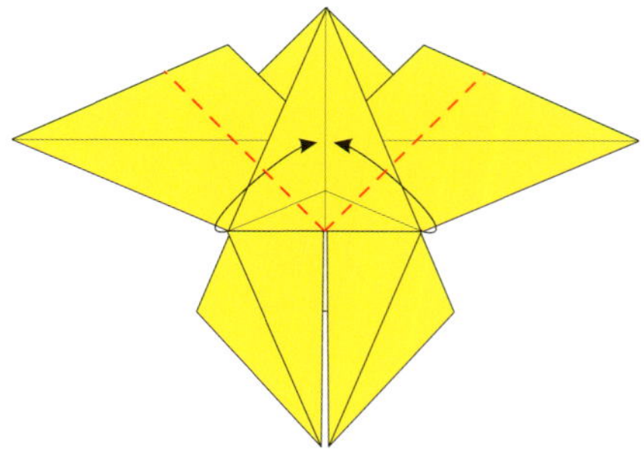

8. Nur mit der oberen Papierlage von der Ecke aus, schräge Linien falten, siehe Pfeil.

Using only the top layer of paper, starting from the corner, fold oblique lines, see arrow.

9. An der mittleren Spitze eine Bergfalte arbeiten und nach innen schieben. Die obere Spitze nach unten falten, liegen lassen.

Form a mountain-fold on the middle point and slide it inwards. Fold the upper point downwards and leave.

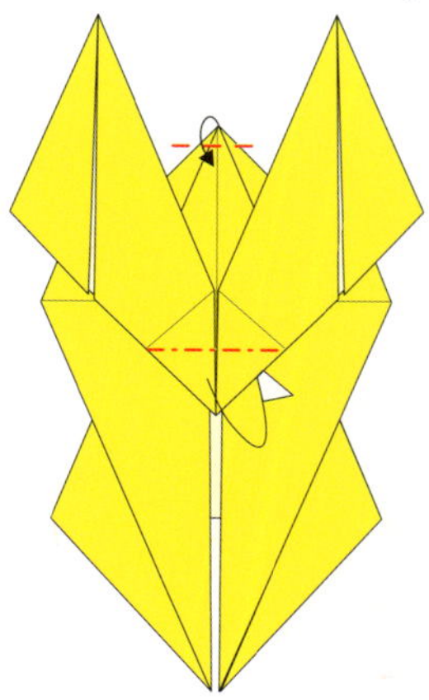

10. An der linken Seite, nur mit der oberen Papierlage so weit wie möglich öffnen. Achtung: Es entsteht eine Papierfalte, siehe auch roter Kreis im Diagramm Nr.11.

On the left side, using only the top layer of paper, open as wide as possible. Attention: A paper fold arises, see also red circle in chart No.11.

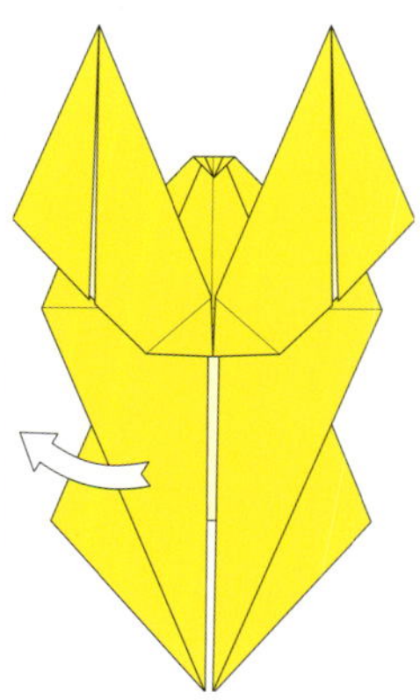

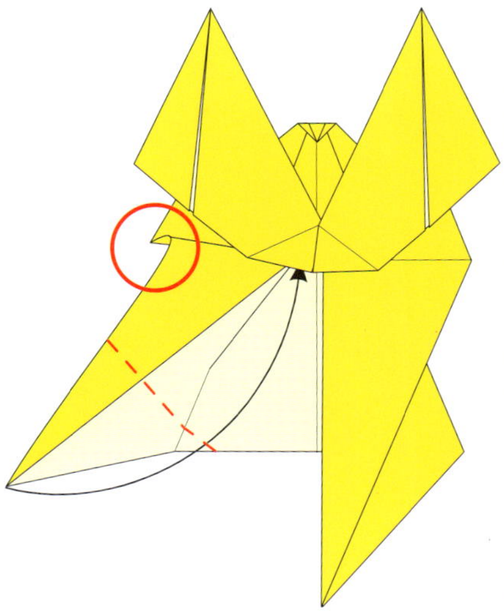

11. Spitze zur Mitte legen, dabei die schräge Linie falten. Die Papierfalte, siehe Kreis, bleibt.
Lay point to the middle and fold the oblique line. The paper fold, see circle, remains.

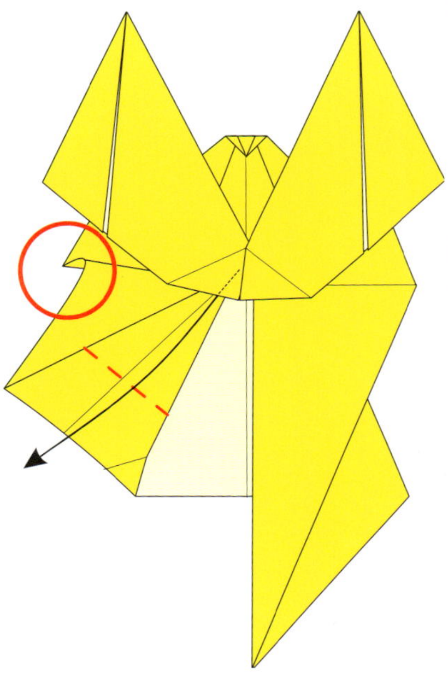

12. Spitze an der schrägen Linie wieder nach unten falten, liegen lassen.
Fold point along the oblique line downwards and leave.

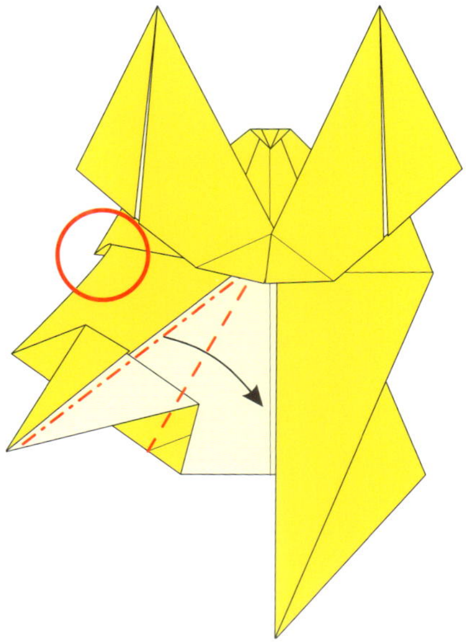

13. Siehe Pfeil, Bergfaltenlinie zur Mitte legen, falten und liegen lassen. Die Papierfalte im Kreis löst sich dadurch auf.
See arrow, lay line of the mountain-fold to the middle, fold and leave. The paper fold in the circle disappears.

14. Arbeitsschritte Nr.10 bis Nr.13 an der rechten Seite wiederholen.
Repeat working steps from No.10 to No.13 on the right side.

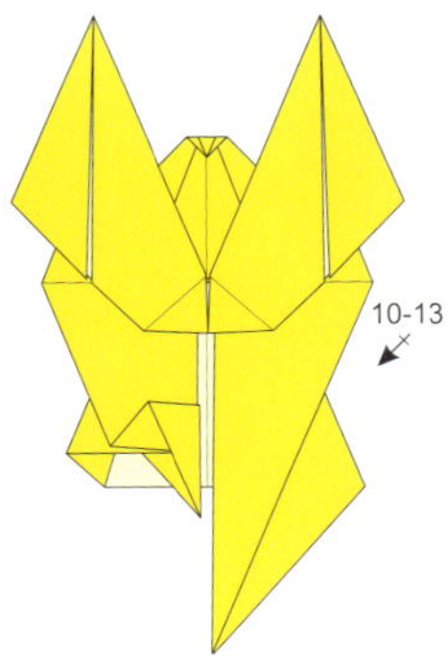

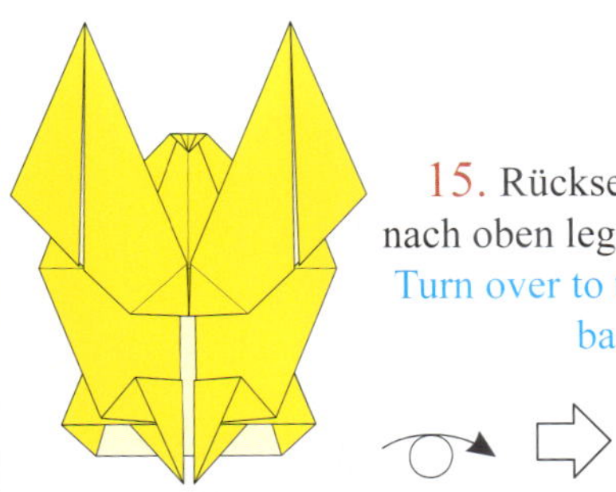

15. Rückseite nach oben legen.
Turn over to the back.

16. Schräge Linien falten, liegen lassen.
Fold oblique lines and leave.

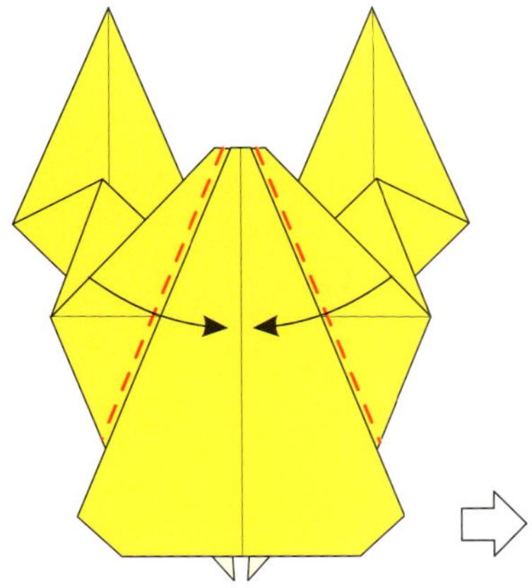

17. Am Kopfbereich, siehe Pfeile, Linien falten und formen. Die Flügel durch eindrücken der Papiere formen, siehe Pfeile.
In the head area, see arrows, fold lines and form. Push in the papers in order to form the wings, see arrows.

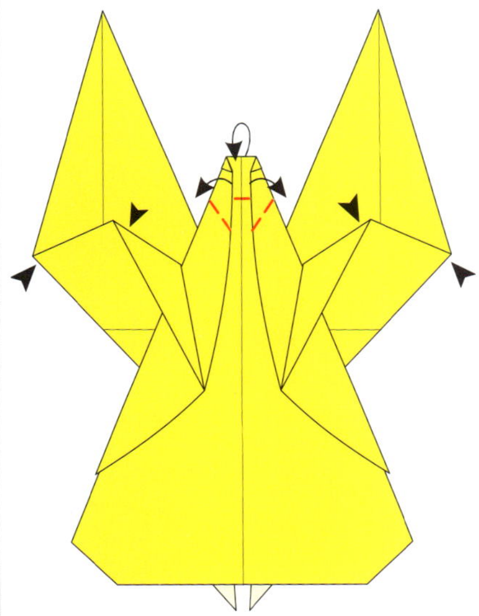

18. Fertiges Modell von vorne gesehen. Der Leuchtkörper wird in der Mitte des Modells von unten nach oben geschoben. Dadurch entsteht das Licht im Kopfbereich.
Finished model viewed from the front. Slide the light bulb in the middle of the model from bottom to top. This way the light inside the head emerges.

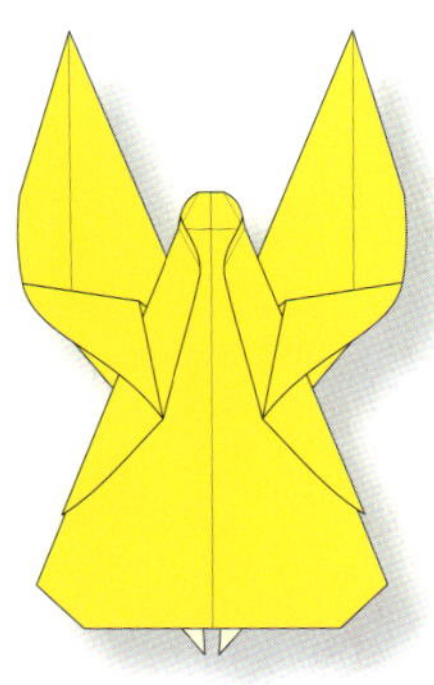

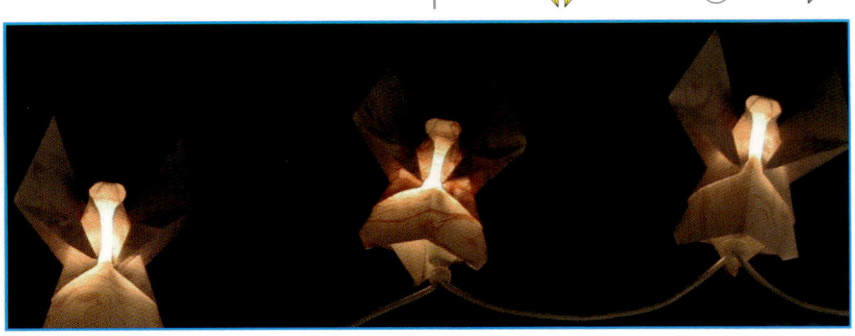

Lichtpost

MATERIAL
1 Bogen Papier im A5 Format für 1 Licht. Es kann jedes Papier ausgewählt werden.
One sheet A5 paper for one light. You can choose any design.

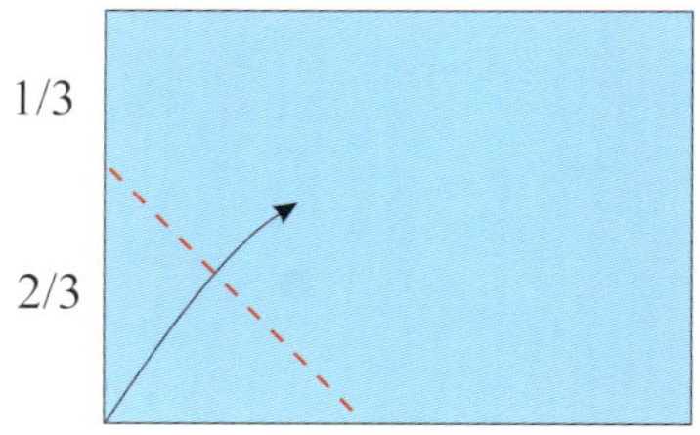

1. Mit der linken unteren Ecke schräge Linie nach oben falten, liegen lassen.
Fold oblique line upwards with the left lower corner and leave.

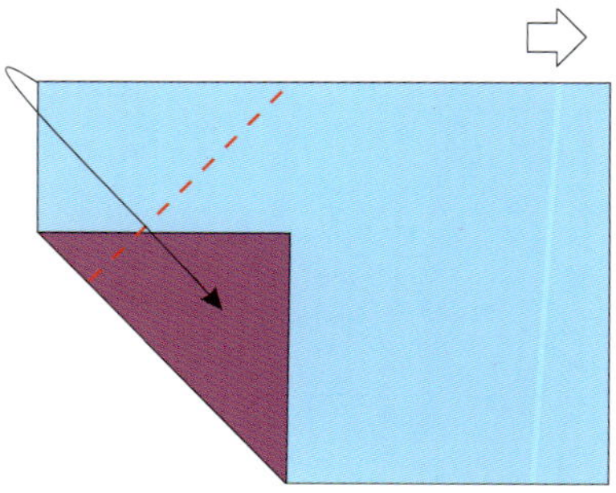

2. Mit der linken oberen Ecke schräge Linie nach unten falten, liegen lassen.
Fold oblique line downwards with the left upper corner and leave.

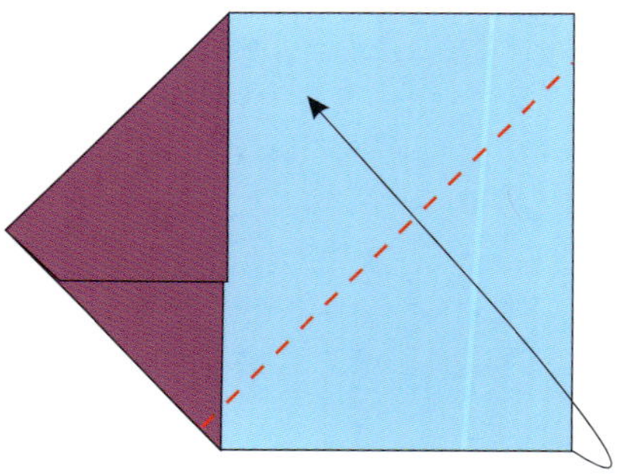

3. Mit der rechten unteren Ecke schräge Linie nach oben falten, liegen lassen.
Fold oblique line upwards with the right lower corner and leave.

4. Rückseite nach oben legen.
Turn over to the back.

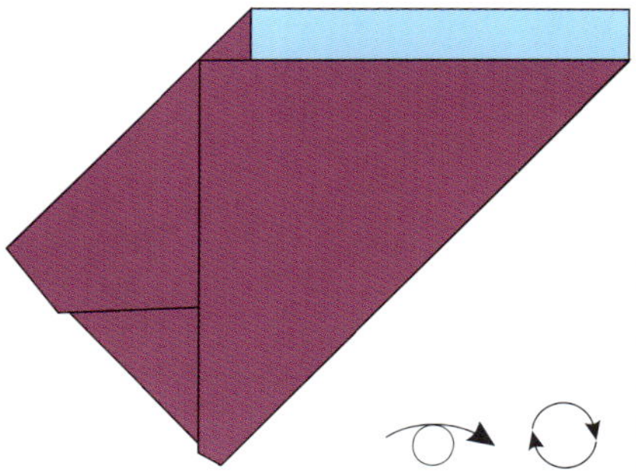

5. Waagerechte Linie von links nach rechts falten, liegen lassen.
Fold horizontal line from left to the right and leave.

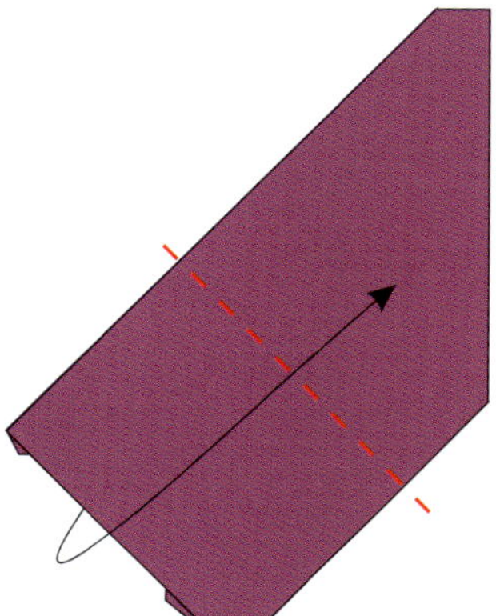

6. Linie von rechts nach links falten, liegen lassen.
Fold line from right to the left and leave.

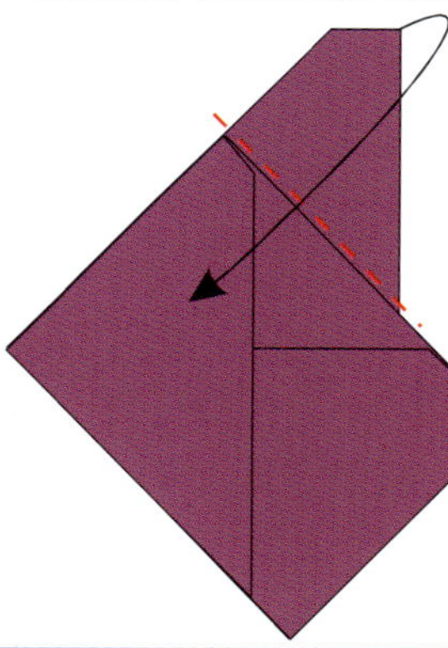

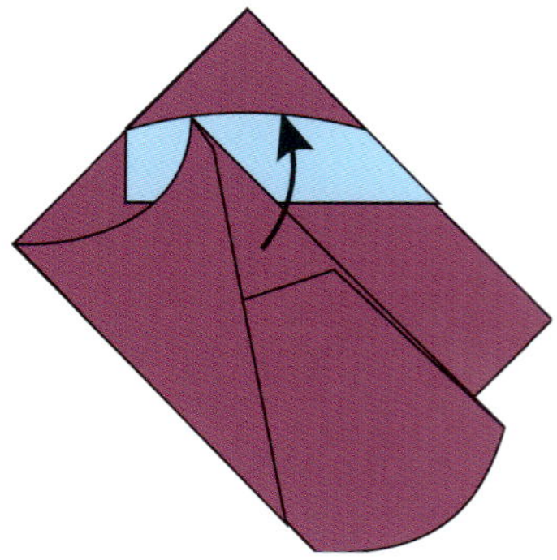

7. Arbeitsgang Nr.5 anheben und zu einer Rundung formen. Die linke Ecke dann in das kleine Dreieck schieben, siehe Pfeil.
Lift working step No.5 and form a round. Push the left corner into the small triangle, see arrow.

8. Fertiges Modell seitlich gesehen. Den Leuchtkörper in eine der Taschen schieben.
Finished model seen from the side. Slide the light bulb in one of the pockets.

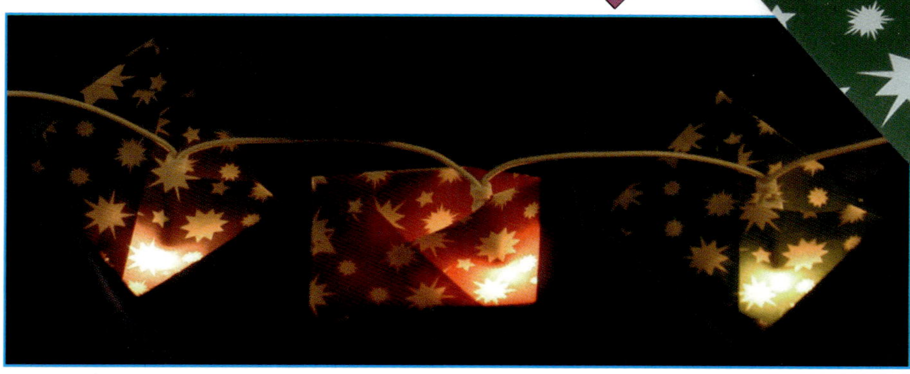

Weihnachtsbaum Lichterkette

MATERIAL

1 Bogen 15x15 cm Papier für 1 Licht. Es kann jedes Papier ausgewählt werden, aber grün sollte es sein.
One sheet 15x15 cm paper for one light. You can choose any paper, but it should be green.

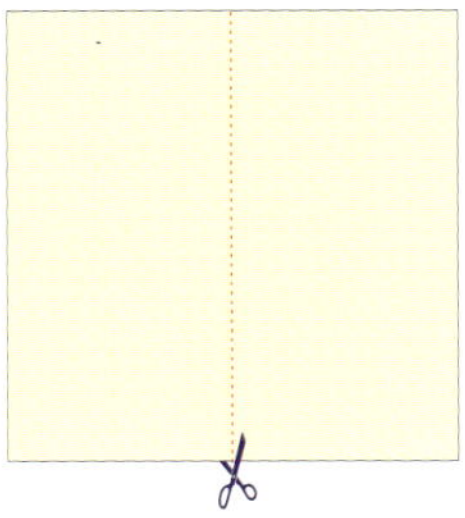

1. Papier an der senkrechten Mitte durchschneiden.
Cut off paper along the vertical middle.

2. Beide Ecken nach unten falten, liegen lassen.
Fold both corners downwards and leave.

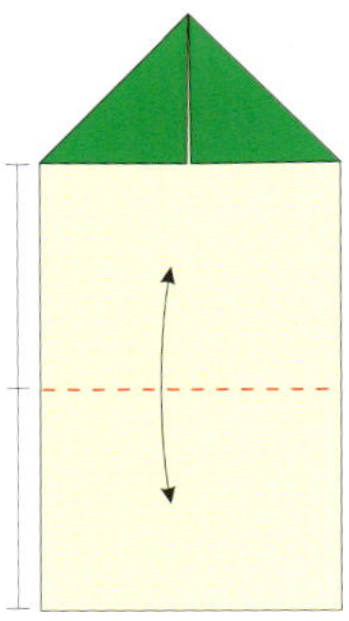

3. Im unteren Teil, waagerechte Mitte falten, wieder öffnen.
On the lower part, fold horizontal middle and open up again.

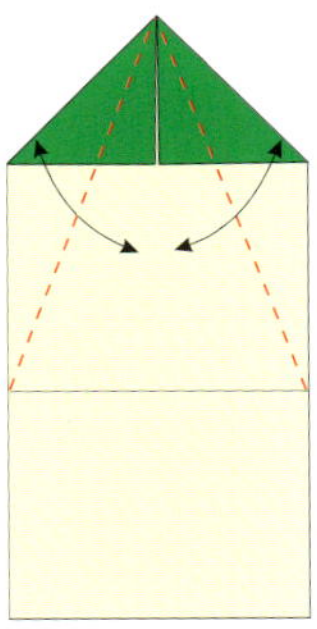

4. Im oberen Teil, schräge Linien zur Mitte falten, wieder öffnen.
On the upper part, fold oblique lines to the middle and open up again.

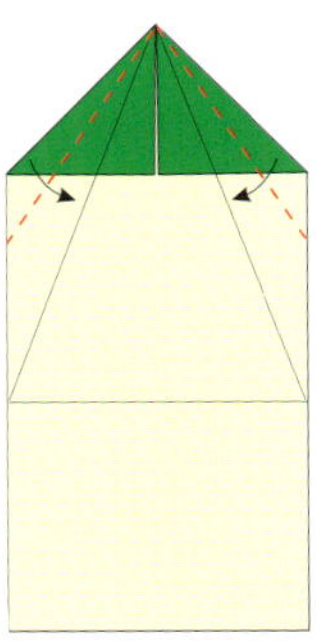

5. Schräge Linien an die neuen Linien falten, liegen lassen.
Fold oblique lines to the new lines and leave.

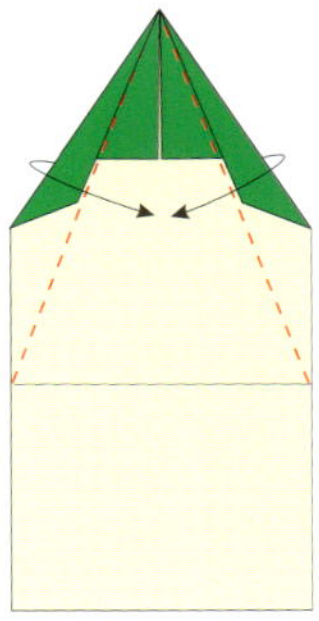

6. Papier von rechts und links zur Mitte legen, liegen lassen.
Lay paper from right and the left to the middle and leave.

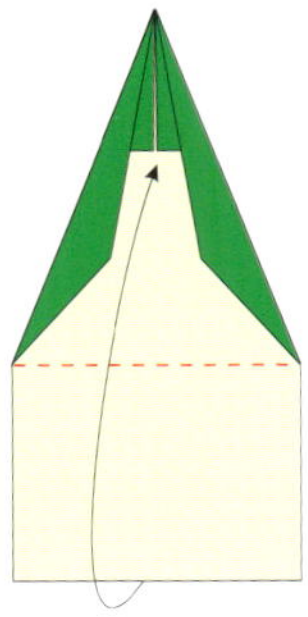

7. An der waagerechten Mitte nach oben legen, liegen lassen.
Lay upwards along the horizontal middle and leave.

8. Nur mit der oberen Papierlage an der Linie nach unten falten, liegen lassen. Achtung: Seitliche Papiereinteilung beachten.
Using only the top layer of paper, fold along the line downwards and leave. Attention: Note the height arrangement on the side.

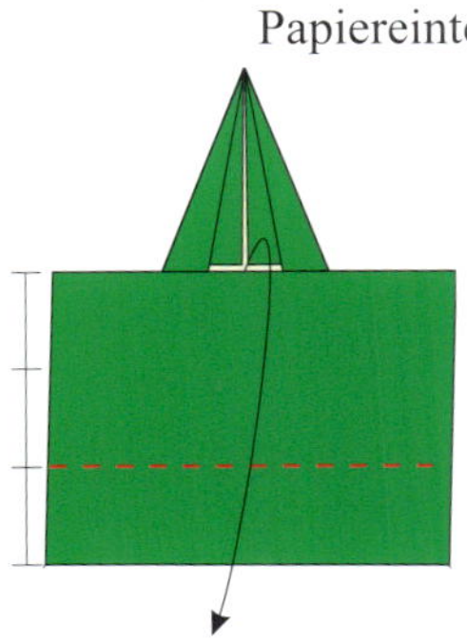

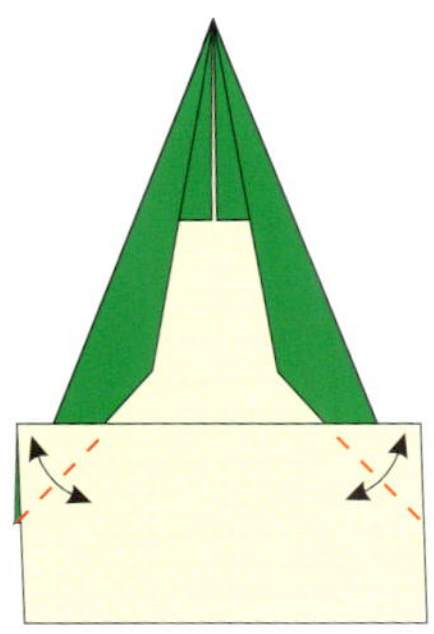

9. Seitliche Ecken nach unten falten, wieder öffnen.
Fold left and right corner downwards and open up again.

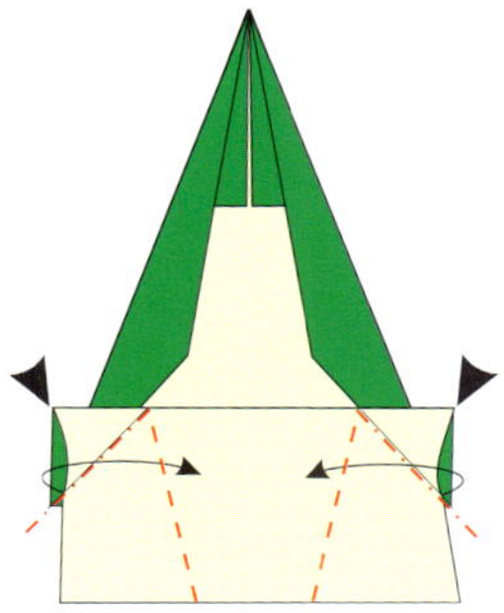

10. Nur mit der oberen Papierlage halb schräge Linien falten, dabei die seitlichen Ecken eindrücken. Es ist hilfreich wenn die schrägen Linien an den Ecken bereits zur Bergfalte geformt sind.
Using only the top layer of paper, fold the half oblique lines and push in corners from the side. It is helpful, if the oblique lines on the corners are already formed as a mountain-fold.

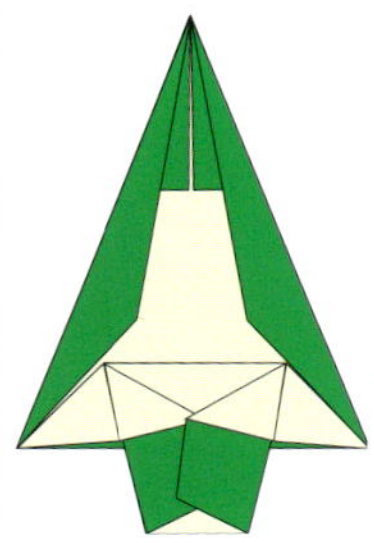

11. Fertiges Modell von vorne gesehen. Es werden zwei gleiche Teile benötigt.
Finished model seen from the front. There are two equal parts needed.

12. Die Weihnachtsbäume im unteren Teil an den Seiten zusammen kleben. Keinen wasserhaltigen Kleber benutzen. Die Baumspitze nach oben halten und über den Leuchtkörper schieben.
Glue the x-mas trees on the sides in the lower part together. Don't use water based glue. Hold the top of the model upwards and slide it over the light bulb.

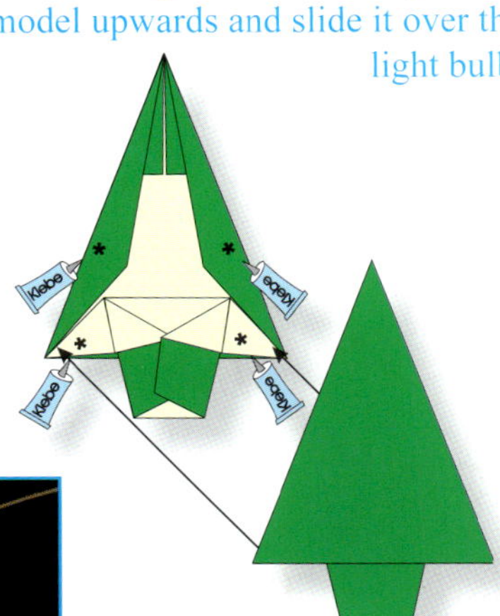

Lichterkette mit Sternen

MATERIAL

1 Bogen 15x15 cm Papier für 1 Licht. Es kann jedes Papier gewählt werden.

One sheet 15x15 cm paper for one light. You can choose any paper.

Start. Diagramme von Seite 52 bis Nr.14 falten.

Fold charts of page 52 until step No.14.

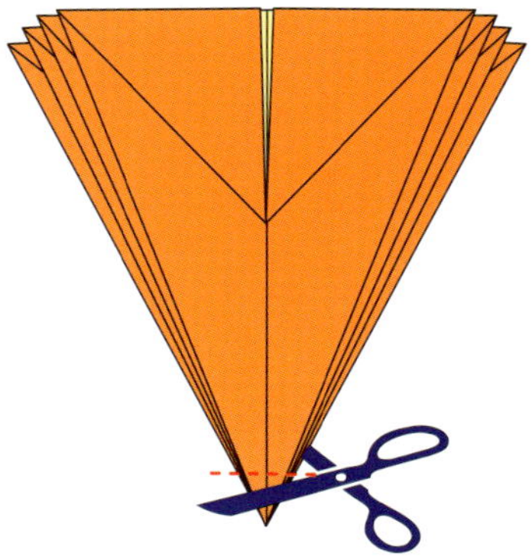

1. Untere Spitze etwas abschneiden.
Cut off the lower point a little bit.

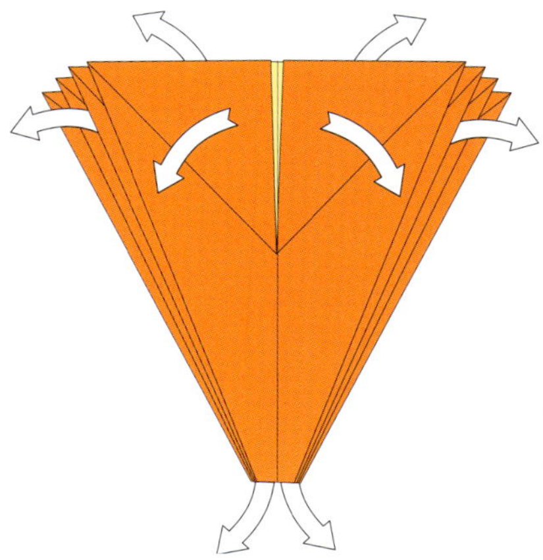

2. Modell von innen auseinanderdrücken.
Push the model from the inside outwards.

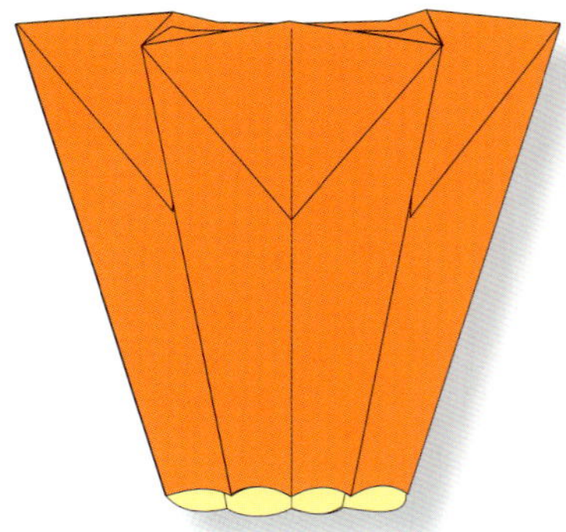

3. Fertiges Modell seitlich gesehen. Das Loch nach oben halten und über den Leuchtkörper schieben.
Finished model seen from the side. Hold the hole upwards and slide it over the light bulb.

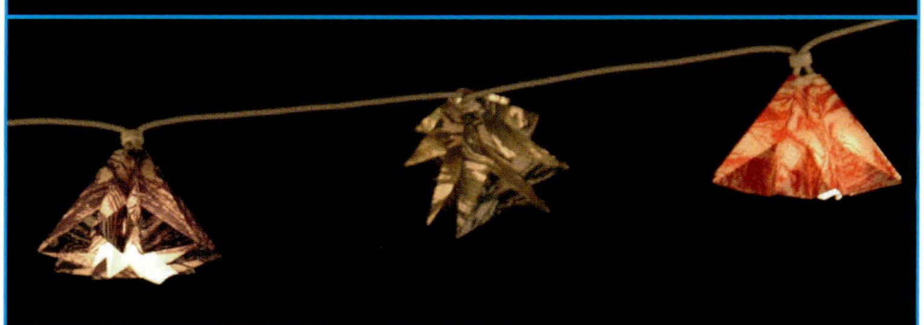

Lieferbare Bücher aus dem Q-Verlag Berlin

Das große ORIGAMI Weihnachtsbuch
Festliche Dekoration aus Papier

In diesem Buch sind Modelle vom Adventskalender über Fenster-, Tür- und Wanddekorationen, sowie ausgefallener Tisch- und Baumschmuck erklärt. Auch die Möglichkeit Geldgeschenke phantasievoll zu gestalten, Geschenkverpackungen, Geschenkanhänger und ausgefallene Weihnachtskarten selber herzustellen wird Schritt-für-Schritt dargestellt.

Eine Besonderheit ist die Stern Lampe, welche mittels einer Glühbirne zu einem außergewöhnlichen Lichtobjekt wird. So taucht ein jedes Zimmer sofort in eine besondere weihnachtliche Stimmung. Extravagant sind auch die schwimmenden Sterne, die in Kombination mit Schwimmkerzen ein echter Hingucker sind.

Sprache: Deutsch Seiten:128 Einband: Gebunden
Schwierigkeitsgrad: Anfänger und Fortgeschrittene
Technik: Papier falten (Origami)

ISBN10: 3-938127-06-6 ISBN13: 978-3-938127-06-3
Preis: 19,90 EUR (D)

ORIGAMI Schiffe
Vom Ruderboot zum Flugzeugträger

Schiff ahoi! Mit dem Buch „ORIGAMI Schiffe“ können Sie in See stechen.
Zur Verfügung stehen Ihnen z.B.: Ruderboot, Tretboot, Katamaran, Speedboot, Segeljacht, Autofähre, Frachtschiff, Lotsenboot und sogar ein ganzer Flugzeugträger incl. Düsenjäger. Oder wandeln Sie auf den Spuren der Geschichte mit dem Cleopatra Schiff, einem Chinesischen Schiff und einem Wikinger Schiff.

Alle Schiffe wurden mit unsinkbaren AQUAPAPIER von Paper Frog gefaltet. Für Kinder ab 6 Jahren und alle jung gebliebenen.

Sprache: Deutsch+Englisch Seiten: 72 Einband: Broschiert

ISBN10: 3-938127-04-X ISBN13: 978-3-938127-04-9
Preis: 12,90 EUR (D)

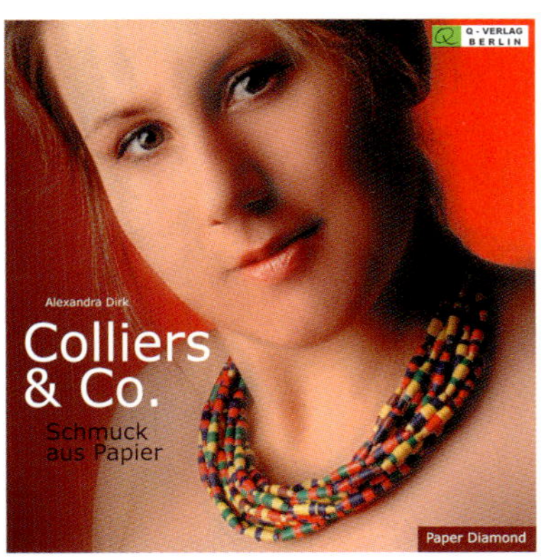

Colliers & Co.
Schmuck aus Papier

Sprache: Deutsch
Seiten: 48
Format: 20 x 20 cm
Einband: Broschiert

ISBN10: 3-938127-05-8
ISBN13: 978-3-938127-05-6
Preis: 8,95 EUR (D)

Paper Diamond
Ohrringe aus Papier

Sprache: Deutsch
Seiten: 48
Format: 20 x 20 cm
Einband: Broschiert

ISBN10: 3-938127-02-3
ISBN13: 978-3-938127-02-5
Preis: 7,95 EUR (D)

Impressum + Quellennachweis

Die Deutsche Bibliothek verzeichnet diese Publikation in der Deutschen Nationalbibliografie;
detaillierte bibliografische Daten sind im Internet über http://dnb.ddb.de abrufbar.
Das große Lichterbuch / The great book of lights
Lichter aus Papier in Origami Technik /
Alexandra Dirk. – Berlin: Q-Verlag Berlin

1. Auflage: Oktober 2005
2. Auflage: November 2006

ISBN10:	3-938127-03-1
ISBN13:	978-3-938127-03-2

ISBN 10: 3-938127-03-1

Autorin: Alexandra Dirk
Herstellung: Q-Verlag Berlin
Umschlaggestaltung: Yves Roger Weber
Aufmacherfotos: R. Huber, Bergisch Gladbach
Arbeitsfotos: Q-Verlag Berlin
Übersetzung: Yves Roger Weber
Diagramme: Jannie van Schuylenburg
Gedruckt in Tschechien

Quellennachweis:

Die Autorin bedankt sich auf diesem Wege bei der Firma nice papers für die Bereitstellung sämtlicher Arbeitsmaterialien.

Alle abgebildeten Papiere, sowie Bücher vom Q-Verlag können im Internet Shop: www.paperfrog.de bestellt werden.